GREEN

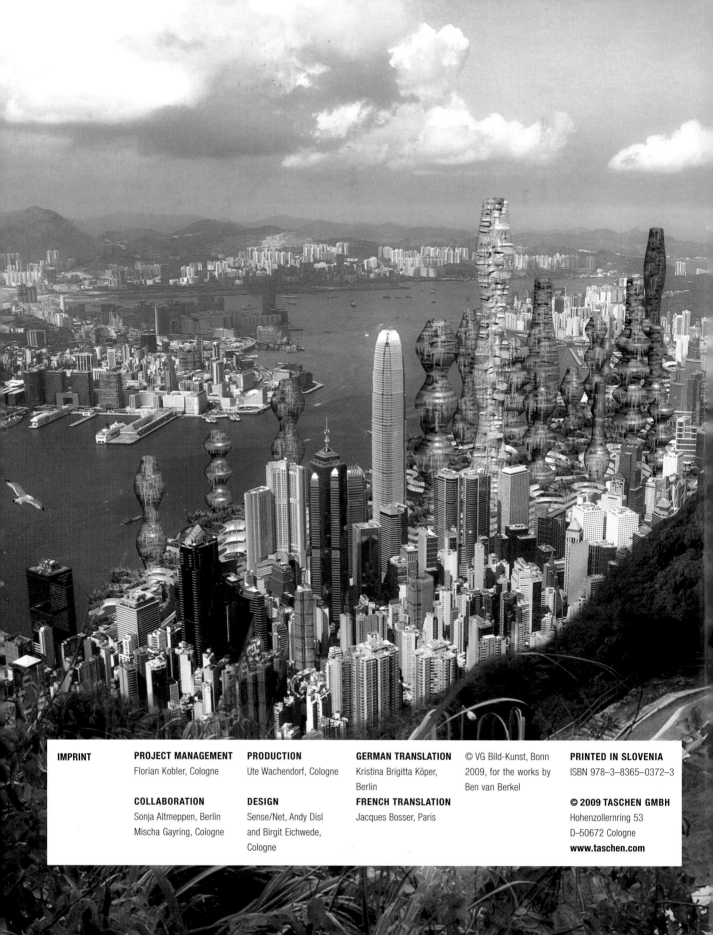

IMPRINT

PROJECT MANAGEMENT
Florian Kobler, Cologne

COLLABORATION
Sonja Altmeppen, Berlin
Mischa Gayring, Cologne

PRODUCTION
Ute Wachendorf, Cologne

DESIGN
Sense/Net, Andy Disl
and Birgit Eichwede,
Cologne

GERMAN TRANSLATION
Kristina Brigitta Köper,
Berlin

FRENCH TRANSLATION
Jacques Bosser, Paris

© VG Bild-Kunst, Bonn
2009, for the works by
Ben van Berkel

PRINTED IN SLOVENIA
ISBN 978–3–8365–0372–3

© 2009 TASCHEN GMBH
Hohenzollernring 53
D–50672 Cologne
www.taschen.com

GREEN

ARCHITECTURE NOW!

GRÜNE *Architektur heute!*
L'architecture VERTE *d'aujourd'hui!*
Philip Jodidio

TASCHEN

HONG KONG KÖLN LONDON LOS ANGELES MADRID PARIS TOKYO

CONTENTS

INTRODUCTION

WAR IN THE ASPHALT JUNGLE

Green is the name of the game, no doubt about it. There has never been so much interest in the ecological impact of buildings as there is today. In the United States alone, the value of green building construction is projected to increase to $60 billion by 2010.[1] Nor is this a negligible fact in the struggle to control pollution and in the search for responsible "sustainable" methods of construction. Buildings are one of the heaviest consumers of natural resources and account for a significant portion of the greenhouse gas emissions that affect climate change. In the United States, buildings account for 39% of all CO_2 emissions.[2] Buildings use 40% of raw materials globally.[3] The difficulty is that green is so fashionable that everyone is jumping on the bandwagon, claiming astonishing sustainability or remarkably low-energy consumption. One effective response to the uncertainty surrounding the complex question of the environmental impact of architecture has been LEED (Leadership in Energy and Environmental Design), the accepted benchmark system of the US Green Building Council (USGBC) for the design, construction, and operation of green buildings. According to the USGBC, "LEED promotes a whole-building approach to sustainability by recognizing performance in five key areas of human and environmental health: sustainable site development, water savings, energy efficiency, materials selection, and indoor environmental quality." The USGBC certifies not only buildings but building professionals. More than 46 000 building professionals from all areas of practice have become LEED Accredited Professionals (APs) since the Professional Accreditation program was launched in the United States in 2001.

The Green Building Council system takes into account the various professions that participate in construction, and not only architects. This broad-based rating organization is undoubtedly much closer to the goal of encouraging real sustainability in architecture than would be individual architects claiming that their structure is greener than the next. It may even be asked, with global warming now a significant international political issue, if architecture itself is not on the brink of very significant changes, where style and matters of aesthetics are placed in a secondary position behind issues of sustainability. At a certain time, "green" buildings were almost obliged to show their colors, as it were, ugly and complicated affairs, usually multicolored as though an entire rainbow in one building might be sufficient to prove a concern for ecology. Technology certainly assists architects by giving them environmentally "correct" materials that are also attractive. Thermal glass, as used by designers such as the German Werner Sobek, allows a glazed house to be as environmentally friendly as one covered in larch shingles. Photovoltaic cells are becoming more efficient as well, though they are not yet often able to provide more than a relatively small percentage of the energy consumption of a building. This of course depends on climate, with gray skies a less propitious to photovoltaic panels than desert sun, of course. As it is, some sustainability methods, be they passive or active, are hardly visible. Turning a building the right way around or organizing its cladding properly to avoid solar gain may have little or no effect on its overall aesthetics. So, too, photovoltaic panels are usually safely tucked away on the roof, unless architects are still trying to make a "statement" with their patchwork sun-seeking technology.

1
David Hertz, 747 Wing House, Santa
Monica Mountains, Malibu, California,
USA, 2007–09

TODAY CALIFORNIA, TOMORROW THE WORLD

The UK Green Building Council (UK-GBC) was launched in February 2007 to bring cohesion to the green building movement in the United Kingdom. The Government's Sustainable Buildings Task Group had earlier reported that no one body or organization concerned with sustainability was providing clear direction for the sector as a whole. The UK-GBC was established to fulfill this role. Both the American and English groups are part of the WorldGBC, which "supports national Green Building Councils whose common mission is to create a sustainable built environment through market transformation." The WorldGBC held its founding meeting in 1999 in San Francisco, with eight countries in attendance. There are currently 12 national councils and a further 16 countries with emerging Green Building Councils. Current members are Australia, Brazil, Canada, Germany, India, Japan, Mexico, New Zealand, Taiwan, the United Arab Emirates, the United Kingdom, and the United States. These nations represent over 50% of global construction activity, though efforts toward sustainability have varying effectiveness in each country.

Other countries have set up similar councils to control the environmental qualities of buildings. One example is MINERGIE®®, "a sustainability brand for new and refurbished buildings… mutually supported by the Swiss Confederation, the Swiss Cantons along with trade and industry, and registered in Switzerland and around the world…" In a ten-year period, 7200 buildings for a total of 6.5 million square meters have received a MINERGIE® rating certificate, and the system is also being employed in France.

Although the GBC system is gaining ground and some communities or government entities are beginning to make their requirements part and parcel of the legal obligations of architects and builders, there are also doubts. Surveys show that many corporate leaders in the United States, for example, are convinced that green architecture costs more than a "normal" building. A GBC study of buildings in California found that "green improvements pay for themselves in three years." The New York Times recently published an article outlining a number of the ideas and issues that pose problems for the advancing green wave. One is that green buildings are ugly. This misconception is probably due to a long history of architects who felt that an environmentally friendly building had to somehow look the prickly part. Kelly Meyer, an environmentalist cited by The New York Times, is trying, with her husband, who is a developer, to prove that "something energy-conscious doesn't have to look as if you got it off the bottom shelf of a health-food store. It doesn't have to smell like hemp."[4]

ON A WING AND A PRAYER

David Hertz, one of the architects selected for this book, feels that the GBC LEED standards are "rigid and cumbersome" and indeed the certification process is complex and potentially costly in itself.[5] Hertz has come up with an innovative way to integrate the wings of a decommissioned 747 aircraft in a new house (747 Wing House, Santa Monica Mountains, Malibu, California, USA, 2007–09, page 185). This sort of reuse, as dramatic as it might be, may not suffice to allow Hertz to garner a precious platinum medal, but he seems set to rebel against the bureaucratic aspects of the GBC rating system. Another architect quoted in the same article in The New York Times, Michael B. Lehrer, is predictably a bit more positive about the LEED certification process since his Water + Life Museum (Hemet, California, USA, 2001–06, page 219) recently became the first LEED Platinum museum: "They have mundane things in there that are pretty nonsensical and other things that

2 3

are pretty profound. At a time when everybody and their sister and brother are saying 'We are green,' it's very important that these things be vetted in a credible way."[6]

On a more positive note, the LEED standards and similar initiatives elsewhere do approach environmental issues in a broad-based or even holistic manner that ranges from encouraging the use of natural light to reducing waste—factors that architects alone can influence but not control totally in many cases. The GBC thus involves not only architects but also a broad variety of "building professionals," all engaged in producing a more "sustainable" result. But this book is not only about LEED-Platinum (the highest rating) buildings, nor about the architects who now tack the unattractive acronyms "LEED AP" to their names wherever they go. Rather, it is about the variety of different efforts that weave a relationship between the built environment and nature, in a positive sense. The *Architecture Now!* series focuses not on the technical aspects of buildings, but precisely on their architectural quality. Though Kelly Meyer is surely right when she says that a green building "doesn't have to smell like hemp," it is also true that not every structure that claims to have some respect for the environment is good architecture. The LEED system may well be a good way to reduce false claims of a "zero carbon footprint" or abusive sales based on "sustainability," but the very fashionable aspects of "green" make all kinds of manipulation of the truth possible. The projects presented in this book range from concept houses to very large complexes, and include parks, a gas station, and a frozen vault for seeds. The point is that there are many ways to approach the issue of the relationship between the environment and architecture.

The broad public appeal of a movie such as Al Gore's *An Inconvenient Truth*, based on the growing evidence of "global warming," together with the proportion of world resources used for construction, makes a clear and pressing case for the need for architects to face up to their own responsibilities. Only one or two of the buildings in this book "smell like hemp" and it has already become obvious that sustainability and good architecture can indeed go hand in hand.

LET A THOUSAND GARDENS BLOOM

One very old method to improve sustainability is to bury architecture, or to cover it with vegetation. A layer of earth serves as insulation and ultimately allows nature to return to its rightful place on a given site. Bringing nature into a city center provides relief from an otherwise artificial environment (a fact that has more psychological impact than real influence on such vast problems as global warming), but it might be said, too, that every little bit helps in a struggle that will surely engage tens of millions of people in the foreseeable future. At opposite ends of the United States two green roofs of very different size show different ways of bringing the strength of nature to bear on an architectural context. In Washington, D. C., Michael Van Valkenburgh has created a 130-square-meter Green Roof for the building of the American Society of Landscape Architects (2005–06, page 385). Using artificial materials to make lightweight mounds, he in a sense invents a new landscape in a very small area, providing users not only with a bit of greenery, but also changing their perspective on the city. Given that roof space is generally underused and ugly in most cities, this project might be seen as a small example of what might be done on a much larger scale, given sufficient public interest and financial incentive. The green roof imagined by Renzo Piano for the new California Academy of Sciences in San Francisco (2005–08, page 277) is on an entirely different scale and has different ambitions. Covering approximately one

2
Tadao Ando, Chichu Art
Museum/Naoshima, Naoshima,
Kagawa, Japan, 2000–04

3
Tadao Ando, Tokyu Toyoko Line
Shibuya Station, Shibuya-ku, Tokyo,
Japan, 2005–08

hectare and planted with 1.8 million native California varieties, the roof is a key element in the environmental strategy of the structure, which is to become the second American museum to receive a LEED Platinum rating. The coating of earth on the building permits a 6° reduction in internal temperatures in summer, leading to an obvious saving on air-conditioning costs, for example.

The French botanist Patrick Blanc has taken a different approach to greening the city. His recent 600-square-meter CaixaForum Vertical Garden (Madrid, Spain, 2006–07, page 91) is located in the heart of the Spanish capital, just across the street from the Prado Museum. It is set on a façade at right angles to the entrance of the new CaixaForum exhibition building designed by the Swiss team Herzog & de Meuron. Blanc has patented a method for growing plants on vertical walls without the use of earth. Aside from the incongruous aspect of seeing a complete garden suspended on a building's façade, there is something to be said for making use of otherwise difficult bits of the urban surface. Just as Michael Van Valkenburgh and many others have taken to greening roofs, so, too, has Patrick Blanc begun to do the same for walls that resemble works of art and bring a breath of fresh air to the congested urban environment.

Although their method is extremely different from that of Patrick Blanc, the Spanish team Ecosistema Urbano has also contributed in Madrid to a growing awareness of problems of pollution and the disappearance of green areas. Their Ecoboulevard of Vallecas (Madrid, Spain, 2006, page 127) consists in a series of three "air trees," conceived as ephemeral installations that use photovoltaic cells to power the dispersion of very fine water vapor near passersby. This water-vapor technique is well known and can lower ambient temperatures by as much as 10°C, a boon in Madrid's sweltering summers, and an encouragement to the congregation of local people. Artificial trees, of course, have a long history in architecture, surely beginning with the column and continuing through Postmodern visitations concocted by such figures as Hans Hollein in Vienna. The Ecosistema Urbano technique takes this architectural metaphor a large step further, making the artificial "tree" do something that a real forest does, lower temperatures and make places agreeable.

FRESH MINT FOR ME

Another young designer, the French-Swiss architect Philippe Rahm, has begun to make a career out of imagining architectural environments in which fundamental factors such as the oxygen content of the air are modified with an aim to alter the physical states of visitors. His latest scheme, called the Digestible Gulf Stream (11th Venice Architecture Biennale, Italy, 2008, page 291), is a small residence in which one level is maintained at 12°C and the other at 28°C, since these are calculated to be the two extremes that are considered "comfortable" by most people. Rahm maintains, rightly, that air conditioning, heating, and other forms of architectural environmental control are systematically geared to maintain a "normal" set of conditions that few people ever bother to question unless they are uncomfortable. He says, on the contrary, that it is precisely by challenging these norms that architecture can branch off into new directions, fundamentally related to physiology, for example. For this project, Rahm also experiments with the idea that edible substances like mint (menthol) can create a sensation of cooling that is unrelated to the usual set of refrigerating machinery that hums just out of sight and out of mind in just about all modern buildings.

ISLANDS IN THE STREAM

The Japanese architect Tadao Ando has long been interested in the idea of building underground, which may indeed sometimes have a bearing on the issue of "green" design. As he said in 2003: "I have an almost unconscious inclination towards underground spaces. Whatever the nature of the site, I try to create architecture that is never imposing on its environment. … Working on underground space links up with the search for the origins of architecture."[7] One of Ando's recent works is the Chichu Art Museum/Naoshima (Naoshima, Kagawa, Japan, 2000–04, page 61). The word *chichu* means "underground" in Japanese, and this building is almost entirely invisible from the neighboring hillsides. The luxuriant vegetation of the island assures that nothing but the skylights and open courtyards betray, at ground level, the presence of a building. Although Ando's declaration makes more reference to an architectural concept than to issues of environmental protection, the Island of Naoshima in Japan's Inland Sea, where he has built other structures, is now in good part a nature reserve after having long served mining interests. It may be interesting to note that Ando does not employ the newly fashionable vocabulary of "green" design very often, but the thick concrete walls he creates, and in the case of the Chichu Art Museum, a layer of earth covering the entire building, make for a very significant passive energy strategy. The inside of the Museum also relies in good part on natural light. A second and more recent project by Ando is his Tokyu Toyoko Line Shibuya Station (Tokyo, Japan, 2005–08, page 66). Here, a 27 725-square-meter subway station in the heart of one of the densest urban areas in the world boasts a natural ventilation system. Thus it is all the more surprising, since Tokyo's extensive subway lines are in large part air conditioned given the high summer temperatures.

SMALL PARK, GREAT CANYON

Although architects are now fond of parading their LEED AP visiting cards, another more traditional way of contributing to environmental quality is simply by encouraging nature, in the form of parks. Two examples of such interventions, one tiny and another massive, show that landscape architecture is part and parcel of any effort to draw attention to issues of sustainability. The small (815 m²) Samir Kassir Square in Beirut (Lebanon, 2004, page 117) by Vladimir Djurovic was designed around two large ficus trees that had somehow survived Beirut's years of civil war—"in essence, to become a small escape dedicated to the city and its people," says Djurovic. Despite its relative modesty, this project did not escape the attention of the jury of the 2007 Aga Khan Award for Architecture that singled out Samir Kassir Square for its contribution to a city where Muslim and Christian populations rarely find new places to rest. On a much larger scale (51 km²), the US-based firm EDAW, where Djurovic first worked, developed the Jinji Lake Landscape Master Plan for the historic city of Suzhou (China, 2002–04, page 135). Situated about 60 kilometers from Shanghai, Suzhou is famed for its canals and gardens. In 514 BC, during the spring and autumn period, King Helu of Wu established the "Great City of Helu," the ancient name for Suzhou, as his capital. When the Grand Canal was completed, Suzhou found itself strategically located on a major trade route. In the course of the history of China, it has been a center of industry and commerce. It has been called "the Oriental Venice," but pollution and rapid development threatened the city until its administration began a concerted effort to clean the water and create new green areas. EDAW's specific projects within the overall master plan include the five-hectare Jinji Lake Cityside Harbor, and the seven-hectare Maple Forest Park. Books on "green" architecture might tend not

4
Ken Smith Landscape Architect,
Orange County Great Park, Irvine,
California, USA, 2007–

4

to mention landscape design, and yet this is one of the most obvious ways to assist other efforts to counter pollution and, indeed, the stress associated with urban life.

Another very large park design, the Orange County Great Park (Irvine, California, USA, 2007–, page 333), is the work of the New York landscape architect Ken Smith. Smith was responsible for the Museum of Modern Art Rooftop Garden (2003–05) on the top of Yoshio Taniguchi's expansion of the MoMA. At least partially for technical reasons, including weight considerations, the MoMA garden is entirely artificial, made of plastic rocks, crushed glass and recycled rubber mulch. Within the 545 hectares of the park in Irvine, Smith plans a more "natural" intervention—including a "great canyon" 3.2 kilometers long and nine meters deep, corresponding to streams that existed on the site before it was a Marine Corps Air Station. A hot air balloon already allows visitors to view the site, but several years of work are necessary before the new complex, including a botanical garden and many biking and walking trails, will be ready.

The play on nature and artifice seen in the work of Ken Smith recalls that just as "green" architecture is difficult to define, so, too, is the presence of nature in architecture. The Japanese, with such figures as Itsuko Hasegawa or Toyo Ito, have long posited that architecture should engage in the creation of an artificial "nature" inspired by the forms of the natural world and yet decidedly manufactured in their aspect. The American specialist in biomimetics, Dennis Dollens, uses Xfrog software, which consists of "botanic, L-system algorithms used in computational biological simulations to grow plants and landscapes for laboratory tests and simulations." Of his various attempts to design towers or bridges that have a relation to the natural world, Dollens says: "The unifying concept behind these projects is that computational growth of architectural structures and systems can be influenced by biomimetic observations without falling into traditional categories of 'organic architecture.' In addition, the potential of biological science, biotechnology, and digital manufacturing, arriving at a union where architectural production and new possibilities for non-toxic architecture come together, begins to make sense" (see his Tree Tower, Los Angeles, California, USA, 2009, page 123). Unlike some architects, who seem content to state that a wooden house is "sustainable," Dollens is looking forward to new applications of computer science that might allow architecture itself to change, becoming somehow more like nature and thus less "toxic."

SMELLS LIKE HEMP
Traditional construction methods employed across a good part of the planet of course produce nowhere near the levels of pollution of a "modern" building. This fact has inspired a number of architects who have sought not only to help people in need, but also to call on their own building techniques to produce structures that are both durable and truly "sustainable." A good example of this approach is that of Anna Heringer and Eike Roswag. Their Handmade School in Bangladesh (Rudrapur, Dinajpur, 2005, page 179) is a 325-square-meter structure made of earth and bamboo for a cost of just 25 000 euros. Another winner of the 2007 Aga Khan Award for Architecture, this project calls on some modern materials such as nylon lashing, but it provides both shelter and a joyous place for children to learn, while having very little negative effect on the environment and boasting low energy consumption. The Salam Center for Cardiac Surgery (Soba, Republic of Sudan, 2006–07, page 351) by the Italian group studio tamassociati was built entirely around two large existing mango trees. A 58-centimeter-thick

5

6

wall made of two layers of bricks separated by an insulating air cavity, 1000 square meters of solar panels, and a water-vapor system used for cooling or keeping dust out are some of the "green" features of a building created where people simply cannot afford to use the typically wasteful construction methods of Western, or developed Eastern, countries. Apparently more "modern" in its appearance than the Handmade School, the Salam Center is nonetheless a creative approach to using local materials to the greatest extent possible, while also calling on more sophisticated technology (solar panels). Christine's House (Mason's Bend, Alabama, USA, 2005–06, page 309) is another example of the creative work done by architecture students at Auburn University, as part of the Rural Studio program founded in 1993 by the late Samuel Mockbee to help poor Alabama residents. Making use of the area's abundant red clay, mixing 70% earth, 25% pulped newspaper, and 5% Portland cement, and pouring it into cardboard boxes of various sizes to make bricks for two main walls of the house, the students showed that simple methods and a good design result in architecture that is both pleasant and environmentally responsible.

AIMING FOR ZERO

Houses of various sorts have been a fruitful area for experimentation with different concepts of sustainability, because well-meaning owners are willing to pay a bit more to be "ecologically responsible." The German engineer Werner Sobek is one of the great specialists of sophisticated architecture that is as close to true sustainability as would appear possible given the present state of technology. His H16 house (Tieringen, Germany, 2005–06, page 337) is larger than ecology might suggest at 454 square meters, but it attains "maximum transparency and a minimum of structure, full recyclability … and zero emissions." The energy consumption of the house is influenced by passive methods such as varying transparent or opaque volumes in function of their exposure to the sun, but geothermal heating with a heat pump, as well as photovoltaic panels, also contribute to the overall sustainability of the residence. Most importantly, Sobek succeeds in creating an attractive modern house while fully respecting the highest standards of regard for the environment—proof that green need not be ugly. Zoka Zola's Rafflesia Zero Energy House (Kuala Lumpur, Malaysia, 2007–09, page 407) is not yet built, but this competition-winning project uses a broad variety of strategies to fit into its environment with minimum disruption to the ecosystem, and also succeeds in using little, if any, energy from the outside grid. A 50-centimeter void in the roof used as insulation, careful study of natural air movements, and extensive surfaces covered by solar panels are amongst the ideas employed here.

With houses like H16 or Rafflesia taking form, it might seem inevitable that architects would engage in a healthy kind of one-up-manship, each trying to outdo the other when it comes to sustainability. In a project for *The New York Times Magazine*, the New York architects Diller Scofidio + Renfro appear to have gone about as far as possible with their Phantom House (southwest USA, 2007, page 113). This house contains not only real technology, but also systems imagined as being practically available, such as exercise bicycles that generate electricity for use in the house when the residents feel like a workout. The drawings of this house do not actually make it look like a masterpiece of contemporary architecture, yet when the goal is to be as energy efficient and environmentally responsible as possible, it is likely that standards of aesthetics will evolve as well, placing emphasis on features that, it is hoped, will ultimately "save" the planet.

5
Diller Scofidio + Renfro, Phantom House, Southwest USA, 2007

6
Rafael de La-Hoz, Telefónica District C, Las Tablas, Madrid, Spain, 2002–07

7
Rural Studio, Christine's House, Mason's Bend, Alabama, USA, 2005–06

7

BIG IS BEAUTIFUL

Although small or even virtual zero-emission houses are interesting exercises for architects with time on their hands or clients with money to burn, large buildings would seem to be a more appropriate target for those who really want to make a difference by reducing their CO_2 footprint. The Spanish architect Rafael de La-Hoz has taken an interesting approach with his new Telefónica District C (Las Tablas, Madrid, Spain, 2002–07, page 213) buildings for Telefónica de España SA. This complex for the largest Spanish company measures no less than 390 000 square meters. With a site covering 19 hectares, this is one of the largest corporate projects undertaken recently in Europe. Passive energy strategies play an important role in the design, with high, elegant canopies shading large parts of the buildings. The architect has also used an unusual system of glass fins that project out, at right angles to the façades, creating not only further shade, but also varying shadow patterns on the buildings—giving the impression that their geometric design actually changes all day long, while also generating further protection from the hot Madrid sun. Silk-screened dots of density determined by the angle of exposure to the sun cover the large glazed panel façades and also reduce solar gain while giving a pleasant, slightly tinted effect when viewed from the interior. Solar panels cover 26 000 square meters of the top of the canopy, transforming enough solar energy into electricity to prevent 2000 tons of CO_2 from being emitted into the atmosphere each year. A garden (not designed by the architect) links the buildings and adds an element of green to the otherwise spacious and airy complex. It is undoubtedly a sign that "green" architecture has finally reached the mainstream when a client like Telefónica becomes conscious of the need to address issues of sustainability. This may be all the more important in a hot climate like that of Madrid, where air conditioning costs can be substantially reduced by an appropriate design. In the case of Rafael de La-Hoz, the client has chosen an architect capable of bringing together sustainable features on a large scale and a high quality of architectural design.

In another, even hotter region with great ambitions in the area of architecture, Adrian Smith and Gordon Gill have designed a new headquarters for Masdar (Abu Dhabi, UAE, 2008–10, page 327). Part of "the world's first zero-carbon, zero-waste city fully powered by renewable energy," the building naturally has a large roof canopy covered with photovoltaics, but it also employs wind turbines and cones to harness another form of natural power. Water and energy use are carefully controlled, while "sustainable materials are utilized throughout and were selected based on life-cycle analysis." At 88 000 square meters, the Masdar Headquarters makes green look sexy, if a little big. Adrian Smith is known in the region as the designer of a number of other large structures, and in particular the world's tallest building, the Burj Dubai (SOM). He and other "star" architects like Lord Norman Foster, who is also involved in the Masdar City initiative, are beginning to prove that sustainability can be something other than a boring set of calculations—it can be genuinely exciting when architecture is not simply an elaborate support for photovoltaic cells covering endless flat roofs.

Norman Foster completed an entire campus in the jungle of Malaysia about four years ago (Petronas University of Technology, Seri Iskandar, Malaysia, 1999–2004, page 147). With a 450-hectare site and gross floor area of 240 000 square meters, this is assuredly a large project, intended for approximately 6000 students. Built into the topography of the site, the buildings have numerous canopies that serve both to shelter from the sun and from frequent rains in the monsoon season. Carefully thought out to encourage social interaction, and executed

8

with the modern rigor that is typical of Foster's office, the Petronas University shows that appropriate design depends in some circumstances as much on climate as it does on clever technology. Foster was, of course, one of the pioneers among better-known architects in adapting to the need to make buildings sustainable; he, unlike some other "star" architects, can thus surely not be accused of "jumping on the green bandwagon" at a late date.

Masdar City (meaning "the source") is meant to rely entirely on solar energy and other sustainable energy sources. It will be built near Abu Dhabi International Airport and, although it is being designed by Foster + Partners, architecture will certainly not be its only original aspect. Such large firms as BP, Royal Dutch Shell, Mitsubishi, Rolls-Royce, Total S. A., Mitsui, and Fiat are grouped together in an initiative dubbed the "Clean Tech Fund," while plans are underway to build a 40 to 60 megawatt solar power plant, wind farms, a hydrogen power plant, and geothermal energy sources. Other initiatives of this type have been announced in the Middle East and in China, which leads to the thought that architecture itself may well be obliged to change if the green wave gets any bigger. Clearly, a number of the most famous architects have relied on their solid aesthetic sense to leave their mark in the past. Huge projects like Masdar and even the GBC LEED rating system necessarily spread the responsibility for sustainability to all of the professions involved in building and beyond, as well as the need to search for and use new technologies that are more related to electrical engineering, for example, than they are to the more traditional sorts of construction engineering. "Good" architects and even some great ones have long been accustomed to using the best and sometimes most expensive materials available, without much concern about where they come from or if their sources are renewable. At the other end of the scale, the great majority of buildings are realized under increasingly money-driven conditions that lead in the worst of circumstances to the kinds of buildings that have absolutely no hope of withstanding an earthquake, for example. The drive for sustainability implies slightly different calculations about cost, perhaps admitting for the first time in several decades that immediate price is not the only way to judge the performance of architecture. Green architecture also implies an increasingly interconnected web of participants in the building process, perhaps in some cases reducing the freedom of action of the architect. The point of this book is to show that "good" architecture and sustainability can indeed go hand in hand, especially if the definition of "green" is a fairly broad one.

PLATINUM DREAMS

The LEED rating system addresses six major categories of questions in establishing its ratings: these are essentially judgments concerning sustainable sites, water efficiency, energy and atmosphere, materials and resources, indoor environmental quality, and, finally, innovation and design process. There are four LEED ratings, which are determined on a basis of a total number of points, with 69 being the maximum where new construction or major renovations of commercial buildings are at issue. The ratings are Certified (26–32 points); Silver (33–38 points); Gold (39–51 points); and, finally, Platinum (52–69 points).

The Grand Rapids Art Museum (Grand Rapids, Michigan, USA, 2004–07, page 395) was designed by wHY Architecture, a firm founded in 2003 by Yo-ichiro Hakomori and Kulapat Yantrasast. Yantrasast worked before 2003 in the office of Tadao Ando, collaborating on such projects as the Fort Worth Museum of Modern Art. The Michigan Museum is an interesting case in point because a major donor for the proj-

9
*Michael B. Lehrer, Water + Life
Museums Campus, Hemet, California,
USA, 2001–06*

9

ect, local philanthropist Peter Wege, made obtaining a LEED certification a condition for giving money to the new project. With 10% of its construction materials recycled and extensive use of natural light or reuse of rainwater, the new structure is both intelligent in terms of sustainability and also boasts a strong, minimalist design that does bring to mind Yantrasast's previous working experience.

Although smaller in size, David Adjaye's first public commission in the United States, the Museum of Contemporary Art/Denver (Denver, Colorado, USA, 2004–07, page 49), became the first museum to attain a LEED Gold rating. Low energy consumption, low greenhouse gas emissions, and the use of environmentally appropriate raw materials contributed to this rating. Adjaye, of course, has a considerable reputation in the United Kingdom, and his arrival in the United States for this project has been a closely watched event. Again, the combination of considerable design skills with an obvious concern for environmental issues proves that green is no longer the ugly duckling of contemporary architecture. Adjaye, though younger than Ando or Piano, for example, is certainly one of the rising stars of world architecture and his very visible participation in the movement toward sustainability is likely to influence many others.

With the likes of Piano (California Academy of Sciences, page 277) and Adjaye "competing" against him to achieve the highest possible LEED rating for a museum, the accomplishment of the Los Angeles architect Michael B. Lehrer, author of the Water + Life Museums complex in Hemet, mentioned above (page 219), is worthy of note. His was the first such structure to obtain a Platinum rating. Intended as a "living example of sustainability and conservation," the Water + Life Museum has a 3000-panel solar array that provides 50% of energy needs, and a water reclamation system for drip irrigation of plants. Abundant natural daylight and extensive use of heat-blocking glass are other features of the structure. Lehrer is surely not as well known as Adjaye, but his powerful design for the Hemet Museum, coupled with the Platinum rating, is likely to earn considerable renown.

CHASING BUTTERFLIES

Although a great deal of defining what green design means has to do with enumerating the different ways that this question is approached by architects or landscape architects, for example, it is also about thinking out the consequences of the built environment for sustainability. Sustainability, too, can be defined in various ways. Should a forest grow back after it is cut? Or should the entire rhythm of human existence on the planet condemn the species, or, indeed, most life on earth, within relatively brief time spans on a geological scale? The answer to the first question depends on how trees are cut and how they are replanted. The second one verges on the philosophical since accurate measurements of remaining resources, global warming, or the progressive extinction of species are the subject of active debate amongst scientists, let alone politicians. There does seem to be growing evidence of global warming, the extinction of certain species, and the depletion of reserves, such as that of petroleum. The very mechanisms that lead to ecological catastrophe are not well understood, surely because of the systemic interdependence of life on earth, but also because of the inaccuracy of weather predictions and analyses of the consequences of given actions.

Despite the existence of the LEED standards, sustainability is not a cut and dried affair. The famous "butterfly effect" seen in chaos theory surely applies to changes in the climate. What seems to be a positive approach on a local scale might well have a greater negative

10
Barlindhaug Consult AS, Svalbard
Global Seed Vault, Longyearbyen,
Svalbard, Norway, 2007–08

10

impact than anyone suspects. Accounting for the real environmental costs of manufacturing photovoltaic cells or biofuels is not a simple affair, as recent news items have shown. Rising costs of certain materials lead to economic adjustments that may obviate carefully calculated gains. When it is cheaper to ship granite from Zimbabwe than to use local stone, are architects and promoters really to blame if their materials come from the other side of the planet?

It seems clear that one consequence of the "green revolution" is that individuals are encouraged to feel responsible not only for their fate by that of others, but also for other life forms. Obviously used to building as they please, some architects are now finding themselves lifting their buildings off the ground in order to reduce their impact not only on the land itself, but also on the various types of plant, animal, or insect life that abounds there. Even the LEED system is not inclusive enough where this logic is concerned. However, a holistic approach that might consider architecture to be part and parcel of the natural world rather than an alien presence imposed by the force of machines is in the cards, perhaps many years off, or perhaps closer than some believe. The young New Zealand architect Chris Tate built his own house (Forest House, Titirangi, Auckland, New Zealand, 2006, page 357) in a protected natural environment. Though inspired by Philip Johnson's splendidly isolated Glass House, Tate's design takes into account all local zoning and environmental restrictions and allows itself to be almost swallowed up by nature. Sustainability, indeed, does not necessarily mean living in a building that smells like hemp or has walls made of rammed earth … even though those options exist as well.

FROM BABYLON TO THE ARCTIC

The extreme range of "green" projects that exist today might be symbolized by the selection of three works in this book, one built and two unbuilt. One unbuilt work is by the French team Agence Babylone. Their Active Nature proposal (Saclay, France, 2007, page 55) was the result of a competition launched by a group of 49 townships in the area of Paris. Although it is unlikely to be built in its proposed form, their idea consists in making radical use of the "productive capacities of nature," while preserving as much farmland as possible given predicted increases in population. Interesting because it is a combined scheme (in collaboration with architects SoA), this landscape and architecture design might well be the most reasonable path to the future, assuming the capacity of townships to impose an overall plan despite the extensive commercial interests involved. Mixing architecture and landscape design, futuristic green technology and a degree of clever presentation, the Active Nature project points, too, at the increasingly necessary collaboration between disciplines, especially when dealing with phenomena that are global rather than local. Indeed, the fact that global factors are now impinging on matters that used to be of strictly local concern is one of the very significant changes facing architecture as the "green revolution" takes hold.

The Belgian architect Vincent Callebaut takes a similarly "utopian" view of a green future. His Anti-Smog design for Paris (France, 2007, page 95) would make use of "all available renewable energy forms to fight against the Parisian smog." This would include windpower, phyto purification of water, photovoltaic cells, and a coating of smog-eating titanium dioxide (TiO_2) for good measure. When large numbers of new technologies are used in single projects, one may legitimately wonder if they are likely to work as well as hoped. There is something of the clever "gadget" about such architecture as well, and yet the imminent arrival of buildings whose real purpose is to fight pollution may not

11
SITE, Fondazione Pietro Rossini
Pavilion, Briosco, Italy, 2000–08

11

be too far off. Callebaut takes a sci-fi approach to his concepts, which, of course, means that they are not entirely serious. These are "what if" projects that may make people think about the ways in which architecture can contribute not only to reducing the pollution it produces directly, but also possibly helping to reduce overall levels of poisonous gases and other dangerous substances in the environment.

The third recent project that illustrates a very different way to approach climate change is the Svalbard Global Seed Vault (Longyearbyen, Svalbard, Norway, 2007–08, page 77) by Peter Søderman of Barlindhaug Consult AS. Essentially a long tunnel and vault carved into a frozen mountain in Norway's Arctic north, this facility is designed to save the diversity of the world's seeds no matter what ecological or military crisis might cross the planet in the years to come. Though it is graced with a glittering work of art by Dyveke Sanne, the Svalbard Global Seed Vault has something of the Doomsday Machine about it—an icy vault that awaits a catastrophe that may well have already been announced. It is not certain that the GBC would grant this facility a platinum rating, but it is hard to imagine a more ecological or "green" gesture in architecture. This building is a pure expression of sustainability—or a guarantee that crop diversity can be protected even as the waters rise and storms roll over the lands.

THE TIMES, THEY ARE A-CHANGIN'

The Malaysian architect Ken Yeang is one of the most committed international professionals in the area of sustainable design. His work in this area consists of very real buildings (see his Mewah Oils Headquarters of 2001–03 in Malaysia, page 401, and his New National Library Board Building in Singapore of 2001–05, page 404), but also of considerable thought and writing. In an essay entitled "What is Green Design?" Yeang states: "If we integrate our business processes and design and everything we do or make in our built environment (which by definition consists of our buildings, facilities, infrastructure, products, refrigerators, toys, etc.) with the natural environment in a seamless and benign way, there will be no environmental problems whatsoever." Ken Yeang is clearly pleading for something much broader than a few photovoltaic cells on a roof—he is making the case for a very specific kind of return to nature, where architecture has often sought to challenge nature. "Ecosystems have no waste," continues Yeang, "everything is recycled within. Thus by imitating this, our built environment will produce no wastes. All emissions and products are continuously reused, recycled within and eventually reintegrated with the natural environment, in tandem with efficient uses of energy and material resources. Designing to imitate ecosystems is ecomimesis. This is the fundamental premise of ecodesign. Our built environment must imitate ecosystems in all respects."[8]

One of Yeang's pet ideas over the years has been to bring nature into cities and buildings. Without going as far as his scheme for generalized ecomimesis, it can be admitted that his analysis of the organic and inorganic components of architecture is sensible and could lead to effective changes, short of turning cities into gurgling swamps of biological activity. "Our myriad of construction, manufacturing and other activities are, in effect, making the biosphere more and more inorganic," says Yeang. "To continue without balancing the biotic content means simply adding to the biosphere's artificiality, thereby making it increasingly more and more inorganic, exacerbating this and other environmentally destructive acts such as deforestation and pollution. This results in the biological simplification of the biosphere and the reduction of its complexity and diversity."[9]

12
Ken Yeang, Mewah Oils Headquarters, Pulau Indah Park, Port Klang, Selangor, Malaysia, 2001–03

12

James Wines of the American group SITE has long had a somewhat bittersweet, or some might say "romantic," vision of nature, designing his early BEST stores in the form of ruins overtaken by a resurgent forest. This idea of nature in architecture seems to be at the heart of his recent proposal, Streetscape in a New World (Beijing, China, 2008, page 324). Here, his drawings depict an increasingly dense web of branch-like paths and intersecting forest areas in the midst of a large urban development. It is, he says, "intended as a metaphor for a growing culture and proposal for environmental improvement in a rapidly burgeoning city." This approach is both a literal one, bringing large trees into the planned complex, but also a poetic one, returning a mixture of concrete and living plants to an environment that is increasingly deprived of anything green.

Although Yeang's program is ambitious, he is getting to the heart of the matter. Might it be that green architecture is not so much about architecture as it is about survival? The aesthetics and internal quarreling of the architectural profession are obviously secondary considerations when it comes to finally stopping the war with nature that has resulted in the creation of "the asphalt jungle."[10] The problem, as Yeang points out, is not specific to architecture: it is systemic and concerns industry as much, if not more, than buildings. It concerns life habits and the use of resources, and the need for change before catastrophe ensues. Making green design fashionable is one tool at the disposition of architects, but it seems clear that it is now time, not to jump on the bandwagon, but to face the inevitable. With soaring gasoline prices and so much evidence of climate change, it is likely that the trend to green will be a lasting one. Architects who ignore this trend might just find they have been replaced by clever builders with a bold LEED AP stamped on their visiting card. Then again, good architecture never represented more than a small proportion of what is built in the world. The times, they are a-changin'.

Philip Jodidio, Grimentz, June 29, 2008

1. "SmartMarket Trends Report," McGraw-Hill Construction Analytics, 2008.
2. "EIA Annual Energy Review 2005," US Energy Information Administration, US Department of Energy.
3. Lenssen and Roodman, "Worldwatch Paper 124: A Building Revolution: How Ecology and Health Concerns are Transforming Construction," Worldwatch Institute, 1995. This reference, as well as the previous two, was noted in "Green Building Facts," published by the US Green Building Council (USGBC), June 2008.
4. Felicity Barringer, "The New Trophy Home, Small and Ecological," in: *The New York Times*, June 22, 2008.
5. Ibid.
6. Ibid.
7. "Reflections on Underground Space," in: *L'Architecture d'aujourd'hui*, May–June 2003.
8. Ken Yeang, "What is Green Design?" in: *Design Does Matter*, Teknion, Mt Laurel, New Jersey, 2005.
9. Ibid.
10. *The Asphalt Jungle* is a 1950 film directed by John Huston, starring Sterling Hayden and Marilyn Monroe.

EINLEITUNG

KRIEG IM ASPHALTDSCHUNGEL

Keine Frage, „Grün" ist das Thema der Stunde. Nie gab es so viel Interesse an den ökologischen Folgen von Bauten wie heute. Allein in den Vereinigten Staaten wird das Volumen „grüner" Bauvorhaben bis 2010 auf voraussichtlich 60 Milliarden Dollar steigen.[1] Dies ist kein unwesentlicher Beitrag im Kampf darum, die Umweltverschmutzung in den Griff zu bekommen, und bei der Suche nach verantwortungsvollen, „nachhaltigen" Baumethoden. Gebäude zählen zu den größten Verbrauchern von natürlichen Ressourcen und sind für einen erheblichen Teil der Treibhausgasemissionen und deren Auswirkungen auf den Klimawandel verantwortlich. In den Vereinigten Staaten verursachen Bauten 39 % aller CO_2-Emissionen.[2] Gebäude machen 40 % des globalen Verbrauchs von Rohmaterialien aus.[3] Das Problem ist jedoch, dass „Grün" so in Mode gekommen ist, dass jeder versucht, auf den Zug aufzuspringen und meint, erstaunliche Nachhaltigkeit und einen außerordentlich niedrigen Energieverbrauch vorweisen zu können. Eine effektive Gegenreaktion auf die vagen Stellungnahmen zu den komplexen ökologischen Auswirkungen von Architektur war die Einführung von LEED (Leadership in Energy and Environmental Design). LEED ist ein anerkanntes Bewertungssystem des US Green Building Council (USGBC), mit dessen Hilfe sich Gestaltung, Bauweise und Betriebsverhalten grüner Bauten beurteilen lassen. Nach Angaben des USGBC „fördert LEED einen nachhaltigen Ansatz, der das gesamte Bauwerk im Blick hat, indem es den Leistungsstandard in fünf Schlüsselbereichen untersucht, die für Gesundheit von Mensch und Umwelt relevant sind: nachhaltige Grundstückserschließung, sparsamer Wasserverbrauch, Energieeffizienz, Materialauswahl sowie das Raumklima im Bau." Dabei zertifiziert der USGBC nicht nur Bauten, sondern auch Fachleute des Bauwesens. Seit Gründung des Akkreditierungsprogramms „LEED Accredited Professionals" (AP) 2001 haben sich über 46 000 Fachleute aller Gebiete registrieren lassen.

Das System des Green Building Council berücksichtigt die unterschiedlichsten Berufsbilder des Bauwesens und damit nicht nur Architekten. Eine solch breit angelegte Bewertungsstruktur ist zweifellos wesentlich besser geeignet, echte Umweltverträglichkeit in der Architektur zu fördern als einzelne Architekten, die behaupten, ihr Bauwerk sei grüner als ein beliebiges anderes. Vielleicht sollte man sogar fragen, ob die Architektur angesichts des Klimawandels, der inzwischen zu einem politischen Schlüsselthema geworden ist, nicht vor einem fundamentalen Wandel steht, der Stil und ästhetische Fragen hinter Fragen der Umweltverträglichkeit auf den zweiten Platz verweist. Es gab Zeiten, als „grüne" Bauten geradezu verpflichtet waren, Flagge zu zeigen. Es waren unansehnliche und komplizierte Kreationen, oft bunt, als habe man sein Umweltbewusstsein schon bewiesen, wenn man das gesamte Regenbogenspektrum in einem Gebäude vereinte. Natürlich erweist sich die Technik als hilfreich, indem sie den Architekten umweltverträgliche Materialien an die Hand gibt, die zugleich attraktiv sind. Dank Wärmeschutzverglasung, wie sie Gestalter wie Werner Sobek verwenden, kann ein verglastes Haus ebenso umweltverträglich sein, wie ein mit Lärchenschindeln verkleideter Bau. Auch Solarzellen werden immer effizienter, selbst wenn sie oft nur einen relativ geringen Prozentsatz des Energieverbrauchs eines Hauses decken. Das hängt natürlich vom Klima ab, und sicherlich ist ein grauer Himmel weniger günstig für Solarmodule als Wüstensonne. So wie die Dinge liegen, sind manche Maßnahmen zur Umweltverträglichkeit, ob nun passiv oder aktiv, ohnehin kaum sichtbar. Ein Gebäude optimal auszurichten oder seine Außenhaut fachgerecht so zu planen, dass die Aufheizung durch die Sonne minimiert wird – solche Maßnahmen haben kaum oder keine Auswirkung auf das ästhetische Erscheinungsbild. Und auch Solarmodule werden üblicherweise dezent auf dem Dach installiert, sofern es den Architekten nicht darum geht, ihr Sonnenenergie-Patchwork zum „Statement" zu machen.

13
Fearon Hay, Shark Alley Retreat,
Great Barrier Island, Auckland, New
Zealand, 2002–03

13

HEUTE KALIFORNIEN, MORGEN DIE WELT

Im Februar 2007 wurde der UK Green Building Council (UK-GBC) gegründet, um auch in Großbritannien Einheitlichkeit in das ökologische Bauen zu bringen. Ein von der Regierung berufenes Komitee für nachhaltiges Bauen hatte zuvor festgestellt, dass keine der mit Nachhaltigkeit befassten Körperschaften oder Organisationen klare Vorgaben für den gesamten Bereich bot. Diese Rolle sollte nun der UK-GBC übernehmen. Sowohl die amerikanische Organisation als auch ihr britisches Pendant gehören zum Dachverband WorldGBC, der „die nationalen Green Building Councils unterstützt, deren allgemeiner Auftrag lautet, durch die Veränderung des Marktes ein nachhaltiges bauliches Umfeld zu schaffen". Der WorldGBC hielt seine Gründungsversammlung, an der acht Staaten teilnahmen, 1999 in San Francisco ab. Gegenwärtig gibt es 12 nationale Gesellschaften und weitere 16 Länder, in denen Green Building Councils im Entstehen sind. Zu den Mitgliedern zählen derzeit Australien, Brasilien, Deutschland, Großbritannien, Indien, Japan, Kanada, Mexiko, Neuseeland, Taiwan, die USA und die Vereinigten Arabischen Emirate. Diese Länder repräsentieren über 50 % der gesamten Bauaktivität weltweit, wobei ihre Bemühungen um Nachhaltigkeit unterschiedlich effektiv ausfallen.

In anderen Ländern wurden ähnliche Organisationen gegründet, um umweltspezifische Qualitäten von Bauten zu kontrollieren. Ein Beispiel hierfür ist MINERGIE®, „ein Qualitätslabel für neue und sanierte Gebäude, ... von der Wirtschaft, den Kantonen und dem [Schweizer] Bund gemeinsam getragen", das in der Schweiz und international als Markenzeichen eingetragen ist. In nur zehn Jahren wurden 7200 Gebäude mit einer Fläche von insgesamt 6,5 Millionen m^2 nach MINERGIE®-Standard zertifiziert. Das System wird auch in Frankreich angewandt.

Obwohl sich das GBC-System zunehmend ausbreitet und manche Gemeinden und Regierungskörperschaften begonnen haben, entsprechende Anforderungen zum festen Bestandteil ihrer Vertragsvereinbarungen mit Architekten und Bauunternehmern zu machen, gibt es auch Zweifel. Umfragen zufolge sind zahlreiche führende Industrievertreter in den USA überzeugt, „grüne" Architektur sei teurer als ein „normales" Gebäude. Eine GBC-Studie zu Bauten in Kalifornien zeigte jedoch, dass sich „grüne Optimierungen innerhalb von drei Jahren amortisieren". Kürzlich veröffentlichte die *New York Times* einen Artikel über verschiedene Vorurteile und Thesen, die der Verbreitung der grünen Welle im Weg stehen – etwa das Vorurteil, grüne Gebäude seien hässlich. Diese Vorstellung ist vermutlich auf eine lange Tradition von Architekten zurückzuführen, die offenbar glaubten, umweltfreundliche Bauten müssten aus irgendeinem Grund unansehnlich sein. Kelly Meyer, eine von der *New York Times* zitierte Umweltschützerin, bemüht sich mit ihrem Mann, einem Bauunternehmer, zu zeigen, dass „etwas Energieeffizientes nicht so aussehen muss, als hätte man es aus dem untersten Regal eines Bioladens gefischt. Es muss nicht zwangsläufig nach Hanf riechen."[4]

FLUGEXPERIMENTE

David Hertz, einer der in diesem Band vorgestellten Architekten, bezeichnet die LEED-Richtlinien des GBC als „unflexibel und schwerfällig". Tatsächlich ist der Zertifizierungsprozess komplex und potenziell kostenaufwendig.[5] Hertz ist es gelungen, die Tragflächen einer ausgemusterten Boeing 747 auf innovative Weise in einen Neubau zu integrieren (747 Wing House, Santa Monica Mountains, Malibu, Kalifornien, 2007–09, Seite 185). Diese Art von Recycling dürfte ihm trotz ihrer Dramatik kaum eine der begehrten LEED-Platinmedaillen bescheren, dennoch scheint er entschlossen, sich gegen die bürokratischen Richtlinien des GBC aufzulehnen. Ein anderer, im gleichen Artikel der *New York*

Times zitierter Architekt, Michael B. Lehrer, äußert sich erwartungsgemäß positiver über den Zertifizierungsprozess; schließlich wurde sein Water + Life Museum (Hemet, Kalifornien, 2001–06, Seite 219) unlängst als erstes Museum mit einer LEED-Platinmedaille ausgezeichnet: „Sie berücksichtigen relativ banale Dinge, die ziemlich unsinnig, aber auch andere, die fundamental wichtig sind. Und in Zeiten, in denen einfach jeder behauptet ‚Wir sind grün', ist es wichtig, dass solche Dinge glaubwürdig beurteilt werden."[6]

Erfreulicher ist die Tatsache, dass die LEED-Richtlinien ebenso wie andere Initiativen umfassend, ja mitunter ganzheitlich an Umweltfragen herangehen. Die Bemühungen reichen von natürlicher Belichtung bis hin zur Abfallreduzierung – Faktoren, die Architekten zwar beeinflussen, jedoch in vielen Fällen nicht allein kontrollieren können. Und so bezieht der GBC nicht nur Architekten, sondern eine ganze Bandbreite verschiedener „Baufachleute" mit ein, die sich gemeinsam um „nachhaltige" Ergebnisse bemühen. Allerdings geht es in diesem Buch weder nur um Gebäude mit LEED-Platinmedaille (der höchstmöglichen Auszeichnung) noch um Architekten, die zu jeder Gelegenheit die unattraktive Abkürzung „LEED AP" hinter ihren Namen setzen. Vielmehr geht es um die verschiedensten Bemühungen, dank derer eine Beziehung zwischen baulicher und natürlicher Umwelt erwächst, und das im positiven Sinn. Die Reihe *Architecture Now!* befasst sich nicht vorrangig mit den technischen Aspekten von Bauten, sondern speziell mit ihrer architektonischen Qualität. Obwohl Kelly Meyer mit ihrer Bemerkung, ein grünes Bauwerk müsse „nicht nach Hanf riechen" sicherlich Recht hat, trifft es ebenso zu, dass nicht jedes Gebäude, das sich Umweltverträglichkeit auf die Fahnen geschrieben hat, gute Architektur ist. Die LEED-Richtlinien mögen ein geeignetes Instrument sein, um irreführende Werbung mit „ausgeglichener CO_2-Bilanz" oder verkaufsfördernden Etikettenschwindel mit „Nachhaltigkeit" zu reduzieren. Dennoch verführt die Tatsache, dass alles „Grüne" in Mode ist, zu Manipulationen jeder Art. Die in diesem Buch vorgestellten Projekte reichen von Konzeptentwürfen bis hin zu Großbauten, vertreten sind Parks, eine Tankstelle ebenso wie eine Tiefkühlkammer für Saatgut. Der springende Punkt dabei ist, dass es viele verschiedene Arten gibt, sich mit dem Verhältnis von Umwelt und Architektur auseinanderzusetzen.

Die breite Publikumswirkung solcher Filme wie Al Gores „Eine unbequeme Wahrheit", die sich auf die immer offensichtlicheren Anzeichen für den Klimawandel stützen, und der hohe Prozentsatz globaler Ressourcen, die die Bauindustrie verbraucht, machen die Dringlichkeit deutlich, mit der Architekten sich weiterentwickeln und Verantwortung übernehmen müssen. In diesem Buch mögen noch ein oder zwei Bauten „nach Hanf riechen", doch inzwischen ist längst klar, dass Nachhaltigkeit und gute Architektur Hand in Hand gehen können.

LASST TAUSEND GÄRTEN BLÜHEN

Eine uralte Methode zur Steigerung der Nachhaltigkeit von Architektur ist ihre Begrünung. Eine Schicht Erde wirkt dämmend und erlaubt der Natur letztendlich, sich ihren Platz auf dem jeweiligen Grundstück zurückzuerobern. Die Natur ins Zentrum der Stadt zurückzuholen bedeutet, das künstlich geschaffene Umfeld aufzulockern (eine Tatsache, die auf so komplexe Probleme wie den Klimawandel allerdings eher psychologische als reale Auswirkungen hat). Dennoch hilft in diesem Kampf, der in absehbarer Zukunft zig Millionen Menschen beschäftigen wird, schon der kleinste Beitrag. Zwei begrünte Dächer von höchst unterschiedlicher Größe, gelegen an zwei entgegengesetzten Enden der USA, veranschaulichen, auf wie unterschiedliche Weise die Natur in einen architektonischen Kontext einbezogen werden kann. In Washington D. C. realisierte Michael Van Valkenburgh ein 130 m² großes begrüntes Dach für den Sitz der American Society of Landscape Architects

14

14
Patrick Blanc, CaixaForum Vertical
Garden, Madrid, Spain, 2006–07

(2005–06, Seite 385). Mit künstlichen Materialien legte er Leichtbauhügel an und erfand in gewisser Weise eine neue Landschaft auf kleinstem Raum, die den Besuchern nicht nur zu etwas Grün verhilft, sondern auch ihren Blick auf die Stadt verändert. Angesichts der Tatsache, dass Dachflächen meistens kaum genutzt werden und unansehnlich sind, kann das Projekt als Beispiel dafür gelten, was sich in größerem Maßstab realisieren ließe, wenn es nur genügend öffentliches Interesse und finanzielle Anreize gäbe. Das von Renzo Piano für die California Academy of Sciences in San Francisco (2005–08, Seite 277) gestaltete Dach hat gänzlich andere Dimensionen und vollkommen andere Ziele. Das Dach hat eine Fläche von fast einem Hektar und wurde mit 1,8 Millionen verschiedenen einheimischen Pflanzen begrünt. In der Umweltstrategie des Baus, der als zweites amerikanisches Museum eine LEED-Platinmedaille erhalten wird, kommt dem Dach eine Schlüsselrolle zu. Die Erdschicht auf dem Gebäude reduziert die Temperatur der Innenräume im Sommer um 6° C, was u. a. die Klimatisierungskosten senkt.

Der französische Botaniker Patrick Blanc verfolgt einen anderen Ansatz zur Begrünung der Stadt. Sein vor Kurzem fertiggestellter, 600 m² großer vertikaler Garten am CaixaForum (Madrid, 2006–07, Seite 91) liegt im Herzen der spanischen Hauptstadt, gegenüber vom Prado. Er befindet sich auf einer Fassade unmittelbar neben dem Eingang zum neuen Ausstellungsgebäude der Schweizer Architekten Herzog & de Meuron, dem CaixaForum. Blanc hat eine Methode patentieren lassen, mit der das Wachstum von Pflanzen auf vertikalen Wandflächen ohne Erde möglich ist. Abgesehen davon, dass es ungewohnt ist, einen ganzen Garten an der Fassade eines Gebäudes hängen zu sehen, spricht einiges dafür, diese ansonsten problematischen Flächen der urbanen Landschaft zu nutzen. So wie Michael Van Valkenburgh und andere sich der Begrünung von Dächern zugewandt haben, hat Patrick Blanc begonnen, sich Wänden und Mauern zu widmen. Sie wirken wie Kunstwerke und bringen frischen Wind in die drangvolle Enge der Stadt.

Obwohl sich seine Methoden extrem von Patrick Blancs Ansatz unterscheiden, hat auch das spanische Team Ecosistema Urbano dazu beigetragen, in Madrid ein Bewusstsein für die Probleme der Umweltverschmutzung und des Schwindens von Grünflächen zu schaffen. Ihr Ecoboulevard in Vallecas (Madrid, 2006, Seite 127) besteht aus drei sogenannten Luftbäumen. Angetrieben mit Solarenergie, versprühen die temporären Bauten fein zerstäubtes Wasser auf die Passanten. Diese Wassersprühtechnik ist durchaus nichts Neues und kann die Umgebungstemperatur um bis zu 10° C senken, eine Wohltat in Madrids drückend heißen Sommern und ein Anreiz für die Anwohner, sich hier zu treffen. Künstliche Bäume haben eine lange Geschichte in der Architektur, angefangen mit der Säule bis hin zu postmodernen Kreationen solcher Gestalter wie Hans Hollein in Wien. Der Ansatz von Ecosistema Urbano entwickelt diese architektonische Metapher weiter und lässt den künstlichen „Baum" etwas tun, was auch reale Wälder tun – die Temperatur senken und angenehme Plätze schaffen.

FRISCHE MINZE, BITTE

Ein anderer junger Gestalter, der französisch-schweizerische Architekt Philippe Rahm, wurde bekannt mit dem Entwurf architektonischer Umgebungen, in denen er so grundlegende Faktoren wie den Sauerstoffgehalt der Luft modifiziert, um die körperliche Befindlichkeit der Besucher zu beeinflussen. Sein jüngstes Projekt, Digestible Gulf Stream (Architekturbiennale Venedig, 2008, Seite 291), ist ein kleines Haus, in dem eine Ebene auf 12° C, eine andere auf 28° C temperiert ist. Berechnungen zufolge werden diese zwei Extreme von den meisten Menschen als „angenehm" empfunden. Rahm behauptet zu Recht, dass Klimaanlagen, Heizsysteme und andere Formen architektonischer

Umweltsteuerung auf „normale" Bedingungen zugeschnitten sind, die nur wenige jemals hinterfragen, es sei denn, sie fühlen sich unwohl. Seiner Ansicht nach kann die Architektur gerade dadurch, dass sie diese Normen hinterfragt, zu neuen Ufern aufbrechen und besipielsweise fundamental an die Physiologie anknüpfen. Bei diesem Projekt experimentiert Rahm auch mit der These, dass essbare Substanzen wie Pfefferminz (Menthol) eine kühlende Wirkung erzeugen, die nichts mit jenen konventionellen Kühlvorrichtungen zu tun hat, die in fast allen modernen Bauten außerhalb unserer Sichtweite und bewussten Wahrnehmung leise vor sich hinsurren.

INSELN IM FLUSS

Der japanische Architekt Tadao Ando interessiert sich schon lange für unterirdisches Bauen, was durchaus einen Bezug zu „grüner" Architektur haben kann. 2003 äußerte er: „Ich habe eine fast unbewusste Neigung zu unterirdischen Räumen. Wie auch immer das Grundstück aussehen mag, versuche ich Architektur zu schaffen, die nie dominanter ist als ihre Umgebung … An unterirdischen Räumen zu arbeiten, schlägt den Bogen zurück zu den Ursprüngen der Architektur."[7] Eines der jüngsten Projekte Andos ist das Chichu Art Museum/Naoshima (Naoshima, Kagawa, Japan, 2000–04, Seite 61). Das japanische Wort „chichu" bedeutet „unterirdisch", und das Gebäude selbst lässt sich von den Hügeln der Umgebung aus kaum ausmachen. Dank der üppigen Vegetation auf der Insel lassen nur die Oberlichter und offenen Innenhöfe ahnen, dass sich hier ein Gebäude verbirgt. Obwohl sich Andos Kommentar eher auf ein architektonisches Konzept als auf Umweltfragen bezieht, ist die in der Seto-Inlandsee gelegene Insel Naoshima, wo Ando auch andere Bauten realisierte, zum Großteil Naturschutzgebiet. Früher wurde hier Bergbau betrieben. Es ist interessant, dass Ando nur selten auf das neuerdings in Mode gekommene Vokabular „grünen" Designs zurückgreift. Dennoch sind die massiven Betonmauern, die er entwirft und – im Fall des Chichu Art Museum – die Erdschicht, die das gesamte Gebäude bedeckt, eine bemerkenswerte Passivenergiestrategie. Hinzu kommt, dass die Innenräume des Museums zum Großteil natürlich belichtet werden. Ein zweites, jüngeres Projekt Andos ist die U-Bahnstation Shibuya auf der Tokyu-Toyoko-Linie in Tokio (2005–08, Seite 66). Die 27 725 m^2 große U-Bahnstation in einer der am dichtesten besiedelten urbanen Regionen der Welt verfügt über ein natürliches Belüftungssystem. Diese Tatsache ist umso erstaunlicher, als Tokios ausgedehntes U-Bahnnetz aufgrund der hohen Temperaturen im Sommer überwiegend künstlich klimatisiert ist.

KLEINER PARK, GROSSE CANYONS

Obwohl Architekten inzwischen gern Visitenkarten mit LEED-Akkreditierung präsentieren, gibt es auch traditionellere Formen, um zur Umweltqualität beizutragen, etwa indem man die Natur ganz einfach durch Parkanlagen unterstützt. Zwei Beispiele für solche Interventionen, eine winzig klein, die andere monumental, stellen unter Beweis, dass Landschaftsarchitektur notwendiger Bestandteil jeglicher Bemühungen um größere Nachhaltigkeit ist. Der kleine (815 m^2 umfassende) Samir-Kassir-Platz in Beirut (Libanon, 2004, Seite 117) von Vladimir Djurovic wurde um zwei große Feigenbäume herum angelegt, die auf wundersame Weise den Bürgerkrieg in Beirut überstanden haben. „Im Grunde soll [der Platz] ein kleiner Zufluchtsort für die Stadt und ihre Menschen sein." Trotz seiner relativen Bescheidenheit entging das Projekt der Jury für den Aga-Khan-Preis für Architektur nicht, die den Samir-Kassir-Platz 2007 als Beitrag für eine Stadt auszeichnete, in der die muslimi-

15
Vladimir Djurovic, Samir Kassir
Square, Beirut, Lebanon, 2004

15

schen und christlichen Bürger selten Orte finden, an denen man verweilen kann. In weitaus größerem Maßstab (51 km²) entwarf die amerikanische Firma EDAW, für die Djurovic zuvor gearbeitet hatte, den Landschaftsmasterplan für den Jinji-See in der historischen Stadt Suzhou (China, 2002–04, Seite 135). Die etwa 60 km von Shanghai entfernte Stadt ist berühmt für ihre Kanäle und Gärten. 514 v. Chr., zur Zeit der Frühlings- und Herbstannalen, hatte der König Helu von Wu die „Große Stadt von Helu", so der alte Name von Suzhou, als Hauptstadt seines Reichs gegründet. Nach Fertigstellung des Großen Kanals lag Suzhou strategisch günstig an einer wichtigen Handelsroute. Durch die gesamte chinesische Geschichte hindurch war die Stadt Industrie- und Handelszentrum. Sie wurde auch „das Venedig des Ostens" genannt, doch Umweltverschmutzung und rapide Entwicklung begannen zur Bedrohung für Suzhou zu werden, bis die Stadtverwaltung konzertierte Anstrengungen unternahm, das Wasser zu klären und neue Grünflächen anzulegen. Die eigentlichen Projekte von EDAW im Rahmen des Masterplans sind der 5 ha große Jinji Lake Cityside Harbor und der 7 ha große Maple Forest Park. Auch wenn Bücher über „grüne Architektur" die Landschaftsplanung oft außer Acht lassen, ist sie doch eine der offensichtlichsten Möglichkeiten, der Umweltverschmutzung und den Belastungen des urbanen Lebens entgegenzutreten.

Ein anderer Großentwurf für einen Park, der Orange County Great Park (Irvine, Kalifornien, 2007–, Seite 333), stammt von dem New Yorker Landschaftsarchitekten Ken Smith. Smith hatte schon für den Dachgarten des Museum of Modern Art (2003–05) auf dem MoMA-Anbau von Yoshio Taniguchi verantwortlich gezeichnet. Der MoMA-Garten ist, zumindest teilweise aus technischen Erwägungen, ein rein künstlicher Garten und besteht aus Kunststofffelsen, Glasbruch und Mulch aus recyceltem Gummi. Auf dem 545 ha großen Parkgelände in Irvine hingegen plant Smith eine „natürlichere" Intervention – u. a. einen „großen Canyon" von 3,2 km Länge und 9 m Tiefe, der Flüsse wiederbelebt, die früher auf dem Gelände verliefen, bevor es als Militärflughafen für ein Korps der Marines genutzt wurde. Schon jetzt können Besucher das Gelände von einem Heißluftballon aus besichtigen, dennoch wird es noch einige Jahre dauern, bis die neue Anlage, einschließlich eines botanischen Gartens und zahlreicher Fahrrad- und Wanderwege, fertiggestellt sein wird.

Das Spiel mit natürlichen und künstlich geschaffenen Umgebungen bei Ken Smith erinnert uns daran, dass nicht nur „grüne" Architektur schwer zu definieren ist – auch die Natur selbst ist in der Architektur nicht immer leicht auszumachen. Die Japaner vertreten mit solchen Persönlichkeiten wie Itsuko Hasegawa oder Toyo Ito schon lange die These, dass sich Architektur mit der Schaffung einer künstlichen „Natur" befassen sollte. Diese lässt sich zwar von Formen der Natur inspirieren, ist aber dennoch eindeutig künstlich. Dennis Dollens, ein amerikanischer Biometrikspezialist, arbeitet mit Xfrog, einer Software mit „botanischen L-System-Algorithmen, die bei biologischen Computersimulationen zum Einsatz kommen, um das Wachstum von Pflanzen und Landschaften für Labortests und Simulationen darzustellen". Dollens sagt über seine verschiedenen Versuche, Hochhäuser zu entwerfen, die von der Natur inspiriert sind: „Das gemeinsame Prinzip hinter diesen Projekten ist, dass computergeneriertes Wachstum von architektonischen Strukturen und Systemen von biomimetischen Erkenntnissen befruchtet werden kann, ohne in die traditionelle Kategorie ‚organische Architektur' zu fallen. Hinzu kommt, dass es sinnvoll ist, die Potenziale von Biowissenschaft, Biotechnologie und digitalen Fertigungsmethoden an einem Punkt zusammenzuführen, an dem sich architektonische Produktion und neue Optionen für nicht toxische Architektur kreuzen." (Vergleiche Dollens' Tree Tower, Los Angeles, Kalifornien, 2009, Seite 123.) Anders als Architekten, die sich mit der Annahme zu begnügen scheinen, ein Haus aus Holz sei „nachhaltig", blickt Dollens auf neue Anwendungen

16
EDAW, Jinji Lake, Suzhou, China,
2002–04

16

der Computerwissenschaften voraus, die es der Architektur möglicherweise erlauben werden, sich fundamental zu verändern, in gewisser Weise naturähnlicher zu werden und damit weniger „toxisch".

DER GERUCH VON HANF

Natürlich erzeugen traditionelle Bauweisen, die in weiten Teilen der Welt Verwendung finden, nicht annähernd den Verschmutzungsgrad „moderner" Bauten. Diese Tatsache hat viele Architekten inspiriert, denen es nicht nur darum ging, Menschen in Not zu helfen, sondern auch deren Bautechniken aufzugreifen, um Gebäude zu realisieren, die sowohl langlebig als auch tatsächlich „nachhaltig" sind. Ein gutes Beispiel für diesen Ansatz sind Anna Heringer und Eike Roswag. Ihre Handmade School in Bangladesch (Rudrapur, Dinajpur, 2005, Seite 179) ist ein 325 m² großes Gebäude aus Lehm und Bambus und kostete nicht mehr als 25 000 Euro. Auch dieses Projekt wurde 2007 mit dem Aga-Khan-Preis für Architektur ausgezeichnet. Das Projekt, das auch moderne Baumaterialien wie Nylonseile nutzt, bietet Kindern Schutz und einen fröhlichen Ort zum Lernen. Dabei hat es kaum negative Auswirkungen auf die Umwelt und verbraucht wenig Energie. Das Zentrum für Herzchirurgie „Salam" (Soba, Sudan, 2006–07, Seite 351) der italienischen Gruppe studio tamassociati wurde um zwei große Mangobäume herum erbaut. 58 cm dicke Mauern aus zwei Backsteinschichten mit einer dazwischen liegenden, isolierenden Luftschicht, 1000 m² Solarmodule und ein Wassersprühsystem, das für Kühlung sorgt und Staub aus dem Gebäude hält, sind nur einige „grüne" Merkmale des Baus, der in einer Gegend errichtet wurde, in der sich die Menschen die typischen, verschwenderischen Baumethoden westlicher oder entwickelter östlicher Länder ganz einfach nicht leisten können. Obwohl das „Salam"-Zentrum moderner wirkt als die Handmade School, verbirgt sich in ihm dennoch ein kreativer Ansatz, der soweit wie möglich ortstypische Materialien nutzt und zugleich neuere Technologien mit einbezieht (Solarmodule). Christine's House (Mason's Bend, Alabama, 2005–06, Seite 309) ist ein Beispiel für die kreative Arbeit der Architekturstudenten an der Auburn University. Ihr Projekt entstand im Rahmen des 1993 gegründeten Rural-Studio-Programms von Samuel Mockbee, das darauf ausgerichtet ist, den einkommensschwachen Bürgern von Alabama zu helfen. Die Studenten arbeiteten mit dem typischen roten Lehmboden der Gegend und mischten 70 % Erde, 25 % Pappmaschee aus Zeitungspapier und 5 % Portlandzement. Diese Mischung gossen sie in unterschiedlich große Pappkartons und fertigten so Ziegel für die beiden Hauptmauern des Hauses. So stellten die Studenten unter Beweis, dass sich mit einfachen Methoden und einem gelungenen Entwurf Architektur realisieren lässt, die ebenso attraktiv wie umweltfreundlich ist.

NULLENERGIE ALS ZIEL

Private Wohnbauten verschiedenster Art haben sich als lohnendes Experimentierfeld für Nachhaltigkeitskonzepte erwiesen. Schließlich sind wohlmeinende Hauseigentümer bereit, auch etwas mehr zu zahlen, um „ökologische Verantwortung" zu zeigen. Der deutsche Ingenieur Werner Sobek ist einer der herausragenden Spezialisten für ausgeklügelte Architektur, die nach dem heutigen Stand der Technik so nachhaltig wie nur möglich ist. Sein Haus H16 (Tieringen, Deutschland, 2005–06, Seite 337) ist mit seinen 454 m² größer, als man bei einem ökologischen Bau erwarten würde, verfügt jedoch über „maximale Transparenz bei minimaler Konstruktion, ist vollständig recycelbar … und emissionsfrei". Der Energieverbrauch des Hauses wird durch passive Strategien unterstützt, etwa durch die Wahl transparenter oder opaker

17

Bauvolumina, je nach ihrer Exponiertheit dem Sonnenlicht gegenüber. Doch auch eine Erdwärmeheizung mit Wärmepumpe und Fotovoltaik-paneele tragen zur Nachhaltigkeit des Wohnhauses insgesamt bei. Am bedeutendsten ist, dass es Sobek gelingt, ein attraktives modernes Haus zu gestalten und zugleich höchste Umweltstandards zu berücksichtigen – was beweist, dass „Grün" nicht unansehnlich sein muss. Das Rafflesia Zero Energy House (Kuala Lumpur, Malaysia, 2007–09, Seite 407) von Zoka Zola wurde bisher nicht realisiert. Das Projekt, das sich in einem Wettbewerb durchsetzen konnte, bedient sich verschiedenster Strategien, um sich bei minimaler Beeinträchtigung des Ökosystems in die Umwelt zu integrieren. Zudem gelingt es ihm, wenige bis keine externen Energiequellen zu nutzen. Zu dem Konzept zählen u. a. ein dämmender, 50 cm großer Hohlraum im Dach, eine exakte Analyse der Windverhältnisse und großflächig installierte Solarmodule.

Wo Häuser wie das H16 oder Rafflesia Gestalt annehmen, scheint es unvermeidlich, dass Architekten in einen gesunden Wettstreit ein-treten und versuchen, einander in puncto Nachhaltigkeit zu übertreffen. Bei ihrem Projekt für das *New York Times Magazine* scheinen die New Yorker Architekten Diller Scofidio + Renfro mit ihrem Phantom House (südwestliche USA, 2007, Seite 113) so weit wie nur möglich gegangen zu sein. Das Haus arbeitet nicht nur mit realer Technik, sondern auch mit fiktiven Systemen, die pragmatisch und realisierbar scheinen, etwa mit Trimmrädern, die Elektrizität erzeugen, wann immer die Hausbesitzer das Bedürfnis nach Fitness haben. Den Zeichnungen nach zu urtei-len ist das Haus nicht gerade ein Meisterwerk zeitgenössischer Architektur, doch da es inzwischen gilt, so energieeffizient und umweltverträg-lich wie möglich zu sein, werden sich wahrscheinlich auch die ästhetischen Ansprüche weiterentwickeln, wobei besonderer Wert auf Eigen-schaften gelegt wird, die unseren Planeten möglicherweise „retten" werden.

JE GRÖSSER, DESTO BESSER

Zwar sind kleinere Nullenergie- oder Fast-Nullenergiehäuser interessante Experimentierfelder für Architekten, die Zeit oder betuchte Auftraggeber haben, dennoch sind es wohl Großbauten, denen sich all jene widmen sollten, die wirklich die CO_2-Emission reduzieren wollen. Für einen interessanten Ansatz entschied sich der spanische Architekt Rafael de La-Hoz mit seinen Bauten für die Telefónica de España SA, dem neuen Telefónica Distrito C (Las Tablas, Madrid, 2002–07, Seite 213). Dieser Komplex für das größte spanische Unternehmen umfasst nicht weniger als 390 000 m^2. Mit einer Grundstücksfläche von 19 ha ist dies eines der größten in jüngster Zeit von einem Unternehmen in Auftrag gegebenen Projekte in ganz Europa. Passivenergiestrategien spielen eine entscheidende Rolle bei diesem Entwurf. Hohe elegante Bal-dachindächer spenden einem Großteil der Bauten Schatten. Außerdem setzte der Architekt ein ungewöhnliches System aus Glaslamellen ein, die lotrecht aus der Fassade herausragen und nicht nur zusätzlichen Schatten spenden, sondern auch Schattenspiele auf die Gebäude malen – fast sieht es aus, als verändere sich das geometrische Profil im Lauf des Tages. Je nach Sonneneinfallswinkel wurden die großflächig verglasten Fassaden mit einem unterschiedlich dichten Muster aus Siebdruckpunkten überzogen, was die Aufheizung durch die Sonne redu-ziert und im Inneren des Baus wie eine angenehme Tönung wirkt. Solarmodule bedecken 26 000 m^2 des Baldachindachs. Sie erzeugen aus-reichend Energie, um den Ausstoß von jährlich 2000 t CO_2 in die Atmosphäre zu verhindern. Eine (nicht vom Architekten entworfene) Garten-anlage verbindet die Gebäude und bringt Grün in den sonst luftig wirkenden Komplex. Es ist zweifellos ein Zeichen dafür, dass „grüne" Architektur den Mainstream erreicht hat, wenn Auftraggebern wie Telefónica die Notwendigkeit bewusst wird, sich Fragen der Nachhaltigkeit

18
Adrian Smith + Gordon Gill Archi-
tecture, Masdar Headquarters,
Abu Dhabi, United Arab Emirates,
2008–10

18

zu stellen. In einem so heißen Klima wie in Madrid, wo sich Kosten für künstliche Klimatisierung durch entsprechendes Design drastisch reduzieren lassen, ist dies von besonderer Bedeutung. Im Fall von Rafael de La-Hoz entschied sich der Auftraggeber für einen Architekten, dem es
gelingt, Nachhaltigkeit in großem Maßstab mit qualitativ hochwertigem Design zu verbinden.

In einer anderen, noch heißeren Region mit großen Ambitionen in puncto Architektur, den Vereinigten Arabischen Emiraten, haben Adrian Smith und Gordon Gill das Zentralgebäude für die Planstadt Masdar entworfen (Abu Dhabi, 2008–10, Seite 327). Das Gebäude ist Teil der
„ersten CO_2-emissions- und abfallfreien Stadt der Welt, die mit erneuerbaren Energien betrieben wird," und verfügt selbstverständlich über
ein großflächiges Fotovoltaikdach, baut jedoch auch auf Windkraftanlagen und Windtürme, um zusätzliche natürliche Energiequellen zu nutzen. Wasser- und Energieverbrauch werden sorgfältig gesteuert, und auch sonst sollen „überall nachhaltige Materialien zum Einsatz kommen,
die ihrer Ökobilanz entsprechend ausgewählt wurden". Mit seinen 88 000 m² wirkt das „grüne" Masdar–Zentralgebäude sexy, wenn auch
etwas überdimensioniert. Adrian Smith hat sich in der Region als Planer verschiedener Großbauten, insbesondere des höchsten Gebäudes der
Welt, des Burj Dubai (SOM), einen Namen gemacht. Smith und andere „Stararchitekten" wie etwa Lord Norman Foster, der ebenfalls am Bauprojekt Masdar City beteiligt ist, stellen mehr und mehr unter Beweis, dass Nachhaltigkeit etwas anderes sein kann als langweilige Berechnungen – und zwar richtiggehend aufregend, sofern man die Architektur nicht darauf reduziert, als aufwendiges Tragwerk für Solarmodule zu
dienen, die endlose Flachdächer bedecken.

Vor vier Jahren konnte Norman Foster einen ganzen Campus im Dschungel von Malaysia fertigstellen (Petronas University of Technology, Seri Iskandar, 1999–2004, Seite 147). Das zweifellos als groß zu bezeichnende Projekt mit seinem 450 ha großen Grundstück und einer
Bruttogeschossfläche von 240 000 m² wurde für rund 6000 Studenten geplant. Die in die Topografie des Grundstücks eingefügten Gebäude
werden von zahlreichen Baldachindächern überspannt, die sowohl vor der Sonne als auch vor den häufigen Regenfällen der Monsunzeit
schützen. Die Petronas-Universität wurde sorgfältig auf soziale Interaktion hin konzipiert und mit der für Fosters Büro typischen modernen
Strenge ausgeführt. Sie zeigt, dass gelungenes Design unter bestimmten Umständen ebenso vom Klima abhängt wie von cleverer Technologie. Foster war ganz offensichtlich einer der ersten prominenten Architekten, die ihre Gebäude auf Nachhaltigkeit ausrichteten. Ihm ist sicher
nicht wie manchen anderen „Stararchitekten" vorzuwerfen, erst spät auf den „grünen Zug aufgesprungen" zu sein.

Die Planstadt Masdar („Masdar" bedeutet so viel wie „Quelle") soll ausschließlich mit Solarenergie und anderen nachhaltigen Energie-
quellen versorgt werden. Erbaut wird die Stadt unweit des Flughafens von Abu Dhabi, und obwohl der Entwurf in den Händen von Foster +
Partners liegt, wird die Architektur sicherlich nicht ihr einziges auffallendes Merkmal sein. Großfirmen wie BP, Royal Dutch Shell, Mitsubishi,
Rolls-Royce, Total S. A., Mitsui und Fiat haben sich zu einer Initiative, dem „Clean Tech Fund" zusammengefunden. Unterdessen plant man ein
Solarkraftwerk mit einer Leistung von 40 bis 60 MW, Windkraftanlagen, ein Wasserkraftwerk und Geothermienutzung. Ähnliche Initiativen
wurden bereits im Mittleren Osten und China angekündigt, und so drängt sich der Gedanke auf, dass sich die Architektur wohl wird wandeln
müssen, wenn die grüne Welle weiter an Schubkraft gewinnt. Ganz offensichtlich haben sich viele berühmte Architekten in der Vergangenheit
auf ihr ästhetisches Gespür verlassen, um sich einen Namen zu machen. Doch monumentale Großprojekte wie Masdar und selbst das LEED-
Bewertungssystem des GBC verteilen die Verantwortung für Nachhaltigkeit auf die Schultern sämtlicher Berufe des Bauwesens und darüber

hinaus. Dasselbe gilt für die Suche nach neuen Technologien, die beispielsweise der Elektrotechnik näher stehen als traditionellen Formen des Bauingenieurwesens. „Gute" und sogar einige der großartigsten Architekten sind seit Langem daran gewöhnt, die besten und mitunter teuersten Materialien nutzen zu können, ohne groß darüber nachzudenken, woher sie kommen oder ob sie erneuerbar sind. Am anderen Ende des Spektrums findet sich die große Mehrzahl aller Bauten, die unter immer gewinnorientierteren Bedingungen realisiert werden, was im schlimmsten Fall zu Bauten führt, die keine Chance haben, etwa ein Erdbeben zu überstehen. Das Streben nach Nachhaltigkeit macht es unerlässlich, die Kostenrechnung zu modifizieren und vielleicht zum ersten Mal seit Jahrzehnten einzuräumen, dass der unmittelbare Preis nicht das einzige Kriterium für die Bewertung der Ausführung von Architektur sein kann. Grüne Architektur setzt zudem eine zunehmende Vernetzung der am Bauprozess Beteiligten voraus, was durchaus die Freiheiten des Architekten einschränken mag. Dieses Buch will zeigen, dass „gute" Architektur und Nachhaltigkeit in der Tat Hand in Hand gehen können, besonders, wenn man den Begriff „grün" weiter fasst.

PLATINTRÄUME

Das LEED-Bewertungssystem berücksichtigt sechs Hauptkategorien: Diese befassen sich mit grundlegenden Fragen der Nachhaltigkeit der Grundstückserschließung, der Effizienz der Wassernutzung, mit Energie und Atmosphäre, Materialien und Ressourcen, dem Raumklima im Bau sowie Innovation und Entwurf. Es gibt vier LEED-Bewertungen, die je nach erlangter Gesamtpunktzahl ermittelt werden, wobei für Neubauten und umfassende Sanierungen von Gewerbebauten 69 Punkte die erreichbare Höchstzahl ist. Die Bewertungsstufen lauten: Zertifikat (26–32 Punkte), Silber (33–38 Punkte), Gold (39–51 Punkte) und schließlich Platin (52–69 Punkte).

Das Grand Rapids Art Museum (Grand Rapids, Michigan, 2004–07, Seite 395) wurde von wHY Architecture entworfen, einem 2003 von Yo-ichiro Hakomori und Kulapat Yantrasast gegründeten Büro. Vor 2003 war Yantrasast für Tadao Ando tätig und hatte an solchen Projekten wie dem Museum of Modern Art in Fort Worth mitgearbeitet. Das Museum in Michigan ist ein interessantes Beispiel, denn der Hauptsponsor des Projekts, der ortsansässige Philanthrop Peter Wege, hatte die LEED-Zertifizierung des Baus zur Bedingung für seine Spende gemacht. 10 % der Baumaterialien des Neubaus sind recycelt, natürliches Licht wird umfassend genutzt und Regenwasser verwendet, und so ist das Gebäude nicht nur im Hinblick auf seine Nachhaltigkeit intelligent, sondern kann darüber hinaus stolz ein eindrucksvolles, minimalistisches Design vorweisen, das an Yantrasasts früheren beruflichen Werdegang erinnert.

David Adjayes erster öffentlicher Bauauftrag in den USA, das Museum of Contemporary Art/Denver (Denver, Colorado, 2004–07, Seite 49), ist zwar kleiner, aber dennoch das erste Museum, das mit einer LEED-Goldmedaille ausgezeichnet wurde. Niedriger Energieverbrauch, niedrige Treibhausgasemissionen und der Einsatz umweltgerechter Rohmaterialien trugen zu dieser Bewertung bei. Adjaye hat sich in Großbritannien bereits einen Namen gemacht, und so wurde sein Einstand in den Vereinigten Staaten aufmerksam beobachtet. Auch hier ist es wieder die Kombination von außerordentlicher gestalterischer Begabung mit einem offensichtlichen Bewusstsein für Umweltbelange, die zeigt, dass „Grün" inzwischen keineswegs mehr das hässliche Entlein der Architektur ist. Auch wenn Adjaye jünger als etwa Ando oder Piano ist, darf man ihn sicherlich zu den aufstrebenden Stars der Architekturwelt rechnen. Sein auffallendes Engagement in Sachen Nachhaltigkeit dürfte Einfluss auf viele andere haben.

19

Die Leistung des in Los Angeles ansässigen Architekten Michael B. Lehrer ist umso bemerkenswerter, wenn man bedenkt, dass Kollegen wie Piano (California Academy of Sciences, Seite 277) und Adjaye mit ihm um die höchstmögliche LEED-Auszeichnung für ein Museum „konkurrieren"; Lehrer entwarf den bereits eingangs erwähnten Water + Life Museumskomplex in Hemet (Seite 219). Sein Bau wurde als Erster mit einer Platinmedaille ausgezeichnet. Das Water + Life Museum, ein „lebendiges Beispiel für Nachhaltigkeit und Umweltschutz", verfügt über eine Fläche mit 3000 Solarmodulen, die 50 % des Energiebedarfs decken, sowie über ein Wasseraufbereitungssystem, das die Tröpfchenbewässerung für die Bepflanzung speist. Weitere Merkmale des Baus sind umfassende natürliche Belichtung und Wärmeschutzverglasung. Auch wenn Lehrer nicht so bekannt ist wie Adjaye, werden ihm sein eindrucksvoller Entwurf für das Museum in Hemet und die Platinmedaille sicherlich einige Bekanntheit bescheren.

AUF DER JAGD NACH SCHMETTERLINGEN

Einerseits hat der Versuch, grünes Design zu definieren, viel damit zu tun, die verschiedenen Arten aufzuzählen, wie sich Architekten und Landschaftsarchitekten dem Thema nähern. Doch andererseits geht es auch darum, wie sich die gebaute Umwelt auf die Nachhaltigkeit auswirkt. Und auch Nachhaltigkeit lässt sich verschieden definieren. Wächst ein Wald nach, nachdem er geschlagen wurde? Oder bedeutet der gesamte Rhythmus menschlicher Existenz auf diesem Planeten das Todesurteil für verschiedene Arten oder gar die meisten Lebensformen auf dieser Erde innerhalb von – nach geologischen Maßstäben – relativ kurzer Zeit? Die Antwort auf die erste Frage hängt davon ab, auf welche Weise ein Wald gefällt und wieder aufgeforstet wird. Die zweite hingegen hat philosophische Dimensionen, schließlich wird die exakte Berechnung der verbleibenden Ressourcen, der Erderwärmung oder des zunehmenden Aussterbens verschiedener Arten intensiv von Wissenschaftlern und erst recht von Politikern diskutiert. Es scheint immer mehr Hinweise für die globale Erderwärmung zu geben, für das Aussterben bestimmter Arten und das Zurneigegehen von Ressourcen, etwa von Erdölreserven. Noch verstehen wir die grundlegenden Mechanismen, die zur ökologischen Katastrophe führen, nicht besonders gut, sicherlich wegen der systemischen Interdependenz der Lebensformen auf dieser Erde, doch auch weil Wettervorhersagen und die Analysen der Folgen bestimmter Handlungen nach wie vor unzuverlässig sind.

Trotz LEED-Richtlinien ist Nachhaltigkeit keine ausgemachte Sache. Der aus der Chaostheorie bekannte „Schmetterlingseffekt" wirkt sich zweifellos auch auf klimatische Veränderungen aus. Was in regionalen Zusammenhängen als positiver Ansatz gilt, kann negativere Folgen haben, als so mancher meint. Die realen ökologischen Kosten für die Herstellung von Solarzellen oder Biokraftstoffen zu beziffern, ist nicht leicht, wie aktuelle Nachrichtenmeldungen zeigen. Steigende Kosten bestimmter Ressourcen führen zu wirtschaftlichen Anpassungen, die sorgfältig kalkulierte Gewinne zunichte machen. Wenn es billiger ist, Granit aus Simbabwe zu verschiffen als heimische Steinarten zu nutzen, kann man Architekten und Bauträgern einen Vorwurf machen, wenn ihre Baumaterialien von der anderen Seite des Planeten kommen?

Es dürfte klar sein, dass eine Konsequenz der sich vollziehenden „grünen Revolution" die Erkenntnis ist, dass der Einzelne nicht nur für sein eigenes Schicksal, sondern auch für das anderer Menschen und Lebensformen verantwortlich ist. Und so beginnen selbst Architekten, die ganz offensichtlich daran gewöhnt sind zu bauen, wie es ihnen gefällt, ihre Gebäude vom Baugrund zu lösen, um nicht nur die Auswirkungen auf den Boden, sondern ebenso auf Pflanzenarten, Tier- und Insektenpopulationen zu minimieren, die es dort zuhauf gibt. Wo es um

20
Chris Tate, Forest House, Titirangi,
Auckland, New Zealand, 2006

20

logische Konsequenzen wie diese geht, ist selbst das LEED-System nicht umfassend genug. Dennoch ist ein ganzheitlicher Ansatz, der Architektur als integralen Bestandteil der Natur begreift und nicht als fremdartige Präsenz, die ihr mit Maschinengewalt aufgezwungen wird, unabwendbar – vielleicht erst in etlichen Jahren, vielleicht auch früher, als manche glauben. Der junge neuseeländische Architekt Chris Tate baute sein eigenes Haus (Forest House, Titirangi, Auckland, Neuseeland, 2006, Seite 357) in einem Naturschutzgebiet. Obwohl sich Tates Entwurf von Philip Johnsons in großartiger Einsamkeit gelegenem Glass House inspirieren ließ, berücksichtigt das Haus sämtliche Bebauungs- und Umweltauflagen und verschmilzt geradezu mit der Natur. Nachhaltigkeit bedeutet keineswegs, in einem Haus wohnen zu müssen, das „nach Hanf riecht" oder Wände aus gestampfter Erde hat … obwohl diese Optionen durchaus bestehen.

VON BABYLON BIS IN DIE ARKTIS

Die extreme Bandbreite „grüner" Projekte heutzutage lässt sich anhand dreier Beispiele aus diesem Band veranschaulichen, eines davon gebaut, zwei bisher unrealisiert. Eines der bisher ungebauten Projekte stammt von dem französischen Team Agence Babylone. Ihr Entwurf Nature Active (Saclay, Frankreich, 2007, Seite 55) war das Ergebnis eines Wettbewerbs, den 49 Stadtgemeinden im Pariser Umland ausgelobt hatten. Zwar ist es unwahrscheinlich, dass das Projekt in der geplanten Form realisiert wird, doch die Idee beruht im Wesentlichen darauf, die „produktiven Kapazitäten der Natur" angesichts eines prognostizierten Bevölkerungswachstums radikal zu nutzen und so viel Ackerland wie möglich zu erhalten. Der Landschafts- und Bauentwurf ist auch deshalb interessant, weil es sich um eine kombinierte Planung handelt (eine Zusammenarbeit mit den Architekten von SoA). Möglicherweise sieht so der sinnvollste Weg in die Zukunft aus, wenn man davon ausgeht, dass Gemeinden weiterhin befugt sein werden, trotz weitreichender wirtschaftlicher Interessen Gesamtbebauungspläne zu beschließen. Das Nature-Active-Projekt verknüpft Architektur und Landschaftsplanung mit kluger Präsentation und macht deutlich, dass es immer zwingender wird, interdisziplinär zu arbeiten, insbesondere bei Phänomenen, die eher globaler als lokaler Natur sind. Im Grunde ist die Tatsache, dass globale Faktoren Dinge beeinflussen, die früher rein lokale Bedeutung hatten, eine der Schlüsselveränderungen, mit denen sich Architektur heute auseinanderzusetzen hat, während die „grüne Revolution" um sich greift.

Der belgische Architekt Vincent Callebaut vertritt eine ähnliche „utopische" Vision von einer grünen Zukunft. Mit seinem Anti-Smog-Projekt für Paris (2007, Seite 95) plant er, „alle verfügbaren Formen erneuerbarer Energien zu nutzen, um den Pariser Smog zu bekämpfen". Hierzu zählen Windkraft, die organische Wiederaufbereitung von Brauchwasser, Solarzellen sowie obendrein eine Beschichtung der Bauhülle mit smogreduzierendem Titandioxid (TiO_2). Wenn innerhalb eines Projekts zahlreiche neue Technologien zum Einsatz kommen, darf man sich zu Recht fragen, ob sie tatsächlich so gut funktionieren wie gehofft. Architektur wie diese hat immer auch etwas von einer cleveren technischen Spielerei. Trotzdem wird es vielleicht nicht mehr lange dauern, bis Bauten realisiert werden, deren primärer Zweck es ist, die Umweltverschmutzung zu bekämpfen. Callebauts Konzepte entstehen aus einem von Science-Fiction inspirierten Ansatz heraus, was natürlich impliziert, dass sie nicht gänzlich ernst gemeint sind. Es sind „Was-wäre-wenn"-Projekte, die Menschen darüber nachdenken lassen, wie Architektur nicht nur die selbst erzeugten Emissionen minimieren kann, sondern möglicherweise dabei helfen könnte, giftige Gase und andere gefährliche Substanzen in der Umwelt insgesamt zu reduzieren.

21
Agence Babylone, Active Nature,
Saclay, France, 2007

Das dritte Projekt, der Global Seed Vault (Longyearbyen, Spitzbergen, Norwegen, 2007–08, Seite 77) von Peter Søderman (Barlindhaug Consult AS), zeigt eine völlig andere Herangehensweise an den Klimawandel. Im Grunde handelt es sich um einen langen Tunnel und einen Tresorraum, die in einen frostsicheren Berg im arktischen Norden geschlagen wurden. Zweck der Einrichtung ist es, die Vielfalt des globalen Saatguts zu schützen, ungeachtet aller ökologischen oder militärischen Krisen, die unseren Planeten in den kommenden Jahren heimsuchen mögen. Trotz des glitzernden Kunstwerks von Dyveke Sanne, das den Global Seed Vault auf Spitzbergen schmückt, scheint der Bau insgesamt eher ein Weltuntergangsszenario heraufzubeschwören – eine eisige Gruft, die auf eine möglicherweise bereits angekündigte Katastrophe wartet. Es bleibt zu bezweifeln, dass der GBC der Einrichtung eine Platinauszeichnung zuerkennt, dennoch lässt sich kaum eine ökologischere oder „grünere" Geste in der Architektur vorstellen. Der Bau ist ein Ausdruck von Nachhaltigkeit in ihrer reinstmöglichen Form. Er ist ein Garant für die Erhaltung der Vielfalt unserer Kulturpflanzen, trotz steigender Wasserpegel und wütender Stürme.

DIE ZEITEN ÄNDERN SICH

Der malaysische Architekt Ken Yeang zählt zu den weltweit engagiertesten Spezialisten im Bereich nachhaltiges Design. Seine Arbeit manifestiert sich ebenso in realen Bauten (etwa der Zentrale von Mewah Oils, 2001–03, in Malaysia, Seite 401, oder seinem New National Library Board Building in Singapur, 2001–05, Seite 404) wie auch in seinen umfangreichen Thesen und Schriften. In seinem Aufsatz „What is Green Design?" führt Yeang aus: „Wenn wir unsere Geschäftsprozesse und unser Design und alles, was wir in unserem baulichen Umfeld (das per definitionem aus Gebäuden, Anlagen, Infrastruktur, Produkten, Kühlschränken, Spielzeug etc. besteht) tun oder fertigen, nahtlos und auf positive Weise in das natürliche Umfeld integrieren, wird es keine Umweltprobleme geben." Yeang plädiert ganz offensichtlich für etwas Umfassenderes als ein paar Solarzellen auf einem Dach – er liefert Argumente für eine sehr spezifische Rückkehr zur Natur, obwohl die Architektur oft darauf bedacht war, die Natur herauszufordern. „Ökosysteme kennen keinen Abfall", fährt Yeang fort, „alles wird systemimmanent recycelt. Wenn wir dieses Prinzip imitieren, wird unsere Umwelt keine Abfälle produzieren. Sämtliche Emissionen und Produkte würden kontinuierlich wiederaufbereitet, systemimmanent recycelt und schließlich in die natürliche Umgebung zurückgeführt, während zugleich Energie und Ressourcen effizient genutzt würden. Mit Design Ökosysteme zu imitieren, ist Ökomimesis. Dies ist die grundlegende Prämisse von Ökodesign. Unser bauliches Umfeld muss Ökosysteme in jeder Hinsicht imitieren."[8]

Eine von Yeangs Lieblingsideen im Lauf der Jahre war, die Natur in Städte und Gebäude zurückzuholen. Ohne dabei so weit zu gehen wie sein Plädoyer für eine allumfassende Ökomimesis, lässt sich durchaus einräumen, dass seine Analyse organischer und anorganischer Komponenten in der Architektur Sinn macht und einen effektiven Wandel bewirken würde, ohne unsere Städte gleich in gurgelnde Sümpfe biologischer Prozesse zu verwandeln. „Unsere zahllosen Bau-, Produktions- und anderen Aktivitäten machen die Atmosphäre im Grunde immer anorganischer", meint Yeang. „So weiterzumachen, ohne die biotischen Umweltfaktoren in ein Gleichgewicht zu bringen, trägt nur dazu bei, die Künstlichkeit der Biosphäre zu verstärken und sie immer anorganischer zu machen, diese und andere umweltschädigende Vorgänge wie etwa die Abholzung und Umweltverschmutzung also zu verschlechtern. Dies führt zu einer Simplifizierung der Biosphäre, der Minderung ihrer Komplexität und Vielfalt."[9]

22
Office dA, Helios House, Los Angeles,
California, USA, 2006–07

22

James Wines, Mitglied des amerikanischen Teams SITE, hat schon lange eine bittersüße, manche würden sagen „romantische" Vision von der Natur. Seine frühen Entwürfe für Ladengeschäfte der Firma BEST waren wie Ruinen gestaltet, die scheinbar von einem zum Leben erwachten Wald überwuchert wurden. In seinem jüngsten Entwurf, Streetscape in a New World (Peking, 2008, Seite 324), scheint die Vorstellung von einer Natur, die in die Architektur eingebettet ist, endgültig zu dominieren. Seine Zeichnungen zeigen ein immer dichter werdendes Netz aus verzweigten Pfaden und sich überschneidenden Waldgebieten inmitten eines riesigen urbanen Erschließungsgebiets. Gedacht ist das Ganze ihm zufolge als „Metapher für eine wachsende Kultur und Vorschlag für die Verbesserung der Umweltqualität in einer rasch wachsenden Stadt". Dieser Ansatz ist ebenso buchstäblich – große Bäume sollen in den geplanten Komplex integriert werden – wie poetisch. Er bringt ein Zusammenspiel aus Beton und lebenden Pflanzen in eine Umwelt zurück, die zunehmend jeglichen Grüns beraubt wird.

Obwohl Yeangs Programm ehrgeizig ist, trifft es den Kern des Ganzen. Könnte es sein, dass es bei grüner Architektur im Grunde weniger um Architektur und vielmehr ums Überleben geht? Ästhetik und interne Streitigkeiten in der architektonischen Berufswelt sind offensichtlich sekundär, wenn es darum geht, endlich den Krieg mit der Natur zu beenden, der erst zur Entstehung des „Asphaltdschungels"[10] geführt hat. Das Problem, wie Yeang deutlich macht, ist kein spezifisch architektonisches, es ist ein systemisches Problem und betrifft die Industrie ebenso sehr (wenn nicht sogar stärker) wie unsere Bauten. Es geht um Lebensgewohnheiten, die Nutzung von Ressourcen und die Notwendigkeit eines Wandels, um einer Katastrophe zuvorzukommen. Grünes Design begehrenswert zu machen, ist ein Mittel, das Architekten zur Verfügung steht. Dennoch ist klar, dass es darum geht, nicht einfach auf den Trendzug aufzuspringen, sondern sich vielmehr dem Unausweichlichen zu stellen. Bei rasant steigenden Benzinpreisen und einer Vielzahl von Anzeichen für den Klimawandel ist damit zu rechnen, dass der grüne Trend von Dauer sein wird. Architekten, die diese Entwicklung ignorieren, werden bald feststellen müssen, dass sie von cleveren Bauunternehmern mit einer stolzen LEED-Akkreditierung auf ihrer Visitenkarte verdrängt worden sind. Andererseits war gute Architektur ohnehin nie mehr als ein kleiner Bruchteil dessen, was weltweit gebaut wird. Nun, die Zeiten ändern sich.

Philip Jodidio, Grimentz, 29. Juni 2008

[1] „SmartMarket Trends Report", McGraw-Hill Construction Analytics, 2008.
[2] „EIA Annual Energy Review 2005", US Energy Information Administration, US Department of Energy.
[3] Lenssen und Roodman, „Worldwatch Paper 124: A Building Revolution: How Ecology and Health Concerns are Transforming Construction", Worldwatch Institute, 1995. Auf diese Quelle, ebenso wie die beiden vorigen, wird in „Green Building Facts" verwiesen, herausgegeben vom US Green Building Council (USGBC), Juni 2008.
[4] Felicity Barringer, „The New Trophy Home, Small and Ecological", in: *New York Times*, 22. Juni 2008.
[5] Ebd.
[6] Ebd.
[7] „Reflections on Underground Space", in: *L'Architecture d'aujourd'hui*, Mai–Juni 2003.
[8] Ken Yeang, „What is Green Design?", in: *Design Does Matter*, Teknion, Mt. Laurel, New Jersey, 2005.
[9] Ebd.
[10] Der Film „Asphalt-Dschungel" unter der Regie von John Huston erschien 1950, in den Hauptrollen waren Sterling Hayden und Marilyn Monroe zu sehen.

INTRODUCTION

LA JUNGLE DE L'ASPHALTE EN QUESTION

Le vert est à la mode. Sans aucun doute. On ne s'est jamais autant intéressé à l'impact de la construction sur l'écologie. Rien qu'aux États-Unis, le poids économique de ce secteur en plein développement devrait représenter 60 milliards de dollars en 2010.[1] C'est un fait qui n'est pas à négliger dans la bataille pour la réduction de la pollution et les recherches sur des méthodes de construction durables. Le bâti est l'un des plus gros consommateurs de ressources naturelles et participe dans une proportion significative aux émissions de gaz à effets de serre qui affectent le changement climatique. Aux États-Unis, il représente 39 % de toutes les émissions de CO_2.[2] Les bâtiments consomment globalement 40 % des matières premières.[3] La difficulté est que le « vert » est si à la mode que tout le monde saute dans le train et annonce des niveaux étonnants de durabilité ou de réduction de la consommation d'énergie. Une des réponses efficaces aux incertitudes qui entourent la question complexe de l'impact environnemental de l'architecture est le LEED (Leadership in Energy and Environmental Design), le système de référence de l'US Green Building Council (USGBC) pour la conception, la construction et la réalisation de bâtiments « verts ». Selon l'USGBC : « LEED permet une approche de la durabilité qui concerne la totalité du bâtiment par l'identification de ses performances dans cinq domaines clés de la santé humaine et environnementale : traitement écologique du site, économie dans l'utilisation de l'eau, efficacité de la consommation énergétique, sélections des matériaux et qualité environnementale intérieure. » L'USGBC certifie non seulement les constructions mais aussi les professionnels. Plus de 46 000 représentants de toutes les professions du bâtiment sont ainsi devenus des « LEED Accredited Professionals » (AP) depuis le lancement de ce programme d'accréditation aux États-Unis en 2001.

Le système du Green Building Council concerne les diverses professions qui participent à l'acte de construire et non seulement les architectes. Ce système de notation à base large est certainement plus opérationnel, si l'on veut encourager réellement le développement durable en architecture, que de laisser des architectes isolés prétendre que leur projet est plus « vert » que celui de leurs voisins. On peut aussi se demander – le réchauffement global devenant un enjeu politique international important – si l'architecture elle-même n'est pas sur le point de connaître des changements très significatifs par lesquels le style et l'esthétique deviendront secondaires par rapport à l'écologie. À une certaine période, il était presque obligé que les bâtiments « verts » affichent leur originalité. Ils étaient laids et compliqués, et même souvent multicolores, comme si toutes les couleurs de l'arc-en-ciel étaient une preuve suffisante de leurs préoccupations écologiques. Aujourd'hui, la technologie vient à l'aide des architectes en leur offrant des matériaux environnementalement « corrects » et séduisants à la fois. Le verre thermique, utilisé par des concepteurs comme l'Allemand Werner Sobek, permet de réaliser une maison entièrement vitrée aussi écologique que si elle était habillée de shingles de bouleau. Les cellules photovoltaïques sont de plus en plus productives, sans être encore capables de produire plus qu'un pourcentage relativement faible de la consommation énergétique d'un bâtiment. Ceci dépend bien sûr du climat, le ciel gris étant moins propice aux panneaux photovoltaïques que le soleil du désert. Par ailleurs, certaines méthodes, passives ou actives, ne se laissent pratiquement pas deviner. Orienter un bâtiment correctement ou imaginer un habillage qui limite le gain solaire peut n'avoir pratiquement aucun effet sur son esthétique. Les panneaux photovoltaïques sont généralement dissimulés en toiture, mais les architectes peuvent décider de s'en saisir et d'en faire un parti pris dans le cadre d'une technologie d'exploitation diversifiée de la ressource solaire.

23

23
Michael Van Valkenburgh, ASLA
Green Roof, Washington, D. C., USA,
2005–06

AUJOURD'HUI LA CALIFORNIE, DEMAIN LE MONDE

Le UK Green Building Council (UK-GBC) a été lancé en février 2007, pour coordonner les initiatives en faveur du mouvement de la construction écologique au Royaume-Uni. Le Sustainable Buildings Task Group du Gouvernement avait auparavant publié un rapport montrant qu'aucun des organismes ou agences concernés par l'écologie ne fournissait d'orientations claires à ce secteur en tant que tel. Le UK-GBC a donc été créé pour remplir ce rôle. Les deux conseils – américain et britannique – font partie du WorldGBC qui « assiste les conseils *Green Building* nationaux dont la mission commune est de créer un environnement bâti durable par des actions de transformation du marché ». Le WorldGBC a tenu son congrès fondateur à San Francisco en 1999, auquel huit pays ont participé. On compte actuellement douze conseils nationaux et seize en cours de constitution. Les membres actuels sont l'Allemagne, l'Australie, le Brésil, le Canada, les Émirats arabes unis, les États-Unis, l'Inde, le Japon, le Mexique, la Nouvelle-Zélande, le Royaume-Uni et le Taïwan. Ces nations représentent plus de 50 % de l'activité mondiale dans le domaine de la construction, mais l'efficacité de leurs efforts en faveur du développement durable varie en fonction des pays.

D'autres pays ont créé des organismes similaires comme, par exemple, en Suisse, MINERGIE®, « un label de qualité destiné aux bâtiments neufs et rénovés ». « La marque est soutenue conjointement par l'économie, les cantons et la Confédération helvétique… et déposée en Suisse et dans le monde… » En dix ans, 7200 bâtiments représentant 6,5 millions de m^2 ont reçu leur certification MINERGIE®. Cette forme de certification est également utilisée en France.

Si le système de notation des GBC commence à s'implanter sérieusement et que certaines administrations locales ou gouvernementales commencent à intégrer ses contraintes dans les cahiers des charges des architectes et des constructeurs, quelques doutes s'élèvent cependant. Des études montrent que beaucoup de responsables d'entreprises aux États-Unis, par exemple, sont convaincus que l'architecture « verte » est plus coûteuse que les méthodes traditionnelles. Une étude, commandée par le GBC en Californie, montre cependant que « les améliorations dues à la conception écologique se remboursent d'elles-mêmes en trois ans ». Le *New York Times* a récemment publié un article soulignant un certain nombre d'idées et d'enjeux qui ralentissent la progression de la vague verte. L'une est que les bâtiments écologiques sont laids. Cette vision fausse est probablement due à une longue histoire d'architectes qui pensaient qu'une construction écologique devait d'une certaine façon montrer ses secrets. Kelly Meyer, une environnementaliste citée par le quotidien, essaie avec son mari, qui est promoteur, de prouver « qu'un projet conscient des problèmes énergétiques ne doit pas avoir l'air d'avoir été trouvé sur l'étagère du bas d'une épicerie bio. Il n'a pas à sentir le chanvre ».[4]

L'ESPOIR FAIT VIVRE

David Hertz, l'un des architectes sélectionnés dans cet ouvrage, pense que les standards GBC LEED sont « rigides et gênants », et il est certain que ce processus de certification est complexe et potentiellement coûteux.[5] Hertz a proposé une façon originale d'intégrer les ailes d'un vieux Boeing 747 dans une maison qu'il est en train de réaliser (747 Wing House, Santa Monica Mountains, Malibu, Californie, 2007–09, page 185). Ce type de réutilisation, aussi spectaculaire puisse-t-il paraître, peut ne pas lui garantir de gagner la précieuse médaille de platine, mais il semble rebelle aux aspects bureaucratiques du système GBC. Un autre architecte, cité dans le même article du *New York Times*, Michael B. Lehrer, est sans doute un peu plus positif sur le processus de certification LEED depuis que son Water + Life Museum à Hemet en Californie (2001–06, page 219) est récemment devenu le premier musée à obtenir le LEED Platine : «On y trouve des choses banales qui n'ont pas beaucoup de sens et d'autres qui sont très profondes. Au moment où n'importe qui dit »je suis écologique« , il est très important que tout ceci soit contrôlé de manière crédible. »[6]

Constatation plus positive, les standards LEED et les initiatives similaires prises ailleurs proposent réellement une approche des enjeux environnementaux qui repose sur une base large, voire holistique. Elle va de l'encouragement à utiliser la lumière naturelle à la réduction des déchets, facteurs que les architectes ne peuvent ni influencer ni contrôler dans de nombreux cas. Le GBC implique non seulement les architectes mais aussi une grande diversité de «professionnels de la construction», tous engagés dans la recherche d'un résultat plus «durable». Mais ce livre ne traite pas seulement du LEED Platine (la plus haute notation), ni des architectes qui arborent maintenant le peu séduisant acronyme de LEED AP. Son objet est de montrer la variété des efforts qui tissent une relation entre l'environnement construit et la nature au sens le plus positif. La série *Architecture Now !* ne s'attache pas aux aspects techniques des réalisations, mais plus précisément à leur qualité architecturale. Si Kelly Meyer a certainement raison lorsqu'elle dit qu'une construction «verte» «n'a pas à sentir le chanvre», il est également vrai que toute construction qui prétend respecter l'environnement n'est pas forcément de la bonne architecture. Le système LEED est sans doute une excellente façon de réduire les fausses affirmations «d'empreinte zéro carbone» ou de propositions commerciales abusives axées sur le développement durable, cependant les aspects très mode de l'écologie ouvrent la porte à toutes sortes de manipulations. Les projets présentés dans cet ouvrage vont de maisons concepts à de très grands ensembles, et comprennent des parcs, une station-service et une chambre forte pour semences. L'idée étant qu'il existe de nombreuses façons d'approcher les enjeux des relations entre l'environnement et l'architecture.

Le vaste succès public d'un film comme *Une vérité qui dérange* d'Al Gore, qui met en lumière les preuves toujours plus nombreuses d'un réchauffement global, ainsi que la forte proportion des ressources consacrées à la construction offrent un argumentaire clair et convaincant aux architectes qui évoluent et veulent prendre leurs responsabilités. Seuls un ou deux de ces projets «sentent le chanvre», mais il est déjà devenu évident que développement durable et bonne architecture peuvent aller main dans la main.

QUE FLEURISSENT MILLE JARDINS

Une très ancienne méthode pour améliorer la durabilité est d'enterrer l'architecture ou de la recouvrir de végétation. Une couche de terre peut servir d'isolant et permettre à la nature de retrouver sa place dans un site. Faire revenir la nature au centre des villes peut alléger un environnement exclusivement artificiel, mais a davantage un impact psychologique qu'une influence réelle sur des problèmes aussi vastes que celui du réchauffement global. On peut dire cependant que chaque petite avancée participe à un combat qui concerne des centaines de millions de personnes dans un futur prévisible. À deux extrémités opposées des États-Unis, deux toitures écologiques de dimensions très différentes montrent diverses manières architecturales de mettre à profit les forces de la nature. À Washington, Michael Van Valkenburgh a créé

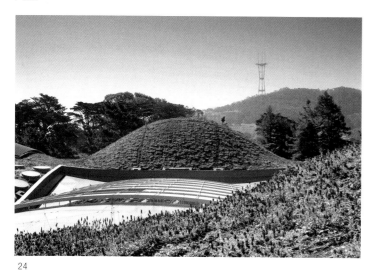

24

un toit vert de 130 m² pour l'immeuble de l'American Society of Landscape Architects (2005–06, page 385). Utilisant des matériaux artificiels pour créer de petits monticules, il invente en un sens un nouveau paysage sur une très petite surface, offrant aux usagers non seulement un peu de verdure mais aussi un changement de perspective sur la ville. Étant donné que les espaces des toitures sont généralement laids et sous-utilisés dans la plupart des villes, ce projet peut être considéré comme un petit exemple de ce que l'on pourrait faire à beaucoup plus grande échelle avec le soutien du public et des incitations financières. Le toit vert imaginé par Renzo Piano pour la nouvelle California Academy of Sciences à San Francisco (2005–08, page 277) se situe à une autre échelle et porte des ambitions différentes. Recouvrant environ un hectare et planté de 1,8 million de plantes locales, cette toiture est un élément clé de la stratégie environnementale du bâtiment, qui sera le second musée américain à recevoir la certification LEED Platine. Cette couche de terre permet de réduire de 6 °C les températures internes en été, ce qui, entre autres avantages, entraîne une réduction évidente des coûts de climatisation.

Le botaniste français Patrick Blanc emprunte des approches différentes pour « verdir » la ville. Son récent jardin vertical de 600 m² pour le CaixaForum (Madrid, 2006–07, page 91) est situé au cœur de la capitale espagnole, juste en face du musée du Prado. Il est installé sur une façade perpendiculaire à l'entrée d'un nouveau lieu d'exposition du CaixaForum conçu par l'équipe suisse Herzog & de Meuron. Blanc a bre-veté une méthode pour faire pousser des plantes sans terre, sur des murs verticaux. Tout comme Michael Van Valkenburgh et de nombreux autres se sont emparés des toits, Patrick Blanc a entrepris la même chose sur des murs, lesquels ressemblent à des œuvres d'art et appor-tent un peu d'air frais dans un environnement urbain congestionné.

Bien que ses méthodes soient extrêmement différentes de celles de Patrick Blanc, l'équipe espagnole Ecosistema Urbano participe également à la prise de conscience par les Madrilènes des problèmes de la pollution et de la disparition des espaces verts. Leur Ecoboulevard de Vallecas (Madrid, 2006, page 127) consiste en une série de trois « arbres à air » qui sont des installations éphémères utilisant des cellules photovoltaïques pour fournir l'énergie nécessaire à la dispersion d'une fine brume. Cette technique bien connue de vaporisation d'eau peut diminuer les températures de près de 10 °C, une véritable aubaine pour les étés madrilènes étouffants, et un encouragement à ce que les gens se réunissent. Les arbres artificiels ont une longue histoire en architecture, qui débute certainement par les colonnes et se poursuit par les explorations postmodernes, dont celles d'Hans Hollein à Vienne, par exemple. La technique d'Ecosistema Urbano fait monter d'un cran cette métaphore architecturale, et donne à l'arbre artificiel l'équivalent d'une vraie forêt qui abaisserait la température et rendrait un lieu plus agréable à vivre.

UN PEU DE MENTHE AVEC ÇA ?

Un autre jeune créateur, l'architecte franco-suisse Philippe Rahm, a débuté sa carrière en imaginant des environnements architectu-raux dans lesquels des facteurs fondamentaux comme le contenu de l'air en oxygène étaient modifiés pour altérer la condition physique des visiteurs. Son dernier projet, Digestible Gulf Stream (Biennale d'architecture de Venise, 2008, page 291) est une petite résidence dans laquelle la température d'un niveau est maintenue à 12 °C, et celle de l'autre à 28 °C, les deux extrêmes de la température « confortable » ressentie pour la plupart des gens. Rahm soutient à juste titre que la climatisation de l'air, le chauffage et d'autres formes architecturales de

25

contrôle environnemental sont systématiquement réglés pour maintenir un ensemble de conditions « normales » que peu de gens prennent la peine de remettre en question à moins de se sentir mal à l'aise. Il prétend au contraire que c'est précisément en remettant en cause ces normes que l'architecture peut trouver de nouvelles directions, liées à la physiologie par exemple. Pour ce projet, Rahm expérimente également la piste de substances comestibles comme la menthe qui peuvent créer une sensation de rafraîchissement sans lien avec ces machineries de réfrigération qui bourdonnent dans presque toutes les constructions modernes.

ÎLES DANS LE COURANT

L'architecte japonais Tadao Ando s'est longtemps intéressé à l'idée de construire sous terre, ce qui peut en effet parfois répondre à des enjeux écologiques. Comme il le disait en 2003 : « J'ai un penchant presque inconscient pour les espaces souterrains. Quelle que soit la nature du site, j'essaie de créer une architecture qui ne s'impose jamais dans son environnement … Travailler sur un espace souterrain est lié à la recherche des origines de l'architecture. »[7] Ando a récemment construit le Musée d'art Chichu (Naoshima, Kagawa, Japon, 2000–04, page 61). Le terme «chichu» signifie «souterrain» en japonais et ce bâtiment est quasiment invisible des collines voisines. La luxuriante végétation de l'île fait que rien, si ce n'est des verrières et des cours, ne trahira au niveau du sol la présence d'une construction. Bien que les déclarations d'Ando se réfèrent davantage à un concept architectural qu'aux enjeux de la protection environnementale, l'île de Naoshima dans la Mer intérieure du Japon, où il a d'ailleurs réalisé d'autres projets, est maintenant en grande partie une réserve naturelle après avoir été longtemps livrée à l'exploitation minière. Il est intéressant de noter qu'Ando n'emploie pas très souvent le nouveau vocabulaire à la mode de « conception verte », mais les épais murs de béton qu'il dessine et, dans le cas de ce musée, la couche de terre qui recouvre l'intégralité du bâtiment sont des stratégies d'énergie passive très efficaces. L'intérieur du musée fait aussi appel pour une bonne part à la lumière naturelle. Un autre projet d'Ando, plus récent encore, est sa station de métro Shibuya pour la ligne Tokyu Toyoko (Tokyo, 2005–08, page 66). Ici, une gare souterraine de 27 725 m^2 au cœur de l'une des zones urbaines les plus denses du monde bénéficie d'un système de ventilation naturelle, ce qui est d'autant plus étonnant que l'important réseau de lignes de métro de la capitale est en grande partie climatisé pour compenser les températures élevées atteintes en été.

PETIT PARC, GRAND CANYON

Bien que les architectes soient maintenant heureux d'arborer le logo LEED AP sur leurs cartes de visite, il reste qu'une manière plus conventionnelle de contribuer à la qualité environnementale est tout simplement d'encourager le développement de la nature, sous forme de parcs. Deux exemples de ce type d'intervention, l'un de dimensions réduites, l'autre massives, montrent que l'architecture du paysage est un composant essentiel de tout effort en faveur des enjeux du développement durable. Le petit square Samir Kassir de 815 m^2 à Beyrouth (Liban, 2004, page 117), conçu par Vladimir Djurovic, s'organise autour de deux grands ficus qui ont réussi à survivre aux années de guerre civile. «Essentiellement, c'est un petit espace dédié à la ville et à ses habitants », explique Djurovic. Malgré sa modestie relative, ce projet n'a pas échappé à l'attention du Prix Aga Khan d'architecture 2007 qui l'a distingué pour sa contribution à une ville dans laquelle les populations

26
Dennis Dollens, Tree Tower, Los
Angeles, California, USA, 2009

26

musulmanes et chrétiennes disposent de peu d'endroits pour se détendre. À beaucoup plus vaste échelle (51 km^2), l'agence américaine EDAW, pour laquelle Djurovic a travaillé à ses débuts, a conçu le plan directeur paysager du lac de Jinji dans la cité historique de Suzhou (Chine, 2002–04, page 135). Située à environ 60 km de Shanghai, cette ville est réputée pour ses jardins et ses canaux. En 514 av. J.-C., au cours du printemps et de l'automne, Helu, le roi de Wu, fonda la « Grande cité d'Helu », ancien nom de Suzhou, qui devait être la capitale du royaume. Lorsque le Grand Canal fut achevé, la ville se retrouva au bord d'une grande voie navigable commerciale. Au cours de l'histoire, elle est resté un centre industriel et commercial. Elle a été appelée la « Venise orientale », mais était menacée par la pollution et un développement rapide jusqu'à ce que l'administration entreprenne des efforts concertés pour nettoyer l'eau et créer des espaces verts. Le projet d'EDAW, inclus dans un plan directeur global, comprend un port de 5 ha et le parc de la forêt d'érables de 7 ha. Les ouvrages sur l'architecture verte tendent à négliger la conception du paysage qui est pourtant l'une des façons les plus évidentes d'aider aux efforts entrepris par ailleurs pour contrer la pollution et les tensions liées à la vie urbaine.

L'architecte paysagiste new-yorkais Ken Smith, auteur d'un très vaste projet de parc, l'Orange County Great Park (Irvine, Californie, 2007–, page 333) avait précédemment réalisé le jardin sur le toit de l'extension du Museum of Modern Art conçue par Yoshio Taniguchi (2003–05). Pour des raisons en partie techniques, incluant celle du poids, le jardin du MoMA est entièrement artificiel, fait de rochers de plastique, de verre brisé et de paillis de caoutchouc recyclé. Pour les 545 ha du parc d'Irvine, Smith prévoit une intervention plus « naturelle », y compris un grand canyon de 3,2 km de long et 9 m de profondeur, correspondant à d'anciens cours d'eau qui existaient avant que le site ne devienne une base aérienne de Marines. Un ballon à air chaud permet déjà aux visiteurs de se faire une idée de l'entreprise, mais plusieurs années seront nécessaires avant que ce nouveau projet, qui comprend aussi un jardin botanique et de nombreuses pistes pour vélos et marcheurs, soit prêt.

Le jeu sur la nature et l'artifice illustré par le travail de Ken Smith rappelle que si l'architecture « verte » est difficile à définir, la présence de la nature dans l'architecture ne l'est pas moins. Les Japonais, dont de grandes figures comme Itsuko Hasegawa ou Toyo Ito, affirment depuis longtemps que l'architecture doit s'engager dans la création d'une « nature » artificielle inspirée par les formes du monde naturel, mais cependant « fabriquées ». Le spécialiste américain de la biomimétique, Dennis Dollens, se sert du logiciel Xfrog qui consiste en « algorithmes botaniques inspirés de systèmes L, utilisés en simulations biologiques computationnelles pour des tests et des travaux en laboratoire sur la croissance des plantes et l'évolution des paysages ». De ses divers projets de tours et de ponts en relation avec l'univers naturel, Dollens précise : « Le concept unificateur derrière ces concepts est que la croissance computationnelle des structures et des systèmes architecturaux peut être influencée par des observations biomimétiques, sans tomber dans les catégories traditionnelles de "l'architecture organique". » Par ailleurs, le potentiel de la science de la biologie, des biotechnologies et de la fabrication assistée par ordinateur en arrive à une fusion à travers laquelle se dessinent et commencent à faire sens conjointement la production architecturale et de nouvelles possibilités d'architecture non toxique (voir sa Tree Tower, Los Angeles, Californie, 2007, page 123). À la différence de certains architectes qui semblent se satisfaire de dire qu'une maison en bois est « durable », Dollens regarde plus avant vers de nouvelles applications des sciences de l'informatique qui pourraient permettre à l'architecture elle-même de changer et de devenir plus proche de la nature et ainsi moins « toxique ».

27
*Anna Heringer and Eike Roswag,
Handmade School, Rudrapur, Dinajpur,
Bangladesh, 2005*

UNE ODEUR DE CHANVRE

Nulle part, les méthodes traditionnelles de construction utilisées sur une grande partie de la planète ne produisent des niveaux de pollution équivalents et même proches de ceux d'une «construction moderne». Cette réalité a inspiré un certain nombre d'architectes qui ont cherché non seulement à assister des gens dans le besoin, mais également à faire appel à leurs techniques de construction pour produire des bâtiments à la fois solides et authentiquement «durables». Un bon exemple de cette approche est donné par Anna Heringer et Eike Roswag. Leur école au Bangladesh (Rudrapur, Dinajpur, 2005, page 179) est une construction de 325 m^2 réalisée en terre et en bambou pour un coût de tout juste 25 000 euros. Récompensé par le Prix Aga Khan d'architecture 2007, ce projet fait appel à certains matériaux modernes comme des lanières en Nylon et offre aux enfants à la fois un abri et un lieu ludique d'enseignement, tout en n'exerçant que très peu d'effets négatifs sur l'environnement sans, logiquement, grande consommation d'énergie. Le centre Salam de chirurgie cardiaque (Soba, Soudan, 2006–07, page 351), réalisé par l'agence italienne studio tamassociati, a été entièrement construit autour de deux manguiers d'origine. Un mur de 58 cm d'épaisseur fait de deux parois de briques séparées par un vide d'isolation, 1000 m^2 de panneaux solaires, un système de vaporisation d'eau utilisé pour rafraîchir l'atmosphère et éloigner la poussière sont quelques-unes des caractéristiques «vertes» de ce petit bâtiment pour un pays dont les habitants ne peuvent tout simplement pas s'offrir les méthodes de construction hyperconsommatrices de l'Occident. Apparemment d'aspect plus «moderne» que l'école du Bangladesh, le centre Salam n'en représente pas moins une approche créative dans le recours maximum aux matériaux locaux, tout en faisant aussi appel à des technologies plus sophistiquées (panneaux solaires). Christine's House (Mason's Bend, Alabama, États-Unis, 2005–06, page 309) est un nouvel exemple du travail créatif exécuté par les étudiants d'architecture de l'université d'Auburn dans le cadre du programme Rural Studio fondé en 1993 par Samuel Mockbee, récemment disparu, pour venir en aide aux habitants pauvres de l'Alabama. En fabriquant des briques composées d'un mélange de 70 % de l'abondante argile rouge locale, de 25 % de pulpe de papier journal et de 5 % de ciment Portland, moulées dans des boîtes en carton de différentes tailles pour les deux murs principaux de la maison, ces étudiants ont montré que des méthodes simples et un bon projet peuvent donner naissance à une architecture à la fois agréable et environnementalement responsable.

OBJECTIF ZÉRO

Toutes sortes de maisons ont fait l'objet d'expérimentations fructueuses de différents concepts de développement durable grâce à des propriétaires «bien-pensants» qui acceptaient de dépenser un peu plus pour se montrer «écologiquement responsables». L'ingénieur allemand Werner Sobek est l'un des grands spécialistes d'une architecture sophistiquée qui se veut, en fonction de l'état actuel des technologies, aussi proche que possible de la durabilité authentique. Sa maison H16 (Tieringen, Allemagne, 2005–06, page 337), est d'une dimension plus importante, 454 m^2, que ce que l'écologie pourrait conseiller, mais elle atteint des objectifs de «transparence maximum, minimum de structure, recyclabilité intégrale… et zéro émissions». La consommation d'énergie de la maison est limitée par des méthodes passives comme l'opacité ou la transparence des volumes selon leur exposition au soleil, mais aussi à des moyens plus actifs comme le chauffage géothermique à pompe à chaleur et des panneaux photovoltaïques. Plus important encore, Sobek a réussi à créer une maison moderne

28

et séduisante tout en respectant les critères de respect de l'environnement les plus rigoureux, preuve que le vert n'est pas forcément laid. La maison Rafflesia Zero Energy (Kuala Lumpur, Malaisie, 2007–09, page 407) de Zoka Zola n'est pas encore construite, mais ce projet qui a remporté un concours utilise une large variété de stratégies pour s'intégrer à son environnement sans troubler – ou presque – l'écosystème; il réussit également à n'utiliser que très peu, voire pas, d'énergie électrique du réseau. Un vide de 50 cm sous le toit faisant office d'isolant et une étude poussée des mouvements naturels de l'air et de vastes surfaces de panneaux solaires sont quelques-unes des solutions employées ici.

Avec ces exemples, il pourrait sembler inévitable que les architectes se lancent dans une sorte de compétition, chacun essayant de dépasser l'autre dans le domaine de la durabilité. Dans un projet mis au point pour le *New York Times Sunday Magazine*, les architectes new-yorkais Diller Scofidio + Renfro semblent être allés aussi loin que possible dans leur projet de la Phantom House (sud-ouest des États-Unis, 2007, page 113). Cette maison fait appel non seulement à des technologies très concrètes, mais aussi à des systèmes dont on peut penser qu'ils sont pratiquement disponibles, comme des vélos d'appartement qui produisent de l'électricité pour la maison lorsque ses résidants décident de se dépenser un peu. Les dessins publiés de cette résidence n'augurent pas vraiment d'un futur chef-d'œuvre de l'architecture contemporaine, mais lorsque l'objectif est d'être aussi écologique que possible, il est probable que les critères esthétiques doivent évoluer et que l'on mettra l'accent sur des caractéristiques qui, peut-on l'espérer, contribueront d'abord à « sauver » la planète.

BIG IS BEAUTIFUL

Bien que les maisons à zéro émissions, petites ou mêmes virtuelles, soient d'intéressants exercices pour les architectes qui ont du temps ou des clients aisés, les grands bâtiments semblent être une cible plus appropriée pour ceux qui veulent vraiment faire la différence et réduire l'empreinte carbone. L'architecte espagnol Rafael de La-Hoz a emprunté une voie intéressante pour les immeubles du Telefónica District C pour Telefónica de España SA (Las Tablas, Madrid, 2002–07, page 213). Ce complexe réalisé pour la plus grande entreprise espagnole ne mesure pas moins de 390 000 m^2. Sur un terrain de 19 ha, c'est l'un des plus grands projets industriels récemment lancés en Europe. Les stratégies énergétiques passives jouent un rôle important dans la conception comme le montrent les élégants auvents de grande hauteur qui protègent de larges surfaces vitrées. L'architecte a également utilisé un système peu courant d'ailettes en verre qui se projettent perpendiculairement vers l'avant, créent davantage d'ombre et font varier l'aspect des façades des bâtiments, en donnant l'impression que leur géométrie se modifie tout au long de la journée. Des pastilles sérigraphiées de densité déterminée par l'angle de leur exposition au soleil recouvrent les vastes parois de verre des façades et réduisent le gain solaire, tout en générant, vues de l'intérieur, un effet agréable, légèrement teinté. Des panneaux solaires, qui occupent 26 000 m^2 des auvents, produisent suffisamment d'énergie électrique pour économiser annuellement 2000 tonnes de rejets de CO_2 dans l'atmosphère. Un jardin (non conçu par l'architecte) relie les bâtiments et ajoute un élément de verdure à ce complexe par ailleurs aéré et spacieux. Qu'un client comme Telefónica ait pris conscience des préoccupations écologiques et de la nécessité de réagir est indiscutablement un signe que l'architecture « verte » est désormais la tendance principale. Ceci est d'autant plus important sous un climat chaud comme celui de Madrid en été, lorsque les coûts de climatisation peuvent être substantiellement réduits

28
Zoka Zola, Rafflesia Zero Energy
House, Kuala Lumpur, Malaysia,
2007–09

29
Foster + Partners, Petronas Univer-
sity of Technology, Seri Iskandar,
Malaysia, 1999–2004

29

par une conception appropriée. Dans le cas de Rafael de La-Hoz, le client a choisi un architecte capable de mettre en œuvre des techniques de durabilité à grande échelle sans renoncer à une haute qualité architecturale.

C'est pour une région encore plus chaude, mais qui affiche de grandes ambitions architecturales, qu'Adrian Smith et Gordon Gill ont conçu le nouveau siège social de Masdar (Abu Dhabi, EAU, 2008–10, page 327). Faisant partie de «la première ville mondiale du zéro car-bone, zéro déchets, entièrement animée par les énergies renouvelables», l'immeuble possède bien sûr un vaste toit en auvent recouvert de panneaux photovoltaïques, mais emploie également des turbines et des cônes à vent pour profiter de cette autre forme d'énergie naturelle. L'utilisation de l'eau et de l'énergie électrique est soigneusement contrôlée, tandis que «des matériaux durables utilisés massivement ont été sélectionnés sur la base de l'analyse de leur cycle de vie». Avec ses 88 000 m^2, le siège de Masdar rend l'écologie «sexy» si ce n'est un peu envahissante peut-être. Adrian Smith est connu dans la région pour avoir conçu un certain nombre d'autres grands immeubles, et en particu-lier la plus haute tour du monde, le Burj Dubaï (SOM). Lui et d'autres architectes «stars» comme Norman Foster, qui participe également au projet de Masdar City, commencent à faire la preuve que la durabilité peut être autre chose qu'un ensemble de calculs ennuyeux – elle peut devenir stimulante lorsque l'architecture ne se contente pas seulement d'être le support élaboré de cellules photovoltaïques recouvrant des hectares de toits plats.

Norman Foster a réalisé il y a quatre ans, dans la jungle de Malaisie, un campus tout entier (Petronas University of Technology, Seri Iskandar, 1999–2004, page 147). Implanté sur un terrain de 450 ha et occupant une surface totale brute de 240 000 m^2, c'est un vaste pro-jet destiné à accueillir environ 6000 étudiants. Insérés dans la topographie, les différents bâtiments sont dotés de multiples et vastes auvents qui protègent à la fois du soleil et des pluies de mousson. Soigneusement étudiée pour encourager les échanges et réalisée dans l'esprit de rigueur moderne typique de l'agence de Foster, cette université montre qu'une conception adaptée peut, dans certaines circonstances, dépendre autant du climat que d'une technologie intelligente. Foster a été l'un des pionniers des architectes connus qui ont décidé de s'intéresser au développement durable. À la différence d'autres confrères stars, il ne pourra pas être accusé d'être monté tardive-ment «dans le train».

Masdar («la source», en arabe) est conçue pour fonctionner entièrement à l'énergie solaire ou d'autres sources d'énergie renouve-lable. La ville sera édifiée près de l'aéroport international d'Abu Dhabi et, bien qu'elle soit conçue par Foster + Partners, son architecture ne sera pas sa seule originalité. De très grandes firmes comme BP, Royal Dutch Shell, Mitsubishi, Rolls-Royce, Total, Mitsui et Fiat se sont regroupées autour d'une initiative appelée «Clean Tech Fund» (Fondation de l'énergie propre), tandis que des plans sont en cours d'étude pour construire une centrale d'énergie solaire de 40 à 60 MW, des fermes éoliennes, une centrale d'énergie à l'hydrogène et des captages d'énergie géothermique. D'autres initiatives de ce type ont été annoncées au Moyen-Orient et en Chine, ce qui fait penser que l'architecture devra évoluer rapidement si la vague verte monte encore. Dans le passé, un certain nombre des plus célèbres architectes comptaient sur leur sens esthétique pour laisser leur marque. Des projets géants comme Masdar et même le système de notation GBC LEED étendent la respon-sabilité de la durabilité à toutes les professions impliquées dans la construction et même au-delà, et stimulent le besoin de rechercher et d'utiliser de nouvelles technologies plus proches de celles de l'électricité, par exemple, que de l'ingénierie traditionnelle de la construction.

30
Michael Reynolds, Hybrid Earthship,
Taos, New Mexico, USA, 2003

Les «bons» architectes et même certains parmi les plus grands sont depuis longtemps habitués à utiliser les matériaux les meilleurs et par-fois le plus coûteux, sans guère se préoccuper d'où ils proviennent ni s'ils sont renouvelables. Sur l'autre plateau de la balance, la grande majorité des constructions actuelles est réalisée sous des contraintes financières de plus en plus fortes, ce qui peut mener, dans les pires cir-constances, à des types de bâtiments qui n'ont aucune chance de résister à un tremblement de terre, par exemple. Ce mouvement vers la durabilité entraîne la nécessité de pratiquer des calculs de coûts légèrement différents et d'admettre pour la première fois depuis plusieurs décennies que le prix payé aujourd'hui n'est pas la seule façon de juger de la performance d'une architecture. L'architecture «verte» implique également un réseau croissant de participants sur la Toile, engagés dans le processus de construction, qui travaillent en collaboration, jusqu'à réduire, dans certains cas, la liberté d'action de l'architecte. L'objet de ce livre est de montrer que la «bonne» architecture et la durabilité peuvent aller de pair, surtout si la définition de ce qui est «vert» est suffisamment large.

RÊVES DE PLATINE

Le système de notation LEED concerne six grandes catégories de problématiques. Ce sont essentiellement le terrain, l'utilisation effi-cace de l'eau, l'énergie, l'atmosphère, les matériaux et les ressources, la qualité environnementale intérieure et enfin l'innovation et le pro-cessus de conception. Il existe quatre niveaux de notation LEED déterminés par des points, 69 points étant le maximum accordé pour la construction neuve ou la rénovation d'immeubles commerciaux. Les certifications attribuées sont : Certifié (26–32 points), Argent (33–38 points), Or (39–51 points) et enfin Platine (52–69 points).

Le Grand Rapids Art Museum (Grand Rapids, Michigan, États-Unis, 2004–07, page 395) a été conçu par wHY Architecture, une agence fondée en 2003 par Yo-ichiro Hakomori et Kulapat Yantrasast qui avait auparavant travaillé chez Tadao Ando et collaboré à des projets comme le Museum of Modern Art de Fort Worth. Le musée du Michigan est intéressant en ce qu'un des principaux mécènes du projet, le philan-thrope local Peter Wege, a fait de l'obtention de la certification LEED la condition d'un don pour le projet. Avec ses 10 % de matériaux de construction recyclés, l'usage généreux de l'éclairage naturel ou encore la réutilisation des eaux de pluie, la nouvelle construction est intel-ligente en terme de développement durable tout en bénéficiant d'une approche minimaliste qui rappelle l'expérience professionnelle anté-rieure de Yantrasast.

Bien que de dimensions plus réduites, la première commande publique reçue par David Adjaye aux États-Unis, le Museum of Con-temporary Art/Denver (Denver, Colorado, États-Unis, 2004–07, page 49) a été le premier musée à obtenir la certification LEED Or. Basse consommation d'énergie, faibles émissions de gaz à effets de serre, utilisation de matériaux bruts environnementalement adaptés ont permis d'atteindre ce niveau élevé. Adjaye jouit déjà d'une réputation considérable au Royaume-Uni et son arrivée aux États-Unis pour ce projet a été un événement particulièrement suivi. Là encore, la combinaison de son énorme talent et de ses préoccupations affichées pour les enjeux environnementaux prouvent que le vert n'est plus le vilain petit canard de l'architecture contemporaine. Adjaye, bien que plus jeune qu'Ando ou Piano, par exemple, est certainement l'une des étoiles montantes de l'architecture internationale et sa participation très visible au mouve-ment en faveur de la durabilité exercera certainement une influence.

Avec des intervenants comme Renzo Piano (California Academy of Sciences, page 277) et Adjaye en « compétition » pour obtenir la plus haute note LEED pour un musée, la réussite de l'architecte angelin Michael B. Lehrer, auteur du Water + Life Museums Campus à Hemet, mentionné plus haut (page 219), est à noter. Son musée a été la première réalisation à obtenir la certification Platine. Se voulant « un exemple vivant de durabilité et de conservation », il dispose d'une armada de 3000 panneaux solaires qui remplissent 50 % de ses besoins énergétiques et d'un système de récupération de l'eau pour l'irrigation des plantes au goutte à goutte. Un éclairage naturel abondant et le recours extensif à un verre bloquant la chaleur font partie des autres dispositifs marquants de ce projet. Lehrer n'est certainement pas aussi connu qu'Adjaye, mais la puissance de son dessin couplée à la certification Platine accéléreront sans doute considérablement sa notoriété.

LA CHASSE AUX PAPILLONS

Si une bonne part des tentatives de définition de la « conception verte » tourne autour de l'énumération des différentes façons dont les problèmes sont abordés par les architectes ou les paysagistes par exemple, elle tient aussi à la réflexion sur les conséquences de l'environnement bâti sur le développement durable. Celui-ci peut également se définir de différentes façons. Une forêt repousse-t-elle après avoir été coupée ? Le rythme de l'existence humaine sur cette planète condamne-t-elle les espèces ou la plus grande partie de la vie sur terre dans un espace de temps relativement court à l'échelle géologique ? La réponse à la première question dépend de la façon dont les arbres sont coupés et replantés. La seconde nous oriente vers la philosophie et la mesure précise des ressources subsistantes, du réchauffement global ou de l'extinction progressive d'espèces – qui font l'objet de débats animés parmi les scientifiques, pour ne pas parler des politiciens. Il semble bien qu'il y ait des preuves croissantes d'un réchauffement de la planète, de l'extinction de certaines espèces et de l'épuisement des réserves naturels comme le pétrole. Les mécanismes mêmes qui conduisent à une catastrophe écologique ne sont pas encore très bien compris, certainement du fait de l'interdépendance systémique de la vie sur Terre, mais aussi de l'imprécision des prévisions météorologiques et des analyses des conséquences des actions décidées.

Malgré l'existence des critères LEED, la durabilité est loin d'être une affaire réglée. Le fameux « effet papillon » de la théorie du chaos s'applique certainement aux modifications du climat. Ce qui semble être une approche positive à l'échelle locale peut avoir un impact négatif beaucoup plus grand que ce que l'on suspecte. Prendre en compte les coûts environnementaux réels de la fabrication des cellules photovoltaïques ou des biocarburants n'est pas une simple affaire, comme l'actualité récente l'a montré. Le coûts croissants de certains matériaux conduisent à des réajustements économiques qui peuvent effacer des gains calculés avec précision. Lorsqu'il est meilleur marché d'importer du granite du Zimbabwe que d'utiliser la pierre locale, peut-on blâmer les promoteurs et les architectes si leurs matériaux viennent de l'autre bout du monde ?

Il semble clair qu'une des conséquences de la « révolution verte » en cours est que les individus sont incités à se sentir responsables non seulement de leur destin mais aussi de celui des autres, ainsi que d'autres formes de vie. Habitués à construire comme ils veulent, certains architectes commencent à surélever leurs bâtiments par rapport au sol pour réduire leur impact non seulement sur la terre elle-même mais sur les divers types de vie animale ou végétale qui y abondent. Même le système LEED est passé à côté de cette logique. Cependant, une approche holistique qui considérerait l'architecture comme un élément de base du monde naturel plutôt qu'une présence étrangère imposée par la force des machines est en vue, et peut-être plus proche que certains ne le pensent. Le jeune architecte néo-zélandais Chris Tate a construit sa propre maison (Forest House, Titirangi, Auckland, Nouvelle-Zélande, 2006, page 357) dans un environnement naturel protégé. Bien qu'inspiré de la fameuse maison de verre de Philip Johnson, au splendide isolement, le projet de Tate prend en compte toutes les restrictions environnementales et de zonage locales et se laisse presque avaler par la nature. La durabilité ne signifie donc pas nécessairement vivre dans une construction qui sent le chanvre ou dont les murs sont en terre battue… même si ces options existent bien.

DE BABYLONE À L'ARCTIQUE

La gamme extrêmement variée des projets « verts » qui existe aujourd'hui peut être symboliquement représentée par trois des projets montrés dans cet ouvrage, un réalisé, deux non construits. Française, l'agence Babylone a signé une proposition qui n'a pas encore passé le cap du chantier. Sa proposition intitulée « Nature Active » (Saclay, France, 2007, page 55) est née d'un concours lancé par un territoire de 49 municipalités de l'Ouest parisien. Bien qu'elle ait peu de chance d'être mise en œuvre sous sa forme actuelle, elle consiste en un recours radical aux « capacités productives de la nature », tout en préservant au maximum les terres arables en prévision de l'accroissement attendu de la population. Intéressant parce qu'il est global (en coopération avec les architectes SoA), ce projet d'architecture et de paysagisme pourrait être la voie la plus raisonnable vers le futur, à condition que les municipalités aient le pouvoir d'imposer un tel plan d'ensemble malgré l'importance des intérêts commerciaux engagés. En mixant architecture et paysage, technologies vertes futuristes et intelligence de présentation, ce projet met le doigt sur la collaboration de plus en plus nécessaire entre les disciplines, en particulier pour traiter de phénomènes qui s'avèrent globaux plutôt que locaux. Le fait que les facteurs globaux influent aujourd'hui sur des problèmes qui n'étaient naguère que strictement locaux est l'un de ces changements significatifs auxquels l'architecture se trouve confrontée au fur et à mesure que progresse la « révolution verte ».

L'architecte belge Vincent Callebaut met en scène une vision similaire dans son « utopie » de futur vert. Son projet Anti-Smog pour Paris (2007, page 95) veut utiliser « toutes les formes d'énergie renouvelables pour combattre le *smog* parisien ». Ceci comprend l'énergie éolienne, la phyto-purification par les plantes, les cellules photovoltaïques et un revêtement de dioxyde de titane (TiO_2) qui cannibalise le *smog* pour faire bonne mesure. Lorsque de nombreuses technologies nouvelles sont mises en œuvre dans un même projet, on peut légitimement se demander si elles seront aussi efficaces qu'on l'espérait. Il y a quelque chose du « gadget » intelligent dans ce type d'architecture, et cependant l'arrivée imminente de bâtiments dont l'objectif réel est de combattre la pollution n'est peut-être pas si lointaine. Callebaut donne à ses concepts une apparence de science-fiction, ce qui signifie qu'ils ne sont pas entièrement sérieux. Ce sont des projets du type « Que se passera-t-il si… ? » qui peut faire réfléchir le public aux façons dont l'architecture peut contribuer non seulement à réduire la pollution qu'elle produit directement, mais aussi peut-être contribuer à réduire les niveaux globaux de gaz toxiques et autres substances dangereuses émis dans l'environnement. Le troisième projet récent qui illustre une approche très différente du changement climatique est le Svalbard Global Seed Vault ou « Caveau international de conservation de semences » (Longyearbyen, Spitzberg / Svalbard, Norvège, 2007–08, page 77)

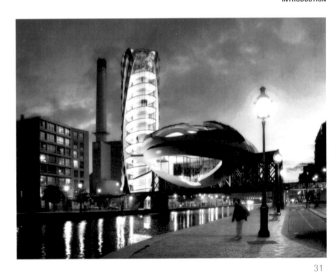

31
Vincent Callebaut Architectures,
Anti-Smog, Paris, France, 2007

31

de Peter Søderman de Barlindhaug Consult AS. Consistant essentiellement en un long tunnel et une chambre forte creusés dans une montagne du nord de l'Arctique norvégien, cette installation a pour objectif de préserver la diversité des semences du monde entier, si une crise écologique ou militaire devait ravager la planète dans les années à venir. Bien qu'il soit décoré d'une œuvre d'art lumineuse de Dyveke Sanne, ce caveau glacé, en attente d'une catastrophe qui semblerait avoir déjà été annoncée, fait un peu penser à un prélude du Jugement dernier. Il n'est pas certain que cette réalisation puisse s'assurer une certification Platine, mais il est difficile d'imaginer geste plus écologique en architecture. Il est une pure expression de la durabilité, la garantie que la diversité des espèces végétales pourra être protégée, même en cas de montée des eaux et de tempêtes apocalyptiques.

LES TEMPS CHANGENT

L'architecte malaisien Ken Yeang est l'un des professionnels internationaux qui s'implique le plus dans la conception durable. Son œuvre dans ce domaine consiste à la fois en constructions réalisées (comme le siège de Mewah Oils en Malaisie, 2001–03, page 401, ou son nouveau bâtiment administratif pour la Bibliothèque nationale de Singapour, 2001–05, page 404), mais aussi en une réflexion approfondie et des écrits. Dans un article intitulé « What is Green Design ? » (Qu'est-ce que la conception verte ?), Yeang écrit : « Si nous intégrons nos processus de travail, de conception et tout ce que nous faisons ou fabriquons dans notre environnement bâti (qui par définition comprend nos bâtiments, nos équipements, nos infrastructures, nos produits, réfrigérateurs, jouets, etc.) à l'environnement naturel de façon non agressive et sans rupture, il n'y aura plus de problème environnemental. » Ken Yeang plaide pour quelque chose de beaucoup plus ambitieux que quelques cellules photovoltaïques sur un toit et défend une sorte de retour très spécifique à la nature. « Les écosystèmes ne produisent pas de déchets », poursuit-il. « Tout se recycle. Ainsi en imitant ce processus, notre environnement bâti ne produira plus de déchets. Tout ce qui est produit et toutes les émissions sont continuellement réutilisés, recyclés et finalement réintégrés dans l'environnement naturel, en tandem avec des modes efficaces de consommation des énergies et des ressources matérielles. Concevoir pour imiter l'écosystème, c'est l'écomimesis. C'est la prémisse fondamentale de l'écoconception. Notre environnement bâti doit imiter en tout les écosystèmes. »[8]

L'une des idées préférées de Yeang au cours des années a été de faire entrer la nature dans les villes et les bâtiments. Sans aller aussi loin que son projet d'écomimesis généralisée, on peut admettre que son analyse des composants organiques et non organiques de l'architecture est sensible et pourrait apporter des changements effectifs, à condition de ne pas transformer les villes en marais bouillonnants d'activités biologiques. « Nos myriades de constructions, fabrications et autres activités rendent en effet la biosphère de moins en moins organique », explique Yeang. « Continuer ainsi sans rééquilibrer le contenu biotique signifie simplement renforcer le caractère artificiel de notre biosphère et donc la rendre de plus en plus inorganique, en exacerbant des actions destructrices de l'environnement comme la déforestation et la pollution. Ceci aboutit à la simplification biologique de la biosphère et à la réduction de sa complexité et de sa diversité », affirme-t-il.[9]

James Wines, de l'agence américaine SITE possède depuis longtemps une vision assez douce-amère – que certains diront romantique – de la nature. Il a conçu ses premiers magasins BEST en forme de ruines envahies par la résurgence d'une forêt. Cette idée de nature en architecture semble être au cœur de sa récente proposition intitulée Streetscape in a New World ou « Paysage de rue dans un monde nou-

32
Sergio Palleroni, Zhong-Xiao
Boulevard Urban Ecological Corridor,
Taipei, Taiwan, 2005–07

veau » (Pékin, 2008, page 324). Ses dessins décrivent un réseau de plus en plus dense de chemins et de clairières au milieu d'une vaste urbanisation. « C'est, dit-il, une métaphore d'une culture en plein développement et une proposition d'amélioration environnementale dans une cité bourgeonnante. » Cette approche est à la fois littérale en faisant intervenir de grands arbres dans le complexe prévu, mais également poétique en ce qu'elle revient à un mariage de béton et de plantes vivantes dans un environnement de plus en plus privé de toute végétation.

Bien que le programme de Yeang soit ambitieux, il est au cœur du sujet. Et si l'architecture verte n'était pas tant un problème d'architecture que de survie ? Les querelles esthétiques et internes de la profession architecturale sont à l'évidence secondaires lorsqu'il s'agit de mettre un terme à la guerre contre la nature qui a abouti à la création d'une « jungle d'asphalte »[10]. Le problème, comme insiste Yeang, n'est pas spécifique à l'architecture, il est de nature systémique et concerne autant si ce n'est plus l'industrie que la construction. Il concerne les habitudes de vie et l'utilisation des ressources et le besoin de changer les choses avant que ne se produise une catastrophe. Faire de la conception verte, ou écoconception, une mode est un outil à la disposition des architectes, mais il semble clair que le temps est venu non pas de sauter dans le train, mais de faire face à l'inévitable. Avec l'augmentation des prix de l'essence et de multiples preuves du changement climatique, il est probable que la tendance écologique durera. Les architectes qui l'ignorent risquent de se retrouver bientôt remplacés par des constructeurs plus intelligents dont la carte de visite arborera l'accréditation LEED AP. Mais là encore, la bonne architecture n'a jamais représenté plus qu'une petite partie de ce qui se construit dans le monde. Les temps vont changer.

Philip Jodidio, Grimentz, 29 juin 2008

[1]   « SmartMarket Trends Report », McGraw-Hill Construction Analytics, 2008.
[2]   « EIA Annual Energy Review 2005 », US Energy Information Administration, US Department of Energy.
[3]   Lenssen and Roodman, « Worldwatch Paper 124 : A Building Revolution : How Ecology and Health Concerns are Transforming Construction », Worldwatch Institute, 1995. Cette référence et les deux précédentes sont tirées de « Green Building Facts », publié par le US Green Building Council (USGBC), juin 2008.
[4]   Felicity Barringer, « The New Trophy Home, Small and Ecological », dans : *New York Times*, 22 juin 2008.
[5]   *Ibid.*
[6]   *Ibid.*
[7]   « Réflexions sur les espaces souterrains », dans : *L'Architecture d'aujourd'hui*, mai-juin 2003.
[8]   Ken Yeang, « What is Green Design ? » dans : *Design Does Matter*, Teknion, Mt Laurel, New Jersey, 2005.
[9]   *Ibid.*
[10] *The Asphalt Jungle* (*Quand la ville dort*) est un film réalisé par John Huston en 1950, avec Sterling Hayden et Marilyn Monroe.

ADJAYE ASSOCIATES

Adjaye Associates
23–28 Penn Street
London N1 5DL
UK

Tel: +44 20 77 39 49 69
Fax: +44 20 77 39 34 84
E-mail: info@adjaye.com
Web: www.adjaye.com

DAVID ADJAYE was born in 1966 in Dar es Salaam, Tanzania. He studied at the Royal College of Art in London (M.Arch, 1993), and worked in the offices of David Chipperfield and Eduardo Souto de Moura, before creating his own firm Adjaye Associates in London in 2000. He has been widely recognized as one of the leading architects of his generation in the United Kingdom, in part because of the talks he has given in various locations such as the Architectural Association, the Royal College of Art, and Cambridge University, as well as Harvard, Cornell, and the Universidad de Luisdad in Lisbon. He was also the co-presenter of the BBC's six-part series on modern architecture "Dreamspaces." His Idea Store library in East London was selected by Deyan Sudjic for the exhibition highlighting "100 Projects that are Changing the World" at the 8th Venice Biennale of Architecture in 2002. His office employs a staff of 35, and some of his key works are: a house extension (Saint John's Wood, 1998); studio/home for Chris Ofili (1999); SHADA Pavilion (2000, with artist Henna Nadeem); Siefert Penthouse (2001); Elektra House (2001); and a studio/gallery/home for Tim Noble and Sue Webster (2002), all in London. Recent work includes the Nobel Peace Center (Oslo, Norway, 2002–05); Bernie Grant Performing Arts Centre (London, 2001–06); Stephen Lawrence Centre (London, 2004–06); a visual arts building for the London-based organizations Iniva and Autograph ABP at Rivington Place (London, 2003–07); and the Museum of Contemporary Art/Denver (Denver, Colorado, USA, 2004–07, published here), all in the UK unless stated otherwise.

DAVID ADJAYE wurde 1966 in Daressalam, Tansania, geboren. Er studierte am Royal College of Art in London (M.Arch., 1993) und arbeitete für David Chipperfield und Eduardo Souto de Moura, bevor er 2000 in London sein eigenes Büro Adjaye Associates gründete, das heute 35 Mitarbeiter beschäftigt. Er gilt weithin als einer der führenden Architekten seiner Generation in Großbritannien, u. a. wegen seiner Vorträge an so verschiedenen Institutionen wie der Architectural Association, dem Royal College of Art, der Universität Cambridge, der Harvard und der Cornell University sowie der Universidad de Luisdad in Lissabon. Darüber hinaus war Adjaye Co-Moderator der sechsteiligen BBC-Serie „Dreamspaces" über moderne Architektur. Seine Bibliothek „Idea Store" in Ost-London wurde von Deyan Sudjic für die Ausstellung „100 Projekte, die die Welt verändern" für die 8. Architekturbiennale 2002 in Venedig ausgewählt. Zu seinen wichtigsten Projekten zählen: eine Hauserweiterung (St. John's Wood, 1998), eine Atelierwohnung für Chris Ofili (1999), der SHADA Pavillon (2000, mit der Künstlerin Henna Nadeem), das Siefert Penthouse (2001), das Elektra House (2001) und eine Kombination aus Atelier, Galerie und Wohnraum für Tim Noble und Sue Webster (2002), alle in London. Zu seinen jüngeren Arbeiten zählen das Nobel-Friedenszentrum (Oslo, Norwegen, 2002–05), das Bernie Grant Performing Arts Centre (London, 2001–06), das Stephen Lawrence Centre (London, 2004–06), ein Haus für visuelle Künste für die Londoner Organisationen Iniva (Institute of International Visual Arts) und Autograph ABP am Rivington Place (London, 2003–07) und das Museum of Contemporary Art/Denver (Denver, Colorado, USA, 2004–07, hier vorgestellt), alle in Großbritannien, sofern nicht anders angegeben.

DAVID ADJAYE est né en 1966 à Dar es-Salaam, Tanzanie. Après des études au Royal College of Art à Londres (M.Arch, 1993), il travaille auprès de David Chipperfield et d'Eduardo Souto de Moura, avant de créer sa propre agence Adjaye Associates à Londres en 2000. Il est reconnu comme l'un des plus brillants architectes de sa génération au Royaume-Uni, en partie du fait des conférences qu'il a données au sein de divers lieux comme l'Architectural Association, le Royal College of Art et Cambridge University, mais aussi Harvard, Cornell et l'Universidad de Luisdad à Lisbonne. Il a aussi été coprésentateur d'une série télévisée de la BBC en six parties sur l'architecture moderne *Dreamspaces*. Sa bibliothèque Idea Store dans l'est de Londres a été sélectionnée par Deyan Sudjic pour l'exposition « 100 Projets qui changent le monde » à la VIIIᵉ Biennale d'architecture de Venise en 2002. Son agence emploie 35 collaborateurs. Parmi ses réalisations les plus notables : l'extension d'une maison (Saint John's Wood, 1998) ; le studio-maison pour Chris Ofili (1999) ; le pavillon SHADA (2000, avec l'artiste Henna Nadeem) ; la Siefert Penthouse (2001) ; la maison Elektra (2001) et un studio-galerie-résidence pour Tim Noble et Sue Webster (2002), le tout à Londres. Plus récemment, il a réalisé le Centre Nobel de la Paix (Oslo, Norvège, 2002–05) ; le Bernie Grant Performing Arts Centre (Londres, 2001–06) ; le Stephen Lawrence Centre (Londres, 2004–06) ; un bâtiment pour les arts plastiques pour Iniva et Autograph ABP à Rivington Place (Londres, 2003–07) et le Musée d'art contemporain/Denver (Denver, Colorado, États-Unis, 2004–07, publié ici).

MUSEUM OF CONTEMPORARY ART/DENVER

Denver, Colorado, USA, 2004–07

Total floor area: 2320 m². Client: Museum of Contemporary Art/Denver.
Cost: not disclosed. Project Director: Joe Franchina. Architect of Record: Davis Partnership

This is the first public commission of Adjaye Associates in the United States. Located on a prominent site, the new museum is at the corner of 15th and Delgany Street. The structure is due to be the first LEED Gold certified museum, thanks to its low energy consumption, greenhouse gas emissions, and use of environmentally appropriate raw materials. The new building includes 1858 square meters of exhibition, education, and lecture spaces, a bookshop, and a roof garden for outdoor art. The announced intention of the building is that it should "support rather than define the museum's mission." The architect has chosen to employ "a limited number of monochromes and textures" because of the "kunsthalle" or temporary-exhibition function to which most of the building is put. With respect to its immediate architectural environment, the structure has four stories in its main volume. As the architects explain: "In order to establish a visual relationship with the traffic moving in and out of the downtown area, the northeast façade is set at a slight angle to 15th Street. The southeastern corner of the building has been pulled forward so that it's visible from the metro station on Delgany Street." Thanks to its sincere modesty and its environmental credentials, the Museum of Contemporary Art/Denver contributes to the emergence of a new generation of cultural facilities in the United States, perhaps less flamboyant but more responsible than its predecessors.

Dieses Museum ist der erste öffentliche Auftrag für Adjaye Associates in den USA und liegt prominent an der Ecke 15th Street und Delgany Street. Das Projekt wird als erstes Museum mit einer LEED-Goldmedaille ausgezeichnet, was es seinem niedrigen Energieverbrauch, den geringen Treibhausgasemissionen und dem Einsatz umweltgerechter Rohmaterialien verdankt. Der Neubau umfasst 1858 m² Fläche für Ausstellungen, Bildungsprogramme und Vorträge, eine Buchhandlung sowie einen Dachgarten für Außenrauminstallationen. Ziel des Baus ist erklärtermaßen, das Museum in seinem Auftrag „zu unterstützen, statt diesen zu definieren". Der Architekt entschied sich für „eine begrenzte Farb- und Materialauswahl", da der Großteil des Baus für temporäre Kunstausstellungen vorgesehen ist. Mit Rücksicht auf das unmittelbare Umfeld präsentiert sich der Hauptbau als vierstöckiges Volumen. Der Architekt führt aus: „Um einen visuellen Bezug zum vorbeifließenden Zentrumsverkehr herzustellen, wurde die Nordostfassade leicht zur 15th Street versetzt. Die südöstliche Ecke des Gebäudes wurde vorgezogen, sodass sie von der U-Bahnstation an der Delgany Street aus zu sehen ist." Dank seiner Bescheidenheit und ökologischen Stärken trägt das Museum of Contemporary Art/Denver unmittelbar dazu bei, dass in den Vereinigten Staaten eine neue Generation kultureller Einrichtungen entsteht, die möglicherweise weniger extravagant, dafür aber verantwortungsbewusster als ihre Vorläufer auftreten.

Il s'agit de la première commande américaine reçue par Adjaye Associates. Ce nouveau musée occupe un site très en vue à l'angle de 15th Street et de Delgany Street à Denver. Il est le premier musée certifié LEED Or, pour sa faible consommation énergétique, son bas niveau d'émissions de gaz à effet de serre et son utilisation de matériaux bruts écologiques. Il comprend 1858 m² de salles pour expositions, conférences et activités éducatives, une librairie et un jardin sur le toit pour l'exposition de sculptures. L'intention affichée est que ce bâtiment « soutienne plutôt que définisse la mission du musée ». L'architecte a choisi d'utiliser « un nombre limité de couleurs et de textures » pour s'adapter à la fonction principale de *Kunsthalle* du musée, c'est-à-dire d'accueil d'expositions temporaires. Respectant son environnement architectural immédiat, le bâtiment ne compte que quatre niveaux dans son volume principal. « Afin de créer une relation visuelle avec l'axe de circulation qui le longe, la façade nord-est est légèrement inclinée par rapport à 15th Street. L'angle sud-est a été tiré vers l'avant pour être visible de la station de métro de Delgany Street », explique l'architecte. Grâce à sa modestie, sa sincérité et sa valeur environnementale, ce musée participe à l'émergence d'une nouvelle génération d'équipements culturels aux États-Unis, peut-être moins flamboyante, mais plus consciente de ses responsabilités que ses prédécesseurs.

Sections, a plan, and images clearly indicate that the museum is made up of basic, rather austere forms, translating a willful modesty and rendering its green program easier to implement than extravagant glass forms might have, for example.

Schnitte, Grundriss und Aufnahmen zeigen deutlich die schlichten, vergleichsweise strengen Formen des Museums. Dies zeugt von bewusster Bescheidenheit und macht es einfacher, das grüne Programm umzusetzen, als dies bei extravaganten Glasformen der Fall gewesen wäre.

Coupes, plan et photographies montrent que le musée est composé de formes basiques assez austères, qui traduisent une modestie volontaire mais facilitent la mise en œuvre de son programme de développement durable par rapport à des formes en verre extravagantes, par exemple.

Interior views and a plan confirm the impression of strict, efficient geometry announced by the façades of the building. Natural light is ample where possible.

Innenansichten und Grundriss bestätigen den Eindruck von einer strengen, effizienten Geometrie, den schon die Fassaden des Baus vermitteln. Wo immer möglich, fällt großzügig natürliches Licht ein.

Les vues de l'intérieur et ce plan confirment l'impression de géométrie stricte et efficace donnée par les façades. La lumière naturelle pénètre en abondance dans les volumes en fonction de l'éclairage souhaité.

AGENCE BABYLONE

Agence Babylone
56 rue de Paradis
75010 Paris
France

Tel: +33 1 49 23 51 01
Fax: +33 1 43 40 31 31
E-mail: contact@agencebabylone.com
Web: www.agencebabylone.com

Jeoffroy de Castelbajac was born in 1957. He obtained his degree in Landscape Architecture from the École Nationale Supérieure du Paysage de Versailles in 2003. He worked from 1980 to 2000 as a composer. Henri de Dreuzy was born in 1974, and also obtained his Landscape Architecture degree in 2003 from the Versailles school. Adrien Fourès was born in 1978, and completed the same studies as Castelbajac and Dreuzy the same year. This is also the case of Vincent Léger, born in 1978. The four landscape architects are co-managers of **AGENCE BABYLONE**. As they explain their work, Agence Babylone "intervenes essentially in the urban environment, be it on the scale of a town square or an entire region, with a passion for ecology that guides them in the development of new synergies between the city and nature." Along with their winning project Active Nature (Saclay, 2007, published here), their current work includes a park in Cormeilles-en-Parisis (2004–09); an avenue, gardens, and a square in Liévin (2006–09); gardens for the ZAC des Ponts Jumeaux (Toulouse, 2006–10); a redesign of public spaces in Rouen (2005–10), Villeneuve-le-Roi (2006–10), and in Chauray (2007–10); and the Saint-Louis Square in Choisy-le-Roi (2007–10), all in France.

Jeoffroy de Castelbajac wurde 1957 geboren. Er schloss sein Studium der Landschaftsarchitektur 2003 an der École National Supérieure du Paysage de Versailles ab. Von 1980 bis 2000 arbeitete er als Komponist. Henri de Dreuzy wurde 1974 geboren und beendete sein Studium der Landschaftsarchitektur ebenfalls 2003 an der École National Supérieure du Paysage de Versailles. Adrien Fourès wurde 1978 geboren und schloss den gleichen Studiengang wie Castelbajac und Dreuzy im selben Jahr ab. Dasselbe gilt für Vincent Léger, der 1978 geboren wurde. Gemeinsam leiten die vier Landschaftsarchitekten die **AGENCE BABYLONE**. Nach eigener Aussage „greift [die Agence Babylone] im Grunde in die urbane Umwelt ein, sei es nun in der Größenordnung eines Marktplatzes oder einer ganzen Region, und zwar mit einer Leidenschaft für Ökologie, die ihr Leitschnur bei der Entwicklung neuer Synergien zwischen Stadt und Natur ist." Neben ihrem preisgekrönten Projekt Nature Active (Saclay, 2007, hier vorgestellt) gehören zu ihren derzeitigen Aufträgen ein Park in Cormeilles-en-Parisis (2004–09), eine Allee, Gärten und ein Platz in Liévin (2006–09), Gärten für die ZAC des Ponts Jumeaux (Toulouse, 2006–10), Umgestaltungen des öffentlichen Raums in Rouen (2005–10), in Villeneuve-le-Roi (2006–10) und in Chauray (2007–10) sowie die Place Saint-Louis in Choisy-le-Roi (2007–10), alle in Frankreich.

Né en 1957, Jeoffroy de Castelbajac est paysagiste DPLG de l'École nationale supérieure du Paysage de Versailles (2003). Il a été compositeur de musique de 1980 à 2000. Henri de Dreuzy, né en 1974, est également paysagiste DPLG de l'École nationale supérieure du Paysage de Versailles (2003). Adrien Fourès, né en 1978, a accompli les mêmes études que Castelbajac et Dreuzy et a été diplômé la même année. C'est également le cas de Vincent Léger, né en 1978. Les quatre architectes paysagistes dirigent ensemble l'**AGENCE BABYLONE**. Celle-ci, expliquent-ils, « intervient essentiellement en milieu urbain, de l'échelle du square à celle du territoire, avec une passion pour l'écologie qui nous guide dans le développement de nouvelles synergies, pérennes et actives, entre ville et nature ». En dehors du projet Nature Active (Saclay, 2007, publié ici), leurs réalisations, toutes en France, comprennent un parc à Cormeilles-en-Parisis (2004–09) ; une avenue, des jardins et une place à Liévin (2006–09) ; des jardins pour la ZAC des Ponts-Jumeaux (Toulouse, 2006–10) ; la remise en forme d'espaces publics à Rouen (2005–10), Villeneuve-le-Roi (2006–10) et Chauray (2007–10) ainsi que la place Saint-Louis à Choisy-le-Roi (2007–10).

ACTIVE NATURE

Saclay, France, 2007

Site area: 360 km². Client: OIN Massy Palaiseau, Saclay, Versailles, Saint-Quentin-en-Yvelines.
Cost: not disclosed. Collaboration: SoA architects, Alter Développement, Biodiversita

The OIN (Opération d'Intérêt National) or Operation of National Interest, a grouping of 49 towns in the suburbs of Paris, launched a competition in 2007 for ideas concerning its development over the next 30 years. With a projected increase in population of 350 000 people during the period, the region has placed a clear emphasis on sustainable development and ecology. Participants were asked to envisage the creation of 5000 homes per year over the 30-year span, while conserving 2000 hectares of existing farmland. Agence Babylone, with an emphasis on landscape design and urban development, worked on this competition with SoA architects, Biodiversita ecological engineers, and Alter Développement engineers. The team won the competition in the category for best use of the resources and natural patrimony of the site. Their idea was to make the maximum possible use of the "productive capacities of nature." Rather than imagining only the overall situation, they used a principle of successively larger zones, each responsible for its own resources. Existing forest areas would be preserved, and agricultural areas for fruit and vegetables added to urban zones. Agricultural zones, crossed by "ecological corridors" intended to protect the natural environment, would be used only for local production. A system of "green batteries" (*piles vertes*) produces energy in the process of treating waste water and garbage. New housing, coupled with retail and office space, would be concentrated in dense 120x160 meter "islands," allowing the overall population density of the region not to exceed 41 inhabitants per hectare.

OIN (Opération d'intérêt national) oder Operation im nationalen Interesse, ein Zusammenschluss von 49 Stadtgemeinden im Umland von Paris, schrieb 2007 einen Wettbewerb aus, um Ideen für die kommenden 30 Jahre zu entwickeln. Prognosen sagen für diese Zeitspanne ein Wachstum der dortigen Bevölkerung um 350 000 Menschen voraus, weshalb die Region besonderen Wert auf eine nachhaltige, ökologische Entwicklung legt. Prämisse für die Wettbewerbsteilnehmer war die Schaffung von 5000 Wohnungen innerhalb der kommenden 30 Jahre und zugleich die Erhaltung von 2000 ha Agrarland. Die Agence Babylone, mit ihrem Schwerpunkt auf Landschaftsgestaltung und Stadtentwicklung, arbeitete für diesen Wettbewerb mit SoA architectes, dem ökologischen Ingenieurbüro Biodiversita sowie dem Ingenieurbüro Alter Développement zusammen. Die Gruppe gewann den Wettbewerb in der Kategorie beste Nutzung von Ressourcen und des landschaftlichen Erbes des Areals. Ihre Idee war es, die „produktiven Kapazitäten der Natur" maximal zu nutzen. Statt nur die Gesamtsituation zu betrachten, arbeiteten sie nach einem Prinzip immer größer werdender Zonen, von denen jede für ihre eigenen Ressourcen verantwortlich ist. Bestehende Waldgebiete sollen erhalten, urbane Zonen um landwirtschaftliche Nutzflächen für Obst und Gemüse ergänzt werden. Landwirtschaftszonen, die ausschließlich der lokalen Versorgung dienen, werden von „ökologischen Korridoren" zum Schutz der Umwelt durchzogen. Ein System „grüner Batterien" („piles vertes") erzeugt Energie durch die Aufbereitung von Brauchwasser und Abfall. Die neuen Wohnanlagen, kombiniert mit Geschäfts- und Büroflächen, sollen sich auf „Inseln" von 120 x 160 m konzentrieren, sodass die Bevölkerungsdichte der Region 41 Bewohner pro Hektar nicht übersteigt.

L'OIN (Opération d'intérêt national) de Massy-Palaiseau, Saclay, Versailles et Saint-Quentin-en-Yvelines regroupant 49 communes de l'ouest de la banlieue parisienne a lancé un concours d'idées en 2007 pour préfigurer l'aménagement de son territoire sur les 30 prochaines années. Pour répondre à un accroissement prévu de la population de 350 000 personnes, l'accent a été mis sur le développement durable. Les participants devaient envisager la création de 5000 logements par an, tout en conservant 2000 ha de terres agricoles. L'agence, spécialisée dans le paysage et le développement urbains, a travaillé pour cette compétition en collaboration avec SoA architectes, les ingénieurs en écologie Biodiversita et les ingénieurs d'Alter Développement. L'équipe a remporté le concours dans la catégorie de la mise en valeur des ressources et du patrimoine naturel. Leur idée était d'utiliser au maximum « les capacités productives de la nature ». Plutôt que de n'imaginer que la situation globale, ils ont défini un principe de zones de plus en plus grandes, chacune en charge de ses propres ressources. Les zones forestières existantes seraient préservées et des secteurs agricoles de maraîchage créés à proximité des zones urbaines. Les terres agricoles, traversées par des « corridors écologiques », protégeraient l'environnement naturel et seraient cultivées pour la consommation locale. Un système de « piles vertes » produirait de l'énergie par le traitement des eaux et des déchets. Les nouveaux logements couplés à des bureaux et des commerces seraient concentrés en « îles » de 120 x 160 m permettant de ne pas dépasser une densité globale de population de 41 habitants par hectare.

An "aerial" view of the project shows its scale and also the close integration of green areas into and around the built-up areas.

Eine „Luftaufnahme" des Projekts macht dessen Dimensionen sowie die enge Integration der Grünflächen in und um die bebauten Zonen deutlich.

Une vue « aérienne » du projet montre son échelle et l'intégration étroite des espaces verts dans et autour du bâti.

NATURE

AGRICULTURE

VILLE

les processus écologiques pour développer la ville

nature active

A diagram and a rendering emphasize the close connection of the complex to nature. In the diagram, the flow of energy and sustenance from field and forest to built up areas is depicted as a natural cycle.

Diagramm und Rendering veranschaulichen die Anbindung des Projekts an die Natur. Das Diagramm stellt den Energie- und Versorgungsfluss zwischen Feld und Wald und bebauten Zonen als natürlichen Zyklus dar.

Ce schéma et l'image de synthèse montrent les interactions entre le projet et la nature. Ci-dessus, les flux d'énergie et de production des cultures et de la forêt vers les zones construites sont représentés comme un cycle naturel.

The biodiverse green areas surrounding the city can assimilate part of the CO_2 it produces and generate 34 percent of the oxygen needs. Forests and farms can provide food for 350 000 people, becoming an "agricultural garden".

Die biologisch vielfältigen Grünflächen um die Stadt absorbieren einen Teil des dort ausgestoßenen CO_2 und produzieren 34% des benötigten Sauerstoffs. Wälder und Bauernhöfe liefern Lebensmittel für 350 000 Menschen und werden zum „landwirtschaftlichen Garten".

Les zones vertes de biodiversité entourant la ville peuvent absorber une partie du CO_2 qu'elle émet et produire 34% de sa consommation d'oxygène. Des forêts et des fermes produisent la nourriture pour 350 000 habitants et deviennent un « jardin agricole ».

TADAO ANDO

Tadao Ando Architect & Associates
Japan

Born in Osaka in 1941, **TADAO ANDO** was self-educated as an architect, largely through his travels in the United States, Europe, and Africa (1962–69). He founded Tadao Ando Architect & Associates in Osaka in 1969. He has received the Alvar Aalto Medal, Finnish Association of Architects (1985); the Medaille d'or, French Academy of Architecture (1989); the 1992 Carlsberg Prize; and the 1995 Pritzker Prize. He has taught at Yale (1987), Columbia (1988), and Harvard (1990). Notable buildings include: Rokko Housing (Kobe, 1983–93); Church on the Water (Hokkaido, 1988); Japan Pavilion Expo '92 (Seville, Spain, 1992); Forest of Tombs Museum (Kumamoto, 1992); and Suntory Museum (Osaka, 1994), all in Japan unless stated otherwise. Recent work includes the Awaji Yumebutai (Awajishima, Hyogo, Japan, 1997–2000); the Pulitzer Foundation for the Arts (St. Louis, Missouri, USA, 1997–2000); and the Modern Art Museum of Fort Worth (Texas, 1999–2002). He completed the Chichu Art Museum/Naoshima on the Island of Naoshima in the Inland Sea in 2004 (published here), part of the continuing project that led him to create the Benesse House Museum and Hotel there beginning in the early 1990s. He is currently working on the Punta della Dogana for François Pinault (Venice, Italy, 2007–). Other recent work includes the Omotesando Hills complex (Tokyo, 2006); 21_21 Design Sight (Tokyo, 2004–07); and Tokyu Toyoko Line Shibuya Station (Shibuya-ku, Tokyo, 2005–08, published here). Tadao Ando is working on an expansion of the Clark Art Institute (Williamstown, Massachusetts); the Abu Dhabi Maritime Museum (Abu Dhabi, UAE, 2006–); and a house for the designer Tom Ford near Santa Fe, New Mexico.

TADAO ANDO wurde 1941 in Osaka geboren. Als Architekt ist er Autodidakt und bildete sich in erster Linie durch seine Reisen in den USA, Europa und Afrika zwischen 1962 und 1969. 1969 gründete er in Osaka das Büro Tadao Ando Architect & Associates. 1985 erhielt er die Alvar-Aalto-Medaille des finnischen Architektenverbands, 1989 die Medaille d'Or der französischen Académie d'Architecture, 1992 den Carlsberg-Preis sowie 1995 den Pritzker-Preis. Er lehrte an den Universitäten Yale (1987), Columbia (1988) und Harvard (1990). Zu seinen beachtenswerten Bauten zählen: die Rokko-Wohnanlage (Kobe, 1983–93), die Kirche auf dem Wasser (Hokkaido, 1988), der japanische Pavillon auf der Expo '92 (Sevilla, Spanien, 1992), das Museum im Gräberwald (Kumamoto, 1992) und das Suntory Museum (Osaka, 1994), alle in Japan, sofern nicht anders vermerkt. Neuere Bauten sind u. a. das Awaji Yumebutai (Awajishima, Hyogo, Japan, 1997–2000), die Pulitzer Foundation for the Arts (St. Louis, Missouri, USA, 1997–2000) und das Modern Art Museum in Fort Worth (Texas, 1999–2002). 2004 konnte das Chichu Art Museum auf der Insel Naoshima in der Seto-Inlandsee fertiggestellt werden (hier vorgestellt), Teil eines fortlaufenden Projekts, für das er Anfang der 1990er-Jahre das Benesse House (Museum und Hotel) realisiert hatte. Seit 2007 realisiert er für François Pinault die Punta della Dogana in Venedig. Weitere jüngere Projekte sind der Omotesando-Komplex (Tokio, 2006), das 21_21 Design Sight (Tokio, 2004–07) sowie der U-Bahnhof Shibuya der Tokyu-Toyoko-Linie (Shibuya-ku, Tokio, 2005–08, hier vorgestellt). Tadao Ando arbeitet derzeit an einer Erweiterung des Clark Art Institute (Williamstown, Massachusetts), dem Meeresmuseum von Abu Dhabi (VAE, 2006–) sowie an einem Haus für den Modedesigner Tom Ford unweit von Santa Fe, New Mexico.

Né à Osaka en 1941, **TADAO ANDO** est un architecte autodidacte formé en grande partie par ses voyages aux États-Unis, en Europe et en Afrique (1962–69). Il fonde Tadao Ando Architect & Associates à Osaka en 1969. Parmi ses prix et distinctions : la médaille Alvar Aalto de l'Association finlandaise des architectes (1985) ; la médaille d'or de l'Académie d'architecture (Paris, 1989) ; le Prix Carlsberg (1992) et le Prix Pritzker (1995). Il a enseigné à Yale (1987), Columbia (1988) et Harvard (1990). Il a notamment réalisé : les immeubles d'appartements Rokko (Kobé, Japon, 1983–93) ; l'église sur l'eau (Hokkaido, Japon, 1988) ; le pavillon japonais d'Expo '92 (Séville, Espagne, 1992) ; le musée de la Forêt des tombes (Kumamoto, Japon, 1992) et le musée Suntory (Osaka, Japon, 1994). Plus récemment, il a conçu le Awaji Yumebutai (Awajishima, Hyogo, Japon, 1997–2000) ; la Fondation Pulitzer pour les Arts (St. Louis, Missouri, USA, 1997–2000) et le Musée d'art moderne de Fort Worth (Texas, 1999–2002). En 2004, il a achevé le Musée d'art Chichu sur l'île de Naoshima en Mer intérieure du Japon, dans le cadre d'un projet à long terme pour lequel il avait déjà conçu le musée et l'hôtel de la maison Benesse au début des années 1990. Il travaille actuellement sur la rénovation de la Punta della Dogana pour François Pinault (Venise, 2007–). Ses interventions récentes comprennent : le complexe Omotesando Hills (Tokyo, 2006) ; le 21_21 Design Sight (Tokyo, 2004–07) ; la station Shibuya/ligne Tokyu Toyoko (Shibuya-ku, Tokyo, 2005–08, publiée ici) ; une extension du Clark Institute (Williamstown, Massachusetts) ; le musée maritime d'Abu Dhabi (Abu Dhabi, EAU, 2006–) ainsi qu'une maison pour le créateur Tom Ford près de Santa Fe, au Nouveau-Mexique.

CHICHU ART MUSEUM/NAOSHIMA

Naoshima, Kagawa, Japan, 2000–04

Site area: 9990 m². Floor area: 2573 m².
Client: Naoshima Fukutake Art Museum Foundation. Cost: not disclosed

A number of Tadao Ando's projects have involved digging into the earth. As he said in 2003: "I have an almost unconscious inclination towards underground spaces. Whatever the nature of the site, I try to create architecture that is never imposing on its environment.... Working on underground space links up with the search for the origins of architecture."[1] Located on a hillside just opposite Benesse House (the Naoshima Contemporary Art Museum), the Chichu Art Museum was intended for a small number of works of art, some of which were designed specifically for the spaces. As the client describes it, the central work of the new Chichu Art Museum is a remarkable six-meter-long *Water Lily* painting by Claude Monet. A large-scale installation by Walter De Maria (*Time/Timeless/No Time*, 2004, granite, mahogany, gold leaf, concrete) has a place of honor here, together with three works by James Turrell, *Afrum, Pale Blue* (1968, projector), *Open Field* (2000, fluorescent light, neon tube), and *Open Sky* (2004, LED, xenon lamp), one of his famous "sky spaces" with an opening to the exterior. Once within the Chichu Art Museum, visitors are invited to follow a circuitous route past strong concrete walls alternating with open courtyards in the purest style of Tadao Ando. The only view to the exterior (aside from the sky seen in the courtyards and in Turrell's installation) comes at the end of the visit in a magnificent café looking out to the Inland Sea. Ando collaborated closely with the client, the curator Yuji Akimoto, Turrell, and De Maria. The result is one of the most astonishing and spiritual of Tadao Ando's works, where architecture, art, and nature truly come together.   [1] "Reflections on Underground Space," in: *L'Architecture d'Aujourd'hui*, May–June 2003.

Bei mehreren Projekten Tadao Andos musste teilweise in die Erde hineingegraben werden. 2003 bemerkte er: „Ich habe eine fast unbewusste Neigung zu unterirdischen Räumen. Wie auch immer das Grundstück aussehen mag, versuche ich Architektur zu schaffen, die nie dominanter ist als ihre Umgebung … An unterirdischen Räumen zu arbeiten, schlägt den Bogen zurück zu den Ursprüngen der Architektur."[1] Das Chichu Art Museum liegt auf einem Hügel unmittelbar gegenüber dem Benesse House (in dem sich das Naoshima Contemporary Art Museum befindet) und war für eine Anzahl von Kunstwerken vorgesehen, von denen einige speziell für die neuen Räume geschaffen wurden. Laut Auftraggeber ist das zentrale Werk des neuen Chichu Art Museum ein beeindruckendes 6 m langes Seerosenbild von Claude Monet. Einen Ehrenplatz haben eine großformatige Installation von Walter De Maria („Time/Timeless/No Time", 2004, Granit, Mahagoni, Blattgold, Beton) sowie drei Arbeiten von James Turrell, „Afrum, Pale Blue" (1968, Projektor), „Open Field" (2000, fluoreszierendes Licht, Neonröhre) und „Open Sky" (2004, LED, Xenonleuchte), eines seiner berühmten „Skyspaces" mit Öffnung nach außen. Haben die Besucher das Chichu Art Museum betreten, werden sie eingeladen, einem kreisförmigen Rundgang zu folgen, der sich an den für Tadao Ando so typischen Betonmauern und offenen Innenhöfen entlangzieht. Der einzige Blick nach draußen (abgesehen vom Himmel, der in den Innenhöfen und in Turrells Installation zu sehen ist) bietet sich am Ende des Rundgangs in einem atemberaubenden Café mit Aussicht auf die Inlandsee. Ando arbeitete eng mit dem Auftraggeber, dem Kurator Yuji Akimoto, mit Turrell und De Maria zusammen. Das Ergebnis ist eines der erstaunlichsten und spirituellsten Werke Andos, in dem Architektur, Kunst und Natur wahrhaft zueinander finden.   [1] „Reflections on Underground Space", in: *L'Architecture d'Aujourd'hui*, Mai–Juni 2003.

Un certain nombre de projets de Tadao Ando ont déjà impliqué le creusement du sol et l'enfouissement. Comme il disait en 2003 : « J'ai un penchant presque inconscient pour les espaces souterrains. Quelle que soit la nature du site, j'essaie de créer une architecture qui ne s'impose jamais dans son environnement … Travailler sur un espace souterrain est lié à la recherche des origines de l'architecture. »[1] Situé à flanc de colline, juste en face de la maison Benesse (Musée d'art contemporain de Naoshima), le Musée d'art Chichu a été conçu pour ne présenter qu'un nombre d'œuvres réduit dont certaines ont été spécialement réalisées pour ses salles. Son commanditaire précise que l'œuvre centrale de ce nouveau musée est un superbe *Nymphéas* de Claude Monet de 6 m de long. Une grande installation de Walter De Maria (*Time/Timeless/No Time*, 2004, granit, acajou, feuille d'or, béton) occupe la place d'honneur, ainsi que trois œuvres de James Turrell, *Afrum, Pale Blue* (1968, projecteur), *Open Field* (2000, lumière fluorescente) et *Open Sky* (2004, LED, lampe xénon) et l'un de ses fameux *sky spaces* qui s'ouvrent sur l'extérieur. Une fois entrés dans le musée, les visiteurs sont invités à suivre un parcours qui se déroule entre de puissants murs de béton alternant avec des cours ouvertes du plus pur style Ando. La seule vue sur l'extérieur (en dehors du ciel visible de la cour et de l'installation de Turrell) est un panorama sur la mer du Japon que l'on admire du magnifique café situé en fin de visite. Ando a étroitement collaboré avec le conservateur, Yuji Akimoto, Turrell et De Maria. C'est l'une de ses réalisations les plus étonnantes et les plus empreintes de spiritualité : l'architecture fusionne ici l'art et la nature.   [1] « Reflections on Underground Space », dans : *L'Architecture d'Aujourd'hui*, mai–juin 2003.

A section (above) shows that the volumes of the museum lie essentially below grade. A view of the hill on which it is sited (top right) shows just how little of the architecture protrudes, but openings still allow light to penetrate the complex.

Ein Schnitt (oben) verrät, dass die Baukörper des Museums zum Großteil unter der Erde liegen. Ein Blick über den Hügel (rechts oben) zeigt, wie geringfügig die Architektur aus dem Boden hervorragt, wenngleich Öffnungen Licht einfallen lassen.

La coupe ci-dessus montre que les salles du musée sont essentiellement situées en sous-sol. Une vue du sommet de la montagne (en haut à droite) montre à quel point l'architecture se fait discrète. Les ouvertures sont des capteurs de lumière.

The plan of the museum shows its
skewed, yet geometric lines. Open
courtyards allow for light and air to
penetrate the entrance sequence
(below).

Anhand des Grundrisses wird die
schiefe und doch geometrische Linienführung des Museums deutlich.
Offene Innenhöfe lassen Licht und
Luft in den Eingangsbereich hinein
(unten).

Le plan du musée est géométrique-
ment articulé en oblique. Les cours
ouvertes laissent pénétrer l'air et la
lumière dans la séquence de l'entrée
(ci-dessous).

Above, the space designed in collaboration between the architect, the artist, and the curator houses Walter De Maria's Time/Timeless/No Time. Below, an opening toward the sea, and a plan showing the museum with the outline of former salt pans leading down the hill to the sea.

Der Raum (oben) wurde in enger Zusammenarbeit zwischen Architekt, Künstler und Kurator gestaltet und präsentiert Walter De Marias Installation „Time/Timeless/No Time". Unten ein Durchblick auf das Meer und ein Grundriss, der das Museum und den Verlauf alter Salzpfannen den Hügel hinunter bis zur See zeigt.

Ci-dessus, un espace conçu en collaboration entre l'architecte, l'artiste et le conservateur du musée accueille Time/Timeless/No Time, œuvre de Walter De Maria. Ci-dessous, une ouverture vers la mer et un plan montrent le musée et les contours d'anciens marais salants descendant de la colline vers la mer.

TOKYU TOYOKO LINE SHIBUYA STATION

Shibuya-ku, Tokyo, Japan, 2005–08

Floor area: 27 725 m². Client: Tokyu Corporation. Cost: not disclosed.

As Tadao Ando points out, the architectural design of subway stations is usually a minimal affair undertaken after the engineering has been completed. In this instance, the architect was able to work with the engineering team from the outset. The resulting project is described as a "hypogenous ship floating deep under the ground." The unusual use of the botanical term "hypogenous," meaning "growing on the underside of something such as a leaf," gives both a natural and a physical context to the design. A void in an egg-shaped shell with an oval plan runs through the site from the 2nd to the 5th levels below grade. This station might be imagined as the first "underground landmark" of contemporary architecture. Ando has also created a natural ventilation system for the space, another unusual feature in subway design. Glass fiber reinforced concrete (GFRC) was used as the material for the shell. Lighter than Ando's favorite concrete, it also allows the use of a panel cooling system consistent with natural ventilation. Shibuya Station, which includes other areas not designed by Tadao Ando, serves three million travelers a day, which means that his facility will be widely seen and used. As the architect says: "Shibuya Station is a major public space within the city and because of this important public nature we wanted to create an urban infrastructure that transcends its functionality, offering people a timeless spatial experience that will remain in their minds and will be embedded in the urban memory."

Tadao Ando weist darauf hin, dass die architektonische Gestaltung von U-Bahnstationen normalerweise ein Minimaleingriff ist, der nach Abschluss der technischen Planung stattfindet. In diesem Fall jedoch konnte der Architekt von Anfang an mit den Ingenieuren zusammenarbeiten. Das so gewachsene Projekt beschreibt er als „hypogenes Schiff, das tief unter der Erde schwebt". Der ungewöhnliche Gebrauch des botanischen Begriffs „hypogen", der soviel bedeutet wie „an der Unterseite von etwas wachsend" (etwa an einem Blatt), ordnet den Entwurf in einen natürlichen und physischen Kontext ein. Durch das gesamte zweite bis fünfte Untergeschoss zieht sich eine schalenartige, eiförmige Aussparung mit ovalem Grundriss. Dieser Bahnhof ist vielleicht der erste „unterirdische Meilenstein" der zeitgenössischen Architektur. Darüber hinaus entwickelte Ando ein natürliches Belüftungssystem, ein weiteres ungewöhnliches Element bei der Gestaltung von U-Bahnhöfen. Für die Schale wurde Glasfaserbeton (GFB) verwendet. Leichter als Andos bevorzugter Beton, erlaubt er zudem den Einsatz einer Deckenkühlung, was einer natürlichen Belüftung entspricht. Der Bahnhof Shibuya, der auch Abschnitte umfasst, die nicht von Ando entworfen wurden, wird täglich von drei Millionen Fahrgästen genutzt, was dem Bau breite Aufmerksamkeit bescheren dürfte. Der Architekt führt aus: „Der Bahnhof Shibuya ist ein wichtiger öffentlicher Raum in der Stadt und gerade wegen seiner bedeutenden öffentlichen Funktion wollten wir eine Infrastruktur schaffen, die über die reine Funktionalität hinausgeht, wollten den Menschen ein zeitloses Raumerlebnis bieten, an das sie sich erinnern und das sich in das urbane Gedächtnis einprägt."

Comme le fait remarquer Tadao Ando, la conception architecturale des stations de métro est généralement une petite intervention entreprise une fois les problèmes d'ingénierie résolus. Ici, l'architecte a pu travailler avec l'équipe d'ingénierie dès le départ. Le résultat de leurs travaux est décrit comme « un bateau symbiotique en suspension dans les profondeurs de la terre ». L'utilisation rare du terme de botanique « symbiotique » qui signifie « pousser en symbiose » fournit à la fois le contexte naturel et physique du projet. Un vide de plan ovale dans une coque ovoïde traverse le site entre les deuxième et cinquième niveaux en sous-sol. Cette station pourrait être qualifiée de premier « monument souterrain » de l'architecture contemporaine. Ando a également créé un système de ventilation naturelle pour ces volumes, autre élément inhabituel dans un projet souterrain. La coque est en béton renforcé de fibre de verre (GFRC). Plus léger que le béton habituel de l'architecte, il permet d'utiliser un système de panneaux refroidissant l'air en conjonction avec la ventilation naturelle. Cette station, qui comprend d'autres parties non conçues par Ando, accueille 3 millions de voyageurs par jour. « La station Shibuya est un espace public majeur à l'intérieur de la ville et du fait de cette nature publique très présente, nous souhaitions créer une infrastructure urbaine qui transcende sa fonctionnalité, offrant aux usagers une expérience spatiale intemporelle qui restera dans leur esprit, comme une incarnation de la mémoire urbaine. »

A plan above shows the oblong form of the new station while the image to the right shows the reality of Ando's soaring curves—an uncommon sight in the subways of Tokyo.

Der Grundriss oben zeigt die längliche Form der neuen Station, während die Abbildung rechts die Wirkung der hohen Kurven zeigt – ein für Tokios U-Bahnsystem untypischer Anblick.

Le plan ci-dessus montre la forme oblongue de la nouvelle gare. À droite, le jaillissement des courbes d'Ando offre une vision étonnante dans le métro de Tokyo.

Oval forms characterize the space, as
can be seen in the openings between
the various levels, assisting in the
natural flow of air that is part of the
design.

Ovale Formen dominieren den Raum,
wie sich an den Öffnungen zwischen
den Geschossebenen zeigt. Zugleich
fördern sie die natürliche Ventilation,
die im Entwurf eingeplant wurde.

Les espaces se caractérisent par des
formes ovales, à l'instar des ouvertures pratiquées entre les niveaux
qui facilitent la ventilation naturelle
prévue dans le projet.

SHIGERU BAN

Shigeru Ban Architects / 5–2–4 Matsubara / Setagaya-ku
Tokyo 156–0043 / Japan
Tel: +81 3 3324 6760 / Fax: +81 3 3324 6789
E-mail: tokyo@shigerubanarchitects.com / Web: www.shigerubanarchitects.com

Born in 1957 in Tokyo, **SHIGERU BAN** studied at SCI-Arc from 1977 to 1980. He attended the Cooper Union School of Architecture, where he studied under John Hejduk (1980–82). He worked in the office of Arata Isozaki (1982–83), before founding his own firm in Tokyo in 1985. His work includes numerous exhibition designs (Alvar Aalto show at the Axis Gallery, Tokyo, 1986). His buildings include the Odawara Pavilion (Kanagawa, 1990); the Paper Gallery (Tokyo, 1994); the Paper House (Lake Yamanaka, 1995); and the Paper Church (Takatori, Hyogo, 1995), all in Japan. He has also designed ephemeral structures, such as his Paper Refugee Shelter made with plastic sheets and paper tubes for the United Nations High Commissioner for Refugees (UNHCR). He designed the Japanese Pavilion at Expo 2000 in Hanover. He installed his Paper Temporary Studio on top of the Centre Georges Pompidou in Paris to work on the new Centre Pompidou in Metz (France, 2004–09). Other recent work includes the Papertainer Museum (Seoul Olympic Park, Songpa-Gu, South Korea, 2003–06, published here); the Nicolas G. Hayek Center (Tokyo, 2005–07); the Takatori Church (Kobe, Hyogo, 2005–07), the last two in Japan; and the disaster relief Post-Tsunami Rehabilitation Houses (Kirinda, Hambantota, Sri Lanka, 2005–07). Current work includes a small museum of Canal History in Pouilly-en-Auxois (France); the Schwartz Residence (Sharon, Connecticut); Forest Park Pavilion, Bamboo Gridshell-02 (St. Louis, Missouri); Mul(ti)houses (Mulhouse, France); Sagaponac House, Furniture House-05 (Long Island, New York); and Hanegi Forest Annex (Setagaya, Tokyo).

SHIGERU BAN, 1957 in Tokio geboren, studierte von 1977 bis 1980 am Southern California Institute of Architecture (SCI-Arc). 1980 bis 1982 besuchte er die Cooper Union School of Architecture in New York, wo er bei John Hejduk studierte. Bevor er 1985 sein eigenes Büro in Tokio gründete, arbeitete er bei Arata Isozaki (1982–83). Sein Werk umfasst zahlreiche Ausstellungsarchitekturen (etwa für die Alvar-Aalto-Ausstellung in der Axis Gallery, Tokio, 1986). Zu seinen Bauten zählen zudem der Odawara-Pavillon (Kanagawa, 1990), die Paper Gallery (Tokio, 1994), das Paper House (Yamanaka-See, 1995) sowie die Paper Church (Takatori, Hyogo, 1995), alle in Japan. Darüber hinaus entwarf Ban temporäre Konstruktionen wie Flüchtlingsquartiere aus Papier, die er aus Plastikplanen und Pappröhren für den UN-Flüchtlingskommissar (UNHCR) realisierte. Für die Expo 2000 in Hannover entwarf er den japanischen Pavillon. Auf dem Dach des Centre Georges Pompidou in Paris hat Ban sich ein temporäres Atelier aus Papier eingerichtet, um dort am neuen Centre Pompidou für Metz arbeiten zu können (2004–09). Andere jüngere Arbeiten sind u. a. das Papertainer Museum (Olympiapark Seoul, Songpa-Gu, Südkorea, 2003–06, hier vorgestellt), das Nicolas G. Hayek Center (Tokio, 2005–07) und die Takatori-Kirche (Kobe, Hyogo, 2005–07), beide in Japan, sowie Einrichtungen für die Katastrophenhilfe nach dem großen Tsunami (Kirinda, Hambantota, Sri Lanka, 2005–07). In Arbeit sind derzeit ein kleines Museum für Kanalgeschichte in Pouilly-en-Auxois (Frankreich), die Schwartz Residence (Sharon, Connecticut), der Forest Park Pavilion, das Bamboo Gridshell-02 (St. Louis, Missouri), die Mul(ti)houses (Mulhouse, Frankreich), das Sagaponac House oder Furniture House-05 (Long Island, New York) sowie ein Anbau im Hanegi-Wald (Setagaya, Tokio).

Né en 1957 à Tokyo, **SHIGERU BAN** a étudié à SCI-Arc de 1977 à 1980 et à la Cooper Union School of Architecture, auprès de John Hejduk (1980–82). Il a travaillé dans l'agence d'Arata Isozaki (1982–83), avant de fonder la sienne à Tokyo en 1985. Son œuvre comprend de nombreuses installations d'expositions (Alvar Aalto Show à la Axis Gallery, Tokyo, 1986) et des bâtiments comme le pavillon Odawara (Kanagawa, 1990) ; la Paper Gallery (Tokyo, 1994) ; la Paper House (Lake Yamanaka, 1995) et la Paper Church (Takatori, Hyogo, 1995), tous au Japon. Il a également conçu des structures éphémères comme un abri en carton pour réfugiés, constitué de films plastiques et de tubes en carton pour le Haut-Commissariat des Nations unies pour les Réfugiés (HCR). Il a dessiné le Pavillon japonais pour l'Expo 2000 à Hanovre. Son Atelier de carton temporaire a été installé au sommet du Centre Georges Pompidou à Paris comme annexe de son agence pour le nouveau Centre Pompidou à Metz (France, 2004–09). Parmi d'autres réalisations récentes : Le Papertainer Museum (Séoul, Parc olympique, Songpa-Gu, Corée du Sud, 2003–06, publié ici) ; le Nicolas G. Hayek Center (Tokyo, 2005–07) ; l'église de Takatori (Kobé, Hyogo, 2005–07), tous deux au Japon, et les maisons de reconstruction post-tsunami (Kirinda, Hambantota, Sri Lanka, 2005–07). Actuellement, il travaille sur le projet d'un petit musée sur l'histoire d'un canal à Pouilly-en-Auxois (France) ; la résidence Schwartz (Sharon, Connecticut) ; le Forest Park Pavilion, Bamboo Gridshell-02 (St. Louis, Missouri) ; les Mul(ti)houses (Mulhouse, France) ; la maison Sagaponac ou Furniture House-05 (Long Island, New York) et l'annexe de la forêt d'Hanegi (Setagaya, Tokyo).

PAPERTAINER MUSEUM

Seoul Olympic Park, Songpa-Gu, South Korea, 2003–06

Floor area: 3454 m². Client: Designhouse Inc. Cost: not disclosed.
Team: Shigeru Ban Architects + KACI International (Kyeong-Sik Yoon, Principal)

This unusual project involves the combination of two of Shigeru Ban's favorite construction elements—structural paper tubes and used shipping containers—both of which represent a significant contribution to the reduction of the overall ecological impact of such a structure. Ban had already designed a temporary art-exhibition facility with these elements (Nomadic Museum, Pier 54, New York, 2005). Composed of a colonnaded, rectangular container structure ten meters high and a semicircular "Paper Gallery" enclosing an arc-shaped inner courtyard, this was a temporary exhibition pavilion for the celebration of the 30th anniversary of the Korean publisher Designhouse. The forested 14 214-square-meter site is located in the Olympic Park of Seoul. The first "container wall" was intended for exhibition booths, while the second housed office and storage areas. The alternating placement of the containers, with regular voids, animated the main façade, while the paper-tube colonnade in front of the structure lent it a gravitas that it might have lacked given the use of such industrial materials. The semicircular Paper Gallery was made of two walls composed of 75-centimeter-diameter paper tube poles, with a roof truss made of 30-centimeter paper tubes.

Dieses ungewöhnliche Projekt kombinierte zwei bevorzugte Bauelemente des Architekten – konstruktive Röhren aus Papier und gebrauchte Schiffscontainer. Beide tragen entscheidend dazu bei, die ökologische Auswirkung eines solchen Bauwerks zu reduzieren. Ban hatte aus denselben Elementen schon einmal eine temporäre Kunsthalle errichtet (Nomadic Museum, Pier 54, New York, 2005). Der zum 30. Geburtstag des koreanischen Verlags Designhouse realisierte temporäre Ausstellungsraum bestand aus einer 10 m hohen, mit Säulen umstandenen rechteckigen Containerkonstruktion und einer halbkreisförmigen „Papiergalerie", die einen bogenförmigen Innenhof umschloss. Das bewaldete 14 214 m² große Grundstück liegt im Olympiapark von Seoul. Die erste „Containerwand" war für Ausstellungsräume vorgesehen, in der zweiten befanden sich Büro- und Lagerräume. Die rhythmische Anordnung der Container mit regelmäßigen Aussparungen belebte die Hauptfassade. Zugleich verliehen die vorgelagerten Kolonnaden aus Papierröhren dem Bau eine Würde, die er wegen der industriellen Baumaterialien sonst wohl nicht gehabt hätte. Die halbrunde Papiergalerie bestand aus zwei Wänden, die wiederum aus Papierröhren mit 75 cm Durchmesser konstruiert waren. Seinen Abschluss fand das Ganze mit einem Dachstuhl aus Papierröhren mit 30 cm Durchmesser.

Cet étonnant projet combine deux des matériaux de construction favoris de Shigeru Ban, les tubes de carton et les conteneurs de transport qui, tous deux, représentent une contribution significative à la réduction de l'impact écologique global de ce bâtiment. Ban avait antérieurement conçu des installations d'expositions temporaires à partir d'éléments semblables (Nomadic Museum, Pier 54, New York, 2005). Ce pavillon temporaire, doté d'une structure composée de conteneurs rectangulaires empilés sur 10 m de haut et d'une « Paper Gallery » semi-circulaire fermant une cour intérieure en demi-cercle, a été construit pour la célébration du trentième anniversaire de la maison d'édition coréenne Designhouse. Son terrain boisé de 14 214 m² se trouve dans le Parc olympique de Séoul. Le premier « mur de conteneurs » servait aux guichets d'entrée, le second abritait bureaux et stockages. La disposition alternée de conteneurs et de vides réguliers animait la façade principale, tandis que la colonnade en tubes de carton lui donnait une *gravitas* qui ne devait *a priori* rien à ce type de matériaux industriels. La Paper Gallery, semi-circulaire, était faite de deux colonnades de piliers de carton de 75 cm de diamètre sur lesquelles venait se poser une ferme de charpente en tubes de carton de 30 cm de diamètre.

The Papertainer Museum, as its name implies, employs both paper tube columns and shipping containers—two elements that Shigeru Ban has employed with success in the past few years.

Das Papertainer Museum besteht, wie schon der Name andeutet, aus Papierröhren und Schiffscontainern – zwei Elemente, die Shigeru Ban in den vergangenen Jahren immer wieder erfolgreich eingesetzt hat.

Ce musée, comme son nom l'indique, utilise à la fois des tubes de carton et des conteneurs d'expédition, deux éléments utilisés avec succès par Shigeru Ban depuis plusieurs années.

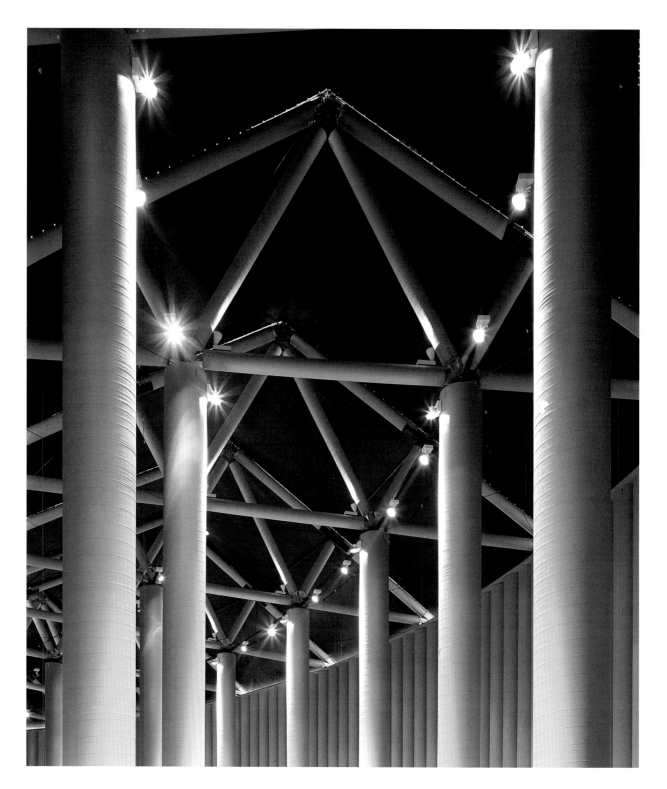

Shigeru Ban's mastery of the use of paper tubes as structural elements in his architecture is visible in this image of the columns and beams that support this building.

Shigeru Bans meisterhafter Einsatz von Papierröhren als konstruktives Element zeigt sich auf dieser Aufnahme: Säulen und Träger stützen den Bau.

La maîtrise dans l'utilisation des tubes de carton comme éléments structurels se constate dans cette image de colonnes et de poutres qui soutiennent le bâtiment.

Die atemberaubende formale Gestaltung des Papertainer Museum ist von
feierlichem, bewusst von Wiederho-
lungen geprägtem Rhythmus. Die
resultierende Erhabenheit bildet einen
Kontrapunkt zu den industriellen Bau-
elementen.

La forme étonnante du musée suit
un rythme processionnel ou volontairement répétitif qui confère une
certaine grandeur à cette utilisation
d'éléments industriels.

BARLINDHAUG CONSULT AS

Barlindhaug Consult AS
Sjølundveien 2
9291 Tromsø
Norway

Tel: +47 77 62 26 00
Fax: +47 77 62 26 99
E-mail: peter.w.soderman@barlindhaug.no
Web: www.barlindhaug.no

The chief architect of this project was Peter Wilhelm Søderman, who works with the firm **BARLINDHAUG CONSULT AS** in Tromsø, Norway. He was born in Vasa, Finland, in 1960, and received his M.Arch degree from the Helsinki University of Technology in 1990. From 1985 to the present, he has worked on public and private projects with Marja & Kari Kyyhkynen Architects, Vasa, Finland; Nyréns Architecture, Stockholm, Sweden; Anderssen+Fremming Architects, Tynset and Hamar, Norway; Hille+Melbye architects and HRTB architects, both Oslo, Norway; Sigurd Hamran architects, Tromsø; Contur Architects, Tromsø; and, most recently, Barlindhaug Consult AS, Tromsø. Recent projects by Peter Søderman include the Reinen Elementary School (Tromsø, 2002); Først og fremst Housing Project (Hammerfest, 2004); Vestre Mortensnes Housing Project (Tromsø, 2004); Breivang High School (Tromsø, 2005); and the Svalbard Global Seed Vault (Longyearbyen, Svalbard, 2007–08, published here), all in Norway. Barlindhaug Consult AS provides engineering services to the Norwegian and international markets. The company's scope of services includes engineering and construction, Arctic technology, energy conservation planning, and impact assessments.

Leitender Architekt des Projekts war Peter Wilhelm Søderman vom Büro **BARLINDHAUG CONSULT AS** in Tromsø, Norwegen. Er wurde 1960 in Vasa, Finnland, geboren und erhielt seinen M.Arch. 1990 an der Technischen Universität Helsinki. Seit 1985 arbeitet er an öffentlichen und privaten Projekten, u. a. für Marja & Kari Kyyhkynen Architekten, Vasa, Finnland, für Nyréns Architecture, Stockholm, für Anderssen+Fremming Architekten, Tynset und Hamar, Norwegen, für Hille+Melbye Architekten und HRTB Architekten, beide Oslo, für Sigurd Hamran Architekten und Contur Architekten sowie in jüngster Zeit für Barlindhaug Consult AS, alle Tromsø. Zu den jüngeren Projekten von Peter Søderman zählen die Grundschule Reinen (Tromsø, 2002), die Wohnanlagen Først og fremst (Hammerfest, 2004) und Vestre Mortensnes (Tromsø, 2004), die Breivang-Schule (Tromsø, 2005) sowie der Global Seed Vault (Longyearbyen, Spitzbergen, 2007–08, hier vorgestellt), alle in Norwegen. Barlindhaug Consult AS bietet ingenieurtechnische Dienstleistungen für den norwegischen und internationalen Markt an. Das Leistungsspektrum der Firma umfasst technische Planung und Bauausführung, arktische Technologie, Planung von Energiesparmaßnahmen und Umweltverträglichkeitsprüfungen.

Peter Wilhelm Søderman, architecte responsable du projet de Svalbard, travaille pour l'agence norvégienne **BARLINDHAUG CONSULT AS** installée à Tromsø. Né à Vasa, Finlande, en 1960, il est architecte diplômé de l'université de Technologie d'Helsinki (1990). De 1985 à aujourd'hui, il a travaillé sur des projets tant privés que publics avec Marja & Kari Kyyhkynen Architects, à Vasa, Finlande ; Nyréns Architecture, Stockholm, Suède ; Anderssen+Fremming Architects, Tynset et Hamar, Norvège ; Hille+Melbye Architects et HRTB Architects à Oslo, Norvège ; Sigurd Hamran Architects, Tromsø ; Contur Architects, Tromsø, et, plus récemment, Barlindhaug Consult AS. Parmi ses réalisations récentes figurent l'école élémentaire de Reinen (Tromsø, 2002) ; les logements Først og fremst (Hammerfest, 2004) et Vestre Mortensnes (Tromsø, 2004) ; le collège Breivang (Tromsø, 2005) et le Svalbard Global Seed Vault (Longyearbyen, Spitzberg / Svalbard, 2007–08, publié ici). Barlindhaug Consult AS est une agence d'ingénierie qui intervient aussi bien en Norvège qu'à l'international. Elle propose des services dans les domaines de la construction, de la technologie arctique, de l'énergie et des études d'impact.

SVALBARD GLOBAL SEED VAULT

Longyearbyen, Svalbard, Norway, 2007–08

Site area: 1720 m². Client: Statsbygg, Norwegian Ministry of Government Administration and Reform.
Cost: $880 000. Team: Peter W. Søderman, Louis Lunde, Trond Hansen (Architects),
Sverre Barlindhaug (Engineer)

The long, rectangular form of the entrance to the Seed Vault is high lighted by a glittering work imagined by the artist Dyveke Sanne.

Die gestreckte Rechtecksform des Eingangs zum Seed Vault wird von einem glitzernden Kunstwerk der Künstlerin Dyveke Sanne unterstrichen.

Le volume rectangulaire allongé de l'entrée du Seed Vault est signalé par une œuvre scintillante de l'artiste Dyveke Sanne.

Located on a remote Island in the Arctic Circle, the Svalbard Global Seed Vault was designed to conserve 100 million seeds of 268 000 plants originating in 100 different countries, making the largest collection of food crop seeds anywhere in the world. As the Norwegian government's declaration on the occasion of the opening of the Vault in February 2008 read: "The seed vault is part of an unprecedented effort to protect the planet's rapidly diminishing biodiversity. The diversity of our crops is essential for food production, yet it is being lost." This "fail-safe" facility, dug deep into the frozen rock of an Arctic mountain, is intended to secure for centuries, or longer, seeds representing every important crop variety available in the world today. As well as protecting against the daily loss of diversity, the vault could also prove indispensable for restarting agricultural production at the regional or global level in the wake of a natural or man-made disaster. Even in the worst-case scenarios of global warming, the vault rooms will remain naturally frozen for up to 200 years. The Global Crop Diversity Trust (www.croptrust.org) is providing support for the ongoing operations of the Vault, which has the capacity to store up to 4.5 million samples or some two billion seeds. The vault consists in three secure rooms located at the end of a 125-meter-long tunnel blasted out of the mountain site. The seeds are stored at a temperature of -18°C in foil pouches, allowing some samples to be usable for as long as 2000 years or more. The artist Dyveke Sanne and KORO, the Norwegian agency overseeing art in public spaces, created a work made of reflective steel, mirrors, and prisms that "acts as a beacon, reflecting polar light in the summer months."

Der Global Seed Vault liegt auf Spitzbergen, einer entlegenen Insel im Polarkreis, und wurde realisiert, um 100 Millionen Arten von Saatgut von 268 000 Nutzpflanzen aus 100 verschiedenen Ländern einlagern zu können – die größte Sammlung von Nutzpflanzensaatgut weltweit. Anlässlich der Einweihung der Einrichtung im Februar 2008 erklärte die norwegische Regierung: „Der Saatguttresor ist Teil einer nie dagewesenen Anstrengung, die rasch schwindende Biodiversität dieses Planeten zu erhalten. Die Vielfalt unserer Nutzpflanzen ist unerlässlich für unsere Nahrungsmittelproduktion und doch verlieren wir sie." Diese tief in den frostsicheren Felsen eines arktischen Bergs geschlagene Sicherheitseinrichtung soll das Saatgut sämtlicher bedeutender, heute weltweit existierender Nutzpflanzenarten jahrhundertelang, wenn nicht gar länger, erhalten. Doch der Tresor ist nicht nur eine Sicherung gegen den täglich wachsenden Verlust an Biodiversität, er könnte sich auch als notwendig erweisen, sollte es je nötig sein, die landwirtschaftliche Produktion regional oder global nach einer von der Natur oder dem Menschen verschuldeten Katastrophe wieder aufzunehmen. Selbst bei Eintreten der schlechtest denkbaren Prognose hinsichtlich der Erderwärmung, dürften die Tresorräume noch bis zu 200 Jahre frostsicher bleiben. Der Global Crop Diversity Trust (www.croptrust.org) unterstützt den aktuellen Betrieb des Tresors, dessen Kapazität auf die Lagerung von bis zu 4,5 Millionen Musterspezies oder etwa 2 Milliarden Samen angelegt ist. Der Tresor besteht aus drei Sicherheitsräumen am Ende eines 125 m langen Tunnels, der in den Berg hineingesprengt wurde. Das Saatgut wird bei einer Temperatur von −18 °C in Folie verpackt gelagert, was erlaubt, die Proben bis zu 2000 Jahre oder länger nutzbar zu erhalten. In Kooperation mit der norwegischen Behörde für Kunst im öffentlichen Raum, KORO, konnte die Künstlerin Dyveke Sanne eine Arbeit aus Spiegelstahl, Spiegeln und Prismen realisieren, die „wie ein Leuchtfeuer wirkt und das polare Licht in den Sommermonaten reflektiert".

Implanté sur une île lointaine de l'intérieur du Cercle arctique, le Svalbard Global Seed Vault (Caveau international de conservation de semences de Spitzberg / Svalbard) a été conçu pour la conservation de 100 millions de semences de 268 000 plantes alimentaires originaires de 100 pays différents ce qui en fait la plus importante collection de ce type dans le monde. La déclaration du gouvernement norvégien, publiée à l'occasion de l'inauguration des installations en 2008, précisait : « Ce caveau de semences fait partie d'un effort sans précédent pour protéger la planète de la diminution rapide de la diversité. Celle-ci qui est essentielle pour la production d'aliments est en cours d'appauvrissement dramatique. » Ces installations à toute épreuve, creusées dans la roche gelée d'une montagne de l'Arctique, devraient protéger pour des siècles ou plus des semences représentant toutes les variétés végétales exploitables importantes existant dans le monde. Leur contenu pourrait se révéler indispensable pour le redémarrage de productions agricoles au niveau régional ou global à la suite de désastres naturels ou provoqués par l'homme. Même dans le pire des scenarii de réchauffement global, les salles devraient rester naturellement gelées pendant au moins deux cents ans. Le Global Crop Diversity Trust (www.croptrust.org) finance les opérations qui consistent à engranger plus de 4,5 millions d'échantillons et quelque 2 milliards de semences. Le caveau se compose de trois salles de sécurité à l'extrémité d'un tunnel de 125 m de long creusé à l'explosif dans la montagne. Les semences sont stockées à -18 °C dans des emballages spéciaux. L'artiste Dyveke Sanne et l'agence norvégienne KORO en charge de l'installation d'œuvres d'art dans des lieux publics ont créé, à l'entrée, une œuvre en acier réfléchissant, miroirs et prises, qui « agit comme un phare, reflétant la lumière polaire pendant les mois d'été ».

The architecture of the Seed Vault is as simple as its function – to provide a protected environment for the seeds of the world, potentially a key to the survival of the human race in the case of some future catastrophe.

Die Architektur des Seed Vault ist ebenso einfach wie sein Zweck – er dient als Schutzraum für Saatgut aus aller Welt – im Falle zukünftiger Katastrophen ein potenzieller Schlüssel zum Überleben der Menschheit.

L'architecture du Seed Vault est aussi simple que sa fonction : offrir un environnement protégé à la conservation de semences venues du monde entier, pour la survie de la race humaine en cas de future catastrophe.

The Vault burrows deep into a mountain to ensure the stability of the collections in terms of temperature, even if global warming should begin to change exterior conditions.

Der Seed Vault reicht tief in den Berg hinein, wohin er verlegt wurde, um Temperaturstabilität für die Bestände zu gewährleisten, selbst bei Veränderung der äußeren klimatischen Gegebenheiten durch die globale Erwärmung.

Le caveau est creusé au plus profond de la montagne pour garantir la constance thermique de la collection de semences, même si le réchauffement climatique doit entraîner la modification des conditions extérieures.

Above, vials and pouches containing seeds and the stacked sample collections.

Oben Ampullen und Beutel mit Saatgut, unten die gestapelten Lagerbestände.

Ci-dessus, ampoules et poches contenant les semences. Ci-dessous, le stockage des collections.

BARTON WILLMORE

Barton Willmore
7 Soho Square
London W1D 3QB
UK

Tel: +44 20 74 46 68 88
Fax: +44 20 74 46 68 89
E-mail: info@bartonwillmore.co.uk
Web: www.bartonwillmore.co.uk

BARTON WILLMORE presents itself as the "UK's leading independent integrated planning and design consultancy." The firm was originally established as an architectural practice 70 years ago. Nick Sweet was born in London in 1957. He studied Landscape Architecture at Thames Polytechnic (now the University of Greenwich, 1981), and worked with the Omrania/Buro Happold/Frei Otto joint venture for the Tuwaiq Palace (Riyadh, Saudi Arabia). He returned to his studies at the University of Westminster, London, obtaining an M. A. in Urban Design (1992–95) while working at Aukett Fitzroy Robinson. He took up an equity partnership at Barton Willmore in 2005. He continues to work in collaboration with such firms as Omrania and Buro Happold. Nick Sweet has obtained a number of commissions through design competitions, including the Salam Park project (Riyadh, Saudi Arabia, 1996); the European Parliament Quarter (Brussels, Belgium, 1998); and the King Abdullah International Gardens project (Riyadh, Saudi Arabia, 2008–11, published here). Further Barton Willmore buildings include Clearwater Court (Reading, 1998); the Honda UK Headquarters (Berkshire, 2002); and the Tonbridge Conference Centre in Kent (2003), all in the UK. In addition, the firm is developing proposals for the new city of Beitun in western China.

BARTON WILLMORE, nach eigener Aussage „die führende, unabhängige und integrierte Beratungsfirma für Planung und Entwurf in Großbritannien" wurde vor 70 Jahren ursprünglich als Architekturbüro gegründet. Nick Sweet wurde 1957 in London geboren. Er studierte Landschaftsarchitektur an der Thames Polytechnic (heute University of Greenwich, 1981) und arbeitete mit Omrania/Buro Happold/Frei Otto am Tuwaiq-Palast (Riad, Saudi-Arabien). Anschließend nahm er sein Studium an der University of Westminster, London, wieder auf und erwarb einen M. A. in Stadtplanung (1992–95), während er parallel bei Aukett Fitzroy Robinson arbeitete. 2005 wurde er Partner bei Barton Willmore. Sweet kooperiert nach wie vor mit Firmen wie Omrania und Buro Happold. Verschiedene Aufträge erhielt er durch Entwurfswettbewerbe, darunter das Salam-Park-Projekt (Riad, Saudi-Arabien, 1996), das Quartier des Europaparlaments (Brüssel, Belgien, 1998) sowie das King-Abdullah-International-Gardens-Projekt (Riad, Saudi-Arabien, 2008–11, hier vorgestellt). Zu den Bauten von Barton Willmore zählen außerdem der Clearwater Court (Reading, 1998), die britische Firmenzentrale von Honda (Berkshire, 2002) sowie das Tonbridge Conference Centre in Kent (2003), alle in Großbritannien. Darüber hinaus entwickelt das Büro Entwürfe für die Planstadt Beitun in Westchina.

BARTON WILLMORE se présente comme « la première agence indépendante d'urbanisme et de conception intégrée ». À l'origine, il y a soixante-dix ans, c'était une agence d'architecture. Nick Sweet, né à Londres en 1957, a étudié l'architecture du paysage à Thames Polytechnic (aujourd'hui université de Greenwich, 1981), et travaillé avec la *joint venture* Omrania/Buro Happold/Frei Otto pour le Tuwaiq-Palace (Riyad, Arabie saoudite). Il est revenu aux études et a obtenu son M. A en urbanisme de l'université de Westminster à Londres (1992–95), tout en travaillant chez Aukett Fitzroy Robinson. Il s'est associé à Barton Willmore en 2005, mais continue à collaborer avec des agences comme Omrania et Buro Happold. Il a gagné un certain nombre de concours dont le projet de Salam Park (Riyad, Arabie saoudite, 1996) ; le quartier du Parlement européen (Bruxelles, Belgique, 1998) et les jardins internationaux du roi Abdallah (Riyad, Arabie saoudite, 2008–11, publiés ici). Parmi les autres réalisations de Barton Willmore figurent Clearwater Court (Reading, 1998) ; le siège de Honda UK (Berkshire, 2002) et le centre de conférences Tonbridge dans le Kent (2003). Par ailleurs, l'agence développe des propositions pour la nouvelle ville de Beitun dans l'ouest de la Chine.

KING ABDULLAH INTERNATIONAL GARDENS

Riyadh, Saudi Arabia, 2008–11

Site area: 170 ha. Floor area: 60 000 m². Client: Riyadh Municipality. Cost: $280 million.
Collaboration: Buro Happold (Consulting Engineers), The Eden Project, The Natural History Museum

Borrowing its sweeping forms from the crescent of Islam, the gardens and greenhouses are intended to be carbon neutral.

Die Gärten und Gewächshäuser, formal in Anlehnung an den islamischen Halbmond gestaltet, sind CO$_2$-neutral konzipiert.

Empruntant leur forme incurvée au croissant islamique, les jardins et les serres présentent une empreinte carbone neutre.

This project involves the creation of a master plan, and an architectural and landscape design concept for the Saudi Arabian city of Riyadh. The brief called for a botanical garden seed bank, visitor attractions, and back-of-house facilities sufficient to accommodate up to 45 000 visitors per day. As the architects explain: "The team's response challenged the idea of creating a conventional botanical collection…. Our response proposed a paleo-botanic timeline, creating authentic interpretations of ecosystems that existed on this precise site in past epochs. The scheme aims to become a unique educational device in the explanation of global climate change and desertification." Seven controlled environments representing past local ecosystems and a final "garden of choices, an exploration of the options available to produce genuinely sustainable development in the future," are contained in a 22-hectare zone. The entire project is to be carbon neutral, using stone, gravel, rainwater, and sun power to sustain the development and operation of the facility.

Das Projekt umfasst einen Masterplan und ein Entwurfskonzept für die Bebauung und Landschaftsgestaltung der saudi-arabischen Stadt Riad. Gefragt waren eine Saatgutbank für einen botanischen Garten, Attraktionen für Besucher und Versorgungseinrichtungen für bis zu 45 000 Besucher pro Tag. Der Architekt führt aus: „Der Entwurf des Teams hinterfragte die Vorstellungen von einem konventionellen botanischen Garten … Unser Entwurf sah eine paläobotanische Zeitleiste vor, die die verschiedenen Ökosysteme, die in vergangenen Epochen an diesem Ort existierten, authentisch illustriert. Der Ansatz ist eine einzigartige Methode, anhand derer sich der globale Klimawandel und die globale Versteppung veranschaulichen lassen." Das 22 ha große Areal umfasst sieben steuerbare Biosphären, die vergangene Ökosysteme repräsentieren, sowie einen „Garten der Möglichkeiten, der auslotet, wie sich eine wirklich nachhaltige Entwicklung in Zukunft gestalten lassen könnte". Das gesamte Projekt wird CO_2-neutral sein und nutzt Stein, Kies, Regenwasser und Solarenergie für eine nachhaltige Bauerschließung und den umweltgerechten Betrieb der Anlage.

Ce projet porte sur la création d'un plan directeur et un concept d'architecture et d'aménagements paysagers pour Riyad, la capitale saoudienne. L'appel d'offre concernait une banque de semences, des attractions pour visiteurs et des installations techniques prévues pour 45 000 visiteurs quotidiens. Comme l'expliquent les architectes : « La réponse de l'équipe a remis en question l'idée de créer une collection botanique conventionnelle… Notre réponse est de proposer un parcours temporel paléobotanique, et de créer des interprétations authentiques d'écosystèmes ayant jadis existé sur ce site précis. Le projet devient ainsi un outil éducatif unique qui explique les changements climatiques globaux et la désertification. » Sept environnements contrôlés représentent ces écosystèmes disparus et un dernier « jardin des choix, exploration des options possibles en faveur d'un développement durable future authentique », occupent une surface d'environ 22 ha. Le projet tout entier n'émettra pas de CO_2 et utilisera la pierre, le gravier, l'eau de pluie et le soleil pour assurer le fonctionnement des installations.

To the left, the entrance level of the covered gardens. On this page, a plan showing the layout of the covered areas, and a perspective giving a sense of the soaring interior volumes.

Links der Eingangsbereich der überdachten Gärten. Auf dieser Seite ein Grundriss der überdachten Zonen sowie eine Innenansicht, die einen Eindruck der hohen Räume vermittelt.

À gauche, le niveau d'entrée des jardins couverts. Le plan de cette page montre la disposition des zones couvertes et une perspective des énormes volumes intérieurs.

PATRICK BLANC

Patrick Blanc
111 rue du Général Leclerc
94000 Créteil
France

Tel: +33 1 42 07 59 95
Fax: +33 1 48 99 86 21
E-mail: info@murvegetalpatrickblanc.com
Web: www.murvegetalpatrickblanc.com

Born in Paris in 1953, **PATRICK BLANC** received his doctorate in Botany in 1989. He does research on the comparative growth rates of plants and their capacity to adapt to extreme environments at the CNRS (Laboratoire d'Écologie, Brunoy). He has published more than 50 articles in scientific journals since 1977. He currently teaches at the University of Paris VI, and has patented his system of "mur vegetal," or vertical gardens. Recent vertical gardens installed by Patrick Blanc include those at the European Parliament (Brussels, Belgium, 2006); the CaixaForum (Madrid, Spain, 2006–07, published here); a concert hall in Taipei (Taiwan, 2007); the Plaza de España (Santa Cruz de Tenerife, Spain, 2008); and the Museum of Natural History in Toulouse (France, 2008). He also installed works in Jean Nouvel's Cartier Foundation (1998) and the Quai Branly Museum (2004), both in Paris, France.

PATRICK BLANC wurde 1953 in Paris geboren und promovierte 1989 in Botanik. Am CNRS (Laboratoire d'Ecologie, Brunoy) erforscht er komparative Wachstumsraten von Pflanzen und deren Fähigkeit, sich extremen Umweltbedingungen anzupassen. Seit 1977 hat er über 50 Artikel in naturwissenschaftlichen Fachzeitschriften veröffentlicht. Derzeit lehrt er an der Universität Paris VI. Sein System vertikaler Gärten, „mur vegetal", ließ er sich patentieren. Zu den unlängst von Patrick Blanc realisierten vertikalen Gärten zählen u. a. die Gärten am Europaparlament (Brüssel, 2006), am CaixaForum (Madrid, 2006–07, hier vorgestellt), an einer Konzerthalle in Taipeh (Taiwan, 2007), an der Plaza de España (Santa Cruz de Tenerife, Spanien, 2008) sowie am Museum für Naturgeschichte in Toulouse (Frankreich, 2008). Darüber hinaus installierte er Arbeiten in Bauten von Jean Nouvel, der Fondation Cartier (1998) sowie dem Museum am Quai Branly (2004), beide in Paris.

Né à Paris en 1953, **PATRICK BLANC** est docteur en botanique (1989). Il effectue des recherches sur le taux de croissance comparatif des plantes et leur capacité à s'adapter à des environnements extrêmes au Laboratoire d'écologie du CNRS, à Brunoy. Il a rédigé plus de cinquante articles pour des publications scientifiques depuis 1977. Il enseigne actuellement à l'université de Paris VI et a breveté son système de « mur végétal ». Parmi ses récents jardins verticaux installés figurent celui du Parlement européen (Bruxelles, Belgique, 2006) ; du CaixaForum (Madrid, Espagne, 2006–07, publié ici) ; d'une salle de concert à Taipei (Taiwan, 2007) ; de la place d'Espagne (Santa Cruz de Tenerife, Espagne, 2008) ; du Museum d'histoire naturelle de Toulouse (France, 2008) et, dans le cadre de deux réalisations de Jean Nouvel (1998), la Fondation Cartier (1998) et le musée du Quai Branly (2004) à Paris.

CAIXAFORUM VERTICAL GARDEN

Madrid, Spain, 2006–07

Floor area: 600 m².
Client: Obra Social Fundacion La Caixa, Madrid.
Cost: € 400 000

Patrick Blancs Vertical Garden is located next to to the entrance of the CaixaForum designed by the Swiss architects Herzog & de Meuron, but on a neighboring structure.

Patrick Blancs vertikaler Garten befindet sich unmittelbar neben dem Eingang des CaixaForum, einem Bau der Schweizer Architekten Herzog & de Meuron, jedoch an einem benachbarten Gebäude.

Le Jardin vertical de Patrick Blanc est implanté à côté de l'entrée du CaixaForum des architectes suisses Herzog & de Meuron, mais sur un bâtiment voisin.

Patrick Blanc's CaixaForum Vertical Garden is located next to to the entrance of a new exhibition building designed by Herzog & de Meuron located close to the Prado in Madrid. The former Mediodía Power Station, an 1899 brick structure, was lifted off the ground by the Swiss architects, allowing for an entrance below its restored façades. A small, sloping square leads down to the Paseo del Prado, and it is here that Blanc's wall of plants and flowers rises on the façade of a neighboring building. Patrick Blanc explains the principles behind his realizations by asking a question: "Do plants need soil?" It turns out that they don't and that a combination of water with minerals dissolved in it is sufficient for their growth. Nor need roots damage walls if the plants are constantly provided with the minerals and water they need. The Madrid installation is 24 meters high and contains 15 000 plants of 250 different species. "The garden is a dialogue with the Botanical Garden on the street and adjacent to the Prado," according to the architect Jacques Herzog. "We love to make new things, to experiment with materials and create a very unusual encounter between the rough and the natural, the smooth and the artificial, to incorporate nature so there can be the smell of a garden where you would not expect it."

Patrick Blancs vertikaler Garten am CaixaForum befindet sich unmittelbar neben dem Eingang des neuen, von Herzog & de Meuron entworfenen Ausstellungszentrums unweit des Prado in Madrid. Das ehemalige Mediodía-Elektrizitätswerk, ein Backsteinbau von 1899, wurde von den Schweizer Architekten vom Boden gelöst und angehoben, wodurch unterhalb der restaurierten Fassaden ein Eingangsbereich entstand. Ein kleiner, leicht abschüssiger Platz führt zum Paseo del Prado, wo Blancs Wand aus Grün- und Blühpflanzen an der Fassade eines benachbarten Gebäudes emporklettert. Patrick Blanc erklärt die Prinzipien seiner Projekte mit einer Frage: „Brauchen Pflanzen Erde?" Wie sich herausstellt, ist dies nicht der Fall. Eine Kombination aus Wasser und Minerallösung reicht, um Wachstum zu ermöglichen. Auch schädigen die Wurzeln das Mauerwerk nicht zwangsläufig, vorausgesetzt, sie werden mit der nötigen Menge an Mineralien und Wasser versorgt. Die Madrider Installation ist 24 m hoch und besteht aus 15 000 Pflanzen von 250 verschiedenen Arten. „Der Garten tritt in einen Dialog mit dem an der Straße gelegenen Botanischen Garten neben dem Prado", erläutert der Architekt Jacques Herzog. „Wir schaffen gern Neues, experimentieren mit Materialien und schaffen ungewöhnliche Dialoge zwischen Rauem und Natürlichem, Glattem und Künstlichem, um die Natur einzubinden, sodass man dem Duft eines Gartens begegnet, wo man ihn nicht erwartet."

Le jardin vertical du CaixaForum de Patrick Blanc est installé à côté de l'entrée de ce lieu d'exposition conçu par Herzog & de Meuron à proximité du musée du Prado à Madrid. L'ancienne centrale électrique de Mediodía, une construction en brique datant de 1899, a été littéralement soulevée par les architectes suisses pour former une entrée sous ses façades restaurées. Une petite place en pente mène au Paseo del Prado, et c'est ici que s'élève, sur la façade d'un immeuble voisin, le jardin de plantes et de fleurs de Blanc. Celui-ci explique les principes de cette réalisation en posant une question : « Les plantes ont-elles besoin du sol ? » Il se trouve qu'elles peuvent s'en passer et qu'une combinaison d'eau et de minéraux peut assurer leur croissance. Leurs racines n'endommagent pas les façades si elles reçoivent continuellement l'eau et les minéraux dont elles ont besoin. L'installation de Madrid mesure 24 m de haut et contient 15 000 plantes de 250 espèces différentes. « Ce jardin est un dialogue avec le Jardin botanique qui s'étend de l'autre côté de la rue, adjacent au Prado », précise Jacques Herzog. « Nous aimons faire des choses nouvelles, expérimenter les matériaux et créer des rencontres très inhabituelles entre le brut et le naturel, le doux et l'artificiel, intégrer la nature de telle façon que l'on sente les odeurs d'un jardin là où vous ne les attendiez pas. »

VINCENT CALLEBAUT ARCHITECTURES

Vincent Callebaut Architectures
119 rue Manin
75019 Paris
France

Tel: +33 1 42 45 11 10
E-mail: vincent@callebaut.org
Web: www.vincent.callebaut.org

VINCENT CALLEBAUT was born in 1977 in Belgium. He graduated from the Institut Victor Horta in Brussels in 2000, where he received the René Serrure Prize for the best diploma project, a proposal for the "Metamuseum of Arts and Civilizations, Quai Branly." He worked as an intern in the offices of Odile Decq and Massimiliano Fuksas in Paris, before opening his own firm in Brussels and Paris. He has collaborated with Jakob + MacFarlane, Claude Vasconi, and Jacques Rougerie. Callebaut seeks to contribute to a "new Ecopolis via 'parasitical' strategies for an investigative architecture, mixing biology with information and communications technologies." His projects (all unbuilt) include Underwater Venice of Beirut, a Master Plan for Martyrs's Square (Beirut, 2004); Fractured Monolith, Hotel and Congress Center (Brussels, 2004); Eye of the Storm, a performing arts center for Seoul (South Korea, 2005); Red Baobab, a project for the New National Library in Prague (2006); as well as Anti-Smog (Paris, 2007); and Perfumed Jungle (Hong Kong, 2007), the last two published here.

VINCENT CALLEBAUT wurde 1977 in Belgien geboren. Sein Studium schloss er 2000 am Institut Victor Horta in Brüssel ab, wo er mit dem René-Serrure-Preis für das beste Diplomprojekt ausgezeichnet wurde, seinen Entwurf „Metamuseum of Arts and Civilizations, Quai Branly". Er war als Praktikant in den Büros von Odile Decq und Massimiliano Fuksas in Paris tätig, bevor er sein eigenes Büro mit Sitz in Brüssel und Paris gründete. Er kooperierte mit Jakob + MacFarlane, Claude Vasconi und Jacques Rougerie. Callebaut geht es darum, zu einer „neuen Ökopolis beizutragen" und zwar „durch ‚parasitäre' Strategien für eine investigative Architektur, in der sich Biologie, Informations- und Kommunikationstechnologien miteinander verbinden". Zu seinen (sämtlich ungebauten) Projekten zählen u. a. ein Unterwasser-Venedig in Beirut, ein Masterplan für einen Märtyrerplatz (Beirut, 2004), das Hotel- und Kongresszentrum Fractured Monolith (Brüssel, 2004), Eye of the Storm, ein Zentrum für darstellende Künste in Seoul (Südkorea, 2005), Red Baobab, ein Projekt für die Neue Nationalbibliothek in Prag (2006), sowie seine Projekte Anti-Smog (Paris, 2007) und Perfumed Jungle (Hongkong, 2007), beide hier vorgestellt.

VINCENT CALLEBAUT, né en 1977 en Belgique, est diplômé de l'Institut Victor Horta à Bruxelles en 2000, qui lui a accordé le prix René Serrure pour le meilleur projet de diplôme avec son « Metamuseum des arts et civilisations, quai Branly ». Il a été stagiaire chez Odile Decq et Massimiliano Fuksas à Paris, avant d'ouvrir sa propre agence à Bruxelles et Paris. Il a collaboré avec Jakob + MacFarlane, Claude Vasconi et Jacques Rougerie. Callebaut cherche à contribuer à la création d'une « nouvelle Ecopolis *via* des stratégies "parasitaires" d'architecture de recherche, mêlant biologie et technologies de l'information et de la communication ». Ses projets (aucun réalisé pour l'instant) comprennent Underwater Venice of Beyrouth, un plan directeur pour la place des Martyrs (Beyrouth, 2004) ; Fractured Monolith, Hotel and Congress Center (Bruxelles, 2004) ; Eye of the Storm, un centre pour les arts de la scène à Séoul (Corée du Sud, 2005) ; Red Baobab, projet pour la Bibliothèque nationale de Prague (2006), ainsi que Anti-Smog (Paris, 2007) et Jungle parfumée (Hong Kong, 2007), ces deux derniers publiés dans ces pages.

ANTI-SMOG

Paris, France, 2007

Floor area: 2065 m². Client: City of Paris. Cost: not disclosed

The architect describes Anti-Smog as an "Innovation Center in Sustainable Development" to be located near the Canal de l'Ourq in the 19th arrondissement of Paris. The complex would make use of "all available renewable energy forms to fight against the Parisian smog." Two distinct museum structures would produce more energy than they consume—the Solar Drop with a superstructure covered in polyester fiber and 250 square meters of photovoltaic cells, and the Wind Tower, a "helical structure incrusted with wind machines." The Solar Drop would be covered with a layer of titanium dioxide (TiO) in the form of anatase, "which, by reacting to ultraviolet rays, allows the reduction of air pollution." Planted arches would allow the collection of rainwater for the complex. As Callebaut describes it: "Below this thermoregulating solar roof, there is a huge exhibition and meeting room organized around a central garden, a phyto-purified aquatic lagoon. It is a didactic place dedicated to new ecological urbanities and renewable energies." The Wind Tower, 45 meters tall, would be topped by a suspended garden with spectacular views of the city. The architect imagines that it might be used to house the "Vélib" bicycles, introduced to Paris by its mayor, or solar cars, in a silo configuration. "This," says Vincent Callebaut, "is a play project, an urban and truly living graft. In osmosis with its surroundings, it is an architecture that interacts with its surroundings in climatic, chemical, kinetic, and social ways to better reduce the ecological footprint in the urban area."

Der Architekt beschreibt Anti-Smog als „Innovationsprojekt für nachhaltige Entwicklung", das in der Nähe des Canal de l'Ourq im 19. Arrondissement von Paris angesiedelt sein soll. Der Komplex soll „alle verfügbaren Formen erneuerbarer Energien nutzen, um den Pariser Smog zu bekämpfen". Zwei separate Museumsbauten würden mehr Energie produzieren als sie verbrauchen – der sogenannte Solar Drop mit einem Überbau aus Polyesterfaser und 250 m² Solarmodulen sowie der Wind Tower, eine „mit Windrädern besetzte Helixkonstruktion". Der Solar Drop würde mit einer Anatasmodifikation von Titandioxid (TiO₂) überzogen werden, „das dank seiner Reaktion mit ultravioletter Strahlung Luftverschmutzung reduzieren" würde. Begrünte Bögen würden Regen für den Komplex sammeln. Callebaut beschreibt sein Projekt wie folgt: „Unter dem wärmeregulierenden Solardach befindet sich ein riesiger Ausstellungs- und Konferenzraum, der um einen zentral angelegten Garten mit einem Teich organisiert ist, dessen Wasser biologisch geklärt wird. Es ist ein didaktischer Ort, der sich mit neuen ökologischen Urbanitäten und erneuerbaren Energien auseinandersetzt." Der 45 m hohe Wind Tower soll oben mit einem hängenden Garten abschließen, der beeindruckende Ausblicke über die Stadt bieten würde. Der Architekt hofft, hier auch die vom Pariser Bürgermeister eingeführten „Vélib"-Fahrräder oder solarbetriebene Autos unterzubringen. Laut Vincent Callebaut handelt es sich um „eine Projektspielerei, ein urbanes und wahrhaft lebendiges Transplantat. Es ist eine Architektur, die in einer Form von Osmose mit ihrem Umfeld in klimatischer, chemischer, kinetischer und sozialer Weise interagiert, um den ökologischen Fußabdruck in der Stadt wirksamer zu reduzieren."

L'architecte présente Anti-Smog comme un « prototype didactique d'expérimentations écologiques » qui pourrait être installé près du canal de l'Ourcq dans le 19ᵉ arrondissement de Paris. Ce complexe utiliserait « toutes les formes disponibles d'énergies renouvelables pour combattre le *smog* parisien ». Deux structures muséales distinctes devraient produire davantage d'énergie qu'elles n'en consomment : la *Solar drop* dont la superstructure est recouverte de fibre de polyester et de 250 m² de cellules photovoltaïques, et la *Wind Tower*, une « structure hélicoïdale incrustées de turbines à vent ». La *Solar Drop* serait recouverte d'une couche de dioxyde de titane (TiO₂) sous forme d'anatase « qui, en réagissant aux rayons ultraviolets, permet de réduire la pollution de l'air ». Des arches plantées permettraient de collecter l'eau de pluie réutilisée par le complexe. « Sous cette couverture solaire thermorégulatrice, se trouve une énorme salle d'expositions et de réunions organisée autour d'un jardin central, un lagon aquatique phyto-épuré. C'est un lieu didactique consacré aux nouvelles urbanités écologiques et aux énergies renouvelables. » La *Wind Tower*, de 45 m de haut, serait surmontée d'un jardin suspendu offrant de superbes vues sur la ville. L'architecte a aussi imaginé abriter les « Vélib' » ou des voitures à énergie solaire dans une configuration de silo. « Il s'agit, précise Callebaut, d'un projet ludique, une greffe urbaine et vivante. En osmose avec son milieu, c'est une architecture qui interagit complètement avec son contexte qu'il soit climatique, chimique, cinétique ou social pour mieux réduire notre empreinte écologique en milieu urbain. »

The Anti-Smog complex takes the idea of the "green" building a step further than usual: the architect proposes to reduce ambient pollution rather than simply taking care not to contribute to energy waste.

Der Anti-Smog-Komplex spinnt das Konzept „grüner" Bauten ein Stück weiter: Der Architekt plant, Umweltverschmutzung aktiv zu reduzieren, statt lediglich Energieverschwendung zu vermeiden.

En proposant de diminuer concrètement la pollution ambiante plutôt que de simplement ne pas contribuer au gaspillage de l'énergie, le complexe Anti-Smog fait progresser le concept de bâtiment « vert ».

The rather futuristic forms proposed by Vincent Callebaut confirm the visionary aspect of his design. Light and open space are grafted onto the existing, less modern environment.

Die vergleichsweise futuristischen Formen von Vincent Callebauts Entwurf betonen seinen visionären Ansatz. Helle und offene Räume werden in das weniger moderne Umfeld eingeschrieben.

Les formes futuristes proposées par Vincent Callebaut confirment l'aspect visionnaire de son projet. L'espace ouvert et lumineux se greffe sur un environnement moins moderne.

PERFUMED JUNGLE

Hong Kong, China, 2007

Site area: 2.7 km². Client: City of Hong Kong. Cost: not disclosed. Team: Vincent Callebaut, Arnaud Martinez, Maguy Delrieu

This is a "Master Plan for the Eco-Design of the Central Waterfront of the Business District of Hong Kong." The architect explains: "Hong Kong is one of the more populated territories in the world with a density of 30 000 inhabitants/per square kilometer. To respond to this overpopulation, the 'Urban Jungle' proposes to re-tame nature and to widen the territory of the ultra-contemporary city." Any new built spaces would be self-sufficient, producing more energies and biodiversity than they consume. A "mesh of irregular cells" brings water into the entire new district, forming open-air swimming pools, marinas, new quays, or lagoons for biological purification. "In front of the skyline of the Kowloon peninsula," says Callebaut, "a true cascade of aquatic and vegetable terraces like the ones of a rice terrace are laid out on this fifth façade. This new topography, without any wall, thus without any limit, is not only meant to be inhabited by the citizens of Hong Kong, but is also designed to be infiltrated, crossed and printed by the numerous species of the fauna and local flora or in migration that will come to install themselves." The towers the architect proposes are modeled on arborescent development and have fishnet skin "closed on a random basis with cushions of substrate and vegetable fertilizers enabling the development of luxuriant vegetation."

Das Projekt ist ein „Masterplan für die ökologische Gestaltung des zentralen Uferabschnitts im Geschäftsviertel von Hongkong". Der Architekt führt aus: „Hongkong zählt mit 30 000 Bewohnern pro Quadratkilometer zu den am dichtest bevölkerten Gegenden der Welt. Um dieser Überbevölkerung entgegenzutreten, geht es dem ‚urbanen Dschungel' darum, die Natur aufs Neue zu zähmen und neues Territorium für eine ultra-zeitgenössische Stadt zu erschließen." Sämtliche Neubauten wären autark und würden mehr Energie und Biodiversität produzieren, als sie verbrauchen. Ein „Geflecht aus unregelmäßigen Zellen" würde Wasser in das gesamte neue Stadtviertel holen, aus denen Freibäder, Jachthäfen, neue Kaianlagen oder Lagunen für biologische Wasseraufbereitung entstehen könnten. „Vor der Skyline der Halbinsel Kowloon", beschreibt Callebaut, „würde eine Kaskade von wassergefüllten oder mit Gemüsekulturen bepflanzten Terrassen, ähnlich wie Reisterrassen, entstehen, die die gesamte fünfte Fassade überziehen würden. Diese neue Art von Topografie, die ohne Mauer und somit ohne Begrenzung auskommt, soll nicht nur von den Bürgern Hongkongs bewohnt werden, sondern ist auch daraufhin angelegt, von den verschiedenen Arten regionaler oder vorbeiziehender Flora und Fauna, die sich hier niederlassen, erobern, passiert und geprägt zu werden." Die vom Architekten geplanten Hochhausbauten basieren auf Wachstumsmodellen von Bäumen und sind mit einer fischnetzartigen Haut überzogen, „die nach dem Zufallsprinzip mit Kissen aus Substrat und Gemüsedünger gefüllt werden, um eine üppige Vegetation anzuregen".

Il s'agit ici d'un « plan directeur pour l'écoconception de la partie centrale du front de mer du quartier d'affaires de Hong Kong ». L'architecte explique : « Avec une densité de 30 000 habitants au km², Hong Kong est l'un des territoires les plus peuplés du monde. Pour répondre à cette surpopulation, la "Jungle urbaine" propose de redomestiquer la nature et d'agrandir le territoire de la cité ultra-contemporaine ». Toute nouvelle construction devrait être autosuffisante et produire plus d'énergie et de biodiversité qu'elle n'en consomme. Une « résille de cellules irrégulières » fournit l'eau au quartier tout entier, formant des piscines en plein air, des marinas, de nouveaux quais ou des lagons d'épuration biologique. « Face au panorama de la péninsule de Kowloon, explique Callebaut, une vraie cascade de terrasses aquatiques et végétalisées, comme celle des cultures rizicoles, est disposée sur cette cinquième façade. Cette topographie nouvelle, sans mur, et donc sans la moindre limite, est non seulement pensée pour les habitants de la ville, mais aussi pour être infiltrée, parcourue et appropriée par les nombreuses espèces de la faune et de la flore locale ou en migration qui viendront s'y installer. » Les tours proposées par l'architecte sont modelées sur des développements de type arborescent et présente une peau en filet « posée sur une base aléatoire avec des coussins de substrats et d'engrais permettant le développement d'une végétation luxuriante ».

The Perfumed Jungle is presented with vast open spaces that might almost give the impression that these towers need not have a precise function, yet they would produce both energy and biodiversity.

Der Perfumed Jungle präsentiert sich mit riesigen Freiflächen, wodurch beinahe der Eindruck entsteht, die Türme hätten keine spezielle Funktion. Tatsächlich sollen sie Energie erzeugen und Biodiversität schaffen.

La « Jungle parfumée » se présente comme de vastes espaces ouverts donnant l'impression que ces tours n'ont pas de fonction précise, or elles produisent de l'énergie et défendent la biodiversité.

Callebaut's fantastic environment seems to suggest that architecture could become an integral part of a living environment.

Callebauts fantastische Umwelt scheint geradezu nahe zu legen, dass Architektur integraler Bestandteil des gesamten Lebensraums werden könnte.

L'environnement fantastique imaginé par Callebaut suggère que l'architecture pourrait devenir partie intégrante d'un environnement vivant.

CEPEZED

Architectenbureau Cepezed
Phoenixstraat 60b
2611 AM Delft
The Netherlands

Tel: +31 15 215 00 00
Fax: +31 15 213 09 08
E-mail: post@cepezed.nl
Web: www.cepezed.nl

Jan Pesman was born in Utrecht in 1951 and studied Architecture at the University of Technology in Delft, where he established **CEPEZED** in 1973. In 1971 he was one of the founders of *Utopia*, a magazine for "scientific amusement," of which he remained an editor and designer until 1977. Pesman was also a co-founder and editor (1983–92) of the design magazine *Items*, which continues to be published. Ronald Schleurholts was born in Roden, The Netherlands, in 1972 and also studied Architecture at Delft University of Technology, where he specialized in construction methods and interior layout. During his studies, he worked for the architectural offices of Claus en Kaan and Koen van Velsen. He has worked with Cepezed since 1999 and became a partner and co-director in 2005. He achieved great success with a personal submission to the Pilkington Glasshouse Competition in 2003. Their joint work includes their own office (Delft, 1999); the Porsche Zentrum Zuffenhausen (Stuttgart, Germany, 2000); Race Planet (Delft, 2000); Station area and Grote Markt Sint-Niklaas (Sint-Niklaas, Belgium, 2004–05); the Dutch Embassy in Rome (Italy, 2007); The Outlook (Schiphol, 2007); Westraven Office Complex (Utrecht, 2005–07, published here); and the Audax Textile Museum (Tilburg, 2008), all in the Netherlands unless stated otherwise.

Jan Pesman wurde 1951 in Utrecht geboren und studierte Architektur an der Technischen Universität in Delft, wo er 1973 **CEPEZED** gründete. Pesman war 1971 einer der Mitbegründer von *Utopia*, einer Zeitschrift für „wissenschaftliche Unterhaltung", für die er bis 1977 als Herausgeber und Gestalter tätig war. Darüber hinaus war Pesman 1983 bis 1992 Mitbegründer und Herausgeber der Designzeitschrift *Items*, die nach wie vor erscheint. Ronald Schleurholts wurde 1972 im niederländischen Roden geboren und studierte ebenfalls Architektur an der Technischen Universität Delft, wo er sich auf Konstruktionsmethoden und Innenraumplanung spezialisierte. Während seines Studiums arbeitete er für die Architekturbüros von Claus en Kaan und Koen van Velsen. Seit 1999 ist er für Cepezed tätig, wurde 2005 Partner und Kodirektor des Büros. Großen Erfolg hatte er 2003 mit einem eigenständigen Wettbewerbsbeitrag für das Pilkington Glasshouse. Zu den gemeinsamen Projekten zählen u. a. das eigene Büro (Delft, 1999), das Porsche-Zentrum Zuffenhausen (Stuttgart, 2000), der Race Planet (Delft, 2000), die Bahnhofsgegend und der Grote Markt in Sint-Niklaas (Belgien, 2004–05), die niederländische Botschaft in Rom (2007), The Outlook (Schiphol, 2007), der Bürokomplex Westraven (Utrecht, 2005–07, hier vorgestellt) sowie das Audax Textilmuseum (Tilburg, 2008), alle in den Niederlanden, sofern nicht anders angegeben.

Jan Pesman, né à Utrecht en 1951, a étudié l'architecture à l'université de Technologie de Delft où il a fondé **CEPEZED** en 1973. En 1971, il a fait partie des fondateurs d'*Utopia*, magazine pour « l'amusement scientifique », dont il est resté rédacteur en chef et directeur artistique jusqu'en 1977. Pesman a également été cofondateur et rédacteur en chef (1983–92) du magazine de design *Items*, toujours publié. Ronald Schleurholts, né à Roden aux Pays-Bas en 1972, a également étudié l'architecture à l'université de Technologie de Delft où il s'est spécialisé dans les méthodes de construction et l'aménagement intérieur. Au cours de ses études, il a travaillé pour les agences d'architecture de Claus en Kaan et de Koen van Velsen, et est entré chez Cepezed en 1999 dont il est devenu associé et codirecteur en 2005. Il a remporté un grand succès pour sa participation au concours de la maison de verre Pilkington en 2003. Parmi les réalisations de l'agence, pour la plupart aux Pays-Bas : les bureaux de Cepezed (Delft, 1999) ; le Porsche Zentrum Zuffenhausen (Stuttgart, Allemagne, 2000) ; Race Planet (Delft, 2000) ; zone de la gare et la grand-place de Saint Nicolas (Belgique, 2004–05) ; l'ambassade néerlandaise à Rome (2007) ; The Outlook (Schiphol, 2007) ; le complexe de bureaux Westraven (Utrecht, 2005–07, publié ici) et le musée du Textile Audax (Tilburg, 2008).

WESTRAVEN OFFICE COMPLEX

Utrecht, The Netherlands, 2005–07

*Floor area: 51 890 m². Client: Dutch Government Buildings Agency.
Cost: €76.975 million. Collaboration: Christaan de Wolf, Erwin Fraikin, Joost Heijnis*

This large project involves both new construction and the reuse of an existing high-rise tower for the Dutch Department of Public Works, located in the Westraven area of Utrecht. The program includes offices, conference facilities, a communications center, and the "Future Center" of the Public Works Department. The high rise was stripped to its concrete skeleton and entirely renovated. Four-story office wings along the Amsterdam-Rhine Canal were added by the architects and inner gardens serve as meeting points between the office blocks. Care was taken to unify the older structure and the new ones in both aesthetic and functional terms. A priority of both the client and the architects was to attain maximum sustainability with this project. Transparency in the architecture is used to maximize daylight and reduce artificial lighting in the day. A "biodynamic" lighting system automatically adjusts artificial light to reduce electricity consumption. Natural ventilation and an underground thermal energy storage system further reduce climate-control expenses. A second skin made of a thin open PTFE (Teflon) fiber weave was used on three sides of the high rise, adding to the building's wind and sun resistance. This large building complex designed for the Dutch government is obviously intended to set an example for the country, and the architects have certainly fulfilled that requirement, adding architectural quality to a largely sustainable design strategy.

Das Großprojekt umfasst sowohl Neubauabschnitte als auch die Integration eines bestehenden Hochhausgebäudes für die Rijkswaterstaat (RWS), eine Behörde des niederländischen Verkehrsministeriums, im Bezirk Westraven in Utrecht. Zum Programm gehören Büros, Konferenzräume, ein Kommunikationszentrum sowie das „Zukunftszentrum" der RWS. Das Hochhaus wurde bis auf sein Betonskelett entkernt und umfassend saniert. Entlang des Amsterdam-Rhein-Kanals erweiterten die Architekten den Bau um vierstöckige Flügel, Innengärten dienen als Treffpunkte zwischen den Büroblocks. Besondere Sorgfalt wurde darauf verwendet, den älteren Bau und die Neubauabschnitte in ästhetischer und funktionaler Hinsicht zu verbinden. Priorität für Auftraggeber und Architekten war es, mit dem Projekt maximale Nachhaltigkeit zu erzielen. Die Transparenz der Architektur wird genutzt, um tagsüber das Tageslicht zu maximieren und künstliche Belichtung zu reduzieren. Ein „biodynamisches" Beleuchtungssystem steuert das Kunstlicht automatisch, um den Stromverbrauch zu drosseln. Kosten für die Klimasteuerung werden durch natürliche Belüftung und ein unterirdisches Wärmespeichersystem weiter reduziert. Eine zweite Gebäudehaut aus dünnem PTFE(Teflon)-Gewebe wurde an drei Seiten des Baus eingesetzt und schützt das Gebäude zusätzlich gegen Wind und Sonne. Natürlich soll der für die niederländische Regierung entworfene Baukomplex landesweit Vorbildcharakter haben. Diese Aufgabe haben die Architekten offensichtlich gemeistert und dabei zudem die primär auf Nachhaltigkeit ausgerichtete Entwurfsstrategie um architektonische Qualität bereichert.

Ce vaste projet consiste en travaux de construction à neuf et de réaménagement d'une tour de grande hauteur existante pour le ministère néerlandais des travaux publics, située dans le quartier de Westraven à Utrecht. Le programme comprend des bureaux, des salles de conférences, un centre de communications et le « Centre du futur » du ministère des travaux publics. La tour, réduite à son squelette de béton, a été entièrement rénovée. Quatre ailes de bureaux le long du canal Amsterdam-Rhin ont été ajoutées par l'architecte, ainsi que des jardins intérieurs qui servent de zone d'échanges entre les blocs de bureaux. Une recherche poussée a été menée pour unifier la construction nouvelle et l'ancienne, aussi bien sur le plan esthétique que fonctionnel. La priorité pour le client et pour l'architecte était d'atteindre un niveau de durabilité optimal. La transparence de l'architecture permet d'utiliser au maximum la lumière naturelle et de réduire la consommation électrique en journée. Un système d'éclairage « biodynamique » règle automatiquement l'éclairage artificiel pour réduire la consommation d'électricité. La ventilation naturelle et un système de stockage souterrain de l'énergie thermique diminuent les dépenses de climatisation. Une seconde peau faite d'une PTFE (Téflon) à maille ouverte posée sur trois côtés de la tour renforce la résistance de l'immeuble aux vents et au soleil. Ce vaste ensemble, réalisé pour l'administration néerlandaise, a manifestement été conçu pour devenir un exemple. Les architectes ont rempli cet objectif en maintenant le niveau de qualité architecturale, tout en proposant une stratégie de conception durable aboutie.

The Westraven Complex demonstrates the capacity of architects to make even very large buildings green— surely an encouraging sign for the future.

Der Bürokomplex in Westraven zeugt von der Fähigkeit der Architekten, selbst Großbauten grün umzugestalten – fraglos ein ermutigender Impuls für die Zukunft.

Le complexe de Westraven témoigne de la capacité des architectes à savoir appliquer les principes de la gestion écologique aux très grands immeubles, signe encourageant pour le futur.

A garden serves as a meeting point for users of the complex—grouped around a renovated tower.

Um das renovierte Hochhaus wurde ein Park angelegt – ein Treffpunkt für die Nutzer des Komplexes.

Autour de la tour rénovée, un jardin sert de point de rencontre aux utilisateurs du complexe.

Transparency, sometimes seen as the opposite of energy efficiency, is used here to maximize natural light and reduce its artificial complement. But then again, the sun is not that strong in Utrecht.

Transparenz, die oftmals als unvereinbar mit energieeffizientem Bauen gilt, dient hier dazu, natürliche Belichtung zu maximieren und ihr künstliches Pendant zu reduzieren. Immerhin ist das Sonnenlicht in Utrecht nicht allzu intensiv.

La transparence peut sembler opposée à l'efficacité énergétique. Elle est utilisée ici pour optimiser l'utilisation de la lumière naturelle et réduire les besoins en éclairage artificiel. Il est à noter que le soleil n'est pas très puissant à Utrecht.

DILLER SCOFIDIO + RENFRO

Diller Scofidio + Renfro / 601 West 26th Street, Suite 1815
New York, NY 10001 / USA
Tel: +1 212 260 7971 / Fax: +1 212 260 7924
E-mail: disco@dsrny.com / Web: www.dsrny.com

ELIZABETH DILLER is Professor of Architecture at Princeton University and **RICARDO SCOFIDIO** is Professor of Architecture at the Cooper Union in New York. The founded Diller + Scofidio in 1979. **CHARLES RENFRO** is a Visiting Professor at Columbia University and became partner in 2004. According to their own description: "DS+R is a collaborative, interdisciplinary studio involved in architecture, the visual arts, and the performing arts. The team is primarily involved in thematically driven experimental works that take the form of architectural commissions, temporary installations, and permanent site-specific installations, multimedia theater, electronic media, and print." Their work includes Slither, 100 units of social housing in Gifu, Japan, and *Moving Target*, a collaborative dance work with Charleroi/Danse Belgium. Installations have been seen at the Cartier Foundation in Paris (*Master/Slave*, 1999); and the Museum of Modern Art in New York. Their completed work includes The Brasserie Restaurant (Seagram Building, New York, 1998–99); the Blur Building (Expo '02, Yverdon-les-Bains, Switzerland, 2000–02); the Institute of Contemporary Art in Boston (2004–06); and they are responsible for the Phantom House (Southwest USA, 2007, published here). They were selected as architects of the Eyebeam Institute in the Chelsea area of Manhattan and Lincoln Center (New York), and they will complete the expansion of the Julliard School and Alice Tully Hall there in 2009. They designed the Viewing Platforms at Ground Zero in Manhattan, and are currently working on the Brown University Creative Arts Center (Providence, Rhode Island); the High Line, a park on three kilometers of elevated train line (New York, in collaboration with Field Operations); the Hudson Riverfront Performing Arts Center (Weehawken, New Jersey); and the Mott Street (Kopp) Townhouse (New York), all in the USA.

ELIZABETH DILLER ist Professorin für Architektur an der Universität Princeton, **RICARDO SCOFIDIO** Professor für Architektur an der Cooper Union in New York. 1979 gründeten sie das Büro Diller + Scofidio. **CHARLES RENFRO** ist Gastprofessor an der Columbia University und wurde 2004 Partner. Eigener Aussage nach verstehen sich DS+R als „kooperierendes, interdisziplinäres Studio, das in den Bereichen Architektur, bildende und darstellende Künste tätig ist. Das Team beschäftigt sich in erster Linie mit thematisch ausgerichteten, experimentellen Projekten, wobei es sich um architektonische Aufträge, temporäre Installationen und permanente, ortsspezifische Installationen handeln kann, um Multimedia-Theater, elektronische Medien und Publikationen." Zu ihren Projekten zählen Slither, 100 Sozialbaueinheiten in Gifu, Japan, und „Moving Target", ein Tanzprojekt mit Charleroi/Danse Belgium. Installationen waren in der Fondation Cartier in Paris zu sehen („Master/Slave", 1999) sowie im Museum of Modern Art in New York. Zu ihren realisierten Bauten zählen das Restaurant The Brasserie (Seagram Building, New York, 1998–99), das Blur Building (Expo '02, Yverdon-les-Bains, Schweiz, 2000–02), das Institute of Contemporary Art in Boston (2004–06), außerdem zeichnen sie verantwortlich für das Phantom House (Südwesten der USA, 2007, hier vorgestellt). Sie erhielten den Auftrag für das Eyebeam Institute in Manhattan (Chelsea) und das Lincoln Center (New York) und werden 2009 die Erweiterung der dortigen Julliard School und Alice Tully Hall abschließen. Das Team entwarf die Aussichtsplattformen für Ground Zero in Manhattan und arbeitet derzeit am Brown University Creative Arts Center (Providence, Rhode Island), der High Line, einem 3 km langen Park auf einem ehemaligen Hochbahnabschnitt (New York, mit Field Operations), am Hudson Riverfront Performing Arts Center (Weehawken, New Jersey) sowie am Mott Street (Kopp) Townhouse (New York), alle in den USA.

ELIZABETH DILLER est professeur d'architecture à l'université de Princeton et **RICARDO SCOFIDIO** enseigne à Cooper Union, New York. Tous deux ont créé en 1979 l'agence Diller + Scofidio. **CHARLES RENFRO** est professeur invité à l'université Columbia et s'associe à eux en 2004. Ils se présentent comme « une agence interdisciplinaire coopérative se consacrant à l'architecture, aux arts plastiques et arts de la scène. L'équipe travaille surtout sur des recherches thématiques expérimentales : commandes architecturales, installations temporaires, installations permanentes adaptées au site, théâtres multimédia, médias électroniques et d'édition ». Parmi leurs projets : Slither, 100 logements sociaux, Gifu, Japon ; *Moving Target*, œuvre chorégraphique avec Charleroi/Danse (Belgique). Ils ont exposé leurs installations à la Fondation Cartier à Paris (*Master/Slave*, 1999) et au MoMA de New York. Autres réalisations : le restaurant The Brasserie du Seagram Building, New York (1998–99) ; le Blur Building à l'Expo '02 (Yverdon-les-Bains, Suisse, 2000–02) ; l'Institut d'Art contemporain à Boston (2004–06) et le Phantom House (sud-ouest des États-Unis, 2007, publié ici). Ils ont été sélectionnés pour l'Institut Eyebeam à Manhattan (Chelsea) et le centre Lincoln (New York), et achèveront l'extension de l'école Julliard et de l'Alice Tully Hall en 2009. Ils ont conçu les plates-formes d'observation de Ground Zero à Manhattan et travaillent actuellement sur le projet du Brown University Creative Arts Center (Providence, Rhode Island) ; la High Line, un parc de 3 km de long sur une ancienne voie ferrée surélevée (avec Filed Operations, New York) ; le Hudson Riverfont Performing Arts Center (Weehawken, New Jersey) et la maison de ville de Mott Street (Kopp) à New York.

PHANTOM HOUSE

Southwest USA, 2007

Floor area: 204 m² (inside); 204 m² (outside). Client: The New York Times Magazine. *Project for print.*
Project Leader: David Allin. Collaboration: Atelier Ten

Designed in conjunction with the May 20, 2007, issue of *The New York Times Magazine*, dedicated to the subject of "Ecotecture," this concept house draws on existing technologies and some imagined ones to create the most sustainable and ecologically conscious residence possible. An indoor, climate-controlled space is located above an outdoor one of the same dimensions. Energy produced in everyday activities is stored for later use, while "ground-coupled heating and cooling uses the steady temperature of the earth" (13°C in the imagined location of the residence) as a source of heat. Double-layer glass called OpaciView by the architects, made with a ventilated cavity between the layers and a porous film of tungsten oxide that lightens or darkens depending on the heat of the sun, is used in the house. Photovoltaic cells are aligned on the roof, and exercise equipment generates electricity when it is used that can be stored. Even the mattresses on the beds are equipped with a similar system that generates and stores electricity generated by "excess human energy," as the architects put it. The house can be put in "hibernation mode" when it is not in use, reducing energy use to a bare minimum. The house would be built from "recycled, remanufactured, and renewable materials. Wood species are selected from the nearest sustainably managed forest." Water sensors on the roof double the areas able to catch rainwater when necessary, and store the water for use in toilets and the garden.

Der Konzeptentwurf für ein Wohnhaus entstand für die Ausgabe des *New York Times Magazine* vom 20. Mai 2007, die sich dem Thema „Ecotecture" widmete. Der Entwurf greift sowohl existierende als auch visionäre Technologien auf, um ein möglichst nachhaltiges und ökologisch bewusstes Wohnhaus zu gestalten. Ein klimatisierter Innenraum liegt über einem ebenso großen Außenbereich. Die bei alltäglichen Verrichtungen erzeugte Energie wird für spätere Nutzung gespeichert, während ein „geothermisches Heizungs- und Kühlsystem die konstante Temperatur des Erdreichs" (bei der geplanten Lage des Hauses 13 °C) nutzt. Im Haus kommt eine Doppelverglasung zum Einsatz, die die Architekten OpaciView nennen. Sie besteht aus zwei Schichten, zwischen denen ein belüfteter Hohlraum und ein poröser Film aus Wolframoxid liegen, der sich je nach Sonnenstrahlung heller oder dunkler tönt. Auf dem Dach sind Solarzellen installiert, Fitnessgeräte erzeugen bei aktiver Nutzung speicherbaren Strom. Selbst die Matratzen der Betten sind mit einem System ausgestattet, das (so die Architekten) „bei exzessiver menschlicher Energie" Strom erzeugt und speichert. Wird das Haus nicht genutzt, kann es in einen „Winterschlafmodus" versetzt werden, der den Energieverbrauch auf ein absolutes Minimum reduziert. Das Haus soll aus „recycelten, wiederaufbereiteten und erneuerbaren Materialien gebaut werden. Holzarten werden aus den nächsten nachhaltig bewirtschafteten Wäldern bezogen". Wassersensoren auf dem Dach verdoppeln die Fläche, auf der sich nach Bedarf Regenwasser sammeln und für Sanitäranlagen und Bewässerung speichern lässt.

Conçue en conjonction avec la parution du numéro du 20 mai 2007 du *New York Times Magazine* consacré à l'*Ecotecture*, cette maison concept s'appuie sur des technologies existantes, et certaines encore imaginaires, pour créer la résidence la plus durable et la plus écologique possible. Le volume intérieur à climatisation contrôlée est posé sur un second volume de dimensions identiques. L'énergie produite par les activités quotidiennes est stockée pour un usage ultérieur tandis que des « systèmes de chauffage et de refroidissement utilisent la température stable de la terre » (13 °C ici) comme source de chaleur. Un vitrage double, appelé OpaciView par les architectes, aux verres séparés par une cavité d'air ventilée est enduit d'un film poreux d'oxyde de tungstène qui s'assombrit ou s'éclaircit au gré de la chaleur solaire. Des panneaux de cellules photovoltaïques équipent le toit, et les équipements de gymnastique utilisés génèrent de l'énergie qui peut être stockée. Même les matelas sont équipés pour stocker l'électricité produite par « l'énergie humaine en excès », comme le précisent les architectes. La maison peut être placée en « mode hibernation » lorsqu'elle n'est pas utilisée pour réduire au minimum la consommation énergétique. Elle sera réalisée en « matériaux recyclés, reconditionnés et renouvelables ». Les variétés de bois sont choisies dans les forêts les plus proches gérées dans un esprit de développement durable ». Les capteurs d'eau du toit doublent les surfaces pouvant recueillir l'eau de pluie, qui est alors récupérée pour les toilettes et l'irrigation.

The Phantom House was designed for The New York Times Magazine as a willful exercise in maximizing environmental responsibility in architecture.

Das Phantom House wurde für das New York Times Magazine *mit dem expliziten Ziel entworfen, Umweltbewusstsein in der Architektur zu erhöhen.*

Le Phantom House a été conçue pour le New York Times Magazine *comme expérimentation pour accroître au maximum le sens de la responsabilité environnementale en architecture.*

VLADIMIR DJUROVIC

Vladimir Djurovic Landscape Architecture (VDLA)
Villa Rizk
Broumana
Lebanon

Tel: +961 4 862 444/555
Fax: +961 4 862 462
E-mail: info@vladimirdjurovic.com
Web: www.vladimirdjurovic.com

VLADIMIR DJUROVIC was born to a Serb father and a Lebanese mother in 1967. He received a degree in Horticulture from Reading University in England in 1989 and his M. A. in Landscape Architecture from the University of Georgia in 1992, after having worked at EDAW in Atlanta. Vladimir Djurovic Landscape Architecture (VDLA) was created in 1995 in Beirut. The office has participated and won several international competitions, such as Freedom Park South Africa (2003). They have completed numerous private residences in Lebanon, including the F House (Dahr El Sawan, Lebanon, 2000–04, with Nabil Gholam). The firm won a 2008 Award of Honor in the residential design category from the American Society of Landscape Architects (ASLA) for its Bassil Mountain Escape project in Faqra, Lebanon. After the work on the award-winning Samir Kassir Square (Beirut, 2004, published here), current work includes the landscaping of the Wynford Drive site in Toronto, Canada, to accomodate the Aga Khan Museum by Fumihiko Maki and the Ismaili Center by Charles Correa. VDLA won the international competition for this design in 2006. Other current work includes Beirut Marina, Solidere, BCD (Lebanon, architect: Steven Holl); and The Edge, a very large multiuse complex in Business Bay (Dubai, UAE, architects: RCR Arquitectes).

VLADIMIR DJUROVIC wurde 1967 als Sohn eines serbischen Vaters und einer libanesischen Mutter geboren. 1989 schloss er zunächst sein Gartenbaustudium an der Universität Reading in England ab, arbeitete für EDAW in Atlanta und absolvierte schließlich 1992 einen M. A. in Landschaftsarchitektur an der Universität von Georgia (USA). Sein Büro Vladimir Djurovic Landscape Architecture (VDLA) gründete er 1995 in Beirut. Das Büro hat mehrfach erfolgreich an internationalen Wettbewerben teilgenommen, etwa für den Freedom Park in Südafrika (2003). Das Team gestaltete zahlreiche Privatwohnbauten im Libanon, darunter das F House (Dahr El Sawan, Libanon, 2000–04, mit Nabil Gholam). Für sein Projekt Bassil Mountain Escape in Fakra, Libanon, wurde das Büro 2008 mit dem Ehrenpreis der American Society of Landscape Architects (ASLA) in der Kategorie Wohnbaugestaltung ausgezeichnet. Nach der Arbeit am preisgekrönten Samir-Kassir-Platz (Beirut, 2004, hier vorgestellt) sind aktuelle Projekte u. a. die Landschaftsgestaltung eines Grundstücks am Wynford Drive in Toronto, Kanada, für das Aga-Khan-Museum von Fumihiko Maki und das Ismaili Center von Charles Correa. Mit diesem Entwurf gewann VDLA 2006 einen internationalen Wettbewerb. Weitere aktuelle Projekte sind die Beirut Marina, Solidere, BCD (Libanon, Architekt: Steven Holl), sowie The Edge, ein Mehrzweck-Großkomplex in der Business Bay von Dubai (VAE, Architekten: RCR Arquitectes).

VLADIMIR DJUROVIC est né d'un père serbe et d'une mère libanaise en 1967. Il est diplômé en horticulture de l'université Reading (G.-B.) en 1989 et a obtenu son M. A. en architecture du paysage de l'université de Géorgie (1992) après avoir travaillé pour l'agence EDAW à Atlanta. L'agence Vladimir Djurovic Landscape Architecture (VDLA) a été fondée en 1995 à Beyrouth. Elle a remporté plusieurs concours internationaux, dont celui du Freedom Park South Africa (2003), et a réalisé de nombreuses résidences privées au Liban, comme la maison F (avec Nabil Gholam, Dahr El Sawan, Liban, 2000–04). En 2008, elle a reçu un Prix d'honneur dans la catégorie « Projets résidentiels » de l'American Society of Landscape Architects (ASLA) pour le chalet de montagne Bassil à Faqra, Liban. Après avoir remporté le Prix Aga Khan pour le jardin Samir-Kassir (Beyrouth, 2004, publiée ici), l'agence travaille sur les aménagements paysagers du site de Wynford Drive à Toronto, Canada, qui regroupe le Musée Aga Khan par Fumihiko Maki et le Centre ismaélien par Charles Correa. VDLA en avait remporté le concours international en 2006. Parmi ses autres projets figurent la Marina de Beyrouth, Solidere, BCD (Liban, architecte : Steven Holl), et The Edge, un très vaste complexe mixte à Business Bay (Dubai, EAU, architectes : RCR Arquitectes).

SAMIR KASSIR SQUARE

Beirut, Lebanon, 2004

*Site area: 815 m². Client: Solidere (Société Libanaise de Développement et Reconstruction).
Cost: $322 000. Team: Vladimir Djurovic (Principal), Paul De Mar Yousef (Design Architect),
Salim Kanaan (Project Architect)*

Vladimir Djurovic has a decidedly minimalist style in his gardens and Samir Kassir Square is no exception. Located in the recently redeveloped Beirut Central District, the small park was conceived around two existing ficus trees that had somehow managed to survive the violence that wracked Beirut for years. "The challenge of this project," says Djurovic, "was to create a quiet refuge on a limited piece of land surrounded by buildings, while addressing the prominent street frontage that it occupies. In essence, to become a small escape dedicated to the city and its people." A raised "water mirror" is a central feature of the Square, faced by a 20-meter-long solid stone bench. This project was a winner of the 2007 Aga Khan Award for Architecture. The jury citation reads: "The Samir Kassir Square is a restrained and serene urban public space that skillfully handles the conditions and infrastructure of its location in a city that has undergone rapid redevelopment. The Award will go to Vladimir Djurovic, the pre-eminent landscape architect working in Lebanon today."

Vladimir Djurovics Gärten zeichnen sich durch einen minimalistischen Stil aus, und der Samir-Kassir-Platz ist keine Ausnahme. Der im kürzlich sanierten Zentrum von Beirut gelegene Park wurde um zwei Feigenbäume herum geplant, die erstaunlicherweise die jahrelang in Beirut wütende Gewalt überstanden haben. Djurovic zufolge lag „die Herausforderung des Projekts darin, einen Zufluchtsort auf einem engen, von Gebäuden umstandenen Grundstück zu schaffen und dabei die prominente Straßenfront des Platzes zu gestalten. Im Grunde sollte es ein kleiner Zufluchtsort für die Stadt und ihre Bewohner werden." Ein erhöhter „Wasserspiegel" ist zentraler Blickpunkt des Platzes, der von einer 20 m langen Steinbank flankiert wird. Das Projekt wurde 2007 mit dem Aga-Khan-Preis für Architektur ausgezeichnet. Die Jury merkte an: „Der Samir-Kassir-Platz ist ein zurückgenommener und heiterer öffentlicher Platz, der gekonnt mit den Bedingungen und der Infrastruktur seines Standorts in einer Stadt umgeht, die sich rasch verändert hat. Der Preis geht an Vladimir Djurovic, den herausragendsten heute im Libanon praktizierenden Landschaftsarchitekten."

Le style des jardins de Vladimir Djurovic est résolument minimaliste et le jardin Samir-Kassir n'y fait pas exception. Situé dans le centre récemment reconstruit de Beyrouth, ce petit square a été conçu autour de deux ficus sauvés des violences qui dévastèrent la ville pendant des années. « Le défi de ce projet, explique Djurovic, était de créer un refuge sur une parcelle de terrain de dimensions limitées et entourée d'immeubles, tout en traitant son importante façade sur rue. Fondamentalement, l'idée était de réaliser un lieu dédié à la ville et à ses habitants. » Un « miroir d'eau » surélevé est l'élément central du projet, face à un banc de pierre massive de 20 m de long. Ce projet a remporté le Prix d'architecture Aga Khan 2007. La citation du jury précisait : « Le jardin Samir-Kassir est un espace public limité et serein qui s'adapte avec talent aux conditions et à l'infrastructure de sa situation dans une ville qui connaît un développement rapide. Le prix ira à Vladimir Djurovic, le plus éminent architecte paysagiste œuvrant actuellement au Liban. »

A central feature of the Square are two ficus trees that symbolize the continuity of the place, in spite of all the events that have marked the history of Beirut in recent years.

Zentrale Elemente des Platzes sind zwei Feigenbäume – Symbol der Kontinuität des Ortes, allen Ereignissen zum Trotz, die die Geschichte Beiruts in den vergangenen Jahren geprägt haben.

Une des caractéristiques importantes de ce square est la présence de deux anciens ficus qui symbolisent la permanence du lieu, malgré les événements récents qui ont marqué l'histoire de Beyrouth.

Dominated by its two old trees, the Square uses the sound of water to create a haven of peace in the middle of the city.

Der von den zwei Bäumen beherrschte Platz wird dank des plätschernden Wassers zum friedlichen Zufluchtsort inmitten der Stadt.

Dominé par ses deux vieux arbres, le jardin profite du bruit de l'eau, créant un havre de paix au cœur de la ville.

DENNIS DOLLENS

Dennis Dollens, Exodesic
40 Camino Cielo
Santa Fe, NM 87506
USA

Tel: +1 505 988 9236
Fax: +1 505 988 5820
E-mail: exodesic@mac.com
Web: www.exodesic.com

Born in Los Angeles in 1950, **DENNIS DOLLENS** has taught Design Biomimetics in the Genetic Architectures Program and in the Department of Ecology and Architecture at the Universitat Internacional de Catalunya's School of Architecture (Barcelona) since 2000. He lectures internationally on Digital-Biomimetic Architecture and his work in schools of industrial design and architecture. He is currently working on a Ph. D. at the University of Strathclyde, Glasgow. His studios are in Santa Fe, New Mexico, and Barcelona, Spain, and his most recent books are *D2A: Digital to Analog* (translated into Spanish and published as *De lo digital a lo analógico*) and *DBA: Digital-Botanic Architecture*. His current architectural work includes a 3D weaving prototype for an apartment building; a passive ventilating and self-shading 14-story tower; and the development of new sensor-embedded biomimetic exterior paneling using adobe, fiber pulp, and bio-resins. See his Tree Tower (Los Angeles, California, 2009), published here.

DENNIS DOLLENS wurde 1950 in Los Angeles geboren und unterrichtet seit 2000 biomimetisches Design im Programm für genetische Architektur an der Architekturfakultät der Universitat Internacional de Catalunya (Barcelona). Er lehrt international an Hochschulen für Industriedesign und Architektur in den Bereichen digital-biomimetische Architektur, wo er auch seine eigene Arbeit vorstellt. Derzeit arbeitet er an seiner Doktorarbeit an der Universität von Strathclyde, Glasgow. Er unterhält Büros in Santa Fe in New Mexico und in Barcelona. Seine jüngsten Publikationen sind *D2A: Digital to Analog* (auf Spanisch erschienen als *De lo digital a lo analógico*) und *DBA: Digital-Botanic Architecture*. Zu seinen aktuellen Architekturprojekten zählen ein 3-D-Gewebeprototyp für ein Apartmenthaus, ein passiv belüftetes und sich automatisch verschattendes 14-stöckiges Hochhaus und die Entwicklung einer neuartigen sensor-integrierten biomimetischen Außenverkleidung, bei der ungebrannte Lehmziegel, Zellstoff und Bioharze zum Einsatz kommen. Vergleiche hierzu auch seinen Tree Tower (Los Angeles, Kalifornien, 2009, hier vorgestellt).

Né à Los Angeles en 1950, **DENNIS DOLLENS** a enseigné le design biomimétique dans le cadre d'un programme sur les architectures génétiques au Département d'écologie et d'architecture de l'École d'architecture de l'Université internationale de Catalogne (Barcelone) depuis 2000. Il donne de nombreuses conférences dans le monde sur « l'architecture numérique-biomimétique » et sur ses recherches dans des écoles d'architecture et de design industriel. Il prépare actuellement un Ph. D. (Université de Strathclyde, Glasgow). Ses bureaux se trouvent à Santa Fe (Nouveau-Mexique) et Barcelone, et ses livres les plus récents sont *D2A : Digital to Analog* (traduit en espagnol sous le titre *De lo digital a lo analógico*) et *DBA : Digital-Botanic Architecture*. Il travaille actuellement à un prototype weaving en 3D pour un immeuble d'appartements, une tour de quatorze niveaux à ventilation passive et autoprotection solaire ; et le développement d'un nouveau type de panneaux à capteurs incrustés extérieur biomimétique utilisant l'adobe, la pâte de fibres et des biorésines. Voir sa Tree Tower (Los Angeles, 2009), publiée ici.

TREE TOWER

Los Angeles, California, USA, 2009

Floor area: 8919 m². Client: Lumen, Inc. Cost: $23 million

Although the final form of the Tower does not really look like a tree, these drawings show how its structure evolved from its biomimetic origins.

Obwohl der Turm in seiner endgültigen Form nicht wirklich wie ein Baum wirkt, illustrieren diese Zeichnungen doch, wie sich die Struktur aus biomimetischen Ursprüngen entwickelt.

Bien que la forme finale de la tour ne soit pas celle d'un arbre, ces dessins montrent l'évolution de la structure à partir de ses origines biomimétiques.

As is the case in much of the work of Dennis Dollens, this project is based on biomimetics. The design features "digitally grown" flexible and therefore earthquake-resistant trusses. Dollens used four software programs to create these forms—Xfrog, ParaCloud, Rhinoceros, and 3DS MAX. Digital simulations of tree, branch, and root growth are the basis for the structure. The underground elements would theoretically be "bio-reactors in the form of underground pods for the harvesting of water and processing sewage with bacteria." The skin, both interior and exterior, is formed with 2200 parametrically designed monocoque panels with an interlocking leaf pattern created with ParaCloud. Each of these panels will have glass elements, though the building itself would have neither traditional windows, nor a normal door, being entered below grade. The skin serves as a sun screen "while also allowing filtered views to the exterior—as if occupants were looking through a tree's leaves." Denis Dollens concludes: "While a first impression of the Tree Tower may not suggest that it is mimicking nature the building's digital heritage is tightly linked to functions found in plants. As the project moves into semifinal phases, environmental sensors for testing air pollution and allergens are being researched, as is the potential for the building's skin panels to filter its incoming air."

Wie viele Arbeiten von Dennis Dollens basiert auch dieses Projekt auf dem Prinzip der Biomimetik. Der Entwurf zeichnet sich durch „digital gezüchtete", flexible und damit erdbebensichere Träger aus. Dollens nutzte vier verschiedene Softwareprogramme, um diese Formen zu entwerfen – Xfrog, ParaCloud, Rhinoceros und 3DS MAX. Grundlage der Konstruktion sind digital simulierte Wachstumsprozesse von Bäumen, Ästen und Wurzeln. Bei den unterirdischen Komponenten handelt es sich um bisher hypothetische, „unterirdische, kapselartige Bio-Reaktoren, die Frischwasser sammeln und mithilfe von Bakterien Abwässer klären sollen". Die Gebäudehaut wurde innen wie außen aus 2200 parametrisch generierten Monocoque-Paneelen gestaltet, die zu einem ineinander zahnenden Blattmuster angeordnet und mit ParaCloud entwickelt wurden. Diese Paneele verfügen über integrierte Glaselemente, wobei der Bau weder traditionelle Fenster noch eine übliche Tür hat, sondern unterirdisch erschlossen wird. Die Außenhaut dient als Sonnenschutz und „filtert zugleich den Ausblick – als würden die Bewohner durch das Laub eines Baumes blicken". Dennis Dollens fasst zusammen: „Auch wenn es auf den ersten Blick nicht so scheint, als ahme der Tree Tower die Natur nach, knüpft das digitale Erbgut des Bauwerks doch eng an pflanzliche Funktionen an. Während sich das Projekt seiner Endphase nähert, experimentieren wir mit umweltsensiblen Sensoren, die Luftverschmutzung und Allergengehalte messen können, sowie mit der Option, einströmende Luft durch die Paneele der Gebäudehaut zu filtern."

Comme souvent chez Dennis Dollens, ce projet repose sur une approche biomimétique. Il présente des poutres « d'origine numérique » souples et donc résistantes aux tremblements de terre. L'architecte a utilisé quatre logiciels pour créer ces formes : Xfrog, ParaCloud, Rhinoceros et 3DS MAX. Des simulations numériques de la croissance d'arbres, de branches et de racines sont à la base de la structure. Théoriquement, des éléments, des « bioréacteurs en forme de cosses souterraines pour capter l'eau et traiter les eaux usées par bactéries », devraient être mis en place dans le sol. La peau, aussi bien externe qu'interne, se compose de 2200 panneaux monocoques de conception paramétrique à motif de feuillage entrelacé créé à l'aide de ParaCloud. Chacun de ces panneaux sera doté d'éléments en verre, bien que le bâtiment ne doive avoir ni fenêtres traditionnelles, ni porte classique et que son accès se fasse par le sous-sol. La peau sert d'écran de protection solaire « tout en autorisant des vues filtrées vers l'extérieur, comme si les occupants regardaient à travers le feuillage d'un arbre ». Denis Dollens conclut : « Si, à première vue, la Tree Tower n'imite pas la nature, le patrimoine numérique de l'immeuble est étroitement lié à des fonctions observées parmi les plantes. Le projet entre dans ses phases semifinales, et nous étudions des capteurs environnementaux pour tester la pollution de l'air et la présence d'allergènes ainsi que le potentiel des panneaux de la peau dans la filtration de l'air entrant. »

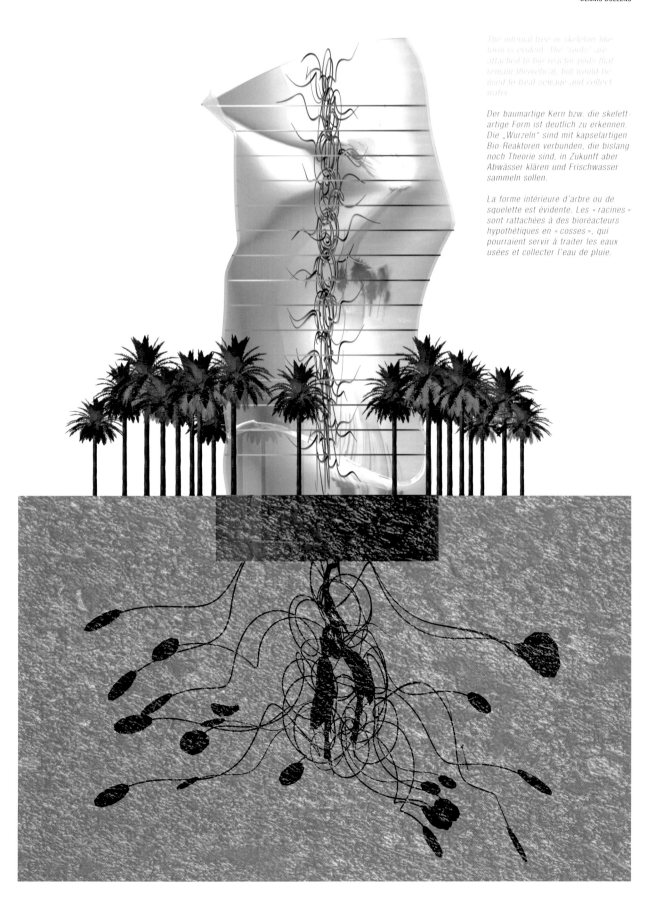

The internal tree or skeleton like form is evident. The "roots" are attached to bio-reactor pods that remain theoretical, but would be used to treat sewage and collect water.

Der baumartige Kern bzw. die skelett-artige Form ist deutlich zu erkennen. Die „Wurzeln" sind mit kapselartigen Bio-Reaktoren verbunden, die bislang noch Theorie sind, in Zukunft aber Abwässer klären und Frischwasser sammeln sollen.

La forme intérieure d'arbre ou de squelette est évidente. Les « racines » sont rattachées à des bioréacteurs hypothétiques en « cosses », qui pourraient servir à traiter les eaux usées et collecter l'eau de pluie.

ECOSISTEMA URBANO

Ecosistema Urbano Arquitectos
Estanislao Figueras 6
Madrid 28008
Spain

Tel: +34 91 559 16 01
E-mail: info@ecosistemaurbano.com
Web: www.ecosistemaurbano.com

ECOSISTEMA URBANO was created in 2000 by two partners: Belinda Tato, born in Madrid in 1971, who studied at the ETSA of Madrid (1999) and the Bartlett School of Architecture, London (1996); and Jose Luis Vallejo, born in Bilbao in 1971, who also studied at the ETSAM (1999) and Bartlett School (1996). Diego Garcia-Setien, born in Madrid in 1974, graduated from the Istituto Universitario di Architettura di Venezia (1997) and the ETSAM (2000) and worked with Tato and Vallejo on the Ecoboulevard project. Ecosistema Urbano has received more than 25 awards since the creation of their firm, in national and international architecture design competitions. In 2007 they were nominated for the European Union Prize for Contemporary Architecture Mies van der Rohe Award for "Emerging European Architects" and they were honored with an *AR* Award for emerging architecture. They received the Silver Award (Holcim Foundation Awards 2008 Europe) for their temporary urban extension in a former landfill, Maribor, Slovenia. Currently the team is involved in research projects concerning the future of city design that they call "eco-techno-logical cities," financed by the Spanish Ministry of Industry. They are working on several urban proposals for different Spanish municipalities (see the Ecoboulevard of Vallecas in Madrid, 2006, published here) and one of their projects will represent Madrid at Shanghai Expo '10.

ECOSISTEMA URBANO wurde 2000 von zwei Partnern gegründet: Belinda Tato, 1971 in Madrid geboren, Studium an der ETSAM in Madrid (1999) und der Bartlett School of Architecture, London (1996), und José Luis Vallejo, 1971 in Bilbao geboren, ebenfalls Studium an der ETSAM (1999) und der Bartlett School (1996). Diego Garcia-Setien, 1974 in Madrid geboren, Abschlüsse am Istituto Universitario di Architettura di Venezia (1997) und der ETSAM (2000), arbeitete mit Tato und Vallejo am Ecoboulevard in Vallecas. Seit Gründung des Büros wurde Ecosistema Urbano mit über 25 Preisen in nationalen und internationalen Entwurfswettbewerben ausgezeichnet. 2007 wurden die Partner für den Mies-van-der-Rohe-Preis für zeitgenössische Architektur der Europäischen Union als „aufstrebende europäische Architekten" nominiert und erhielten einen *AR* Award for Emerging Architecture der britischen Zeitschrift *Architectural Review*. Für ihr temporäres Stadterweiterungsprojekt auf einer ehemaligen Deponie in Maribor, Slowenien, wurden sie mit dem Silver Award (Europapreis 2008 der Holcim Foundation) ausgezeichnet. Zurzeit entwickeln sie Zukunftsperspektiven für die Stadtplanung und arbeiten an einer von ihnen als „öko-techno-logisch" bezeichneten Stadt, Untersuchungen, die vom spanischen Ministerium für Industrie finanziert werden. Das Team arbeitet an einer Reihe von Stadtplanungsentwürfen für verschiedene spanische Gemeinden (u. a. Ecoboulevard in Vallecas, Madrid, 2006, hier vorgestellt). Ein Projekt des Büros wird Madrid auf der Expo '10 in Shanghai vertreten.

L'agence **ECOSISTEMA URBANO** a été créée en 2000 par deux associés : Belinda Tato, née à Madrid en 1971, qui a étudié à l'ETSA de Madrid (1999) et à l'École Bartlett d'Architecture de Londres (1996), et Jose Luis Vallejo, né à Bilbao en 1971, qui a également étudié à l'ETSA (1999) et à l'École Bartlett (1996). Diego Garcia-Setien, né à Madrid en 1974, diplômé de l'Institut universitaire d'architecture de Venise (1997) et de l'ETSA de Madrid (2000), a travaillé avec Tato et Vallejo au projet de l'Ecoboulevard de Vallecas. Ecosistema Urbano a obtenu plus de 25 distinctions à des concours d'architecture nationaux ou internationaux depuis la création de leur agence. En 2007, ils ont été nominés pour le Prix d'architecture contemporaine de l'Union Européenne-Mies van der Rohe dans la catégorie « Jeunes architectes européens » et ont reçu un *AR* Award pour l'architecture émergente. En 2008, l'European Holcim Awards (organisé par la Holcim Foundation) leur a décerné un Silver Award pour l'extension urbaine temporaire dans une ancienne déchetterie (Maribor, Slovénie). Actuellement, ils se consacrent à des projets de recherche sur le futur des villes qu'ils appellent les « cités éco-techno-logiques », financées par le ministère espagnol de l'Industrie. Ils travaillent sur plusieurs projets pour diverses villes espagnoles, tels que l'Ecoboulevard de Vallecas à Madrid (2006) publié ici, et représenteront l'Espagne à Expo '10 à Shanghai.

ECOBOULEVARD OF VALLECAS

Madrid, Spain, 2006

Site area: 500 m x 45 m.
Client: Empresa Municipal de Vivienda y Suelo de Madrid. Cost: € 2.6 million

According to the architects: "The proposal for the Ecoboulevard of Vallecas can be defined as an operation of urban recycling that consists of the installation of three socially revitalizing air trees placed in the existing urban pattern, the densification of trees within their existing concourse, the reduction and asymmetric disposition of the traffic routes…" The "air trees," powered with photovoltaic cells, are considered "temporary prostheses," to be dismantled, "leaving remaining spaces that resemble forest clearings." The architects were selected through a competition with a social and environmental program intended to improve daily life in the area. The "air trees" occupy space that should eventually be populated with mature real trees and are intended as gathering places. The "air trees" contain a system that uses water vapor with power generated by the photovoltaic cells to create a space that is "8° to 10°C cooler than the rest of the street in summer."

Die Architekten erklären: „Der Entwurf für den Ecoboulevard in Vallecas lässt sich als urbane Recyclingoperation definieren, bei der drei sozial stimulierende ‚Luftbäume' in ein bestehendes urbanes Raster integriert werden, sowie als Steigerung der Baumdichte in ihrer unmittelbaren Umgebung und zugleich als Reduzierung und asymmetrische Verschiebung der Verkehrswege …" Die mit Solarzellen betriebenen „Luftbäume" sind als „temporäre Prothesen" gedacht, die letzendlich wieder abgebaut werden und „Räume entstehen lassen, die an Waldlichtungen erinnern". Den Zuschlag erhielten die Architekten im Rahmen eines sozial und umweltpolitisch orientierten Wettbewerbs, dessen Ziel es war, den Alltag im Stadtviertel zu verbessern. Die „Luftbäume" besetzen Flächen, auf denen später große Bäume gepflanzt werden sollen, und dienen als Treffpunkte. Die Bäume sind mit Solarzellen zur Stromerzeugung und einem Wasserzerstäubungssystem ausgestattet. So entsteht ein Ort, der „im Sommer 8 bis 10 °C kühler ist als der übrige Teil der Straße".

« La proposition de l'Ecoboulevard de Vallecas peut se définir comme une opération de recyclage urbain qui consiste en l'installation de trois "arbres d'air" insérés dans le tissu urbain, censés dynamiser les relations sociales. Ils s'accompagnent d'une densification des plantations d'arbres existantes, ainsi que d'une réduction et d'une implantation en asymétrie des axes de circulation… », expliquent les architectes. Ces « arbres d'air », alimentés par des cellules photovoltaïques, sont considérés comme des « prothèses temporaires » prévues pour être ultérieurement démantelées « en laissant les espaces subsistants ressembler à des clairières en forêt ». Les architectes ont été retenus, après concours, sur un programme social et environnemental destiné à améliorer la vie quotidienne du quartier. Les « arbres d'air » occupent un espace qui devrait sans doute être davantage planté d'arbres venus à maturité, et deviendra un lieu public agréable. Ils contiennent un système de diffusion de vapeur d'eau dont l'énergie est fournie par des cellules photovoltaïques pour créer un volume dont la température est de « 8 à 10 °C plus basse que le reste de la rue en été ».

The sculptural installations of Eco-sistema Urbano are arrayed in the central area of an avenue, providing islands of coolness and greenery in the dry city of Madrid.

Die skulpturalen Installationen von Ecosistema Urbano sind auf der Mittelachse einer Allee angeordnet und schaffen kühle, grüne Inseln inmitten der Trockenheit von Madrid.

Les installations sculpturales d'Eco-sistema Urbano se répartissent le long de la zone centrale du boulevard. Ils constituent des îlots de fraîcheur et de verdure dans l'air sec de Madrid.

The round volumes of the pavilions house nothing but vegetation and serve no "real" purpose in the usual sense of architecture. They might thus be compared to ecological sculptures.

In den runden Baukörpern der Pavillons sind ausschließlich Pflanzen untergebracht, sie dienen keinem „wirklichen" Zweck im üblichen architektonischen Sinn. Man könnte sie also als ökologische Skulpturen verstehen.

Les volumes circulaires des pavillons n'abritent que de la végétation mais ne répondent à aucun objectif concret en termes d'architecture. On pourrait les comparer à des sculptures écologiques.

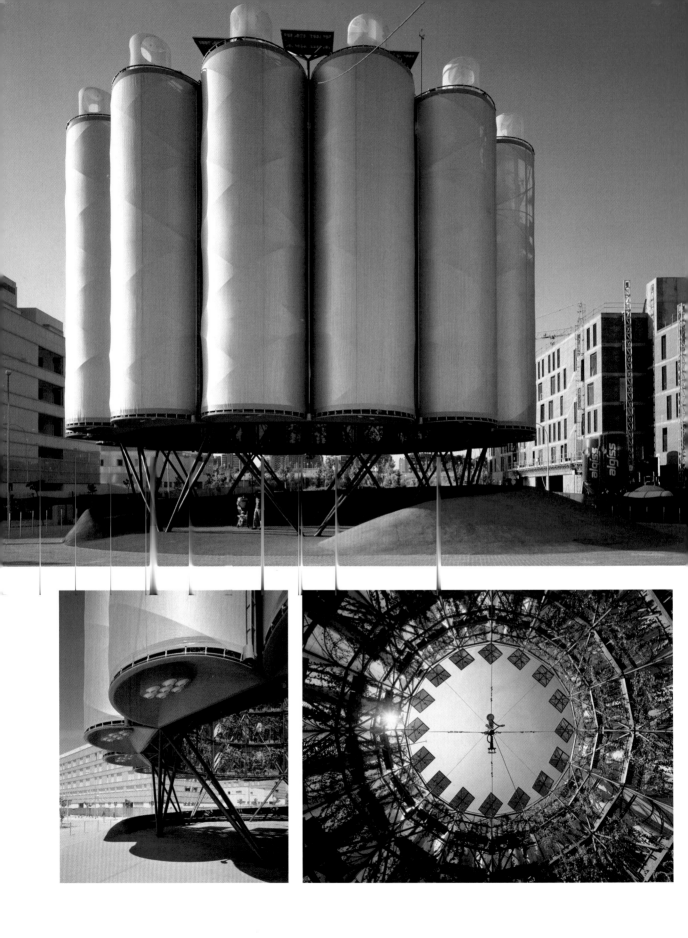

Another pavilion borrows its formal vocabulary from industrial architecture, but like the others is lifted off the ground, making it function like a tree or perhaps a wind chimney.

Ein weiterer Pavillon orientiert sich formal an industrieller Architektur, ist jedoch wie die übrigen über dem Boden aufgeständert und „funktioniert" am ehesten wie ein Baum oder Windturm.

Un autre pavillon emprunte son vocabulaire à l'architecture industrielle. Comme les autres, il est surélevé par rapport au sol, et opère comme un arbre, ou une cheminée à vent.

evapotranspiración

gestión energética

reciclando la no ciudad

FERCABER

EDAW

EDAW
20/F China Merchants Tower / Shun Tak Centre
168–200 Connaught Road Central / Hong Kong / China
Tel: +852 2833 5580 / Fax: +852 2833 5584
E-mail: erik.miller@edaw.com / Web: www.edaw.com

EDAW is one of the largest firms involved in "reshaping the built and natural environment." Founded 70 years ago, its head office is in San Francisco and there are branch offices in 32 other cities. Frank Chow is Regional Creative Director and Principal of EDAW. He is a graduate of the Rhode Island School of Design (1992) and the Harvard GSD (1995). Alfred Fulton is a Senior Landscape Designer. He received his Bachelor of Landscape Architecture from SUNY College of Environmental Science and Forestry (Syracuse, New York, 1983). David Jung is Director of Landscape Design and a Principal of EDAW. He received his E chelor of Landscape Architecture from UC Berkeley (1987) and his Master of Landscape Architecture from the Harvard GSD (1993). Sean Chiao is Senior Vice Preside t and Regional Chair of Asia at EDAW. He received his M.Arch degree from UC Berkeley (1986) and an M.Arch in Urban Design from Harvard (1988). Yaping Chai is a enior Associate and Senior Landscape Designer. She received her Master of Landscape Architecture degree from Ohio State University (Columbus) and a B. A. in Wester Language and Literature from the University of Chengchi, Taiwan. As well as Jinji Lake (Suzhou, China, 2002–04, published here), their recent landscape work include : Chongming Island North Lake Master Plan (Shanghai, China, ongoing, master plan completed 2007); Tokyo Midtown (Tokyo, Japan, 2007); Kigali Master Plan ar Countrywide Land Planning Projects (Rwanda, 2007); the North-South Bypass Tunnel Urban Design (Brisbane, Australia, 2007); the Singapore Sports Hub (Singapore, 010); Saadiyat Island (Abu Dhabi, UAE, ongoing, first phase, 2010); and the Olympic Park Design and Site-Wide Infrastructure (London, UK, 2012).

EDAW zählt zu den größten Firmen, die sich mit der „Umgestaltung der gebauten und natürlichen Umwelt" beschäftigen. Hauptsitz des vor 70 Jahren gegründeten Büros ist San Francisco, Zweigstellen gibt es in 32 weiteren Städten. Frank Chow ist regionaler Creative Director und leite der Kopf von EDAW. Seine Abschlüsse machte er an der Rhode Island School of Design (1992) sowie der Harvard Graduate School of Design (1995). Alfred Fulton zählt zu den leitenden Landschaftsarchitekten des Teams. Er absolvierte seinen Bachelor of Landscape Architecture am SUNY College of Environmental Science and Forestry (Syracuse, New York, 1983). David Jung ist Direktor für Landschaftsarchitektur und einer der Geschäftsführer von EDAW. Er erhielt seinen Bachelor of Landscape Architecture in Berkeley (1987) und seinen Master of Landscape Architecture an der Harvard Graduate School of Design (1993). Sean Chiao ist Seniorvizepräsident und Regionalvorsitzender für Asien bei EDAW. Er absolvierte seinen M.Arch. in Berkeley (1986) sowie seinen M.Arch. in Stadtplanung in Harvard (1988). Yaping Chai ist Seniorgesellschafterin und eine der leitenden Landschaftsarchitektinnen. Sie absolvierte ihren Master of Landscape Architecture an der Ohio State University (Columbus) sowie einen B. A. in Westlicher Philologie und Literatur an der Universität von Chengchi, Taiwan. Neben dem Projekt am Jinji-See (Suzhou, China, 2002–04, hier vorgestellt), gehören derzeit folgende Landschaftsplanungen zu den Aktivitäten des Teams: Masterplan für den North Lake District auf der Insel Chongming (Shanghai, China, im Bau, Abschluss des Masterplans 2007), Tokyo Midtown (Tokio, Japan, 2007), Masterplan für Kigali und landesweite Landschaftsplanungsprojekte (Ruanda, 2007), Stadtplanung des Tunnels der Nord-Süd-Umgehungsstraße (Brisbane, Australien, 2007), der Singapore Sports Hub (Singapur, 2010), die Insel Saadijat (Abu Dhabi, VAE, im Bau, erste Phase, 2010) sowie der Entwurf für den Olympiapark in London und die gesamte Infrastruktur des Geländes (2012).

EDAW est l'une des plus importantes agences à se consacrer à « la reformulation de l'environnement bâti et naturel. » Fondée il y a 70 ans, son siège se trouve à San Francisco et elle possède des bureaux dans trente-deux autres villes. Frank Chow est le dirigeant et le directeur de création régional d'EDAW. Il est diplômé de la Rhode Island School of Design (1992) et de l'Harvard GSD (1995). Alfred Fulton est paysagiste senior, diplômé en architecture paysagère du SUNY College of Environmental Science and Forestry (Syracuse, New York, 1983). David Jung est directeur des projets d'architecture paysagère et l'un des dirigeants d'EDAW. Il est diplômé en architecture du paysage de UC Berkeley (1987) et a passé son mastère dans la même discipline à la Harvard GSD (1993). Sean Chiao est vice-président senior et président régional pour l'Asie d'EDAW. Il est M. Arch de UC Berkeley (1986) et M. Arch en urbanisme d'Harvard (1988). Yaping Chai est associée senior et architecte paysagiste senior, diplômée d'architecture du paysage de l'université de l'État de l'Ohio (Columbus) et B. A. en langues et littératures occidentales de l'université de Chengchi à Taiwan. En dehors du projet pour le lac de Jinji (Suzhou, Chine, 2002–04, publié ici), leurs récentes réalisations comprennent : le plan directeur de l'île de Chongming sur le lac du Nord (Shanghai, Chine, 2007) ; le quartier de Tokyo Midtown (Tokyo, 2007) ; le plan directeur de Kigali et des projets d'aménagement ruraux dans tout le pays (Rwanda, 2007) ; le plan d'urbanisme du tunnel de la rocade nord-sud (Brisbane, Australie, 2007) ; une plate-forme sportive à Singapour (2010) ; l'île de Saadiyat (Abou Dhabi, EAU, première phase en cours, 2010) ainsi que le Parc olympique et le plan des infrastructures des futurs Jeux olympiques de Londres (2012).

JINJI LAKE

Suzhou, China, 2002–04

Site area: 51 km². Client: Suzhou Industrial Park Administrative Committee. Cost: $40 million

This substantial project in the city of Suzhou, known for its gardens and canals and located near Shanghai, is made up of several different elements, all related to the 550-hectare Jinji Lake Industrial Park. The result of a joint venture between Singapore and China, the project was described by *The New York Times* as "a sort of fusion cuisine that adapted contemporary design techniques to traditional Chinese landscape and horticultural traditions."[1] EDAW was responsible for the Jinji Lake Landscape Master Plan, developed with the idea of creating green areas for the new areas that are rapidly overwhelming the historic city. The Jinji Lake Cityside Harbor Plaza is a five-hectare "ceremonial space ... designed to accommodate festive events throughout the year." The seven-hectare Maple Forest Park, located between the Science Exposition at the edge of Jinji Lake and the new Suzhou Convention Center, is planted with red maples, which are considered to be a symbol of prosperity. The Jinji Lake Waterfront Promenade is another of the eight elements that comprise the Jinji Lake district. As the architects write: "The Waterfront District is a 513-hectare land area that circles Jinji Lake and is the most prominent natural feature of the New Suzhou development. EDAW's task was to reference an unparalleled visual resource by providing a variety of experiential qualities."   [1] Paula Deitz, "Where Progress Is Just a Walk in the Park," in: *The New York Times*, September 16, 2007.

Das Großprojekt in Suzhou, einer für ihre Gärten und Kanäle bekannten Stadt unweit von Shanghai, setzt sich aus verschiedenen Elementen zusammen, die an den 550 ha großen Industriepark am Jinji-See angeschlossen sind. Das Projekt, ein Jointventure von Singapur und China, wurde von der *New York Times* als "eine Art Fusionfood" beschrieben, "das zeitgenössische Designstrategien mit traditionellen chinesischen Landschafts- und Gartenbautraditionen verbindet"[1]. EDAW war für den Masterplan des Jinji-See-Projekts verantwortlich, der grüne Nischen in den neuen Stadtvierteln schaffen sollte, die die historische Stadt zu ersticken drohen. Die sogenannte Jinji Lake Cityside Harbor Plaza ist ein 5 ha großes "Gelände ... angelegt, um das ganze Jahr über Platz für festliche Veranstaltungen zu bieten". Der 7 ha große Maple Forest Park mit seinen Rotahornbäumen, einem Symbol für Wohlstand, liegt zwischen dem Wissenschaftspark am Ufer des Jinji-Sees und dem neuen Messe- und Kongresszentrum von Suzhou. Die Uferpromenade am Jinji-See ist ein weiteres der insgesamt acht Elemente, aus denen sich das Jinji-See-Projekt zusammensetzt. Die Architekten schreiben: "Der Uferbereich ist ein 513 ha großes Landstück, das sich um den Jinji-See zieht und zugleich eines der eindruckvollsten Naturgebiete der neuen Erschließungsareale von Suzhou. Aufgabe von EDAW war es, durch eine ganze Bandbreite sinnlicher Qualitäten eine visuell unverwechselbare Inspirationsquelle zu schaffen."   [1] Paula Deitz, "Where Progress Is Just a Walk in the Park", in: *New York Times*, 16. September 2007.

Ce vaste projet pour la ville de Suzhou, située à proximité de Shanghai, connue pour ses jardins et canaux, se compose de divers éléments, tous liés à la présence du Parc industriel du lac de Jinji d'une surface de 550 ha. Fruit d'une collaboration entre Singapour et la Chine, ce projet a été décrit par le *New York Times* comme « une sorte de cuisine de style fusion qui adapte des techniques de conception contemporaines aux traditions de l'art du paysage et de l'horticulture chinoises. »[1] EDAW a été chargée du plan directeur des aménagements paysagers du lac de Jinji dont l'objectif est de créer des espaces verts pour les nouvelles zones qui cernent de plus en plus la ville historique. La Cityside Harbour Plaza est un espace cérémoniel [de 5 ha]... conçu pour accueillir des évènements festifs tout au long de l'année ». Le parc de la forêt d'érables de 7 ha, situé entre l'Exposition les Sciences en bordure de lac et le nouveau centre de congrès de Suzhou, est planté d'érables rouges, symboles de prospérité. La promenade en bordure du lac fait partie des huit éléments du projet. Comme l'expliquent les architectes : « Le quartier du front de lac est une zone de 513 ha qui entoure le lac de Jinji et constitue le plus important composant naturel du nouveau Suzhou. La tâche d'EDAW a été de mettre en valeur cette richesse naturelle et visuelle exceptionnelle en multipliant les occasions de la découvrir. »   [1] Paula Deitz, « Where Progress Is Just a Walk in the Park », dans : *New York Times*, 16 septembre 2007.

As the architects are fully aware, in creating gardens in Suzhou, they are working in the very cradle of Chinese garden design. This places a particular burden on their work, to be at once modern and respectful of this tradition.

Den Architekten war durchaus bewusst, dass die Gartenanlagen, die sie in Suzhou gestalteten, in der Wiege der chinesischen Gartenkunst liegen. Dies verpflichtete sie ganz besonders dazu, der Tradition bei aller Modernität respektvoll zu begegnen.

En créant ces jardins à Suzhou, les architectes étaient parfaitement conscients d'intervenir dans le berceau même de l'art du jardin chinois. Ils étaient placés sous la double pression de la modernité et du respect de la tradition.

The interventions of EDAW include
actual garden spaces but also numerous walkways and water features,
animating the space along the lake
for public recreation.

Zu den Interventionen von EDAW
zählen die eigentlichen Gartenanlagen, jedoch auch zahlreiche Wege
und Wasserelemente, die das Ufergelände des Sees als öffentliches
Naherholungsgebiet erschließen.

L'intervention d'EDAW comprenait
de nombreux jardins mais aussi des
promenades et des installations
sur l'eau afin d'animer cette rive du
lac très fréquentée par le public.

Shark Alley Retreat

FEARON HAY

Fearon Hay Architects Ltd.
70 Sale Street
Auckland Central 1010
New Zealand

Tel: +64 9 309 0128
Fax: +64 9 309 0827
E-mail: contact@fearonhay.com
Web: www.fearonhay.com

JEFFREY FEARON was born in 1972 in Auckland. He received his B.Arch degree from the University of Queensland (1990–95). **TIM HAY** was born in 1973, also in Auckland, and received a B.Arch degree from Auckland University (1993–97). They established Fearon Hay Architects in 1998. They describe their own practice and its largely residential work as follows: "Fearon Hay projects include commissions in diverse environments—coastal, urban, rural, lakeside, and alpine. Works are located in both North and South Islands of New Zealand." Their projects include: the Coromandel Beach House (Coromandel Peninsula, 2000); Kellands Commercial Office Building (Auckland, 2001); Parnell House (Auckland, 2002); Darling Point Apartment (Sydney, 2002); Shark Alley Retreat (Great Barrier Island, Auckland 2002–03 published here); Lake Wakatipu House (Queenstown, 2003); reworking Sargent House (1973) to Dunn House (Auckland, 2005); Clooney Restaurant (Auckland, 2006); Northland Beach House (Rawhiti, 2007); Yates-Allison House (Tutukaka Coast, 2007); Sandhills Road House (Great Barrier Island, Auckland, 2007); Closeburg Station Guest House (Queenstown, 2008); Wintergarden @ The Northern Club (Auckland, 2008); and Tribeca Loft (New York, New York, USA, 2008), all in New Zealand and Australia unless stated otherwise.

JEFFREY FEARON wurde 1972 in Auckland geboren. Er schloss sein Studium an der Universität von Queensland (1990–95) mit einem B.Arch. ab. **TIM HAY** wurde 1973 ebenfalls in Auckland geboren und absolvierte seinen B.Arch. an der Universität von Auckland (1993–97). 1998 gründeten die beiden ihr Büro Fearon Hay Architects. Sie beschreiben ihre Firma und deren überwiegendes Engagement im Wohnungsbau wie folgt: „Zu den Projekten von Fearon Hay zählen Aufträge in den verschiedensten Kontexten – an der Küste, in der Stadt, auf dem Land, an Seen und in den Bergen. Die Projekte liegen auf der Nord- ebenso wie auf der Südinsel Neuseelands." Zu ihren Arbeiten zählen: das Haus am Coromandel Beach (Coromandel-Halbinsel, 2000), Kellands Commercial Office Building (Auckland, 2001), Haus Parnell (Auckland, 2002), Darling Point Apartment (Sydney, 2002), Shark Alley Retreat (Great-Barrier-Insel, Auckland, 2002–03, hier vorgestellt), das Haus am Wakatipu-See (Queenstown, 2003), Umbau des Hauses Sargent (1973) zum Haus Dunn (Auckland, 2005), das Restaurant Clooney (Auckland, 2006), Haus am Northland Beach (Rawhiti, 2007), Haus Yates-Allison (Tutukaka Coast, 2007), Haus Sandhills Road (Great-Barrier-Insel, Auckland, 2007), Gästehaus Closeburg Station (Queenstown, 2008), Wintergarden @ The Northern Club (Auckland, 2008) sowie ein Loft in Tribeca (New York, USA, 2008), alle in Neuseeland und Australien, sofern nicht anders vermerkt.

JEFFREY FEARON, né en 1972 à Auckland, est B. Arch de l'université du Queensland (1990–95). **TIM HAY**, né en 1973, également à Auckland, est B. Arch de l'université d'Auckland (1993–97). Ils ont créé Fearon Hay Architects en 1998. Ils présentent ainsi leur agence et leurs interventions, essentiellement dans le domaine résidentiel : « Les projets de Fearon Hay comprennent des commandes pour divers types d'environnement : côtier, urbain, rural, lacustre et montagneux. Leurs réalisations sont situées aussi bien dans l'île Nord que dans l'île Sud de la Nouvelle-Zélande. » Parmi leurs réalisations : la maison Coromandel Beach (Coromandel Peninsula, 2000) ; l'immeuble de bureaux Kellands (Auckland, 2001) ; la maison Parnell (Auckland, 2002) ; l'appartement de Darling Point (Sydney, 2002) ; le chalet de Shark Alley (Great Barrier Island, Auckland, 2002–03, publié ici) ; la maison de Lake Wakatipu (Queenstown, 2003) ; la transformation de la maison Sargent (1973) en la maison Dunn (Auckland, 2005) ; le restaurant Clooney (Auckland, 2006) ; la maison de Northland Beach (Rawhiti, 2007) ; la maison Yates-Allison (Tutukaka Coast, 2007) ; la maison de Sandhills Road (Great Barrier Island, Auckland, 2007) ; la maison d'hôtes de Closeburg Station (Queenstown, 2008) ; le Wintergarden @ The Northern Club (Auckland, 2008) et un loft à Tribeca (New York, États-Unis, 2008).

SHARK ALLEY RETREAT

Great Barrier Island, Auckland, New Zealand, 2002–03

Floor area: 250 m². Client: not disclosed. Cost: €400 000

Wie der topografische Geländeplan
(oben) und die Fotos rechts zeigen,
liegt das Shark Alley Retreat auf
einem kargen, steil abfallenden
Grundstück direkt am Ufer.

Comme le montrent le plan topo-
graphique du site ci-contre et les
photos à droite, cette résidence est
implantée sur un terrain en pente et
vierge, au bord de l'océan.

Great Barrier Island is located 90 kilometers to the northeast of central Auckland in the outer Hauraki Gulf. It is the fourth-largest island of New Zealand's main chain of islands and has a population of about 850 people. The architects describe this house as a "comfortable shelter from a potentially hostile exposure." The hilly, 6.5-hectare site is set at the southern end of Medlands Bay on the east coast of Great Barrier Island. Their strategy was to "set an outdoor courtyard into the side of the hill and use the resulting retaining terraces to nest the overall composition." An open verandah around the courtyard provides the main living areas. Sliding glass doors and sliding aluminum shutters provide a combination of openness and protection from the prevailing sea winds. Given its exposed and rather remote location, the architects had to take into account issues related to the house's environment. Tim Hay explains: "Sustainability and respect for the site were drivers for the house at Shark Alley. The house is completely off the grid and has no connections to utilities. Power is generated by a solar array hidden in the surrounding bush. Sewage is treated by an onsite bio-cycle system and water is harvested from the roof and stored in tanks."

Die Great-Barrier-Insel liegt 90 km nordöstlich von Auckland im äußeren Hauraki-Golf. Sie ist die viertgrößte Hauptinsel Neuseelands und hat 850 Bewohner. Die Architekten beschreiben das Haus als „behaglichen Zufluchtsort in einer potenziell exponierten und feindlichen Lage". Das hügelige, 6,5 ha große Grundstück liegt am südlichen Ende der Medlands-Bucht an der Ostküste der Great-Barrier-Insel. Die Strategie der Architekten war es, „den Hof in der Senke des Hügels zu positionieren und die Terrassen ringsum zu nutzen, um die Gesamtkomposition einzurahmen". Die Hauptwohnbereiche liegen an einer offenen Veranda, die den Hof umgibt. Durch ver-schiebbare Glastüren und Fensterläden aus Aluminium ergibt sich eine Mischung aus Offenheit und Schutz vor den vorherrschenden Seewinden. Angesichts der expo-nierten und vergleichsweise entlegenen Lage musste sich das Haus zwingend mit seiner Umwelt auseinandersetzen. Tim Hays erklärt: „Nachhaltigkeit und respektvoller Umgang mit dem Grundstück waren Impulse für das Haus in Shark Alley. Das Haus liegt vollkommen jenseits jeglicher Infrastruktur und hat keinerlei Anschluss an die Energieversorgung. Strom wird durch eine Solaranlage erzeugt, die in der umgebenden Buschlandschaft verschwindet. Abwässer fließen vor Ort in einen biologischen Aufbereitungskreislauf; Wasser wird auf dem Dach gesammelt und in Tanks gespeichert."

Great Barrier Island se trouve à 90 km au nord-est d'Auckland dans le golfe d'Hauraki. Peuplée de 850 habitants, c'est la quatrième plus grande île de la chaîne d'îles de la Nouvelle-Zélande. Les architectes décrivent cette résidence comme « un abri confortable face à une exposition potentiellement hostile ». Le terrain vallonné de 6,5 ha est situé à l'extrémité sud de Medlands Bay sur la côte est de l'île. La stratégie adoptée était « d'implanter une cour extérieure dans le flanc de la colline et d'utiliser les terrasses de soutènement qui en résultent pour intégrer la composition globale ». Une véranda ouverte tout autour de la cour constitue en fait les espaces de vie principaux. Des portes en verre et des volets d'aluminium tous coulissants offrent une combinaison d'ouverture et de protection par rapport aux vents dominants venus de la mer. Étant donnée sa position exposée et assez isolée, la maison a dû prendre en compte son propre environnement. Tim Hay explique : « La dura-bilité et le respect du site nous ont guidés dans la conception de cette maison. Entièrement en dehors de la trame urbanistique, elle n'est reliée à aucun réseau. L'élec-tricité provient d'un dispositif solaire dissimulé dans le bush environnant. Les eaux usées sont traitées par un système à cycle biologique et l'eau de pluie est récupérée par les toits et conservée dans un réservoir. »

*The house is exceedingly simple
in its lines and plan. Its modernism
is undeniable, as is its openness
to the natural environment.*

*Linienführung und Grundriss des
Hauses sind ausgesprochen schlicht.
Der moderne Einfluss ist ebenso
wenig zu leugnen, wie die Offenheit
zum landschaftlichen Umfeld.*

*La maison est d'apparence et
de plan extrêmement simples.
Son modernisme est indéniable,
de même que son ouverture sur
l'environnement naturel.*

Given the climate, the house boasts the capacity to be exceptionally open to the outdoors, making the distinction between inside and outside sometimes difficult to discern.

Dank des Klimas kann sich das Haus außergewöhnlich stark nach außen öffnen, wodurch die Grenzen zwischen Innen- und Außenraum mitunter zu verschwimmen scheinen.

Étant donné le climat, la maison peut se permettre de s'ouvrir largement sur la nature, ce qui rend parfois la distinction entre l'intérieur et l'extérieur difficilement perceptible.

FOSTER + PARTNERS

Foster + Partners / Riverside / 22 Hester Road
London SW11 4AN / UK
Tel: +44 20 77 38 04 55 / Fax: +44 20 77 38 11 07
E-mail: enquiries@fosterandpartners.com / Web: www.fosterandpartners.com

Born in Manchester in 1935, **NORMAN FOSTER** studied Architecture and City Planning at Manchester University (1961). He was awarded a Henry Fellowship to Yale University, where he received his M.Arch degree and met Richard Rogers, with whom he created Team 4 He received the RIBA Gold Medal for Architecture (1983) and was knighted in 1990. The American Institute of Architects granted him their Gold Medal for Architecture in 1994. Lord Norman Foster has notably built: the IBM Pilot Head Office (Cosham, UK, 1970–71); the Sainsbury Centre for Visual Arts and Crescent Wing, University of East Anglia (Norwich, UK 1976–77; 1989–91); the Hong Kong and Shanghai Banking Corporation Headquarters (Hong Kong, 1981–86); London's third airport, Stansted (1987–91); the Faculty of Law at the University of Cambridge (Cambridge, UK, 1993–95); and the Commerzbank Headquarters, Frankfurt (Germany, 1994–97). Recent projects include: the airport at Chek Lap Kok (Hong Kong, 1995–98); the new German Parliament, Reichstag (Berlin, Germany, 1995–99); Millennium Bridge (London, 1996–2000); the British Museum Redevelopment (London, 1997–2000); Greater London Authority (1998–2002); Petronas University of Technology (Seri Iskandar, Malaysia, 1999–2004, published here); Millau Viaduct (Millau, France, 1993–2005); 126 Philip Street (Sydney, Australia, 1997–2005); Wembley Stadium (London, 1996–2006); and Beijing Airport (China, 2003–08). Current work includes the Aldar Central Market Towers (Abu Dhabi, UAE, 2006–10); and the 78-story 200 Greenwich Street Tower (World Trade Center, New York, 2006–12).

NORMAN FOSTER wurde 1935 in Manchester geboren, wo er später bis 1961 Architektur und Stadtplanung studierte. Ein Henry Fellowship ermöglichte ihm das Studium in Yale, wo er seinen M.Arch. absolvierte und Richard Rogers begegnete, mit dem er das Büro Team 4 gründete. Er wurde mit der RIBA-Goldmedaille für Architektur ausgezeichnet (1983) und 1990 in den Adelsstand erhoben. 1994 verlieh ihm das American Institute of Architects die Goldmedaille für Architektur. Zu Lord Norman Fosters besonders hervozuhebenden Bauten zählen: der IBM-Hauptsitz in Cosham (Cosham, Großbritannien, 1970–71), das Sainsbury Centre for Visual Arts und der Crescent Wing, Universität von East Anglia (Norwich, Großbritannien, 1976–77, 1989–91), der Hauptsitz der Hong Kong and Shanghai Banking Corporation (Hongkong, 1981–86), Londons dritter Flughafen Stansted (1987–91), die Fakultät für Rechtswissenschaften der Universität Cambridge (Großbritannien, 1993–95), sowie der Hauptsitz der Commerzbank, Frankfurt am Main (1994–97). Jüngere Projekte sind u. a. der Flughafen Chek Lap Kok (Hongkong, 1995–98), der Umbau des Reichstagsgebäudes (Berlin, 1995–99), die Millennium Bridge (London, 1996–2000), der Umbau des British Museum (London, 1997–2000), die Greater London Authority (1998–2002), die Technische Universität Petronas (Seri Iskandar, Malaysia, 1999–2004, hier vorgestellt), das Viadukt von Millau (Frankreich, 1993–2005), 126 Philip Street (Sydney, Australien, 1997–2005), das neue Wembley-Stadion (London, 1996–2006) und der Flughafen Peking (China, 2003–08). Aktuelle Projekte sind u. a. die Aldar Central Market Towers (Abu Dhabi, VAE, 2006–10) sowie das 78-stöckige Hochhaus 200 Greenwich Street (World Trade Center, New York, 2006–12).

Né à Manchester en 1935, **NORMAN FOSTER** a étudié l'architecture et l'urbanisme à l'université de Manchester (1961). Il a bénéficié d'une Henry Fellowship pour l'université Yale, où il a passé son M. Arch et rencontré Richard Rogers avec lequel il a créé l'agence Team 4. Il a reçu la médaille d'or de l'Institut royal des architectes anglais (RIBA) en 1983, et a été anobli en 1990. L'Institut américain des architectes lui a accordé sa médaille d'or en 1994. Lord Norman Foster a construit en particulier : le siège pilote d'IBM (Cosham, G.-B., 1970–71) ; le Sainsbury Centre for Visual Arts et le Crescent Wing, université de East Anglia (Norwich, G.-B., 1976–77 ; 1989–91) ; le siège de la Hong Kong and Shanghai Banking Corporation (Hong Kong, 1981–86) ; Stansted, troisième aéroport de Londres (1987–91) ; la faculté de droit de l'université de Cambridge (Cambridge, G.-B., 1993–95) et le siège de la Commerzbank à Francfort (Allemagne, 1994–97). Parmi ses récentes commandes : l'aéroport de Chek Lap Kok (Hong Kong, 1995–98) ; le nouveau Parlement allemand, le Reichstag (Berlin, 1995–99) ; le Millenium Bridge (Londres, 1996–2000) ; les nouveaux aménagements du British Museum (Londres, 1997–2000) ; l'immeuble de la Greater London Authority (1998–2002) ; la Petronas University of Technology (Seri Iskandar, Malaisie, 1998–2004, publié ici) ; le viaduc de Millau (Millau, France, 1993–2005) ; l'immeuble du 126 Philip Street (Sydney, Australie, 1997–2005) ; le Wembley Stadium (Londres, 1996–2006) et l'aéroport de Pékin (Chine, 2003–08). Actuellement, son agence travaille, entre autres, sur les projets des tours du Aldar Central Market (Abu Dhabi, EAU, 2006–10) et la tour de 78 niveaux du 200 Greenwich Street (World Trade Center, New York, 2006–12).

PETRONAS UNIVERSITY OF TECHNOLOGY

Seri Iskandar, Malaysia, 1999–2004

Site area: 450 ha. Gross floor area: 240 000 m². Client: Universiti Teknologi Petronas.
Cost: not disclosed. Collaboration: GDP Architects

The large canopies of the University and its curving patterns demonstrate its respect for nature and capacity to function efficiently even in periods of very heavy rain.

Die monumentalen Baldachindächer der Universität mit ihrer geschwungenen Zeichnung zeugen mehr als deutlich vom Respekt für die Natur und gewährleisten selbst in der Regenzeit effiziente Funktionalität.

Les vastes auvents incurvés de l'université traduisent une volonté de respecter la nature et de fonctionner efficacement même en période de fortes pluies.

This project includes teaching facilities for 6000 students studying civil, mechanical, chemical, and electrical engineering. Funded in large part by the Malaysian oil company Petronas, the campus is located in the jungle, 300 kilometers north of Kuala Lumpur. A curved roof held up by tall, thin columns marks the pedestrian routes within the complex, acknowledging the frequent heavy rains. Four-story buildings placed under this canopy contain labs, lecture halls, and other communal facilities. The entrance to the campus is singled out by a large drum-shaped resource center containing a library and a multipurpose theater with a capacity for 3000 people. The master plan for the campus takes into account the likelihood of future expansion. A winner of the 2007 Aga Khan Award for Architecture, this project was described by the Jury in glowing terms: "A soaring, crescent-form roof supported by steel columns winds around the edge of the site, covering pedestrian routes and providing a defined, shaded zone for social interaction and circulation. To preserve the natural topography, the core academic buildings are wrapped around the base of a series of knolls; viewed from a distance, the university's canopy elevation echoes the tree canopy of the densely forested site. This is an exemplary use of a performance-based approach to architectural design that goes beyond the diagram. The design has been carried through to completion with meticulous detail, rigor, and persistence, and engendered a transfer of knowledge, process, and technology between Foster + Partners and the Malaysian firm GDP Architects, which has in turn led to their collaboration on other projects."

Das Projekt umfasst Unterrichtsräume für 6000 Studenten in den Studiengängen Bauingenieurwesen, Maschinenbau, Verfahrenstechnik und Elektrotechnik. Der zum Großteil von der malaysischen Ölfirma Petronas finanzierte Campus liegt im Dschungel, 300 km nördlich von Kuala Lumpur. Ein von schlanken, hohen Säulen getragenes, geschwungenes Baldachindach schützt die Fußgängerwege des Komplexes, was aufgrund der häufigen Regenfälle erforderlich ist. Die unter dem Dach gelegenen vierstöckigen Gebäude bieten Raum für Labors, Vorlesungssäle und andere Gemeinschaftseinrichtungen. Der Eingang zum Campus wird von einem großen Rundbau markiert, in dem sich die Bibliothek und ein Mehrzwecktheater mit 3000 Plätzen befinden. Der Masterplan für den Campus berücksichtigt vorhersehbare Erweiterungen. Das Projekt, 2007 mit dem Aga-Khan-Preis für Architektur ausgezeichnet, wird von der Jury überschwänglich gelobt: „Ein hoch aufragendes, halbmondförmiges, von Stahlsäulen getragenes Dach schmiegt sich an die Grundstücksgrenze, schützt die Fußgängerwege und definiert eine schattenspendende Zone als Ort für soziale Interaktion und Verkehrsfläche. Um die natürliche Topografie zu erhalten, gruppieren sich die akademischen Hauptgebäude um mehrere kleinere Hügel. Aus der Ferne betrachtet wirkt der Aufriss der Dachlandschaft wie ein Echo des Laubdachs des dicht bewaldeten Geländes. Hier kommt ein zweckorientierter architektonischer Entwurfsansatz, der über das Schematische hinausgeht, auf vorbildlichste Weise zum Tragen. Der Bau wurde vom Entwurf bis zu seiner Fertigstellung sorgfältig, strikt, konsequent und bis ins Detail umgesetzt. Der Wissens-, Prozess- und Techniktransfer zwischen Foster + Partners und dem malaysischen Büro GDP Architects führte zu Kooperationen bei weiteren Projekten."

Financé en grande partie par la compagnie pétrolière malaisienne Petronas, ce campus pour 6000 étudiants en ingénierie civile, mécanique, chimique et électrique, est situé dans la jungle, à 300 km au nord de Kuala Lumpur. Les circulations piétonnières à l'intérieur du complexe sont abritées des pluies fréquentes par un auvent incurvé reposant sur de fines colonnes. Les bâtiments de quatre niveaux également placés sous cette protection réunissent laboratoires, salles de conférences et autres équipements communs. L'entrée principale est signalée par un important centre de ressources en forme de tambour contenant une bibliothèque et un auditorium polyvalent de 3000 places. Le plan directeur prend en compte la possibilité de futures extensions. Ce projet, qui a remporté en 2007 le prix Aga Khan d'architecture, a été présenté par le jury en ces termes flatteurs : « Un toit aux formes arrondies et soutenu par des colonnes de métal épouse les formes du site, protège les espaces de déplacement et crée des zones bien définies pour les interactions sociales et la circulation. Afin de préserver la topographie naturelle du lieu, les bâtiments académiques se déroulent au pied d'une série de petites collines et, vus à distance, les auvents de l'université font écho à la canopée de la forêt environnante. C'est un usage exemplaire d'une approche du design architectural qui va au-delà du plan. La conception a été menée jusqu'à l'achèvement avec un soin méticuleux des détails, une grande rigueur et le sens de la persistance. Ce projet a permis un transfert de connaissances, de processus et de technologies entre Foster + Partners et l'agence Malaisienne GDP qui a conduit à leur collaboration sur d'autres projets. »

The soaring spaces and genuine lightness of the architecture give it an originality that responds intelligently to the climatic conditions of Malaysia.

Die hohen Räume und große Leichtigkeit der Architektur verleihen dem Bau eine Originalität, die intelligent auf die klimatischen Bedingungen von Malaysia eingeht.

Les énormes espaces couverts et la légèreté de l'architecture confèrent une originalité qui répond avec intelligence aux conditions climatiques de la Malaisie.

PETER GLUCK

Peter Gluck and Partners, Architects
646 West 131st Street
New York, NY 10027
USA

Tel: +1 212 690 4950
Fax: +1 212 690 4961
E-mail: info@gluckpartners.com
Web: www.gluckpartners.com

PETER GLUCK received both his B.Arch (1962) and M.Arch (1965) degrees from Yale University. He founded his present firm in New York in 1972. He has been the chairman of AR/CS Architectural Construction Services, a firm that integrates architectural design and construction, since 1992. He is also a co-founder of Aspen GK (1997), a development partnership intended to build "well-designed high-quality housing." After Little Ajax Affordable Housing (Aspen, Colorado, 2005–06, published here), current projects include the East Harlem School (New York, New York, 2008); House on the Bluff (Winnetka, Illinois, 2008); Olive Bridge Tower (Olive Bridge, New York, 2008); Legal Outreach Afterschool Program (New York, New York, 2009); Manes Tuscany Project (Tuscany, Italy, 2009); Bolton Landing/Terraced Family Retreat (Lake George, New York, 2009); Center for Discovery (Harris, New York, 2008–10); an athletic facility for Roosevelt Island (Bronx, New York, 2010); and Mink Building (New York, New York, 2008–14), all in the USA unless stated otherwise.

PETER GLUCK schloss sein Studium in Yale mit einem B.Arch. (1962) und schließlich einem M.Arch. (1965) ab. Sein Büro gründete er 1972 in New York. Seit 1992 ist er Vorsitzender von AR/CS Architectural Construction Services, einem integrierten Architektur- und Bauunternehmen. Darüber hinaus ist er Mitbegründer von Aspen GK (1997) einem Bauunternehmen, das „anspruchsvoll entworfene, qualitativ hochwertige Wohnbauten" realisiert. Neben dem Projekt Little Ajax Affordable Housing (Aspen, Colorado, 2005–06, hier vorgestellt) zählen zu seinen aktuellen Projekten auch eine Schule in East Harlem (New York, 2008), das House on the Bluff (Winnetka, Illinois, 2008), das Tower House in Olive Bridge (New York, 2008), das Legal Outreach Afterschool Program (New York, 2009), das Projekt Manes in der Toskana (2009), die Familienferienhäuser Bolton Landing (Lake George, New York, 2009), das Center for Discovery (Harris, New York, 2008–10), eine Leichtathletikeinrichtung auf der Roosevelt–Insel (Bronx, New York, 2010) sowie das Mink Building (New York, 2008–14), alle in den USA, sofern nicht anders angegeben.

PETER GLUCK est B. Arch (1962) et M. Arch (1965) de l'université Yale. Il a créé son agence actuelle à New York en 1972. Il est président des AR/CS Architectural Construction Services, agence intégrant conception architecturale et construction depuis 1992. Il est également cofondateur d'Aspen GK (1997), un partenariat de promotion immobilière qui propose de construire « des logements bien conçus de haute qualité ». Après Little Ajax Affordable Housing (Aspen, Colorado, 2005–06, publié ici), ses projets actuels comprennent l'école de East Harlem (New York, 2008) ; House on the Bluff (Winnetka, Illinois, 2008) ; la tour d'Olive Bridge (Olive Bridge, New York, 2008) ; le Legal Outreach Afterschool Program (New York, 2009) ; le projet Manes Tuscany (Toscane, Italie, 2009) ; la maison familiale Bolton, à terrasses (Lake George, New York, 2009) ; le Center for Discovery (Harris, New York, 2008–10) ; des équipements d'athlétisme pour Roosevelt Island (Bronx, New York, 2010) et l'immeuble Mink (New York, 2008–14).

LITTLE AJAX AFFORDABLE HOUSING

Aspen, Colorado, USA, 2005–06

*Floor area: 2322 m². Client: City of Aspen and private developers. Cost: $4 million.
Collaborators: Charlie Kaplan, Jason LaPointe*

Located on a site previously deemed difficult to develop because of its steep inclination, this project is set close to the center of Aspen. Peter Gluck explains: "We acted as developer, architect, and contractor, providing housing for 14 working families that previously could not afford to live close to their workplace. An open space parcel was created as part of the planning process, linking together the many public trails that surround the site." The particular geometry of the architecture was a solution to the problems posed by the site, and numerous bridges and lookouts give a sense of continuity and relationship to the location, creating a "physical and visual connection to the mountains." High-performance glass in a floor-to-ceiling configuration and colorful, insulated panels were used. The architect writes: "Using multiple strategies, including a compact design, an efficient centralized mechanical system, and a super-insulated building complemented by the use of green building products like bamboo floors, low VOC paints, recycled-content carpets, and laminates that did not require finishing, resulted in a building that complied with and far exceeded the strict sustainability code of the City of Aspen."

Das Projekt liegt auf einem Grundstück, das man seiner Steillage wegen bis dato für problematisch gehalten hatte, und befindet sich unweit des Stadtzentrums von Aspen. Peter Gluck führt aus: „Wir fungierten als Bauunternehmer, Architekt und Baufirma und realisierten Wohnraum für 14 berufstätige Familien, die es sich bisher nicht leisten konnten, in der Nähe ihres Arbeitsplatzes zu wohnen. Im Zuge des Planungsprozesses entstand ein offenes Grundstück, das die zahlreichen öffentlichen Wanderwege, die das Gelände umgeben, verbindet." Das spezifische, geometrische Design der Architektur war Antwort auf die Probleme, die sich durch das Grundstück ergaben. Zahlreiche Brücken und Aussichtspunkte vermitteln Kontinuität und stellen Bezüge zum Umfeld her, schaffen eine „physische und visuelle Anbindung an die Berge". Zum Einsatz kamen deckenhohe Fenster mit hochisolierender Verglasung und farbige Dämmpaneele. Der Architekt schreibt: „Dank verschiedener Maßnahmen – einem kompakten Entwurf, einer effizienten zentralisierten Haustechnik und hochdämmender Bauweise – gekoppelt mit grünen Baumaterialien wie Bambusböden, emissionsarmen Farben, Teppichböden mit Recyclinganteil und Laminaten, die keine Versiegelung erfordern, entstand ein Wohnbau, der den strengen Nachhaltigkeitsanforderungen in Aspen mehr als entsprach."

Implanté sur un site jugé longtemps difficile du fait de sa pente, cet ensemble de logements se trouve à proximité du centre d'Aspen. « Nous sommes intervenus en tant que promoteurs, architectes et constructeurs pour réaliser ces appartements pour quatorze familles de travailleurs qui, jusque-là, ne pouvaient se permettre de vivre près de leur lieu de travail. Une parcelle ouverte a été dégagée, qui fait lien entre les nombreux cheminements publics qui entourent le terrain », explique Peter Gluck. La géométrie particulière de l'architecture apporte une solution aux problèmes posés par le site. De nombreuses passerelles et plates-formes d'observation donnent un sentiment de continuité et de relation avec le lieu, créant « une connexion physique et visuelle avec les montagnes ». Un verre à hautes performances est utilisé pour les baies du sol au plafond, ainsi que des panneaux d'isolations de couleur. « Le recours à de multiples stratégies, do un p n comp un système de ventilation mécanique centralisé efficace, une isolation renforcée complétée par des matériaux de construction "vert comme les s en mbou, beintures à fait le contenu de composants organiques volatiles (VOC), des tapis en matières recyclées et des bois lamifiés qui ne req èrent pas de f tion a permi réaliser un im meuble qui répond aux codes très stricts de développement durable de la ville d'Aspen et même au-delà. »

Making housing affordable and environmentally friendly at the same time represents a challenge to any architect in the best of circumstances. Peter Gluck succeeds here in also making these residences attractive.

Selbst unter den besten Voraussetzungen ist es für jeden Architekten eine Herausforderung, Wohnraum zu realisieren, der erschwinglich und umweltfreundlich zugleich ist. Peter Gluck gelingt es hier zudem, die Bauten attraktiv zu gestalten.

Faire un logement abordable et respectueux de l'environnement est un défi pour tout architecte même dans les meilleures circonstances. Peter Gluck a réussi le pari avec ces maisons séduisantes.

Gluck's use of a typology that might well bring to mind a trailer perched on a garage is a testimony to efficiency, but it also results in a cheerful lightness.

Glucks Typologie, die durchaus an einen Wohnwagen erinnern könnte, der auf einer Garage sitzt, zeugt von Effizienz, schafft jedoch auch fröhliche Leichtigkeit.

L'utilisation par l'architecte d'une typologie qui pourrait évoquer un mobile home perché sur un garage est une solution efficace qui crée également un effet de légèreté.

The houses are at once individual and separate, but also connected by stairways and ramps. Interiors are bright and simple in their design.

Die Häuser sind zwar individuell und separat gestaltet, jedoch über Treppen und Rampen miteinander verbunden. Das Interieur ist hell und schlicht gehalten.

Les maisons individuelles sont séparées, tout en étant reliées par des escaliers et des rampes. Les intérieurs sont de conception simple et lumineuse.

MONIKA GOGL

Architekten Gogl & Partner
Dorfstr. 44
6072 Lans/Tirol
Austria

Tel: +43 512 37 72 13
Fax: +43 512 37 72 13 77
E-mail: office@gogl-architekten.at
Web: www.gogl-architekten.at

MONIKA GOGL was born in 1969 in St. Johann in the Tyrol region of Austria. She received her M.Arch degree under Peter Cook at the Bartlett School of Architecture in London (1996–97), after studying at the University of Innsbruck (1988–95). She created her own office in Linz in 2000. As she describes it, her practice covers "all aspects of design and management," and has included several partnerships, for example with Isabel Hamm for the design of lamps and with Bartel & Gaffal for furniture and interior design. She has lectured in Innsbruck and Linz. Her current and recent work includes the Schweiger House (Sistrans, 2005, published here); Obereder House (Kitzbühel, 2006); an office for Dr. Wagner (Salzburg, 2007); Head Office for Andreas Wieser (Lans, 2007); Strolz House (Fano, Italy, 2008); Hotel Schwarzer Adler (Kitzbühel, 2008); Walde House (Kitzbühel, 2008–10); and the Lanserhof Health Center (Innsbruck, construction starting 2009), all in Austria unless stated otherwise.

MONIKA GOGL wurde 1969 in St. Johann in Tirol, Österreich, geboren. Sie schloss ihr Studium bei Peter Cook an der Bartlett School of Architecture in London (1996–97) mit einem M.Arch. ab, nachdem sie zuvor an der Universität Innsbruck studiert hatte (1988–95). 2000 gründete sie ihr eigenes Büro in Linz. Nach eigenen Angaben deckt ihre Praxis „sämtliche Aspekte vom Entwurf bis hin zur Bauleitung" ab und umfasst auch Kooperationen, etwa das gemeinschaftliche Entwerfen von Leuchten mit Isabel Hamm oder von Möbeln und Innenarchitekturprojekten mit Bartel & Gaffal. Monika Gogl hat in Innsbruck und Linz gelehrt. Jüngere und aktuelle Projekte sind u. a. Haus Schweiger (Sistrans, 2005, hier vorgestellt), Haus Obereder (Kitzbühel, 2006), Büroräume für Dr. Wagner (Salzburg, 2007), Büroräume für Andreas Wieser (Lans, 2007), Haus Strolz (Fano, Italien, 2008), Hotel Schwarzer Adler (Kitzbühel, 2008), Haus Walde (Kitzbühel, 2008–10) und das Gesundheitszentrum Lanserhof (Innsbruck, Baubeginn 2009), alle in Österreich, sofern nicht anders angegeben.

MONIKA GOGL, née en 1969 à St. Johann dans le Tyrol autrichien, a passé son diplôme de M.Arch sous la direction de Peter Cook à la Bartlett School of Architecture à Londres (1996–97), après avoir étudié à l'université d'Innsbruck (1988–95). Elle a créé son agence à Linz en 2000. Selon sa description, son agence intervient sur « tous les aspects de la conception et de la gestion de chantier », et a participé à de nombreux partenariats comme, par exemple, avec Isabel Hamm pour la conception de lampes, et avec Bartel & Gaffal pour celle de meubles et d'aménagements intérieurs. Elle a enseigné à Innsbruck et Linz. Parmi ses travaux récents et actuels : la maison Schweiger (Sistrans, 2005, publiée ici) ; la maison Obereder (Kitzbühel, 2006) ; le bureau du Dr. Wagner (Salzbourg, 2007) ; le siège d'Andreas Wieser (Lans, 2007) ; la maison Strolz (Fano, Italie, 2008) ; l'hôtel Schwarzer Adler (Kitzbühel, 2008) ; la maison Walde (Kitzbühel, 2008–10) et le Centre de santé de Lanserhof (Innsbruck, 2009–).

SCHWEIGER HOUSE

Sistrans, Austria, 2005

Floor area: 149 m². Client: Gebhard Schweiger. Cost: not disclosed.
Collaboration: Hildegard Platzer-Rieder, Richard Steger

This single-family house was built on a sloped, narrow site to the south of the center of Sistrans. Clad in larch and generously glazed, the long house runs parallel to the southwestern edge of the site, blending "harmoniously and seamlessly into the landscape." Designed to be wheelchair accessible, the house includes an entrance level, living floor, and attic, culminating in a landscaped green roof. Monika Gogl explains the sustainability strategy of the house: "It is a low-energy house, which is to say that it uses less than 0.15 kWh/square meter/year. Its design corresponds to the highest possible standards of thermal insulation. The penthouse and roof were built with a prefabricated wood structure that is a sustainable method. As an alternative heat source in the spring and autumn, a masonry heater has been placed in the living area." Finally, the architect underlines the fact that the handicapped owner of the house "preserves nature by sitting in his wheelchair, floating over a green vista, with nature at eye level."

Das Einfamilienhaus wurde auf einem abschüssigen schmalen Grundstück südlich des Ortskerns von Sistrans gebaut. Das mit Lärchenholz verblendete und großzügig verglaste Haus liegt parallel zur südwestlichen Grundstücksgrenze und fügt sich „harmonisch und nahtlos in die Landschaft ein". Das barrierefrei angelegte Haus besteht aus einer Zugangsebene und einem Wohn- und Dachgeschoss, das mit einem begrünten Dach abschließt. Monika Gogl erläutert die nachhaltigen Strategien des Hauses: „Es ist ein Niedrigenergiehaus mit einem Verbrauch von unter 0,15 kWh/m² pro Jahr. Der Entwurf entspricht höchsten Dämmstandards. Penthouse und Dach wurden mithilfe eines nachhaltigen Holzfertigbausystems errichtet. Als alternative Heizquelle im Frühjahr und Herbst wurde ein Kachelofen in den Wohnbereich integriert." Schließlich weist die Architektin darauf hin, dass der Bauherr, wenn er „in seinem Rollstuhl über dem grünen Panorama zu schweben scheint und die Natur auf Augenhöhe hat", diese Natur zugleich schützt.

Cette résidence familiale est édifiée sur un étroit terrain en pente au sud du centre de Sistrans. Habillée de bouleau et généreusement vitrée, cette construction tout en longueur se développe en limite sud-ouest du terrain et se fond « harmonieusement et sans rupture avec le paysage ». Conçue pour être accessible en chaise roulante, la maison comprend un niveau d'entrée, un niveau de séjour et un grenier, culminant dans un toit végétalisé paysagé. Monika Gogol explique ainsi la stratégie de durabilité utilisée : « C'est une maison à basse consommation d'énergie, ce qui veut dire qu'elle consomme moins de 0,15 kWh/m² par an. Sa conception répond aux normes d'isolation thermique les plus strictes. Le toit et la *penthouse* font appel à une ossature en bois préfabriquée, méthode durable en soi. Une chaudière en maçonnerie a été installée dans le séjour qui sert de chauffage alternatif au printemps et à l'automne. » L'architecte souligne également que le propriétaire de la maison, handicapé, « a tenu à préserver la nature laquelle est au niveau du regard depuis sa chaise roulante, par cette maison qui flotte au-dessus d'un panorama de verdure. »

The Schweiger House is set in an inclined site as shown by the elevation drawings above and the photos to the right.

Das Haus Schweiger wurde in den Hang hineingebaut, wie die Aufrisse oben und die Fotos rechts zeigen.

La maison Schweiger est implantée sur un terrain incliné, comme le montrent les dessins d'élévations ci-dessus et les photos à droite.

The house combines carefully
wrapped interior spaces, and ample
open areas, including terraces.

Das Haus kombiniert präzise inein-
ander greifende Innenräume mit
großzügigen Außenbereichen, wie
etwa Terrassen.

La maison associe à la fois des
volumes intérieurs enveloppés et
d'amples zones ouvertes dont
ses terrasses.

The house lies on a base that includes the garage, and its main façades wrap around in a continuous flow, opening progressively as they rise, forming a fully glazed upper level.

Das Haus ruht auf einem Sockel, in dem auch die Garage untergebracht ist. Die Hauptfassaden wirken wie fließend umeinander gefaltet und öffnen sich mit zunehmender Höhe. Das oberste Geschoss ist vollständig verglast.

La maison repose sur un socle qui contient le garage. Les façades principales sont enveloppées dans un bandeau continu, qui s'ouvre progressivement en s'élevant. Le niveau supérieur est entièrement vitré.

ZAHA HADID

Zaha Hadid Architects
Studio 9 / 10 Bowling Green Lane / London EC1R OBQ / UK
Tel: +44 20 72 53 51 47 / Fax: +44 20 72 51 83 22
E-mail: mail@zaha-hadid.com / Web: www.zaha-hadid.com

ZAHA HADID studied architecture at the Architectural Association (AA) in London beginning in 1972 and was awarded the Diploma Prize in 1977. She then became a partner of Rem Koolhaas in the Office for Metropolitan Architecture (OMA) and taught at the AA. She has also taught at Harvard, the University of Chicago, in Hamburg and at Columbia University in New York. Well-known for her paintings and drawings, she has had a substantial influence, despite having built relatively few projects. She has completed the Vitra Fire Station (Weil am Rhein, Germany, 1990–94); and exhibition designs such as the one for "The Great Utopia" (Solomon R. Guggenheim Museum, New York, 1992). Significant competition entries include her design for the Cardiff Bay Opera House (1994–96); the Habitable Bridge (London, 1996) and the Luxembourg Philharmonic Hall (1997). More recently, Zaha Hadid has entered a phase of active construction with such projects as the Bergisel Ski Jump (Innsbruck, Austria, 2001–02); Lois & Richard Rosenthal Center for Contemporary Art (Cincinnati, Ohio, 1999–2003); Phaeno Science Center (Wolfsburg, Germany, 2001–05) and the Central Building of the new BMW Assembly Plant in Leipzig (Germany, 2005). She has recently completed the MAXXI National Center of Contemporary Arts in Rome (Italy, 2008) and is working on the Guangzhou Opera House (Guangzhou, China, 2006–09); the Sheik Zayed Bridge (Abu Dhabi, UAE, 2005–10); and the E.ON Energy Research Department, RWTH Aachen (Aachen, Germany, 2009–10, published here). In 2004 Zaha Hadid became the first woman to win the coveted Pritzker Prize.

ZAHA HADID studierte ab 1972 an der Architectural Association (AA) in London und erhielt 1977 den Diploma Prize. Anschließend wurde sie Partnerin von Rem Koolhaas im Office for Metropolitan Architecture (OMA) und unterrichtete an der AA. Darüber hinaus lehrte sie in Harvard, an der Universität von Chicago, in Hamburg sowie an der Columbia University in New York. Hadid wurde besonders durch ihr Gemälde und Zeichnungen bekannt. Obwohl nur wenige ihrer Entwürfe realisiert wurden, zählt sie zu den einflussreichsten Vertreterinnen ihrer Zunft. Realisiert wurden u. a. die Feuerwache für Vitra (Weil am Rhein, Deutschland, 1990–94) und Ausstellungsarchitekturen wie „The Great Utopia" (Solomon R. Guggenheim Museum, New York, 1992). Zu ihren wichtigsten Wettbewerbsbeiträgen zählen der Entwurf für das Cardiff Bay Opera House (1994–96), die Habitable Bridge in London (1996) und die Philharmonie in Luxemburg (1997). In jüngerer Zeit begann eine Phase des aktiven Bauens für Hadid, etwa mit der Skisprungschanze Bergisel (Innsbruck, Österreich, 2001–02), dem Lois & Richard Rosenthal Center for Contemporary Art (Cincinnati, Ohio, 1999–2003), dem Wissenschaftszentrum Phaeno (Wolfsburg, 2001–05) und dem Zentralgebäude des neuen BMW-Werks in Leipzig (2005). Unlängst fertiggestellt wurde das MAXXI, das Nationalmuseum für Kunst des 21. Jahrhunderts in Rom (2008). Derzeit arbeitet Hadid am Opernhaus in Guangzhou (China, 2006–09), der Scheich-Zajed-Brücke (Abu Dhabi, VAE, 2005–10) sowie dem E.ON Institut für Energieforschung an der RWTH Aachen (2009–10, hier vorgestellt). 2004 wurde Zaha Hadid als erste Frau mit dem begehrten Pritzker-Preis ausgezeichnet.

ZAHA HADID a étudié à l'Architectural Association (AA) de Londres de 1972 à 1977, date à laquelle elle a reçu le Prix du diplôme. Elle devient ensuite partenaire de Rem Koolhaas, à l'Office for Metropolitan Architecture (OMA), et enseigne à l'AA. Elle a également enseigné à Harvard, à l'université de Chicago, à Hambourg et à l'université Columbia de New York. Célèbre pour ses peintures et dessins, elle a exercé une réelle influence, même si elle n'a construit que relativement peu pendant longtemps. Parmi ses réalisations anciennes : un poste d'incendie pour Vitra (Weil am Rhein, Allemagne, 1990–94) et des projets pour des expositions comme « La Grande utopie » au Solomon R. Guggenheim Museum à New York (1992). Elle a participé à de nombreux concours dont les plus importants sont le projet pour l'Opéra de la baie de Cardiff (Pays de Galles, 1994–96) ; la Habitable Bridge (Londres, 1996) et la salle de concerts philharmoniques de Luxembourg (1997). Plus récemment, elle est entrée dans une phase active de grands chantiers, avec des réalisations comme le tremplin de ski de Bergisel (Innsbruck, Autriche, 2001–02) ; le Centre d'art contemporain Lois & Richard Rosenthal (Cincinnati, Ohio, 1999–2003) ; le Centre de la science Phaeno (Wolfsburg, Allemagne, 2001–05) et le bâtiment central de la nouvelle usine BMW de Leipzig (Allemagne, 2005). Elle a récemment achevé le Centre national des arts contemporains de Rome MAXXI (2008) et travaille sur les projets de l'Opéra de Guangzhou (Guangzhou, Chine, 2006–09) ; du pont Cheikh Zayed (Abu Dhabi, EAU, 2005–10) et du Centre de recherches d'E.ON, RWTH (Aix-la-Chapelle, Allemagne, 2009–10, publié ici). En 2004, Zaha Hadid a été la première femme à remporter le très convoité Pritzker Prize.

E.ON ENERGY RESEARCH DEPARTMENT

RWTH Aachen, Aachen, Germany, 2009–10

Floor area: 3700 m². Client: Building and Real Estate NRW, Aachen. Cost: €17.4 million.
Collaboration: Philipp Vogt, Gernot Finselbach

Set between rail tracks and a four-lane road at the RWTH University in Aachen, the E.ON Energy Research Department building makes use of structural and aerodynamic fins and a wind turbine on its roof to "allow for the modulation both of daylight and wind stream over the roof, maximizing the provision of natural light and ventilation to the building interior." Other sustainable features of the building include its orientation, use of thermal mass and minimal volume to surface ratio, and the use of geothermal energy (constant ground temperature of 10°C), wind, and sun (1500 m² of conventional opaque and monocrystalline solar panels). Interior, manually operated sun and glare roller blinds increase the potential protection from solar gain. Careful calculations lead the architects to affirm that the building will produce more energy than it consumes. With this structure, Zaha Hadid shows that her unique design process can be fruitfully adapted to the issue of sustainability—an element that is clearly desired by the client in this instance and also part of the very purpose of energy research. As she says: "Architecture and energy determine and complement one another, the components of the building have more than one function, performing and multi-tasking as hybrid forms."

Das E.ON Institut für Energieforschung an der RWTH Aachen liegt zwischen Gleisanlagen und einer vierspurigen Bundesstraße. Strukturgebende, aerodynamische Grate und eine Windturbine auf dem Dach „erlauben die Modulation von Tageslicht und Windströmen durch das Dach und maximieren die natürliche Belichtung und Belüftung des Gebäudeinneren". Weitere nachhaltige Merkmale sind die Ausrichtung des Baus, die Nutzung der thermischen Masse, ein geringes Volumen-Oberflächen-Verhältnis, die Nutzung von Erdwärme (bei einer konstanten Erdtemperatur von 10 °C), Wind- und Sonnenenergie (mit 1500 m² konventionellen opaken sowie monokristallinen Solarmodulen). Im Innern schützen manuell bedienbare Sonnen- und Blendschutzrollos zusätzlich vor potenziellem solarem Wärmegewinn. Ausgehend von sorgfältigen Berechnungen geht die Architektin davon aus, dass das Gebäude mehr Energie erzeugen als verbrauchen wird. Mit diesem Bau stellt Zaha Hadid unter Beweis, dass sich ihr unverwechselbarer Entwurfsprozess gewinnbringend an Fragen der Nachhaltigkeit anpassen lässt – was in diesem Fall explizites Anliegen des Auftraggebers war und natürlich Kernthema der Energieforschung überhaupt ist. Die Architektin merkt an: „Architektur und Energie bedingen und ergänzen sich, die einzelnen Komponenten des Baus haben jeweils mehr als eine Funktion und erfüllen als hybride Formen mehrere Aufgaben."

Implanté entre des voies de chemin de fer et une route à quatre voies en limite du terrain de l'école technique supérieure RWTH à Aix-la-Chapelle, l'immeuble du Centre de recherches sur l'énergie d'E.ON utilise des ailettes structurelles et aérodynamiques et une éolienne en toiture pour « permettre la modulation à la fois de l'éclairage naturel et du flux d'air sur le toit, et d'optimiser l'apport d'éclairage et de ventilation naturels à l'intérieur du bâtiment ». Parmi les autres dispositifs durables utilisés figurent l'orientation du bâtiment, la mise à profit de la masse thermique, le rapport minimum entre surfaces et volumes, l'utilisation de la géothermie (la température du sol est en permanence à 10 °C), du vent et du soleil (1500 m² de panneaux solaires conventionnels opaques monocristallins). À l'intérieur, des volets roulants commandés manuellement protègent du gain solaire et de l'éblouissement. Des calculs poussés ont permis aux architectes d'affirmer que l'immeuble produira plus d'énergie qu'il n'en consomme. Par cette réalisation, Zaha Hadid montre que son processus très particulier de conception peut s'adapter avec succès aux enjeux de la durabilité, élément qui fait évidemment partie des souhaits de son client dans ce domaine et aux fonctions de recherche du département. Zaha Hadid a déclaré : « L'architecture et l'énergie se déterminent et se complètent mutuellement, les composantes du bâtiment remplissent plus d'une fonction, ce sont des formes hybrides actives et multitâches. »

Zaha Hadid's design here, as is often the case, is intimately related to its site, and seems almost in the basic models and drawings to be rising directly up out of the earth.

Zaha Hadids Entwurf ist wie so oft eng mit seinem Standort verwoben und scheint in den schlichten Modellen und Zeichnungen fast direkt aus dem Erdboden herauszuwachsen.

Le projet de Zaha Hadid, comme souvent dans son œuvre, est intimement lié au site et, dans les dessins et maquettes, semble même jaillir directement du sol.

Interior spaces are amply lit and flow together much as the exterior forms give a strong impression of continuous movement.

Die Innenräume sind großzügig belichtet und gehen fließend inein-ander über. Auch die Formen des Außenbaus bilden ein dynamisches Kontinuum.

Les volumes intérieurs amplement éclairés s'inscrivent dans une confi-guration de flux, de même que les formes extérieures, ce qui laisse une puissante impression de mouve-ment continu.

The bands of light shown in the night view (right) underline the strong horizontal lines of the project and indeed its unity. Interior hallways and walkways (below) animate the space and intertwine its volumes.

Die sich in der Nachtansicht abzeichnenden Lichtbänder (rechts) unterstreichen die ausgeprägt horizontale Linienführung des Projekts und betonen seine Einheit. Korridore und Rampen im Innern des Baus (unten) beleben den Raum und verflechten die Volumina miteinander.

Les bandes de lumière qui apparaissent dans cette vue nocturne (à droite) mettent en valeur la forte horizontalité du projet et renforcent son unité. Les halls intérieurs et les passages (ci-dessous) animent l'espace et relient les volumes.

Lindale Beach House

HERBST ARCHITECTS

Herbst Architects Ltd.
Unit 9 "G" Building
114 St. Georges Bay Road
Parnell, Auckland
New Zealand

Tel: +64 9 377 9106
Fax: +64 9 377 9103
E-mail: office@herbstarchitects.co.nz
Web: www.herbstarchitects.co.nz

HERBST ARCHITECTS was established in 2001 and has a staff of seven people. Its Principals are the husband and wife team Lance and Nicola Herbst. Their work includes residential, commercial, mixed-use, healthcare, and educational work, but, as Lance Herbst says, they are best known for their "bach" (New Zealand word for beach house) work, which has been widely published in the country. Both Principals studied at the University of Cape Town in South Africa, with Lance Herbst graduating in 1988 and Nicola Herbst in 1990. They moved to New Zealand in 1994, worked with Leuschke Group Architects for one year and returned to South Africa for three years. Their notable work includes the Herbst Bach (2001); Island Bach (2001); and Aotea Bach 3 (2003), all on Great Barrier Island, Auckland; Wonderview House (Leigh, Auckland, 2002); Parnell School Library (Auckland City, 2003); Hammerhead House (Mangawhai, Auckland, 2004); Alberon Apartments (Auckland City, 2005); and Lindale Beach House (Great Barrier Island, Auckland, 2006–07, published here), all in New Zealand.

HERBST ARCHITECTS wurde 2001 gegründet und hat sieben Mitarbeiter. Geleitet wird das Büro von dem Ehepaar Lance und Nicola Herbst. Zu ihren Projekten zählen Wohnbauten, gewerbliche und Mehrzweckbauten sowie Projekte im Gesundheits- und Bildungsbereich. Lance Herbst zufolge beruht die Bekanntheit des Büros in erster Linie auf ihren „Bachs" (in Neuseeland die Bezeichnung für Strandhäuser), die landesweit umfassend publiziert wurden. Beide Partner studierten an der Universität Kapstadt, wo Lance Herbst 1988 und Nicola Herbst 1990 ihren Abschluss machte. 1994 zogen sie nach Neuseeland, arbeiteten ein Jahr lang mit Leuschke Group Architects und kehrten zunächst für drei weitere Jahre nach Südafrika zurück. Besonders zu erwähnen sind folgende Projekte: Herbst Bach (2001), Island Bach (2001) und Aotea Bach 3 (2003), alle auf der Great-Barrier-Insel, Auckland, sowie das Haus Wonderview (Leigh, Auckland, 2002), die Bücherei der Parnell-Schule (Auckland, 2003), Haus Hammerhead (Mangawhai, Auckland, 2004), die Alberon Apartments (Auckland, 2005) und das Strandhaus Lindale (Great-Barrier-Insel, Auckland, 2006–07, hier vorgestellt), alle in Neuseeland.

L'agence **HERBST ARCHITECTS** a été fondée en 2001 et emploie sept personnes. Elle est dirigée par un couple, Lance et Nicola Herbst. Ils interviennent sur des projets résidentiels, commerciaux, mixtes et des secteurs de la santé et de l'éducation mais, comme le précise Lance Herbst, ils sont surtout connus pour leur *bach* (mot néo-zélandais désignant une maison de plage) qui a été beaucoup publiée dans leur pays. Tous deux ont étudié au Cap, en Afrique du Sud, Lance Herbst étant diplômé en 1988 et Nicola en 1990. Ils se sont installés en Nouvelle-Zélande en 1994, ont travaillé avec Leuschke Group Architects pendant un an avant de revenir en Afrique du Sud pour trois ans. Parmi leurs réalisations notables : la Herbst Bach (2001) ; l'Island Bach (2001) et l'Aotea Bach 3 (2003), toutes sur la Great Barrier Island, Auckland ; la maison Wonderview (Leigh, Auckland, 2002) ; la bibliothèque de la Parnell School (Auckland City, 2003) ; la maison Hammerhead (Mangawhai, Auckland, 2004) ; l'immeuble d'appartements Alberon (Auckland City, 2005) et la maison de plage Lindale (Great Barrier Island, Auckland, 2006–07, publiée ici).

LINDALE BEACH HOUSE

Great Barrier Island, Auckland, New Zealand, 2006–07

Floor area: 112 m² (interior); 78 m² (covered decks); 25 m² (boat shed). Client: Marc Lindale. Cost: not disclosed

This house is a composition of three forms, a horizontal living spac a tower that incl des be rooms and baths, and a shed r storag A wall de fr locally quarried stone is set at right angles to the site, providing shelter from t e wind for the mai deck. nce the island has no ectricit sewage water- pply s vices, the sustainability of the house is of greater immediate importance than most other locati s. The uilding is powered by hotovol c cells wage is eated site, and water is collected and stored in the house as well. Aside from the l al stone, the hous uses N w Zealand Radiata pi and w tern re dar, wh are, the architect says, "certified renewable resources." He goes on to say: "The ladding has been hosen r its ability to self-w ther wit ut the ed for a paint surface treatment and requires no ongoing maintenance." Heat is provided wood fires and, a Herbs concludes, "importan in term of sust bility, tl buildi challenges preconceptions of amenity and convenience. The form of the buil g is a direct resp nse to e context." The hous won a w Zeal Institu of Arc tects National Award.

Das Haus ist eine Komposition aus drei formalen Elementen, einem orizontalen Wohnb eich, e em Turm, in dem sic Schlafzi mer un äder be den u einem als Stauraum dienenden Schuppen. Eine Mauer aus Steinen der Gegen verläuft im rechten Winkel ur Grundstücksgrenze nd schü t die Ha terrass or Wi Da die Insel keinerlei Strom- und Wasserversorgung hat, ist die Nachhaltigkeit des Hauses von größerer unmittelbarer Bedeutung, als sie es an anderen Standorten wäre. Das Haus gewinnt Strom durch Solarzellen, Abwässer werden auf dem Grundstück aufbereitet, und auch Frischwasser wird direkt am Haus gesammelt und gespeichert. Abgesehen vom örtlichen Stein kommen am Haus auch neuseeländische Monterey-Kiefer und Riesenlebensbaum zum Einsatz, die dem Architekten zufolge „zertifizierte erneuerbare Ressourcen" sind. Außerdem erklärt Herbst: „Die Holzverkleidung der Fassade wurde gewählt, weil sie natürlich witterungsbeständig ist, nicht gestrichen oder behandelt werden muss und keine permanente Pflege erfordert". Geheizt wird mit Holzkaminen. Herbst merkt abschließend an: „Das Haus hinterfragt die üblichen Vorstellungen von Annehmlichkeit und Komfort, ein entscheidender Faktor, wenn es um Nachhaltigkeit geht. Die formale Gestaltung des Baus knüpft unmittelbar an den vorgefundenen Kontext an." Das Haus wurde mit dem Nationalpreis des New Zealand Institute of Architects ausgezeichnet.

Cette maison est une composition de trois volumes : un espace de séjour horizontal, une tour qui regroupe les chambres et les salles de bains et un abri pour le rangement. Un mur en pierre locale implanté à angle droit protège la terrasse principale du vent. Comme l'île n'a ni réseaux d'eau ou d'électricité ni tout-à-l'égout, le caractère écologique durable de cette maison prend encore plus d'importance. Son énergie provient de cellules photovoltaïques, les rejets sont traités sur place, et l'eau est captée et stockée dans la maison même. En dehors de la pierre locale, la construction fait appel à du pin radiata de Nouvelle-Zélande et au cèdre rouge, qui sont, comme le précisent les architectes « des ressources renouvelables… le bardage a été choisi pour sa capacité à se patiner sans recours à aucune peinture ou traitement de surface, et ne demande aucun entretien ». Le chauffage est procuré par des feux de bois. Herbst conclut : « Importante en terme de durabilité, cette construction remet en jeux les préjugés sur les services et le pratique. Sa forme est une réponse directe à son contexte. » Elle a remporté un prix national de l'Institut des architectes de Nouvelle-Zélande.

The Lindale Beach House has a strong "shed" aesthetic that translates a willful desire to make it light on the ground in terms of its environmental impact.

Die „Schuppen"-Ästhetik des Lindale Beach House zeugt von der bewussten Entscheidung, ökologisch so wenig Spuren wie nur möglich zu hinterlassen.

La maison de plage Lindale affiche une nette esthétique de hangar qui exprime une volonté d'alléger sa présence sur le sol et donc son impact environnemental.

The images and site plan on this
page give a clear idea of the strong
presence of nature around the house.

Die Bilder und der Geländegrundriss
auf dieser Seite vermitteln die starke
Präsenz der Natur um das Haus.

Les photographies et le plan
du terrain montrent bien la forte
présence de la nature autour.

Natural stone walls, wood structural elements, and an open terrace speak to the ecological viability of this architecture.

Natursteinmauern, konstruktive Elemente aus Holz und eine offene Terrasse zeugen von der gelungenen ökologischen Funktionalität der Architektur.

Des murs en pierre naturelle, des éléments en bois de construction et la terrasse ouverte expriment la qualité écologique de cette architecture.

The basic forms of the house, as seen in the plan to the right, are decidedly rectilinear or indeed rectangular. Though somewhat industrial in appearance, it is efficiently comfortable.

Die Grundformen des Hauses sind, wie der Grundriss rechts zeigt, rechtwinklig, zum Teil rechteckig. Obwohl der Bau beinahe industriell anmutet, ist er ohne Frage behaglich.

Comme le montre le plan à droite, les formes basiques de cette maison sont résolument orthogonales. Bien que d'apparence quasi industrielle, elle est efficacement confortable.

ANNA HERINGER AND EIKE ROSWAG

Roswag & Jankowski Architekten
Lehrter Str. 57 Haus 4
10557 Berlin
Germany

Tel: +49 30 89 73 37 73
Fax: +49 30 89 73 37 72
E-mail: kontakt@werk-a.de
Web: www.werk-a.de

ANNA HERINGER was born in 1977 in Rosenheim, Germany. She studied Architecture at the University of Linz in Austria (1999–2004) and is currently a visiting professor at the University of Stuttgart. She is also working on the BASEhabitat studio for building in developing countries at the University of Art and Design in Linz. She has been involved in rural development work with the NGOs Shanti and Dipshikha since 1997. **EIKE ROSWAG** was born in 1969 in Gießen, Germany. He obtained his Dipl.-Ing. Architecture degree from the Technical University in Berlin (1992–2000). He worked as a partner of ZRS Architekten Ingenieure in Berlin, beginning in 2003 on projects using earth as a building material. In 2003–04 he worked on the design and construction of a rammed-earth house near Berlin (Ihlow House). Since 2006 he has been a partner of Roswag & Jankowski Architekten in Berlin and has taught at the Technical University there. Heringer and Roswag worked together on the Handmade School published here (Rudrapur, Dinajpur, Bangladesh, 2005), a recipient of the 2007 Aga Khan Award for Architecture.

ANNA HERINGER wurde 1977 in Rosenheim geboren. Sie studierte Architektur an der Kunstuniversität Linz in Österreich (1999–2004) und ist derzeit Gastprofessorin an der Universität Stuttgart. An der Kunstuniversität Linz ist sie zudem am Projekt BASEhabitat beteiligt, das sich mit Architektur in Entwicklungsländern befasst. Seit 1997 engagiert sie sich für ländliche Entwicklungsprojekte der Nichtregierungsorganisationen Shanti und Dipshikha. **EIKE ROSWAG** wurde 1969 in Gießen geboren. Er schloss sein Architekturstudium an der Technischen Universität Berlin (1992–2000) als Diplom-Ingenieur ab. Er arbeitete als Partner bei ZRS Architekten Ingenieure in Berlin und begann 2003, Erde als Baumaterial bei seinen Projekten zu nutzen. 2003 bis 2004 arbeitete er am Entwurf und Bau eines Stampflehmhauses in der Nähe von Berlin (Haus Ihlow). Seit 2006 ist er Partner bei Roswag & Jankowski Architekten in Berlin und unterrichtet an der dortigen Technischen Universität. Heringer und Roswag realisierten gemeinsam die hier vorgestellte Handmade School (Rudrapur, Dinajpur, Bangladesch, 2005), die 2007 mit dem Aga-Khan-Preis für Architektur ausgezeichnet wurde.

ANNA HERINGER, née en 1977 à Rosenheim, Allemagne, a étudié l'architecture à l'université de Linz (Autriche, 1999–2004) et est actuellement professeur invitée à l'université de Stuttgart. Elle travaille également au studio BASEhabitat de l'université des arts et du design industriel de Linz, lequel conçoit des bâtiments pour les pays en voie de développement. Elle s'implique enfin dans des projets de développement rural avec les ONG Shanti et Dipshikha depuis 1997. **EIKE ROSWAG**, né en 1969 à Gießen, Allemagne, est Dipl.-Ing. Architekt de l'Université Polytechnique de Berlin (1992–2000). Il a travaillé comme associé pour ZRS Architekten Ingenieure à Berlin, à partir de 2003, sur des projets utilisant la terre comme matériau de construction. En 2003–04, il a travaillé à la conception et la construction d'une maison en béton de terre près de Berlin (maison Ihlow). Depuis 2006, il est un des associés de Roswag & Jankowski Architekten à Berlin et enseigne à l'Université Polytechnique berlinoise. Heringer et Roswag ont collaboré sur le projet de l'école publié ici (Rudrapur, Dinajpur, Bangladesh, 2005) qui a reçu le prix Aga Khan d'architecture en 2007.

HANDMADE SCHOOL

Rudrapur, Dinajpur, Bangladesh, 2005

Floor area: 325 m². Client: Dipshikha/METI, Bangladesh. Cost: €25 000. Team: Anna Heringer and Eike Roswag

"We believe that architecture is more than simply shelter. It is intimately connected with the creation of identity and self-confidence. And this is the basis of sustainable development," declare Anna Heringer and Eike Roswag. Their school made of earth and bamboo was built for and with the Modern Education and Training Institute (METI) and its NGO mother organization, Dipshikha, in 2005 in Rudrapur in northern Bangladesh. The project was undertaken in cooperation with Shanti Bangladesh and the Papal Children's Mission (PMK). The ground floor of the structure has thick earth walls, while the upper story, where colorful saris are stretched on the ceiling, is made of bamboo. Three classrooms and six organically shaped "caves" are located on the ground floor, and two large, flexible class areas are on the upper floor. Twelve thousand five hundred bamboo strips were used to make the porous façades of the upper level. Made with the assistance of 25 local laborers, the structure makes use of traditional building techniques with "technical improvements." The school is used by 168 children. The jury citation of the 2007 Aga Khan Award for Architecture given to the Handmade School reads: "This joyous and elegant two-story primary school in rural Bangladesh has emerged from a deep understanding of local materials and a heartfelt connection to the local community. Its innovation lies in the adaptation of traditional methods and materials of construction to create light-filled celebratory spaces, as well as informal spaces for children. Earthbound materials, such as loam and straw, are combined with lighter elements like bamboo sticks and nylon lashing to shape a built form that addresses sustainability in construction in an exemplary manner."

„Wir glauben, dass Architektur mehr ist als nur ein Obdach. Sie ist eng verknüpft mit der Bildung von Identität und Selbstbewusstsein. Und sie ist Grundlage einer nachhaltigen Entwicklung", erklären Anna Heringer und Eike Roswag. Ihre Schule aus Bambus und Lehm wurde 2005 für das Modern Education and Training Institute (METI) und dessen NGO-Mutterorganisation Dipshikha in Rudrapur in Nord-Bangladesch erbaut. Das Projekt entstand in Kooperation mit Shanti Bangladesch und dem Päpstlichen Missionswerk der Kinder (PMK). Das Erdgeschoss des Baus hat massive Lehmmauern, während das obere Stockwerk, in dem bunte Saris unter der Decke hängen, aus Bambus gefertigt wurde. Im Erdgeschoss liegen drei Klassenzimmer und sechs organisch geformte „Höhlen", im Obergeschoss befinden sich zwei große flexible Schulräume. Die lichtdurchlässigen Fassaden des Obergeschosses wurden aus 12 500 Bambusstäben gefertigt. Der mithilfe von 25 ortsansässigen Arbeitern errichtete Bau bedient sich regionaler Bautechniken, die „technisch optimiert" wurden. Die Schule wird von 168 Kindern genutzt. In der Begründung der Jury des Aga-Khan-Preises für Architektur, den die Handmade School 2007 erhielt, heißt es: „Die fröhliche und elegante zweistöckige Grundschule im ländlichen Bangladesch entstand aus einem tiefen Verständnis für regionale Materialien und einer zutiefst empfundenen Bindung an die örtliche Gemeinschaft. Ihre Neuheit liegt in der Abwandlung traditioneller Baumethoden und -materialien, um lichterfüllte, festliche und informelle Räume für Kinder zu schaffen. Erdverbundene Materialien wie Lehm und Stroh wurden mit leichteren Materialien wie Bambusstäben und Nylonseilen kombiniert, um einen Raum zu gestalten, der nachhaltiges Bauen exemplarisch umsetzt."

« Nous pensons que l'architecture doit être davantage qu'un simple abri. Elle est intimement liée à la création d'une identité et de la confiance en soi. C'est la base du développement durable », expliquent Anna Heringer et Eike Roswag. Leur école en terre et bambou a été édifiée pour l'Institut moderne d'éducation et de formation (METI) et son organisation non gouvernementale mère, Dipshikha, en 2005 à Rudrapur dans le nord du Bangladesh. Le projet a été initié en coopération avec Shanti Bangladesh et la mission papale pour l'enfance (PMK). Le rez-de-chaussée du bâtiment présente d'épais murs de terre tandis que l'étage, au plafond duquel pendent des saris de couleurs vives, est en bambou. Trois salles de classe et six « cavernes » de forme organique se trouvent au rez-de-chaussée et deux grandes salles d'utilisation souple à l'étage. 12 500 lattes de bambou ont été utilisées pour la façade du niveau supérieur. Mené avec l'aide de 25 paysans locaux, le chantier a fait appel à des techniques traditionnelles « techniquement améliorées ». L'école reçoit 168 enfants. La citation du jury du Prix Aga Khan d'architecture 2007 précisait : « Cette élégante école de deux niveaux dans le Bangladesh rural est le résultat d'une profonde compréhension des matériaux locaux ainsi que d'un rapport sincère avec les populations locales. Son innovation réside dans son adaptation aux méthodes et aux matériaux de constructions traditionnels pour créer d'agréables espaces lumineux ainsi que des espaces informels pour les enfants. Les matériaux issus de la terre, tels que le limon et la paille, sont combinés avec des éléments plus légers tels que les branches de bambou et les cordes de nylon pour réaliser une construction dont la durabilité est exemplaire. »

Originality in architecture may well have to do with first anchoring a structure in local tradition and materials and then making it modern through details in design and construction.

Die Originalität von Architektur hat sicherlich viel damit zu tun, zunächst lokale Traditionen und Materialien zu berücksichtigen und erst dann durch gestalterische und bauliche Details modern zu interpretieren.

Souvent en architecture l'originalité tient à l'ancrage du projet dans les traditions et les matériaux locaux. L'apport de la modernité s'affirme alors dans les détails de conception et de construction.

The flow of light and air through the building is obvious in these images. Nor does an emphasis on simple local materials give any sense that the building was made on a restricted budget.

Die Bilder veranschaulichen, wie ungehindert Licht und Luft durch das Gebäude strömen. Die einfachen lokalen Baumaterialien lassen dennoch nicht ahnen, dass das Budget für dieses Projekt knapp war.

Les flots d'air et de lumière qui pénètrent dans l'école sont évidents sur ces images. L'accent mis sur des matériaux locaux simples ne trahit en rien la faiblesse du budget de construction.

747 Wing House

DAVID HERTZ

David Hertz Architects, Inc.
SEA, Studio of Environmental Architecture
1920 Olympic Boulevard
Santa Monica, CA 90404
USA

Tel: +1 310 829 9932
Fax: +1 310 829 5641
E-mail: info@studioea.com
Web: www.syndesisinc.com; www.studioea.com

DAVID HERTZ, born in 1960 in Los Angeles, received his B.Arch degree from SCI-Arc in 1983. He worked as an apprentice in the offices of John Lautner and Frank Gehry before founding his own firm in 1984. He is the founder and president of SEA, the Studio of Environmental Architecture (formerly Syndesis Inc.). He is a member of the Los Angeles Chapter of the American Institute of Architects Committee on the Environment, the Environmental Affairs Committee of the Construction Specifications Institute, the Environmental Committee of Concrete Organizations, and the California Energy Commission's High Performance Wall Systems Collaborative. In 2004 he became a LEED AP, administered by the US Green Building Council. His work includes the Panel House, a single-family residence made of prefabricated refrigeration panels (Venice, California, 2006), and his own office, installed in a renovated market and restaurant using "cutting-edge green building technology" (Santa Monica, California, 2007, LEED Platinum registered). Current work includes the 747 Wing House (Santa Monica Mountains, Malibu, 2007–09, published here); the Mullin Collection Automotive Museum (Oxnard, California, 2009); the North Cache Project, a sustainable mixed-use complex (Jackson Hole, Wyoming, 2010); and Living Homes, the "design of a systemized aluminum frame and panel prefab house design that is ordered as a kit of parts and integrated systems" (no location, ongoing).

DAVID HERTZ, 1960 in Los Angeles geboren, erhielt seinen B.Arch. 1983 an der SCI-Arc. Bevor er 1984 sein eigenes Büro gründete, war er Praktikant bei John Lautner und Frank Gehry. Er ist Gründer und Direktor von SEA, dem Studio of Environmental Architecture (vormals Syndesis Inc.). Er ist Mitglied des Ortsverbands Los Angeles des Umweltkomitees des American Institute of Architects, des Komitees für Umweltfragen des Construction Specifications Institute, des Umweltkomitees der Betonverbände sowie der Arbeitsgemeinschaft Hochdämmende Wandsysteme der kalifornischen Energiekommission. 2004 wurde er für das LEED-AP-Programm des amerikanischen Green Building Council akkreditiert. Zu seinen Projekten zählen das Panel House, ein Einfamilienhaus aus vorgefertigten Kühlpaneelen (Venice, Kalifornien 2006), sowie sein eigenes Büro, das nach „neuesten grünen Baumethoden" in ein saniertes Markt- und Restaurantgebäude integriert wurde (Santa Monica, Kalifornien, 2007, registriert für eine LEED-Platin-Medaille). Zu seinen aktuellen Projekten gehören das 747 Wing House (Santa Monica Mountains, Malibu, 2007–09, hier vorgestellt), das Mullin Collection Automotive Museum (Oxnard, Kalifornien, 2009), das North Cache Project, ein nachhaltiger Gebäudekomplex mit gemischter Nutzung (Jackson Hole, Wyoming, 2010), sowie Living Homes, der „Entwurf für ein Fertighaussystem aus Aluminiumrahmen und -paneelen, das als Bausatz aus Einzelteilen und integrierten Haustechnikelementen bestellt werden kann" (ohne Ort, in Arbeit).

DAVID HERTZ, né en 1960 à Los Angeles, est B. Arch de SCI-Arc (1983). Il a été apprenti dans les agences de John Lautner et Frank Gehry avant de fonder sa propre agence dès 1984. Il est fondateur et président de SEA, Studio of Environmental Architecture (anciennement Syndesis Inc.). Il est membre du comité pour l'environnement de la section de Los Angeles pour l'Institut américain des architectes, du Comité des affaires environnementales de l'Institut des normes de la construction, du Comité environnemental des professions du béton et membre de la Commission californienne de l'énergie pour le projet collaboratif sur les systèmes de murs à hautes performances. En 2004, il a reçu l'accréditation 2004 LEED AP, gérée par l'US Green Building Council. Parmi ses réalisations : la Panel House, résidence familiale en panneaux réfrigérants préfabriqués (Venice, Californie, 2006) et ses propres bureaux, installés dans un marché et restaurant rénovés au moyen de « technologies vertes d'avant-garde » (Santa Monica, Californie, 2007, LEED Platine). Actuellement, il travaille sur la maison 747 Wing (Santa Monica Mountains, Malibu, 2007–09, publiée ici) ; le Mullin Collection Automotive Museum (Oxnard, Californie, 2009) ; le projet North Cache, complexe mixte durable (Jackson Hole, Wyoming, 2010), et Living Homes, la « conception d'une maison à ossature et panneau d'aluminium systémisés, qui se commandera en kit et sera livrée accompagnée de systèmes intégrés ».

747 WING HOUSE

Santa Monica Mountains, Malibu, California, 2007–09

*Site area: 22 ha. Floor area: 464 m². Client: Francie Rehwald.
Cost: not disclosed*

The client for this project asked the architect to design a house with "curvilinear, feminine shapes." The architect's original idea of a curved roof that would appear to float gave way to the use of the 230-square-meter wings of a decommissioned 747–200 aircraft purchased for a price of just $40 000. Considering the ecology of the entire site, Hertz decided to use components of the aircraft for several structures on the property, all of which are designed with passive solar orientation and natural ventilation strategies. As he says: "The recycling of some of the 4.5 million parts of this 'big aluminum can' is seen as an extreme example of sustainable reuse and appropriation." The strength and lightness of aircraft components is, of course, something that other architects have made use of before, but none has gone as far as Hertz in their direct reuse. Both of the main wings of the aircraft, as well as its two horizontal stabilizers from the tail section, are employed as roof elements, while the ailerons and elevators of the plane "are proposed to be made operational and will be used as kinetic solar shades as well as airfoils to regulate airflow of the prevailing breezes for ventilation."

Der Bauherr bat den Architekten um ein Haus mit „weichen, femininen Formen". Die ursprüngliche Idee des Architekten eines geschwungenen, scheinbar schwebenden Dachs wurde schließlich durch den Einsatz der 230 m² großen Tragflächen einer ehemaligen Boeing 747–200 abgelöst, die für nur 40 000 US-Dollar erworben werden konnten. Nachdem Hertz die Ökologie des gesamten Geländes analysiert hatte, beschloss er, Flugzeugkomponenten für verschiedene bauliche Elemente auf dem Grundstück einzusetzen, die durch ihre Ausrichtung als Passivbauten angelegt sind und natürlich belüftet werden. Er merkt an: „Das Recycling verschiedener Elemente der insgesamt 4,5 Millionen Teile einer solchen ‚gigantischen Aluminiumdose' kann als Extrembeispiel für nachhaltige Wiederverwertung und Umnutzung gelten." Natürlich wurden die Stabilität und Leichtigkeit von Flugzeugteilen bereits von anderen Architekten erkannt, doch niemand trieb die unmittelbare Wiederverwertung bisher soweit wie Hertz. Die beiden Haupttragflächen des Flugzeugs ebenso wie die beiden Höhenflossen vom Heck dienen als Dachelemente, während die Querruder und Höhenruder „funktional erhalten bleiben, um als kinetische Sonnensegel und aerodynamisches Profil zu fungieren, mit deren Hilfe die vorherrschenden Windströme reguliert und für die Belüftung nutzbar gemacht werden können".

Le client avait demandé à l'architecte une « maison de formes curvilignes, féminines ». L'idée d'origine d'un toit incurvé qui aurait semblé suspendu a laissé place aux 230 m² d'ailes d'un vieux 747–200 achetées pour à peine 40 000 dollars. Prenant en compte l'écologie du site, Hertz a décidé d'utiliser des éléments de l'avion pour plusieurs constructions édifiées sur la propriété, toutes conçues selon des stratégies d'orientation solaire et de ventilation naturelle. « Le recyclage de quelques-unes des 4,5 millions de pièces de cette "grosse boîte d'aluminium" est un exemple extrême de réutilisation et d'appropriation durables », a commenté l'architecte. La résistance et la légèreté de ces pièces d'avion étaient conçues par d'autres architectes avant lui, mais personne n'était allé aussi loin dans leur réutilisation. Les deux ailes et les deux stabilisateurs horizontaux de la section de queue ont servi pour la toiture, tandis que les ailerons et les gouvernails de l'avion « devraient être rendus fonctionnels pour servir d'écrans solaires cinétiques ou de régulateurs de flux des brises dominantes récupérées pour la ventilation ».

The wing forms of the house are clearly visible in the aerial view above. Separated in this way, the wings might even resemble those of a bird in flight.

Im Luftbild (oben) sind die Tragflächen des Hauses deutlich zu erkennen. So voneinander getrennt mögen sie vielleicht sogar an die Flügel eines fliegenden Vogels erinnern.

Les ailes de la maison sont clairement reconnaissables dans cette vue aérienne. Ainsi séparées, elles font presque penser à évoquer un oiseau en vol.

Other drawings and plans give a less literal impression of the wing design, sublimating it rather than rendering it fully explicit.

Andere Zeichnungen und Grundrisse zeigen weniger offensichtlich, wie die Tragflächen in den Entwurf eingearbeitet wurden – eher verhalten als explizit.

D'autres plans et dessins affichent beaucoup moins clairement les aîles, les sublimant plutôt que de les rendre explicites.

HOTSON BAKKER BONIFACE HADEN

Hotson Bakker Boniface Haden architects + urbanistes
406–611 Alexander Street
Vancouver, BC, V6A 1E1
Canada

Tel: +1 604 255 1169
Fax: +1 604 255 1790
E-mail: design@hbbharc.com
Web: www.hbbharc.com

HOTSON BAKKER BONIFACE HADEN has long been involved in what they call "sustainable city-shaping," for example in the progressive adaptive reuse and urbanism of Vancouver's Granville Island. Their Capers building in Vancouver was the first commercial application of geothermal technology in western Canada. The firm has recently completed the campus plan and academic buildings for the new Quest University in Squamish, British Columbia, Canada, where sustainable design "infuses the site planning, the building design, and the curriculum." Further, in contrast with some other approaches to green architecture, HBBH "believes in the importance of making buildings 'visibly green' as a means of fostering public knowledge about key environmental issues, such as greenhouse gas emissions, and the significant role buildings play in global environmental health." Bruce Haden, the partner in charge of the Nk'Mip project published here (Osoyoos, British Columbia, Canada, 2004–06), grew up in Kingston, Ontario, and studied architecture at the University of Waterloo, receiving his M.Arch degree from the University of British Columbia. He has been involved in a number of projects that concern native Indian tribes, as can be seen in his work with Haida Gwaii and bands in the Northwest Territories.

Das Büro **HOTSON BAKKER BONIFACE HADEN** engagiert sich schon lange für „nachhaltige Stadtgestaltung", etwa mit Projekten wie der fortschrittlichen, fle-xiblen Umnutzung und Stadtplanung der zu Vancouver gehörenden Granville-Insel. Das Capers Building in Vancouver war das erste kommerzielle Bauprojekt in West-kanada mit Erdwärmetechnik. Kürzlich stellte das Team Lehrgebäude für die neue Quest University in Squamish, British Columbia, Kanada, fertig, wo nachhaltiges Design „die Planung des Geländes, den baulichen Entwurf und den Lehrplan" beeinflusst. Im Gegensatz zu anderen Ansätzen ist HBBH „überzeugt, dass es entscheidend ist, Bauten ‚sichtbar grün' zu gestalten, um der Öffentlichkeit Schlüsselfragen des Umweltschutzes zu vermitteln, etwa Wissen über Treibhausgase und die bedeutende Rolle, die Bauten für die Gesundheit unseres Planeten spielen". Bruce Haden, verantwortlich für das hier vorgestellte Nk'Mip-Projekt (Osoyoos, British Columbia, Kanada, 2004–06), wuchs in Kingston, Ontario, auf, studierte Architektur an der Universität Waterloo und erwarb seinen M.Arch. an der Universität von British Columbia. Er war an zahlreichen Projekten für heimische Indianerstämme beteiligt, wie seine Arbeit mit Haida Gwaii und verschiedenen Stammesgruppierungen in den Northwest Territories zeigt.

L'agence **HOTSON BAKKER BONIFACE HADEN** s'est longtemps intéressée à ce qu'elle appelle « la mise en forme durable des villes », par exemple dans la démarche de réutilisation progressive adaptée pour l'urbanisme de Granville Island à Vancouver. Son immeuble Capers Building à Vancouver est la première application des technologies géothermiques dans l'ouest du Canada. Elle a récemment réalisé le plan du campus ainsi que les bâtiments universitaires de la nouvelle université Quest à Squamish, Colombie britannique, Canada, pour laquelle la conception durable « touche l'ensemble de la planification, la conception des bâtiments et le cours des études ». De plus, à la différence de certaines approches de l'architecture verte, HBBH « croit en l'importance de constructions visiblement "vertes" pour promouvoir la prise de conscience par le public d'enjeux environnementaux clés, comme les conséquences des gaz à effet de serre, et le rôle significatif du bâti dans la santé glo-bale de l'environnement ». Bruce Haden, associé en charge du projet Nk'Mip publié ici (Osoyoos, Colombie britannique, Canada, 2004–06), a grandi à Kingston, Ontario, et a étudié l'architecture à l'université de Waterloo. Il est M. Arch de l'université de Colombie britannique. Il a travaillé sur un certain nombre de projets concernant les tribus indiennes, comme le montre son travail dans les Haida Gwaii et pour les tribus des territoires du Nord-Ouest.

NK'MIP DESERT CULTURAL CENTRE

Osoyoos, British Columbia, Canada, 2004–06

*Floor area: 1115 m². Client: Osoyoos Indian Band. Cost: $2.9 million.
Project Architect: Brady Dunlop*

Hotson Bakker Boniface Haden was hired by the Osoyoos Indian Band to master plan the Nk'Mip Desert Cultural Centre's 81-hectare site, part of a new resort that includes a winery, an 18-hole golf course with clubhouse, and tourist accommodations. The site is located at the far northern end of the American deserts that extend southward to the Sonoran Desert in Mexico. In an unusual climate for Canada, summer temperatures can rise as high as 40°C and fall to -18°C in winter. The program of the center includes indoor and outdoor exhibition spaces, a theater, gift shop, administrative offices, rattlesnake research facilities, and 50 kilometers of hiking trails. The green features of the project include its main rammed-earth wall, its orientation and choice of site, radiant heating and cooling based on ceiling and floor slabs, a habitable green roof, water-use management, and support for endangered-species research. Bluestain pine was used for the cladding because an infestation of pine beetles in British Columbia led to an excess of this type of tree. The center's earthen wall—80 meters long, 5.5 meters high, and 60 centimeters thick—is the largest rammed-earth wall in North America. Made from local soil mixed with concrete, it retains warmth in winter and cools the building in summer.

Die Gruppe der Osoyoos-Indianer beauftragte Hotson Bakker Boniface Haden mit der Erstellung des Masterplans für das 81 ha große Gelände des Nk'Mip Desert Cultural Centre, das Teil eines neuen Erholungsgebiets ist und zu dem auch ein Weingut, ein 18-Loch-Golfplatz mit Klubhaus und Touristenunterkünfte gehören. Das Gelände markiert das nördlichste Ende der amerikanischen Wüstengegenden, die sich nach Süden bis zur Sonora-Wüste in Mexiko ziehen. In einem für Kanada ungewöhnlichen Klima können die Temperaturen hier auf 40 °C steigen und im Winter auf bis zu −18 °C fallen. Das Programm des Zentrums umfasst Ausstellungsbereiche im Innen- und Außenraum, ein Theater, einen Souvenirladen, Verwaltungsbüros, eine Klapperschlangen-Forschungsstation und insgesamt 50 km Wanderwege. Grüne Merkmale des Projekts sind u. a. die große Hauptmauer aus Stampflehm einschließlich ihrer Standortwahl und Ausrichtung sowie eine in Decken- und Bodenpaneele integrierte Strahlungsheizung und -kühlung, ein begehbares begrüntes Dach, Wassersparsysteme und schließlich das Engagement für die Erforschung bedrohter Arten. Für die Holzverkleidung wählte man Küstenkiefer, da eine Käferepidemie in British Columbia zu Bauholzüberschuss geführt hatte. Die Mauer des Zentrums – 80 m lang, 5,5 m hoch und 60 cm stark – ist die größte Stampflehmmauer Nordamerikas. Die aus einer Mischung aus regionaler Erde und Beton gefertigte Mauer dient im Winter als Wärmespeicher und kühlt das Gebäude im Sommer.

L'agence Hotson Bakker Boniface Haden a été engagée par les Indiens Osoyoos pour réaliser le plan directeur du Centre du patrimoine du désert de Nk'Mip, site de 81 ha qui fait partie de nouvelles installations touristiques comprenant un chai, un golf de 18 trous avec *club-house* et des hébergements pour visiteurs. Le lieu se trouve à l'extrémité nord des grandes étendues désertiques américaines qui partent du désert de Sonora au Mexique. Inhabituelles pour le Canada, les températures d'été peuvent s'élever jusqu'à 40 °C et descendre jusqu'à -18 °C en hiver. Le programme du centre comprend des espaces d'expositions couverts et en plein air, un auditorium, une boutique de cadeaux, des bureaux administratifs, un centre de recherche sur les serpents à sonnettes et 50 km de pistes de randonnée. Les aspects durables du projet comprennent le mur principal en béton de terre, l'orientation et le choix de l'emplacement, le chauffage et le rafraîchissement radiant par les sols et les plafonds, un toit végétalisé habitable, la gestion de l'eau et le soutien à la recherche sur les espèces en voie de disparition. On a utilisé un bardage en pin Bluestain très abondant, car le pin local est infesté de parasites. Le mur de terre du bâtiment du Centre – 80 m de long, 5,5 m de haut et 60 cm d'épaisseur – est le plus grand mur en béton de terre jamais monté en Amérique du Nord. Réalisé en terre locale mélangée à du béton, il retient la chaleur en hiver et conserve la fraîcheur en été.

The basic structure is inserted into the hillside and fronted by the strong rammed-earth wall.

Das schlichte Gebäude wurde in den Abhang hineingebaut und liegt hinter einer mächtigen Stampflehmmauer.

La structure de base est insérée dans le flanc de la colline et comme bloquée par un puissant mur de terre.

0m   10m

The layered effect of the rammed-earth wall makes it blend into its natural setting, as the site plan with its topographic lines (above) shows from a different perspective. Right, Indian heritage…

Dank ihres Schichteffekts verschmilzt die Stampflehmmauer geradezu mit ihrem Umfeld, wie auch der topografische Geländeplan (oben) aus einer anderen Perspektive deutlich macht. Rechts indianische Artefakte…

L'effet de stratification du mur de terre l'intègre encore mieux dans son cadre naturel, comme le plan du site et les courbes de niveaux (ci-dessus) le montrent sous une perspective différente. À droite, témoignage de la tradition indienne…

The modern volumes of the center lie behind its long, visible wall, as seen in the plan below.

Die modernen Baukörper des Centers liegen hinter der lang gestreckten, nach außen hin sichtbaren Mauer, wie der Grundriss unten zeigt.

Comme le montre le plan ci-dessous, les volumes modernes qui composent le centre sont protégés par le long mur de terre.

A sense of earthy solidity pervades
the architecture and makes it contex-
tual without any sense of pastiche.

Die Architektur ist von erdiger Boden-
ständigkeit und dabei kontextuell,
ohne je zur Pastiche zu werden.

Cette architecture qui diffuse un
sentiment de grande solidité maté-
rielle joue le contexte sans tomber
pour autant dans le pastiche.

CHRIS JACOBS

Chris Jacobs
United Future / 8500 Steller Drive, Building 5
Culver City, CA 90232 / USA
Tel: +1 310 280 7778 /E-mail: chris@unitedfuture.com
Web: www.unitedfuture.com

CHRIS JACOBS is the co-founder and Executive Creative Director of United Future, a design firm founded in 2005. The goal of the company "is to create cross-culture, cross-platform solutions that unite people and business processes through the use of transparent-technology ideologies." He worked previously as a creative director with Equus (Singapore, 2002) and Lemon Asia (Hong Kong). Jacobs has also worked as an independent consultant for companies such as SAP, Time Warner and Universal Music. He attended the Art College Center of Design (1991–95) and is thus not an architect. He explains: "I've always had a love of architecture, and have designed a few homes while working in the field professionally. My true loves are industrial design and graphic design, with an emphasis on Interface design and usability for Internet applications. I always felt that a good designer can design anything, from a shower curtain ring to a movie poster to an automobile. I've always pushed myself to be multidisciplined in a multitude of fields, including typography, digital illustration, 3D, interface usability, etc., etc. Because of my love of industrial design, I forced myself to learn Rhino3D. When I was tasked to design a Vertical Farm [published here], I worked around the clock and designed it in one sitting (using Rhino3D), with the idea that this structure had to be stackable and modular. I then had it remodeled in 3D Studio Max by Dean Fowler with further detail design assistance by Rolf Mohr, an architect we work with on occasion."

CHRIS JACOBS ist Mitbegründer und leitender Creative Director von United Future, einem 2005 gegründeten Designbüro. Ziel der Agentur ist es, „kultur- und grundsatzübergreifende Lösungen zu finden, die Menschen und Geschäftsprozesse durch eine transparente technische Weltanschauung verbinden". Zuvor war er als Creative Director für Equus (Singapur, 2002) und Lemon Asia (Hongkong) tätig. Darüber hinaus war Jacobs als freier Berater für Firmen wie SAP, Time Warner und Universal Music aktiv. Er studierte am Art College Center of Design (1991–95) und ist somit kein Architekt. Er erklärt: „Ich hatte schon immer eine Leidenschaft für Architektur und habe im Lauf meiner beruflichen Tätigkeit in diesem Bereich auch einige Häuser entworfen. Doch meine wahre Leidenschaft ist das Produkt- und Grafikdesign, mit einem Schwerpunkt auf Interfacedesign und dessen Umsetzung für Internetanwendungen. Ich war schon immer der Meinung, dass ein guter Designer alles gestalten kann, von Ringen für Duschvorhänge über Kinoplakate bis hin zu Autos. Ich habe mich immer bemüht, multidisziplinär in einer ganzen Bandbreite von Bereichen arbeiten zu können, etwa in der Typografie, der digitalen Illustration, in 3D, benutzerfreundlichen Interfaces etc. etc. Wegen meiner Leidenschaft für Produktdesign war ich gezwungen, mir Rhino3D zu erschließen. Als ich den Auftrag erhielt, einen vertikalen Bauernhof [hier vorgestellt] zu entwerfen, arbeitete ich rund um die Uhr und entwarf das Projekt (mit Rhino3D) in einem Zug. Die Idee war, dass die Konstruktion stapelbar und modular sein sollte. Schließlich musste der Entwurf von Dean Fowler mit 3D Studio Max neu modelliert werden, weitere Unterstützung beim Entwurf von Details kam von Rolf Mohr, einem Architekten, mit dem wir gelegentlich zusammenarbeiten."

CHRIS JACOBS est cofondateur et directeur de création de United Future, une agence de design créée en 2005. L'objectif de cette société est de « trouver des solutions trans-cultures, trans-plates-formes qui réunissent des personnes et des processus économiques à travers l'utilisation d'idéologies de technologies transparentes ». Il a été précédemment directeur de création d'Equus (Singapour, 2002) et de Lemon Asia (Hong Kong). Jacobs a également été consultant indépendant pour des entreprises comme SAP, Time Warner et Universal Music. Il a étudié au Art College Center of Design (1991–95) et n'est donc pas un architecte. Il explique ainsi : « J'ai toujours éprouvé un grand amour pour l'architecture et j'ai dessiné quelques maisons pendant que je travaillais professionnellement dans ce secteur. J'aime surtout le design industriel et le design graphique, avec un accent sur la conception d'interfaces et leur utilisation dans les applications Internet. J'ai toujours pensé qu'un bon designer pouvait tout concevoir, d'un anneau de rideau de douche à une affiche de film ou automobile. Je me suis toujours efforcé d'être multidisciplinaire dans une multitude de domaines, dont la typographie, l'illustration numérique, la 3D, la convivialité des interfaces, etc. Dans cette passion pour le design industriel, je me suis forcé à apprendre le logiciel Rhino3D. Lorsque l'on m'a demandé de concevoir une Ferme verticale [publiée ici], j'ai travaillé 24/24 h et je l'ai conçue en une fois (avec Rhino3D), sur l'idée que cette structure devait être modulaire et empilable. Puis je l'ai fait retravailler en 3D Studio Max par Dean Fowler avec l'assistance en conception de détail de Rolf Mohr, un architecte avec lequel nous travaillons occasionnellement. »

VERTICAL FARM

Harlem, New York, New York, USA, 2007

Floor area: not disclosed. Client: Chris Jacobs. Cost: $200 million.
Collaboration: Rolf Mohr

The concept behind this research project is that of bringing an actual farming space to the core of inner cities, from Los Angeles to New York, where Chris Jacobs imagines installing it in Harlem. Jacobs says: "Close your eyes; now imagine 30 stories of contemporary architecture designed to show off the real green with floor-to-ceiling windows, specialized equipment—solar panels everywhere. Put it next to a freeway; make it a 24-hour operation glowing brightly from the inside. A beacon of green technology. Would this technologically advanced 'greenscraper' spawn a new type of Agro-tourism?" Despite dreaming of such a project on a very large scale, Jacobs admits that "a two-story hydroponic structure atop a multistory affordable housing project might be the most pragmatic way to start." Chris Jacobs has thought through the potential for such a structure in the United States, where venture capital or philanthropic foundations might be persuaded to participate in the cost, with the goal of bringing jobs and fresh produce to America's underprivileged inner cities.

Das Konzept dieses Forschungsprojekts war es, eine reale Landwirtschaftsfläche in das Zentrum von Großstädten zu integrieren – von Los Angeles oder New York, wo Chris Jacobs sie an einen fiktiven Standort in Harlem verlegte. Jacobs führt aus: „Schließ deine Augen und stell dir ein 30-stöckiges zeitgenössisches Gebäude vor, das gebaut wurde, um echtes Grün zu präsentieren, mit geschosshohen Fenstern, spezieller technischer Ausstattung – überall Solarmodule. Stell es dir direkt neben einer Stadtautobahn vor, lass es als 24-Stunden-Fabrik hell von innen leuchten. Ein Leuchtfeuer grüner Technologie. Könnte dieser technisch anspruchsvolle ‚Greenscraper' zu einer neuen Art von Agro-Tourismus führen?" Trotz seiner Träume von einem Projekt in monumentaler Größenordnung räumt Jacobs ein, dass „eine zweistöckige Hydrokultur-Konstruktion auf einem mehrstöckigen Gebäude mit subventionierten Sozialbauwohnungen zu Anfang wohl der pragmatischere Weg wäre". Chris Jacobs hat die Chancen für ein solches Bauwerk in den USA sehr wohl durchdacht: Möglicherweise ließen sich Risikokapitalgeber und karitative Stiftungen überzeugen, Kosten zu übernehmen, um neue Arbeitsplätze zu schaffen und frisches Obst und Gemüse in die unterprivilegierten Innenstädte Amerikas zu bringen.

Le concept de ce projet de recherche est d'installer de vrais espaces agricoles au cœur des villes, de Los Angeles à New York où Jacobs imagine son implantation à Harlem. «Fermez les yeux et imaginez trente étages d'architecture contemporaine conçus pour montrer cette verdure authentique à travers des baies toute hauteur, des équipements spécialisés, y compris des panneaux solaires dans tous les sens. Placez-le tout près d'une autoroute, faites qu'on le voit de jour comme de nuit, brillamment éclairé de l'intérieur. Un concentré spectaculaire de technologie verte! Ce "gratte-vert" de haute technologie ne pourrait-il pas lancer un nouveau type d'agro-tourisme?» Tout en rêvant à ce projet à très grande échelle, Jacobs admet qu'«une structure hydroponique de deux niveaux au sommet d'un immeuble de logements accessibles à tous pourrait être un point de départ plus pragmatique». Il a réfléchi au potentiel d'une structure de ce type aux États-Unis, où les investisseurs et les fondations philanthropiques pourraient être convaincus de participer au coût de l'opération dans le but de créer des emplois et de fournir des produits frais aux habitants défavorisés des centres des villes.

Chris Jacobs addresses the question of just how agriculture might well enter the urban environment in a coherent way, assisted by an intelligent use of architecture.

Chris Jacobs setzt sich mit der Frage auseinander, wie sich Landwirtschaft dank intelligenter Architektur schlüssig in ein urbanes Umfeld integrieren lässt.

Chris Jacobs traite le problème de l'introduction éventuelle de l'agriculture dans un cadre urbain de manière cohérente, aidé par une mise en œuvre intelligente de l'architecture.

KEMPE THILL

Atelier Kempe Thill Architects and Planners
Van Nelleweg 8065, Building 8
3044 BC Rotterdam
The Netherlands

Tel: +31 10 750 37 07
Fax: +31 10 750 36 97
E-mail: info@atelierkempethill.com
Web: www.atelierkempethill.com

ANDRÉ KEMPE was born in 1968 in Freiberg, in former East Germany. He attended the Technical University in Dresden (1990–96) and did "Urban Studies" thereafter in Paris (1993–94) and in Tokyo (1994). He worked in the offices of Frits van Dongen (Amsterdam, 1996–97) and Karelse van der Meer (Rotterdam, 1997–2000), before co-founding Atelier Kempe Thill in Rotterdam (2000). **OLIVER THILL** was born in 1971 in Karl-Marx-Stadt (today Chemnitz), in former East Germany. He also attended the Technical University in Dresden (1990–96) before undertaking similar Urban Studies in Paris and Tokyo. He worked in the office of Frits van Dongen (1996–97) and DKV (Rotterdam, 1997–2000), before joining Kempe in the creation of their firm in 2000. Kempe Thill is specialized in public projects, housing, and urban planning. They seek to create "architecture that is neutral and inexpensive, as well as enjoyable and innovative." Their projects include the Hedge Building (Rostock, Germany, 2003, published here); a museum in Veenhuizen (2005–08); a housing estate (Zwolle, 2005–08); the Railwayline Building (Rotterdam, 2007–); Eco Housing (Tienen, Belgium, 2007–); the Confucius Tower (Amsterdam, 2008–); and the Drug Addict's Hotel (Amsterdam, 2008–), all in the Netherlands unless stated otherwise.

ANDRÉ KEMPE wurde 1968 in Freiberg, DDR, geboren. Er besuchte die Technische Universität Dresden (1990–96) und studierte Städtebau in Paris (1993–94) und Tokio (1994). Er arbeitete für Frits van Dongen (Amsterdam, 1996–97) und Karelse van der Meer (Rotterdam, 1997–2000), bevor er in Rotterdam das Atelier Kempe Thill mitbegründete (2000). **OLIVER THILL** wurde 1971 in Karl-Marx-Stadt (heute Chemnitz) geboren. Auch er besuchte die Technische Universität Dresden (1990–96), bevor er sich ähnlichen Studien wie Kempe in Paris und Tokio widmete. Er arbeitete für Frits van Dongen (1996–97) und DKV (Rotterdam, 1997–2000), bevor er mit André Kempe 2000 das gemeinsame Büro gründete. Kempe Thill ist auf öffentliche Bauten, Wohnungsbau und Stadtplanung spezialisiert. Ihr Ziel ist es, „Architektur zu gestalten, die sowohl neutral und erschwinglich als auch angenehm und innovativ ist". Zu ihren Projekten zählen u. a. der niederländische Pavillon für die Internationale Gartenbauausstellung in Rostock, das Hedge Building (2003, hier vorgestellt), ein Museum in Veenhuizen (2005–08), ein Sozialbauprojekt in Zwolle (2005–08), die Umnutzung von Gleisunterbauten (Rotterdam, 2007–), ein Ökohausprojekt (Tienen, Belgien, 2007–), der Confucius-Turm (Amsterdam, 2008–) sowie eine Unterkunft für Drogenabhängige (Amsterdam, 2008–), alle in den Niederlanden, sofern nicht anders vermerkt.

ANDRÉ KEMPE, né en 1968 à Freiberg, dans l'ex-Allemagne de l'Est, a étudié à l'université polytechnique de Dresde (1990–96) et effectué des études d'urbanisme à Paris (1993–94) et Tokyo (1994). Il a travaillé dans les agences de Frits van Dongen (Amsterdam, 1996–97) et de Karelse van der Meer (Rotterdam, 1997–2000), avant de fonder l'Atelier Kempe Thill à Rotterdam (2000). **OLIVER THILL**, né en 1971 à Karl-Marx-Stadt (aujourd'hui Chemnitz), ex-Allemagne de l'Est, a également étudié à l'université polytechnique de Dresde (1990–96) et effectué les mêmes études d'urbanisme à Paris et Tokyo. Il a travaillé dans les agences de Frits van Dongen (1996–97) et DKV (Rotterdam, 1997–2000), avant de rejoindre Kempe pour créer ensemble leur agence en 2000. Kempe Thill est spécialisée dans les projets publics, le logement et l'urbanisme. Elle cherche à créer une « architecture neutre et inexpressive, mais en même temps novatrice et agréable à vivre ». Parmi leurs réalisations : le Hedge Building (Rostock, Allemagne, 2003, publié ici) ; un musée à Veenhuizen (Pays-Bas, 2005–08) ; un ensemble de logements (Pays-Bas, Zwolle, 2005–08) ; l'immeuble de la gare (Rotterdam, 2007–) ; des logements écologiques (Tirlemont, Belgique, 2007–) ; la tour Confucius (Amsterdam, 2008–) et l'hôtel Drug Addict's (Amsterdam, 2008–).

HEDGE BUILDING

Rostock, Germany, 2003

Floor area: 200 m². Client: IBC Hillegom/NL. Cost: € 400 000.
Team: André Kempe, Cornelia Sailer, Ruud Smeelen, Oliver Thill, Takashi Nakamura.
Landscape Architect: Niek Roozen, Weesp, NL

This building served as the Dutch Pavilion at the IGA international garden exhibition in Rostock, Germany, and is now used as a cultural building by the city of Rostock. As the architects write: "The project demonstrates the logic and rationality of Dutch agriculture and unearths surprisingly romantic qualities within its limited conditions." The so-called smart screen, an ivy hedge grown in Dutch greenhouses in sections 1.2x1.8 meters in size, can be assembled in sections. Described by the architects as a pergola, the structure is outfitted precisely to allow these smart screens to be used as 10-meter-high green walls. A screen made of translucent plastic covers the interior. The architects insist on the "neutral" aspect of the design, which allows it to be used for different functions. They also insist on the ambiguity thus created between interior and exterior. "The result is a game played between inside and outside," they say. "The light from above makes the space feel like an interior, while the light entering through the hedges gives the space the character of an exterior space. What's more, the gentle sway of the leaves and their shadows enhances the perception of the space."

Der als niederländischer Pavillon auf der Internationalen Gartenbauausstellung (IGA) in Rostock realisierte Bau dient inzwischen als städtische Kultureinrichtung. Die Architekten schreiben: „Das Projekt veranschaulicht die Logik und Rationalität der niederländischen Landwirtschaft und entfaltet im Rahmen seiner begrenzten Möglichkeiten erstaunlich romantische Qualitäten." Der „smart screen", eine in niederländischen Gewächshäusern in 1,2 x 1,8 m großen Segmenten gezogene Efeuhecke lässt sich aus Einzelteilen montieren. Die von den Architekten als Pergola bezeichnete Konstruktion ermöglicht es, diese „smart screens" zu 10 m hohen grünen Mauern aufzurichten. Eine transparente Kunststoffdecke schützt den Raum. Besonders wichtig ist den Architekten die „Neutralität" des Entwurfs, der eine Nutzung für unterschiedlichste Zwecke erlaubt. Darüber hinaus betonen sie die Mehrdeutigkeit von Innen- und Außenraum: „Auf diese Weise ergibt sich ein Spiel zwischen Innen- und Außenraum. Durch die Belichtung von oben wirkt der Raum wie ein Innenraum, dabei verleiht das Licht, das seitlich durch die Hecken fällt, dem Inneren etwas von einem Außenraum. Hinzu kommt, dass das zarte Rascheln der Blätter und ihr Schattenspiel das Raumempfinden verstärkt."

Ce bâtiment a été le pavillon néerlandais pour l'exposition internationale de jardins IGA à Rostock en Allemagne où il sert maintenant de centre culturel. Comme le précise l'architecte : « Ce projet démontre la logique et la rationalité de l'agriculture néerlandaise et révèle des qualités étonnamment romantiques dans ses conditions de vie limitée. » L'ainsi nommé « écran intelligent », composé de haies de lierre venant de serres néerlandaises par section de 1,2 x 1,8 m, a été assemblé. Cette structure, présentée par les architectes comme une pergola, a été montée avec précision pour créer des murs verts de 10 m de haut. Un écran en plastique translucide vert recouvre l'intérieur. Les architectes insistent sur l'aspect « neutre » de cette installation, ce qui lui permet de remplir différentes fonctions et de créer une ambiguïté entre l'intérieur et l'extérieur. « C'est finalement un jeu entre l'intérieur et l'extérieur, disent-ils, la lumière tombant du haut donne l'impression que l'on se trouve à l'intérieur, tandis que celle qui pénètre par les haies donne à l'espace le caractère de salon extérieur. De plus, le léger balancement des feuilles et de leurs ombres accroît la perception de cet espace. »

The Hedge Building is almost more of a cage than it is a building, with its high walls filled out with an ivy screen. Here vegetation and architecture are united.

Das Hedge Building ist mit seinen hohen Wänden, in denen Efeurankgitter angebracht sind, fast mehr Käfig als Gebäude. Hier finden Vegetation und Architektur wirklich zueinander.

Le Hedge Building est autant une cage qu'un bâtiment. Ses hautes parois sont recouvertes de lierre : union de l'architecture et de la végétation.

KIERANTIMBERLAKE

KieranTimberlake
420 North 20th Street / Philadelphia, PA 19130.3828 / USA
Tel: +1 215 922 6600 / Fax: +1 215 922 4680
E-mail: kta@kierantimberlake.com / Web: www.kierantimberlake.com

Founded in Philadelphia in 1984 by Stephen Kieran and James Timberlake, **KIERANTIMBERLAKE** comprises a staff of 60. Kieran graduated from Yale University and got his M.Arch from the University of Pennsylvania. Timberlake graduated from the University of Detroit before receiving his M.Arch from the University of Pennsylvania. The firm's projects include programming, planning, and design of all types of new structures and their interiors; and the renovation, reuse, and conservation of existing structures. KieranTimberlake has received over 80 design awards, including the 2008 Architecture Firm Award from the American Institute of Architects. In 2003 the firm developed SmartWrapTM: The Building Envelope of the Future, a mass customizable, high-performance building façade that was initially exhibited at the Smithsonian Institution, Cooper-Hewitt National Design Museum. Structures completed in 2007 include: the Sculpture Building Gallery, Yale University (New Haven, Connecticut), and the Suzanne Roberts Theatre, Philadelphia Theatre Company (Philadelphia, Pennsylvania). Buildings by KieranTimberlake completed in 2008 include the Sidwell Friends Middle School (Washington, D. C., 2005–06, published here); and the Multi-Faith Center and Houghton Memorial Chapel Restoration, Wellesley College (Wellesley, Massachusetts). Currently in design are the Northwest Campus Student Housing, University of California (Los Angeles, California); the Center City Building, University of North Carolina at Charlotte (Charlotte, North Carolina); and the Morse and Stiles Colleges, Yale University (New Haven, Connecticut), all in the USA.

KIERANTIMBERLAKE wurde 1984 von Stephen Kieran und James Timberlake in Philadelphia gegründet und hat 60 Mitarbeiter. Kieran schloss sein Studium in Yale ab und erwarb seinen M.Arch. an der University of Pennsylvania. Timberlake machte seinen Abschluss an der University of Detroit und absolvierte seinen M.Arch. ebenfalls an der University of Pennsylvania. Das Büro befasst sich mit Programmentwicklung, Planung und Gestaltung von Neubauten aller Art und deren Innenraumgestaltung sowie der Sanierung, Umnutzung und Erhaltung von Altbauten. KieranTimberlake erhielt über 80 Designpreise, darunter den Architecture Firm Award 2008 des American Institute of Architects. 2003 entwickelte das Büro SmartWrapTM, die Gebäudehülle der Zukunft, eine technisch ausgeklügelte Gebäudefassade, die maßgeschneidert, aber in Massenfertigung hergestellt werden kann und erstmals im Cooper-Hewitt National Design Museum der Smithsonian Institution präsentiert wurde. Zu den 2007 realisierten Bauten zählen die Sculpture Building Gallery an der Yale University (New Haven, Connecticut) sowie das Suzanne Roberts Theatre für die Philadelphia Theatre Company (Philadelphia, Pennsylvania). 2008 wurden folgende Bauten bezugsfertig: die Sidwell Friends Middle School (Washington D. C., 2005–06, hier vorgestellt) sowie das Multi-Faith Center und die Sanierung der Houghton Memorial Chapel am Wellesley College (Wellesley, Massachusetts). In Planung sind derzeit ein Studentenwohnheim für den Northwest-Campus der University of California (Los Angeles), das Center City Building der University of North Carolina (Charlotte, North Carolina) sowie das Morse und das Stiles College, Yale University (New Haven, Connecticut), alle in den USA.

Fondée à Philadelphie en 1984 par Stephen Kieran et James Timberlake, l'agence **KIERANTIMBERLAKE** emploie 60 collaborateurs. Kieran est diplômé de Yale et M. Arch de l'université de Pennsylvanie. Timberlake, diplômé de l'université de Detroit, est également M. Arch de l'université de Pennsylvanie. L'agence se consacre à la programmation, l'urbanisme et la conception de tous types de constructions et à leurs aménagements intérieurs ainsi qu'à la rénovation, la réutilisation et la restauration de bâtiments existants. KieranTimberlake a reçu plus de 80 prix, dont celui de l'agence 2008 de l'Institut américain des architectes. En 2003, l'agence a créé SmartWrapTM, « L'enveloppe du bâtiment du futur », façade préfabriquée personnalisable à hautes performances qui a été présentée pour la première fois au Cooper-Hewitt National Design Museum à Washington. Parmi leurs réalisations : la Sculpture Building Gallery de l'université Yale (New Haven, Connecticut) et le théâtre Suzanne Roberts de la Philadelphia Theatre Company (Philadelphie, Pennsylvanie). Parmi leurs projets achevés très récemment : le collège de Sidwell Friends (Washington, D. C., 2005–06, publié ici) et la restauration du Centre œcuménique et du Houghton Memorial Chapel du Wellesley College (Wellesley, Massachusetts). Ils travaillent actuellement à divers projets : logements pour étudiants du Northwest Campus, université de Californie (Los Angeles, Californie) ; le Center City Building de l'université de Caroline du Nord (Charlotte, Caroline du Nord) et les Morse et Stiles Colleges, université Yale (New Haven, Connecticut), tous au États-Unis.

SIDWELL FRIENDS MIDDLE SCHOOL

Washington, D.C., USA, 2005–06

*Floor area: 3623 m² (addition); 3112 m² (renovation). Client: Sidwell Friends School. Cost: $21.5 million.
Collaboration: Andropogon Associates (Landscape), CVM Engineers (Structural Engineers),
Bruce E. Brooks & Associates (Mechanical Engineers)*

The architects have developed a master plan for this Quaker independent school that places a strong emphasis on environmental responsibility. A new building adds 3623 square meters to the existing facility. The building was awarded a LEED Platinum rating, the highest level of certification attainable from the USGBC, and it is the first school of its type in the United States to receive such a rating. Exterior sunscreens, and classrooms that place an emphasis on natural lighting, are part of the environmental strategy. Occupancy sensors and automatic dimmers reduce electricity consumption. Exterior walls of the addition and the third floor of the existing building are clad in recycled wood from red cedar fermentation barrels. Operable windows encourage the use of natural ventilation. Solar chimneys are designed for mechanically assisted natural ventilation to minimize the need for artificial cooling. A "wetland" zone integrated into the landscaping recycles building wastewater for future "graywater" use, thus reducing water consumption from municipal sources by 94%. A "vegetated roof" collects rainwater, and photovoltaic panels generate 5% of electrical requirements.

Für diese freie Quäkerschule entwickelten die Architekten einen Masterplan, der besonderen Wert auf ökologische Verantwortung legt. Ein Neubau erweitert die bestehende Schuleinrichtung um 3623 m². Das Gebäude wurde als erste Schule in den Vereinigten Staaten mit einer LEED-Platinmedaille ausgezeichnet, der höchstmöglichen Zertifizierungsstufe des USGBC. Teil des ökologischen Konzepts sind Sonnenschutzvorrichtungen an der Außenfassade und den Klassenräumen, die besonders auf natürliche Belichtung hin ausgelegt sind. Infrarotsensoren und automatische Dimmer reduzieren den Stromverbrauch. Die Außenmauern des Anbaus und der dritte Stock des Altbaus wurden mit Holz von recycelten Fässern aus Riesenlebensbaum verblendet. Fenster, die sich öffnen lassen, fördern die natürliche Belüftung. Zusätzlich wurden Solarkamine installiert, um die mechanische natürliche Belüftung zu unterstützen und den Bedarf an künstlicher Kühlung zu minimieren. Ein in das Gelände integriertes „Feuchtgebiet" soll Brauchwasser aus den Gebäuden aufbereiten, um das „Grauwasser" in Zukunft nutzen zu können, wodurch sich der Wasserbedarf aus städtischen Quellen um 94 % senken lässt. Ein begrüntes Dach sammelt Regenwasser, Solarzellen generieren 5 % des Strombedarfs.

Les architectes ont conçu pour cette école quaker un plan qui met un fort accent sur la responsabilité environnementale. Le nouveau bâtiment de 3623 m² complète des installations existantes. Il a reçu la certification LEED Platine, le plus haut niveau accordé par l'USGBC, et est la première école de ce type aux États-Unis à le recevoir. Les écrans extérieurs et les salles de classe qui bénéficient fortement de l'éclairage naturel relèvent de la stratégie environnementale retenue. Des capteurs d'occupation des locaux et des rhéostats automatiques réduisent la consommation d'électricité. Les murs extérieurs du nouveau bâtiment et le troisième niveau des constructions existantes sont habillés de bois recyclé venant de barriques de fermentation en cèdre rouge. Des fenêtres ouvrables encouragent le recours à la ventilation naturelle. Des cheminées solaires facilitent mécaniquement les flux d'air pour réduire les besoins en climatisation. Une zone de lagunage a été intégrée dans les aménagements paysagers pour recycler les eaux usées, ce qui réduit la consommation de l'eau du réseau municipal de 94 %. Un toit végétalisé recueille l'eau de pluie et des panneaux photovoltaïques produisent 5 % de l'électricité consommée.

The addition to this prestigious school by the architects provides a large efficient volume with a clear emphasis on environmental concerns.

Der Anbau an die renommierte Schule ist ein großer, effizienter Baukörper, der dabei ausdrücklich ökologische Belange berücksichtigt.

L'extension de cette prestigieuse école est un vaste volume efficace conçu qui met clairement l'accent sur ses ambitions écologiques.

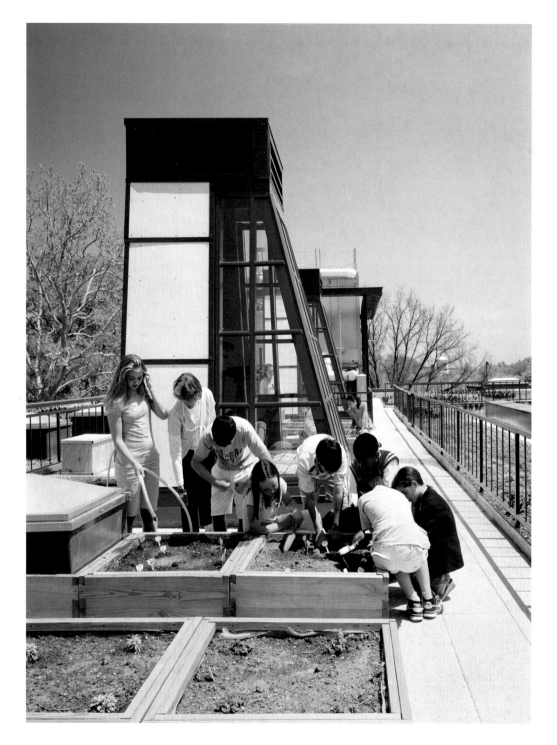

Roottop planters allow young students to be educated not only about plants but also about environmental concerns and ways to address them.

Pflanzkübel auf dem Dach erlauben nicht nur, die Schüler an Pflanzen heranzuführen, sondern ebenso an Umweltfragen und Möglichkeiten, wie man diesen gerecht werden kann.

Les jardinières du toit permettent aux élèves d'être sensibilisés non seulement à la culture des plantes mais aussi aux préoccupations environnementales et aux façons d'y répondre.

The bright, open classrooms seem
very much in harmony with banks
of solar arrays seen to the right.

Die hellen offenen Klassenzimmer
scheinen hervorragend mit den auf-
gereihten Solarmodulen auf dem
Dach (rechts) zu harmonieren.

Les salles de cours largement ouvertes
paraissent en harmonie avec les
installations de panneaux solaires
(à droite).

RAFAEL DE LA-HOZ

Rafael de La-Hoz Arquitectos
Paseo de la Castellana, 82–2ºA / 28046 Madrid / Spain
Tel: +34 91 745 35 00 / Fax: +34 91 561 78 03
E-mail: estudio@rafaeldelahoz.com / Web: www.rafaeldelahoz.com

Born in Córdoba in 1955, **RAFAEL DE LA-HOZ** studied Architecture at the ETSA in Madrid and got his M.Arch degree from the city's Polytechnic University (1981). His recent built work includes: "Encina Real," 60 housing units in Encinar de los Reyes (2002); the headquarters of Vodafone (Madrid, 2002); the "Parque Norte" (Madrid, 2001) and "Bilma" Business Parks (Madrid, 2003); the main offices of Endesa (Madrid, 2003); special planning for the high speed train at Vigo Airport (Vigo, 2004); the Headquarters of the Chamber of Commerce in Madrid (2004); the Master Plan for Vilamoura (Algarve, Portugal, 2004); the Pentax offices (Madrid, 2004); the BMW Dealership (Madrid, 2005); the main offices of the Madrid legal firm Uría & Menéndez (2005); the Municipal Meeting facilities of the District of Retiro (Madrid, 2004); the Auditorium of the Spanish Olympic Committee (Madrid, 2005); the sustainable office building "Pórtico" (Madrid, 2005); offices of the Madrid legal firm Garrigues (2004–06); District C of Telefónica (Madrid, 2002–07, published here); and "Rafael del Pino" Foundation offices (Madrid, 2001–08). As well as winning the competition for Chamartín Island Tower (Madrid, 2008–11), his current work includes the Hércules Towers in "Los Barrios" (Cádiz, 2005–09); lecture rooms for the University of Córdoba (2005–09); a sports complex in Central Bus Station (Granada, 2006–09); "El Paraíso" Foundation (Córdoba, 2007–09); Gran Via 48 (Madrid, 2007–09); building for the Juvenile Court (Madrid, 2007–10); AMA Headquarters (Madrid, 2007–10); Repsol Headquarters (Madrid, 2008–10); Residential Complex and Hotels (Warsaw, Poland, 2007–11); Extension for the Vilamoura Marina (Algarve, Portugal, 2008–11); and a building for the Criminal Court (Madrid, 2008–11).

RAFAEL DE LA-HOZ wurde 1955 in Córdoba geboren. Er studierte zunächst Architektur an der ETSAM in Madrid und erwarb einen M.Arch. an der Polytechnischen Hochschule von Madrid (1981). Jüngere realisierte Bauten sind u. a. „Encina Real", 60 Wohneinheiten in Encinar de los Reyes (2002), die Verwaltungszentrale für Vodafone (Madrid, 2002), die Gewerbegebiete „Parque Norte" (Madrid, 2001) und „Bilma" (Madrid, 2003), die Verwaltungszentrale für Endesa (Madrid, 2003), Spezialplanungen für den Hochgeschwindigkeitszug am Flughafen Vigo (Vigo, 2004), die Hauptniederlassung der Handelskammer in Madrid (2004), der Masterplan für Vilamoura (Algarve, Portugal, 2004), ein Bürogebäude für Pentax (Madrid, 2004), die BMW-Niederlassung (Madrid, 2005), das Hauptbüro der Anwaltskanzlei Uría & Menéndez (Madrid, 2005), das Stadtratsgebäude für den Madrider Bezirk Retiro (Madrid, 2004), der Versammlungssaal des spanischen Olympischen Komitees (Madrid, 2005), das umweltfreundliche Bürogebäude „Pórtico" (Madrid, 2005), Büros für die Madrider Anwaltskanzlei Garrigues (2004–06), der Distrito C für Telefónica (Madrid, 2002–07, hier vorgestellt) sowie Büros für die Stiftung Rafael del Pino (Madrid, 2001–08). Aktuelle Projekte sind neben einem gewonnenen Wettbewerb für das Hochhaus Isla Chamartín (Madrid, 2008–11) das Hércules-Hochhaus in „Los Barrios" (Cádiz, 2005–09), Hörsäle für die Universität Córdoba (2005–09), ein Sportkomplex im Zentralen Busbahnhof (Granada, 2006–09), die Stiftung El Paraíso (Córdoba, 2007–09), das Gebäude Gran Vía 48 (Madrid, 2007–09), ein Neubau für das Jugendgericht (Madrid, 2007–10), die AMA-Hauptverwaltung (Madrid, 2007–10), die neue Hauptniederlassung für Repsol (Madrid, 2008–10), ein Wohnbaukomplex mit Hotels in Warschau (2007–11), der Erweiterungsplan für den Jachthafen in Vilamoura (Algarve, Portugal, 2008–11) und ein Neubau für das Strafgericht in Madrid (2008–11).

Né à Cordoue en 1955, **RAFAEL DE LA-HOZ** a étudié architecture à l'ETSA à Madrid et a obtenu son M. Arch de l' Université polytechnique de la même ville (1981). Parmi ses réalisations: «Encina Real», 60 logements à Encinar de los Reyes (2002) ; le siège de Vodafone (Madrid, 2002) ; les parcs d'affaires «Parque Norte» (Madrid, 2001) et «Bilma» (Madrid, 2003) ; les bureaux d'Endesa (Madrid, 2003) ; la planification du TGV à l'aéroport de Vigo (2004) ; le siège de la Chambre de commerce de Madrid (2004) ; le plan directeur de Vilamoura (Algarve, Portugal, 2004) ; les bureaux de Pentax (Madrid, 2004) ; la concession principale BMW (Madrid, 2005) ; le siège du cabinet juridique madrilène Uría & Menéndez (2005) ; des installations municipales dans le quartier du Retiro (Madrid, 2004) ; l'auditorium du Comité olympique espagnol (Madrid, 2005) ; un immeuble «vert», le Pórtico (Madrid, 2005) ; les bureaux du cabinet juridique madrilène Garrigues (2004–06) ; les bureaux «District C» de Telefónica (Madrid, 2002–07, publié ici) et les bureaux de la Fondation Rafael del Pino (Madrid, 2001–08). Parmi les projets en cours, la tour de l'île de Chamartín (Madrid, 2008–11) ; les tours Hércules à «Los Barrios» (Cádiz, 2005–09) ; un bâtiment de salles de conférences pour l'université de Cordoue (2005–09) ; un complexe sportif dans la gare routière (Grenade, 2006–09) ; la Fondation «El Paraíso» (Cordoue, 2007–09) ; l'immeuble Gran Via 48 (Madrid, 2007–09) ; le nouveau bâtiment du tribunal pour enfants (Madrid, 2007–10) ; le siège d'AMA (Madrid, 2007–10) ; le nouveau siège de Repsol (Madrid, 2008–10) ; un complexe résidentiel et hôtelier (Varsovie, Pologne, 2007–11) ; l'extension de la marina de Vilamoura (Algarve, Portugal, 2008–11) et un nouveau bâtiment pour la Cour criminelle de Madrid (2008–11).

TELEFÓNICA DISTRICT C

Las Tablas, Madrid, Spain, 2002–07

Floor area: 390 000 m². Client: Telefónica de España SA. Cost: €490 million.
Team: Hugo Berenguer, Francisco Arévalo, Siegfried Bürger

The District C buildings are very large in scale, a fact that belies their landscaping and division into distinct volumes, which are nonetheless joined together by the large canopy roofs.

Die Bauten des Distrito C sind ungewöhnlich groß, ein Eindruck, der durch die landschaftliche Gestaltung und die Aufteilung des Komplexes in einzelne, durch monumentale Baldachindächer miteinander verbundene Baukörper gemildert wird.

Les bâtiments du District C sont de très vastes dimensions, que font presque oublier les aménagements paysagers et leur division en volumes séparés mais néanmoins reliés par d'immenses auvents.

As part of its corporate strategy, the Telefónica Group, the largest company in Spain, decided to build a new headquarters in order to bring together all of its companies and divisions, which were previously spread in different locations in Madrid. The site selected measures 19 hectares, has its own subway station, and is intended for up to 12 000 employees. The program required at least ten buildings measuring between three and 11 stories, with each floor offering at least 2500 square meters of space. The architect chose to make glass the predominant visible material, and to base the composition on a square grid, with a linking landscape. Very large, high roof canopies cover large parts of the complex. According to the architect: "None of the buildings actually imposes its identity on the rest; instead, each building submits its volume to the whole, just as all the buildings are protected under the same canopy that unifies them and brings them together." Clear glass with a strict pattern of silk-screen dots that make it appear opaque from the interior, while users can still see out with little impression that the glass is even tinted, is used with different degrees of opacity throughout the complex in 4x2 meter panes. With glass fins set at right angles to the façades, angular shadows play across the surface of the buildings in patterns dictated by the movements of the sun. Indeed, the strong sun of Madrid is an essential element in the sustainability strategy of the architect. Rafael de La-Hoz writes: "Finally and fundamentally, the roof is photovoltaic, constituting the largest horizontal surface for collecting solar energy in Europe. The solar panels that cover 26 000 square meters of the top of the canopy, transform solar thermal energy into electricity, at the rate of 4 389 000 kWh/year, which represents a reduction of 2000 tons of CO_2 emitted into the atmosphere. The roof's shadow, cast over the façades, cloisters and entrances, unifies and protects."

Aus firmenpolitischen Gründen beschloss die Telefónica-Gruppe, das größte Unternehmen Spaniens, einen neuen Hauptsitz zu bauen, in dem alle Unterfirmen und Abteilungen zusammengelegt werden sollten, die bis dato über verschiedene Standorte in Madrid verstreut waren. Das ausgewählte Grundstück hat eine Größe von 19 ha, eine eigene U-Bahnstation und wird 12 000 Angestellten Platz bieten. Das Programm erforderte mindestens zehn drei- bis elfstöckige Gebäude mit je 2500 m² Geschossfläche. Der Architekt entschied sich für Glas als dominierendes sichtbares Baumaterial und gestaltete den Entwurf auf Grundlage eines quadratischen Rasters, in das er landschaftliche Elemente integrierte. Monumentale hohe Baldachindächer überspannen weite Teile des Komplexes. Der Architekt erklärt: „Keiner der Einzelbauten stellt mit seinem Profil die übrigen Gebäude in den Schatten, vielmehr trägt jedes Gebäude mit seinem Volumen zum Ganzen bei, ebenso werden die Gebäude von einem Baldachindach geschützt, das sie eint und zusammenführt." Im gesamten Komplex wurden 4 x 2 m große Klarglastafeln mit einem strengen Muster aus Siebdruckpunkten eingesetzt, das das Glas von innen opak und dennoch kaum getönt erscheinen lässt, wobei der Opazitätsgrad variiert. Lotrecht zur Fassade stehende Glaselemente lassen je nach Sonnenstand scharfkantige Schatten über die Fassaden spielen. Das intensive Sonnenlicht in Madrid ist ein wesentliches Element in der nachhaltigen Strategie des Architekten. Rafael de La-Hoz schreibt: „Von entscheidender Bedeutung ist schließlich das Fotovoltaikdach, insgesamt die größte horizontale Fläche zur Erzeugung von Solarenergie in ganz Europa. Die Solarmodule, die 26 000 m² Dachfläche bedecken, erzeugen durch Sonnenenergie 4 389 000 kWh Strom pro Jahr, was einer Reduzierung der CO_2-Emissionen in die Atmosphäre um 2000 t gleichkommt. Der auf die Fassaden, ‚Kreuzgänge' und Eingänge fallende Schatten des Dachs wirkt einend und schützend zugleich."

Dans le cadre de sa stratégie institutionnelle, le groupe Telefónica, la plus grande entreprise espagnole, a décidé d'édifier un nouveau siège afin de rassembler ses multiples sociétés et divisions dispersées dans Madrid. Le site de 19 ha a sa propre station de métro et a été conçu pour accueillir 12 000 employés. Le programme portait sur au moins dix immeubles de trois à onze niveaux, chaque niveau offrant 2500 m² chacun de surface au minimum. L'architecte a décidé de faire du verre le matériau dominant et d'appuyer sa composition sur une trame carrée et des aménagements paysagers qui unifient l'ensemble. D'importants auvents de grande hauteur recouvrent une vaste partie du complexe. Selon l'architecte : « Aucun immeuble n'impose son identité par rapport aux autres. Au contraire, chacun est soumis aux volumes de l'ensemble, de même que tous sont protégés par un même auvent qui les regroupe et les unifie. » Les panneaux de verre clair de 4 x 2 m sont sérigraphiés de pastilles qui les font sembler opaques, depuis l'extérieur, mais restent translucides et légèrement teintées, depuis l'intérieur. Leur degré d'opacité varie selon l'exposition au soleil. Des ailettes de verre verticales perpendiculaires aux façades créent des jeux d'ombres anguleux sur les façades selon la course du soleil. Particulièrement fort à Madrid, celui-ci est un élément essentiel de la stratégie de durabilité adoptée par l'architecte. Rafael de La-Hoz explique : « Très important, le toit photovoltaïque est la plus grande surface horizontale de captation de l'énergie solaire mise en œuvre en Europe. Les panneaux solaires, qui couvrent 26 000 m² de l'auvent, transforment l'énergie thermique en électricité au taux de 4 389 000 kWh par an, soit une diminution de 2000 tonnes de rejets de CO_2 dans l'atmosphère. L'ombre de la toiture se projette sur les façades, les patios et les entrées. Elle unifie et protège. »

The glass fins that protrude at right angles to a number of the façades reduce solar gain and also create varied patterns on the building according to the movement of the sun.

Glasgrate, die lotrecht aus den Fassaden einzelner Bauten herausragen, reduzieren den Wärmegewinn und lassen zudem je nach Sonnenstand unterschiedlichste Muster über die Fassaden spielen.

Les ailettes de verre qui se projettent perpendiculairement d'un certain nombre de façades réduisent le gain solaire et créent des effets visuels variés selon la course du soleil.

MICHAEL B. LEHRER

Lehrer Architects
2140 Hyperion Avenue
Los Angeles, CA 90027–4708
USA

Tel: + 1 323 664 4747
Fax: + 1 323 664 3566
E-mail: architect@lehrerarchitects.com
Web: www.lehrerarchitects.com

MICHAEL B. LEHRER received a B.A. degree from the College of Environmental Design, UC Berkeley, in 1975. He received his M.Arch degree at the Harvard GSD in 1978. Michael B. Lehrer worked as a Senior Project Architect in the office of Frank O. Gehry (1984–85), and created his own firm, Lehrer Architects, in 1985. He is an Adjunct Associate Professor of Architecture at the University of Southern California, School of Architecture, and President of the American Institute of Architects Los Angeles. His work includes the Water + Life Museums Campus (Hemet, 2001–06, published here); his own office in Los Angeles (2006), a converted warehouse that won an AIA National Honor Award; Registrar Recorder Clerk, County of Los Angeles (Los Angeles, 2008); Westwood United Methodist Church Master Plan (Los Angeles, 2009); Canyon Residence (Santa Monica, 2009); Westside Jewish Community Center Natatorium (Los Angeles, 2009); and Lofts on Croft Court (West Hollywood, 2010), all in California, USA.

MICHAEL B. LEHRER schloss sein Studium am College of Environmental Design in Berkeley 1975 mit einem B.A. ab. Seinen M.Arch. erhielt er 1978 an der Harvard Graduate School of Design. Michael B. Lehrer war als leitender Projektarchitekt bei Frank O. Gehry tätig (1984–85) und gründete 1985 sein eigenes Büro, Lehrer Architects. Er ist außerordentlicher Professor für Architektur an der Universität von Southern California und Präsident des American Institute of Architects Los Angeles. Zu seinen Projekten zählen der Water + Life Museums Campus (Hemet, 2001–06, hier vorgestellt), seine eigenen Büroräume in Los Angeles (2006), ein umgebautes Lagerhaus, ausgezeichnet mit dem AIA National Honor Award, das Amtsgebäude des Registrar Recorder Clerk für Los Angeles (Los Angeles, 2008), der Masterplan für die Westwood United Methodist Church (Los Angeles, 2009), die Canyon Residence (Santa Monica, 2009), die Schwimmhalle des Gemeindezentrums der Westside Jewish Community (Los Angeles, 2009) sowie Lofts am Croft Court (West Hollywood, 2010), alle in Kalifornien.

MICHAEL B. LEHRER est B.A. du College of Environmental Design d'UC Berkeley (1975) et a passé son M. Arch à la Harvard GSD en 1978. Il a travaillé comme architecte de projet senior chez Frank O. Gehry (1984–85) et crée son agence, Lehrer Architects, en 1985. Il est professeur adjoint d'architecture à l'École d'architecture de l'université de Californie du Sud, et président de l'Institut américain des architectes à Los Angeles. Parmi ses réalisations : le Water + Life Museums Campus (Hemet, 2001–06, publié ici) ; ses propres bureaux à Los Angeles (2006), la conversion d'un entrepôt qui a remporté un Prix d'honneur national de l'AIA ; le siège du Registrar Recorder Clerk du comté de Los Angeles (Los Angeles, 2008) ; le plan directeur de l'église méthodiste unifiée de Westwood (Los Angeles, 2009) ; la résidence Canyon (Santa Monica, 2009) ; le Westside Jewish Community Center Natatorium (Los Angeles, 2009) et les Lofts sur Croft Court (West Hollywood, 2010), toutes en Californie.

WATER + LIFE MUSEUMS CAMPUS

Hemet, California, USA, 2001–06

*Floor area: 6340 m². Client: The Center for Water Education and Western Center for Archeology and Paleontology.
Cost: $40 million. Collaboration: Mark Gangi, AIA, Lehrer + Gangi Design + Build*

Built on a 6.9-hectare site near Diamond Valley Lake, the program for this project required the design of "an engaging museum campus that celebrates the link between southern California's water infrastructure and the evolution of life. Phase 1 of the campus includes two museums, laboratories, classrooms, administrative offices, support facilities, gift shop, café, and interpretive/educational landscape." The program further stipulated that the architecture should be a "living example of sustainability and conservation." The design with five 12-meter-high steel towers was inspired by architecture created for the Los Angeles Metropolitan Water District, such as Gordon B. Kaufman's pump buildings at the Parker Dam near Lake Havasu. The complex was the first museum to receive a LEED Platinum rating, the highest bestowed by the USGBC. Abundant natural light is used, and a 540-kilowatt, 3000-panel photovoltaic installation provides the complex with almost half of its total power needs. Heat-blocking glass and a network of electronic sensing devices and timers optimize energy consumption, while heating and cooling are run through a sophisticated mechanical system of radiant flooring and forced-air units.

Das Programm für dieses Projekt, das unweit des Diamond Valley Lake auf einem 6,9 ha großen Gelände liegt, erforderte den Entwurf „eines lebendigen Museumscampus, der sich mit der Wasserversorgung Südkaliforniens ebenso wie mit der Evolutionsgeschichte auseinandersetzt. Die erste Bauphase des Campus umfasst zwei Museen, Labors, Lehrräume, Verwaltungsbüros, technische Einrichtungen, einen Museumsshop, ein Café sowie eine suggestive/bildungsorientierte Landschaftsgestaltung". Darüber hinaus forderte das Programm eine Architektur als „lebendiges Beispiel für Nachhaltigkeit und Naturschutz". Der Entwurf mit seinen fünf 12 m hohen Stahltürmen wurde von Bauten des Los Angeles Metropolitan Water District inspiriert, etwa den Pumpenhäusern von Gordon B. Kaufman am Parker-Staudamm in der Nähe von Lake Havasu. Der Komplex wurde als erstes Museum mit einer LEED-Platinmedaille ausgezeichnet, der höchstmöglichen vom US Green Building Council verliehenen Auszeichnung. Das außerordentlich helle Licht wird für natürliche Belichtung genutzt, 3000 Solarmodule mit einer Leistung von je 540 kW versorgen den Komplex mit nahezu 50 % seines Energiebedarfs. Wärmeschutzverglasung und ein Netzwerk elektronischer Sensoren optimieren den Stromverbrauch. Heizung und Kühlung erfolgen über ein ausgeklügeltes System aus Fußbodenheizung und Luftschächten.

Réalisé sur un terrain de 6,9 ha près du lac de Diamond Valley, ce projet répond à un programme précis de création d'« un musée séduisant qui célèbre le lien entre les infrastructures hydrauliques californiennes et l'évolution de la vie. La Phase 1 du campus comprend deux musées, des laboratoires, des salles de cours, des bureaux administratifs, des installations techniques, une boutique, un café et un environnement paysager aménagé pour l'interprétation et l'éducation ». Il stipulait également que l'architecture devait être « un exemple vivant de durabilité et de préservation ». La conception des cinq tours d'acier de 12 m de haut s'inspire des réalisations architecturales du Los Angeles Metropolitan Water District, et en particulier des bâtiments des pompes de Gordon B. Kaufman pour le barrage Parker près du lac Havasu. Le complexe a été le premier musée à recevoir la certification LEED Platine, le plus haut niveau accordé par l'US Green Building Council. L'éclairage naturel est privilégié et une installation de 3000 panneaux photovoltaïques de 540 kW fournit près de la moitié de la consommation électrique du complexe. Des verres thermiques et un réseau de capteurs électroniques et de minuteries optimisent la consommation d'électricité tandis que le chauffage et le refroidissement sont fournis par un système mécanique sophistiqué de sols radiants et d'unités à air pulsé.

This complex makes it clear that green design can go hand-in-hand with crisp, modern forms.

Dieser Komplex macht deutlich, dass grünes Design Hand in Hand gehen kann mit klarer moderner Formgebung.

Ce complexe montre clairement qu'une conception écologique peut aller de pair avec des formes modernes.

The vertical blocks of the building, divided into two groups of five, form a strong horizontal continuity that was inspired by California dam design.

Die vertikalen Blöcke, die in zwei Fünfergruppen angeordnet sind, bilden ein ausdrucksstarkes horizontales Kontinuum, das vom kalifornischen Staudammbau inspiriert wurde.

Les blocs verticaux, divisés en deux groupes de cinq, présentent une forte continuité horizontale inspirée des barrages californiens.

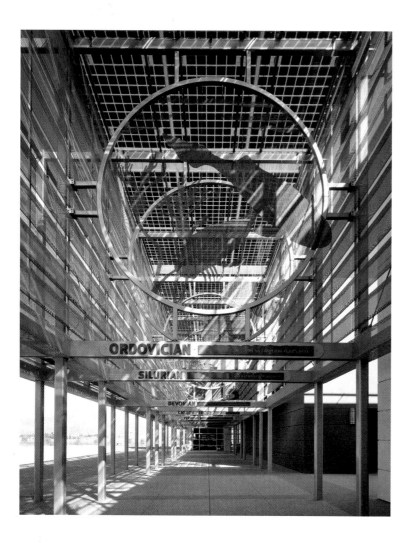

The complex is defined by repetitive
volumes, alternating between light
and more opaque, heavier elements.

Der Komplex ist von sich wiederho-
lenden Volumina und einem Wechsel
heller und dunkler, schwererer Elemente geprägt.

Le complexe est défini par des
masses répétées, alternant des éléments légers et d'autres plus lourds
et plus opaques.

Vast surfaces covered by photovoltaic cells are visible in the image above, which also emphasizes the industrial origin of the architectural vocabulary.

Das Bild oben zeigt weitläufige Solarmodulfelder, was die industriellen Wurzeln der architektonischen Formensprache zusätzlich betont.

Les importantes étendues de panneaux solaires photovoltaïques visibles ci-dessus expriment également l'origine industrielle du ton architectural employé.

MIII ARCHITECTEN

MIII architecten
Generaal Berenschotlaan 211–213
2283 JM Rijswijk
The Netherlands

Tel: +31 70 394 43 49
Fax: +31 70 394 42 34
E-mail: info@m3architecten.com
Web: www.m3architecten.com

MIII ARCHITECTEN is an architectural design firm created in 1990 in Rijswijk, the Netherlands, and directed by Leendert Steijger, Edwin Smit, and Remko van Buren. Leendert Steijger, born in 1961 in Delft, attended the Faculty of Architecture of the Technical University in Delft (1981–90). He was Assistant Designer at the architectural office of Hoogstad Weeber en Van Tilburg and worked as an architect at KOW architects, before co-founding MIII in 1990. Edwin Smit was born in 1963 in Hoorn. He attended the Faculty of Architecture of the Technical University in Delft (1981–88) and worked in several architectural offices, including Broek & Bakema, before co-founding MIII. Remko van Buren was born in Sittard in 1966, attended the Faculty of Architectural Design at the Academy of Art and Design, St. Joost, Breda (1982–87), and gained experience in the office of Morphosis in Santa Monica, before working in the Netherlands (1987–99). He became a partner of MIII in 1999. Their design of the Quantum Homes gave them in the Netherlands the status of pioneers in the area of sustainable building. Their work includes the Environmental Education Center (Hoorn, 2001–03, published here); a housing project in Zoetermeer (2005); a Waterfront Restaurant (Capelle a/d IJssel, 2007); the Chess Office Building (Haarlem, 2008); and a district police station (Utrecht, 2008). Current projects are a facility center and hotel at Eindhoven Airport (2009), and housing projects in the Hague and Amsterdam (2009), all in the Netherlands.

MIII ARCHITECTEN ist ein 1990 in Rijswijk in den Niederlanden gegründetes Architekturbüro unter der Leitung von Leendert Steijger, Edwin Smit und Remko van Buren. Leendert Steijger, geboren 1961 in Delft, besuchte von 1981 bis 1990 die Fakultät für Architektur der Technischen Universität Delft. Anschließend war der Assistent-Designer im Architekturbüro Hoogstad Weeber en Van Tilburg. Bevor er 1990 MIII mitgründete, arbeitete er als Architekt bei KOW Architecture. Edwin Smit wurde 1963 in Hoorn geboren. Er studierte Architektur an der Technischen Universität Delft (1981–88) und war in verschiedenen Architekturbüros tätig, darunter auch Broek & Bakema, bevor er MIII mitgründete. Remko van Buren wurde 1966 in Sittard geboren, studierte Architektur an der Akademie für Kunst und Design St. Joost in Breda (1982–87) und arbeitete für Morphosis in Santa Monica, bevor er verschiedentlich in den Niederlanden tätig war (1987–99). 1999 wurde auch er Partner bei MIII. Der Entwurf der Quantum Homes machte MIII in den Niederlanden als Pioniere für nachhaltiges Bauen bekannt. Zu ihren Projekten zählen das Umweltbildungszentrum (Hoorn, 2001–03, hier vorgestellt), eine Wohnanlage in Zoetermeer (2005), ein Restaurant am Meer (Capelle aan den IJssel, 2007), das Bürogebäude Chess (Haarlem, 2008) sowie ein Polizeirevier (Utrecht, 2008). Aktuelle Projekte sind u. a. ein Funktionsgebäude und ein Hotel am Flughafen Eindhoven (2009) sowie Wohnbauprojekte in Den Haag und Amsterdam (2009), alle in den Niederlanden.

MIII ARCHITECTEN est une agence d'architecture créée en 1990 à Rijswijk, Pays-Bas, dirigée par Leendert Steijger, Edwin Smit et Remko van Buren. Leendert Steijger, né en 1961 à Delft a étudié à la faculté d'architecture de l'Université Polytechnique de Delft (1981–90). Il a été concepteur assistant dans l'agence Hoogstad Weeber en Van Tilburg et travaillé comme architecte chez KOW Architects avant de co-fonder MIII en 1990. Edwin Smit, né en 1963 à Hoorn, à étudié à la faculté d'architecture de l'Université Polytechnique de Delft (1981–88) et travaillé dans plusieurs agences, dont Broek & Bakema, avant de cofonder MIII. Remko van Buren, né à Sittard en 1966, a étudié à la faculté d'architecture de l'Académie d'art et de design de St. Joost à Breda (1982–87), et travaillé chez Morphosis à Santa Monica, puis dans plusieurs agences aux Pays-Bas (1987–99). Il est associé de MIII depuis 1999. Leur projet pour les Quantum Homes a fait d'eux des pionniers de la construction durable dans leur pays. Parmi leurs réalisations : le Centre d'éducation environnementale (Hoorn, 2001–03, publié ici) ; un projet d'immeuble de logements à Zoetermeer (2005) ; un restaurant en front de mer (Capelle a/d IJssel, 2007) ; l'immeuble de bureaux Chess (Haarlem, 2008) ; et un commissariat de police de quartier (Utrecht, 2008). Actuellement, ils travaillent sur les projets d'un hôtel et centre de services à l'aéroport d'Eindhoven (2009) et des immeubles de logements à La Haye et à Amsterdam (2009), le tout aux Pays-Bas.

ENVIRONMENTAL EDUCATION CENTER

Hoorn, The Netherlands, 2001–03

Floor area: 511 m². Client: City of Hoorn. Cost: € 500 000

"For this project," according to the architects, "by order of the local government, the premise was to create a presence close to 'no intervention' in the landscape." Approximately 85% of the building is covered with a thick layer of soil, meaning that it disappears partially, and takes advantage of a particularly efficient form of natural insulation. A single, large, curved window emerges on one side, where there is a pond, and visitors are invited to observe the underwater habitat. On the opposite side of the structure, a single concrete door is incised into the hill that forms the visible volume of the structure. The architects write: "Ecological considerations affect the design, as well as the positioning of required functions, the technologies used, the building physics, and the choice of materials, in order to establish a coherent presence within the original scenery." In a sense, this is an extreme example of ecological and landscape considerations dictating the form of an architectural realization.

„Die Vorgaben der Kommunalregierung für dieses Projekt" hatten es den Architekten zufolge „zur Bedingung gemacht, einen Bau zu schaffen, der so gut wie ‚keinen Eingriff' in die Landschaft darstellte." Rund 85 % des Gebäudes sind mit einer dicken Erdschicht bedeckt, sodass der Bau teilweise verschwindet und zugleich von der besonders effizienten, natürlichen Dämmweise profitiert. Auf einer Seite, zum Teich hin, befindet sich ein großes, gewölbtes Fenster, durch das die Besucher das Leben unter Wasser beobachten können. Auf der gegenüberliegenden Seite des Baus wurde eine einzelne Betontür in den Hügel eingelassen, der das sichtbare Volumen des Gebäudes ausmacht. Die Architekten schreiben: „Einfluss auf den Entwurf hatten sowohl ökologische Überlegungen als auch die Positionierung der erforderlichen Funktionen, die zum Einsatz gebrachte Technik, die Bauphysik sowie die Materialwahl, um eine schlüssige Erscheinung in der ursprünglichen Landschaft gestalten zu können." In gewisser Weise ist dies ein Extrembeispiel, wie ökologische und landschaftliche Überlegungen die formale Gestaltung eines architektonischen Entwurfs diktieren können.

« À la demande de la municipalité, expliquent les architectes, les nouvelles constructions se devaient d'avoir dans le paysage une présence proche de la "non-intervention". » Environ 85 % du bâtiment sont recouverts d'une épaisse couche de terre qui le fait disparaître en partie et assure une forme naturelle et efficace d'isolation. Une grande et unique fenêtre sur un côté donne sur un étang, et les visiteurs sont invités à observer le biotope aquatique. Sur l'autre façade, une unique porte de béton est découpée dans la colline que forme le volume de la structure. « Les considérations écologiques ont influé sur le projet, ainsi que le positionnement des fonctions prédéfinies, les technologies utilisées, les contraintes physiques du bâti et le choix des matériaux afin d'établir une présence cohérente avec le paysage d'origine », précise l'agence. En un sens, il s'agit d'un exemple extrême dans lequel les considérations écologiques et paysagères ont dicté la forme d'une réalisation architecturale.

The form of the building is integrated into the landscape with the rather traditional device of the green roof here functioning as a central part of the architectural design.

Formal wurde der Bau mit einem eher traditionellen Stilmittel in die Landschaft integriert: einem begrünten Dach, das hier integraler Bestandteil des architektonischen Entwurfs ist.

Le centre est comme enveloppé dans le paysage. Le recours assez traditionnel à la couverture végétalisée manifeste l'ambition écologique de ce projet architectural.

Wood House

MARCHI ARCHITECTES

Adelaïde & Nicola Marchi Architectes
20 rue Sainte-Croix de la Bretonnerie
75004 Paris
France

Tel: +33 6 63 49 31 99
E-mail: contact@anmarchi.com
Web: www.anmarchi.com

NICOLA MARCHI was born in 1968 in Milan and received a degree in Architecture from Milan Polytechnic in 1996, after benefiting from an Erasmus scholarship at the Architecture Faculty in Porto (Portugal, 1991–94) and studying with Eduardo Souto de Moura and Álvaro Siza. In Paris, he worked in the office of Christian de Portzamparc (1997–99), and Manuelle Gautrand (2001–02). **ADELAÏDE MARCHI** was born in Paris in 1973, and also studied at the Faculty of Architecture in Porto (1995–96), before obtaining her Architecture degree (DPLG) from UP9 in Paris. She worked in the offices of Brunet Saunier in Paris (1997–98) and Dusapin Leclercq (2000–02), before creating her own office with Nicola Marchi in 2004. Their recent work includes a number of residential projects such as a house in Brittany (2006); a house in Bandol (collaboration with Rudy Ricciotti, 2008); the Wood House, Ville-d'Avray (near Paris, 2006–, published here); and a house made of steel that can be dismantled (collaboration with the artist Thomas Schütte, ongoing), all in France. They have also participated in a number of international competitions, such as that for the Shenzhen Museum of Contemporary Art (with SG Partners, MOCAPE, 2007).

NICOLA MARCHI wurde 1968 in Mailand geboren und schloss sein Architekturstudium 1996 an der Polytechnischen Hochschule in Mailand ab. Zuvor hatte er mit einem Erasmus-Stipendium an der Architekturfakultät in Porto (Portugal, 1991–94) bei Eduardo Souto de Moura und Álvaro Siza studieren können. In Paris war er für Christian de Portzamparc (1997–99) und Manuelle Gautrand (2001–02) tätig. **ADELAÏDE MARCHI** wurde 1973 in Paris geboren und studierte ebenfalls an der Architekturfakultät in Porto (1995–96), bevor sie ihren Abschluss in Architektur (DPLG) an der UP9 in Paris absolvierte. Sie arbeitete für Brunet Saunier in Paris (1997–98) und Dusapin Leclercq (2000–02), bevor sie 2004 mit Nicola Marchi ihr eigenes Büro gründete. Jüngere Projekten sind u. a. verschiedene Wohnbauten, darunter ein Haus in der Bretagne (2006), ein Haus in Bandol (zusammen mit Rudy Ricciotti, 2008), das Holzhaus in Ville-d'Avray (bei Paris, 2006–, hier vorgestellt) sowie ein demontierbares Haus aus Stahl (mit dem Künstler Thomas Schütte, in Arbeit), alle in Frankreich. Darüber hinaus haben sie an verschiedenen internationalen Wettbewerben teilgenommen, etwa für das Museum für zeitgenössische Kunst in Shenzhen (mit SG Partners, MOCAPE, 2007).

NICOLA MARCHI, né à Milan en 1968, est diplômé en architecture du Politecnico di Milano en 1996, après avoir bénéficié d'une bourse Erasmus à la Faculté d'architecture de Porto (Portugal, 1991–94) où il a étudié auprès d'Eduardo Souto de Moura et Álvaro Siza. À Paris, il a travaillé dans les agences de Christian de Portzamparc (1997–99) et de Manuelle Gautrand (2001–02). **ADELAÏDE MARCHI**, née à Paris en 1973, a également étudié à la Faculté d'architecture de Porto (1995–96). Elle est architecte DPLG de l'UP9 Paris. Elle a travaillé dans les agences de Brunet Saunier à Paris (1997–98) et Dusapin Leclercq (2000–02), avant de créer Marchi Architectes avec Nicola Marchi en 2004. Parmi leurs récentes interventions : un certain nombre de projets résidentiels dont une maison en Bretagne (2006) ; une autre à Bandol (en collaboration avec Rudy Ricciotti, 2008) ; la maison en bois, Ville-d'Avray (près de Paris, 2006–, publiée ici) et une maison en acier démontable (en collaboration avec l'artiste Thomas Schütte, en cours de réalisation). Ils ont également participé à plusieurs concours internationaux comme celui du Musée d'art contemporain de Shenzhen (avec SG Partners, MOCAPE, 2007).

WOOD HOUSE
Ville-d'Avray, France, 2006–

Floor area: 170 m². Client: not disclosed. Cost: €340 000

This house was designed for a 5700-square-meter site near the Parc de Saint-Cloud to the west of Paris. An existing, main house on the site was designed in the Neoclassical style. The integration of the house into the site was a priority for the architects, and they have lifted it off the ground to preserve trees and their roots. The natural slope of the site means that the entry façade is one meter off the ground, while terraces on the forest side are at the level of the ground. Large glazed surfaces allow for views toward the neighboring forest, and give the house a real sense of transparency and communion with nature. Wood strips are used for the roof and entry façade. The architects have provided for ample insulation and state that "the house is the result of a careful reflection on sustainable development. It will be a 'passive' house, practically autonomous insofar as energy use is concerned."

Das Haus wurde für ein 5700 m² großes Grundstück in der Nähe des Parc de Saint-Cloud westlich von Paris entworfen. Ein bestehendes Gebäude auf dem Grundstück ist im klassizistischen Stil gehalten. Die Einbindung des Hauses in das Gelände hat Priorität für die Architekten, und so planten sie, den Bau anzuheben, um Bäume und Wurzeln zu schützen. Durch das natürliche Gefälle des Grundstücks befindet sich die Eingangsfassade einen Meter über dem Boden, während die Terrassen auf der Waldseite ebenerdig liegen. Die großzügige Verglasung erlaubt Ausblicke in den benachbarten Wald und verleiht dem Haus greifbare Transparenz und das Gefühl besonderer Nähe zur Natur. Für Dach und Eingangsfassade werden Holzlatten verarbeitet. Die Architekten haben das Haus umfassend gedämmt und führen aus: „Das Haus ist Ergebnis eines sorgfältigen Nachdenkens über Nachhaltigkeit. Es wird als ,Passivhaus' praktisch autark, was den Energieverbrauch betrifft."

Cette maison a été conçue pour un terrain de 5700 m² à proximité du parc de Saint-Cloud, dans la banlieue ouest de Paris, sur lequel existait déjà une résidence de style néoclassique. L'intégration du projet dans le site a constitué une priorité des architectes. Ils ont surélevé la maison par rapport au sol pour préserver les arbres et leurs racines. La pente naturelle fait que la façade d'entrée se trouve à 1 m du sol, alors que les terrasses côté forêt sont au niveau de celui-ci. De vastes baies vitrées donnent sur la forêt avoisinante et créent un réel sentiment de transparence et de communion avec la nature. Des lattes de bois recouvrent le toit et la façade d'entrée. Les architectes ont insisté sur la qualité de l'isolation et précisent que « la maison est l'aboutissement d'une réflexion soigneuse sur le développement durable. Ce sera une maison "passive", pratiquement autonome en terme d'énergie ».

Although the virtual images of the house almost give the impression of a real building, it remains a concept. Sitting lightly on the earth, and making use of large glazed surfaces where exposure to the sun allows, the design preserves existing trees.

Obwohl die virtuellen Bilder fast vermuten lassen, es handele sich um ein reales Gebäude, so ist das Haus bislang nur Konzept. Der Entwurf sitzt leichtfüßig auf dem Baugrund, nutzt große Fensterflächen, wo immer es der Sonneneinfall erlaubt, und schützt den vorhandenen Baumbestand.

Si les images virtuelles de cette maison donnent une quasi impression de réalité, le projet reste encore à l'état de concept. Posée avec légèreté sur le sol, utilisant d'amples surfaces vitrées lorsque l'exposition le permet, son implantation préserve les arbres existants.

San Francisco Federal Building

MORPHOSIS

Morphosis
2041 Colorado Avenue
Santa Monica, CA 90404
USA

Tel: +1 310 453 2247
Fax: +1 310 829 3270
E-mail: studio@morphosis.net
Web: www.morphosis.net

MORPHOSIS Principal Thom Mayne, born in Connecticut in 1944, received his B.Arch in 1968 from the University of Southern California, Los Angeles, and his M.Arch degree from Harvard in 1978. He created Morphosis in 1979 with Michael Rotondi, who later left to create his own firm, RoTo. He has taught at UCLA, Harvard, Yale, and SCI-Arc, of which he was a founding Board Member. Thom Mayne was the winner of the 2005 Pritzker Prize. Some of the main buildings by Morphosis are the Lawrence House (Hermosa Beach, California, 1981); Kate Mantilini Restaurant (Beverly Hills, California, 1986); Cedar's Sinai Comprehensive Cancer Care Center (Beverly Hills, California, 1987); Crawford Residence (Montecito, 1987–92); Yuzen Vintage Car Museum (project, West Hollywood, 1992); Blades Residence (Santa Barbara, California, 1992–97); and International Elementary School (Long Beach, California, 1997–99). More recent work includes the University of Cincinnati Student Recreation Center (Cincinnati, Ohio, 1999–2005); the NOAA Satellite Operation Facility in Suitland (Maryland, 2001–05); the San Francisco Federal Building (San Francisco, California, 2003–07, published here); a proposal for the 2012 Olympics in New York City made prior to the selection of London; and the Phare Tower (Paris, France, 2006–12). They are also participating in Brad Pitt's "Make It Right" initiative in New Orleans with their "Floating Prototype House," and are working on the Museum of Nature and Science (Dallas, Texas) and the Alexandria Bay Port of Entry (Alexandria Bay, New York), all in the USA unless stated otherwise.

Thom Mayne, Direktor von **MORPHOSIS**, wurde 1944 in Connecticut geboren. 1968 erlangte er den Abschluss eines B.Arch. an der University of Southern California, Los Angeles (UCLA), sowie 1978 seinen M.Arch. in Harvard. 1979 gründete er mit Michael Rotondi das Büro Morphosis. Rotondi machte sich jedoch später mit seiner eigenen Firma RoTo selbstständig. Mayne lehrte an der UCLA, in Harvard, Yale und am Southern California Institute of Architecture (SCI-Arc), zu dessen Gründungsmitgliedern er zählt. 2005 wurde Mayne mit dem Pritzker-Preis ausgezeichnet. Zu den wichtigsten Bauten von Morphosis zählen das Lawrence House (Hermosa Beach, Kalifornien, 1981), das Kate Mantilini Restaurant (Beverly Hills, Kalifornien, 1986), die Cedar's-Sinai-Krebsklinik (Beverly Hills, Kalifornien, 1987), die Crawford Residence (Montecito, Kalifornien, 1987–92), das Yuzen-Oldtimermuseum (Projekt, West Hollywood, Kalifornien, 1992), die Blades Residence (Santa Barbara, Kalifornien, 1992–97) sowie die International Elementary School (Long Beach, Kalifornien, 1997–99). Jüngere Arbeiten sind das Freizeitzentrum für Studenten der University of Cincinnati (Cincinnati, Ohio, 1999–2005), das NOAA-Satellitenzentrum in Suitland (Maryland, 2001–05), das San Francisco Federal Building (San Francisco, Kalifornien, 2003–07, hier vorgestellt), ein Entwurf für die Olympischen Spiele 2012 in New York (vor der Entscheidung für London aus Austragungsort entstanden) sowie das Hochhaus Phare (Paris, 2006–12). Darüber hinaus ist das Büro mit seinem „Floating Prototype House" an Brad Pitts Initiative „Make It Right" in New Orleans beteiligt und arbeitet an einem Museum für Naturkunde (Dallas, Texas) sowie am Hafen Alexandria Bay (Alexandria Bay, New York).

Le dirigeant de **MORPHOSIS**, Thom Mayne, né dans le Connecticut en 1944, est B. Arch de USC, Los Angeles (1968) et M. Arch de Harvard (1978). Il fonde l'agence en 1979 avec Michael Rotondi qui la quitte pour créer par la suite sa propre structure, RoTo. Il a enseigné à UCLA, Harvard, Yale, et SCI-Arc dont il est un des fondateurs. Thom Mayne a reçu le Prix Pritzker en 2005. Parmi ses principales réalisations : la maison Lawrence (Hermosa Beach, Californie,1981) ; le restaurant Kate Mantilini (Beverly Hills, Californie, 1986) ; le Cedar's Sinai Comprehensive Cancer Care Center (Beverly Hills, Californie, 1987) ; la résidence Crawford (Montecito, Californie, 1987–92) ; le Yuzen Vintage Car Museum (projet, West Hollywood, 1992) ; la résidence Blades (Santa Barbara, Californie, 1992–97) ; et l'International Elementary School de Long Beach (Californie, 1997–99). Plus récemment, il a réalisé le Student Recreation Center de l'université de Cincinnati (Ohio, 1999–2005) ; le NOAA Satellite Operation Facility (Suitland, Maryland, 2001–05) ; le San Francisco Federal Building (San Francisco, 2003–07, publié ici) ; il a soumis une proposition pour la candidature de New York aux Jeux olympiques 2012 (faite avant la sélection de Londres) et mis au point le projet de la tour Phare (Paris La-Défense, 2006–12). Morphosis participe à l'initiative de Brad Pitt « Make It Right » à la Nouvelle-Orléans à travers sa proposition de « maison flottante prototype » et travaille sur les projets du musée de la nature et de la science (Dallas, Texas) et de l'entrée du port d'Alexandria Bay (Alexandria Bay, New York).

SAN FRANCISCO FEDERAL BUILDING

San Francisco, California, USA, 2003–07

*Floor area: 41 806 m². Client: US General Services Administration (GSA). Cost: $144 million.
Team: Tim Christ (Project Manager), Brandon Weiling (Project Architect)*

Morphosis worked in this instance with the GSA, which seeks "to reduce consumption of natural resources, minimize waste, and create a healthy and productive work environment for all tenants who occupy federal workspace." Eighteen stories high (73 m) and intended for 1500 employees, the Federal Building is occupied by a number of US government offices, including the Departments of Defense, Labor, and Agriculture. The methods employed to render the building sustainable are numerous. Computer systems open and close windows, vents, and sunscreens according to temperature conditions. The thermal mass of exposed concrete columns is used to cool or warm the building. The GSA attempts to use no more than 55 000 Btu of energy/square foot/year in its buildings. The San Francisco Federal Building surpasses the GSA's target as well as California's restrictive Title 24 Energy Code. The naturally ventilated floors have an average energy consumption of less than 25 000 Btu/square foot/year. 85% of the structure's interior receives natural light, resulting in a further reduction in electricity consumption. The GSA mandated that 75% of materials used during construction be recycled. Currently, the project is recycling 87% of its waste material. In 2007 Morphosis won the first international Zumtobel Group Award for Sustainability and Humanity in the Built Environment for the Federal Building. Thom Mayne states: "Our primary interest was to produce a performance-driven building that would fundamentally transform its urban surroundings, the nature of the workplace, and the experiences of the people who use it, while making intelligent use of natural resources. For me, this project represents the epitome of an optimistic architecture…"

Bei diesem Projekt arbeitete Morphosis mit der amerikanischen Regierungsagentur General Service Administration (GSA) zusammen, die sich dafür einsetzt, „den Verbrauch natürlicher Ressourcen zu reduzieren, Abfall zu minimieren und ein gesundes, produktives Umfeld für all jene zu schaffen, die in Arbeitsräumen der Bundesverwaltung tätig sind". Das Federal Building, 18 Stockwerke hoch (73 m) und für 1500 Angestellte vorgesehen, wird von verschiedenen Bundesbehörden wie den Ämtern für Verteidigung, Arbeit und Landwirtschaft genutzt. Verschiedenste Methoden kamen zum Einsatz, um das Gebäude umweltfreundlich zu gestalten. Computersysteme öffnen und schließen Fenster, Lüftungsschächte und Sonnenblenden je nach Temperatur. Die thermische Masse der frei liegenden Betonsäulen wird genutzt, um das Gebäude zu kühlen oder zu erwärmen. Die GSA strebt an, in ihren Gebäuden nicht mehr als 55 000 Btu (British thermal units) jährlich pro 0,09 m² zu verbrauchen. Das Federal Building in San Francisco unterschreitet diese Grenze ebenso wie die strengen Vorgaben in Kalifornien, den „Title 24 Energy Code". Die natürlich belüfteten Etagen haben einen durchschnittlichen Energieverbauch von jährlich unter 25 000 Btu pro 0,09 m². 85 % des Innenraums werden mit Tageslicht versorgt, was zu einer weiteren Reduzierung des Stromverbrauchs führt. Die GSA forderte, dass die verwendeten Baumaterialien zu 75 % recyclingfähig sein müssten. Derzeit recycelt das Projekt 87 % seiner Abfälle. 2007 gewann Morphosis mit seinem Federal Building den ersten Internationalen Zumtobel Group Award for Sustainability and Humanity in the Built Environment (Preis der Zumtobel-Gruppe für Nachhaltigkeit und Menschlichkeit in der gebauten Umwelt). Thom Mayne erklärt: „Unser primäres Ziel war es, ein leistungsorientiertes Gebäude zu gestalten, das sein urbanes Umfeld fundamental verändern würde, ebenso wie die Art des Arbeitsplatzes und die Erfahrung derjenigen, die dort arbeiten. Zugleich sollten natürliche Ressourcen auf intelligente Weise zum Einsatz kommen. Für mich ist dieses Projekt der Inbegriff einer optimistischen Architektur…"

Morphosis a étroitement collaboré avec son client, l'Administration générale des services fédéraux, qui cherche « à diminuer la consommation des ressources naturelles, réduire les déchets et créer un environnement de travail sain et productif pour les utilisateurs des lieux de travail fédéraux ». Prévu pour 1500 employés, ce Federal Building de 18 niveaux (73 m de haut) est occupé par divers bureaux et agences fédérales dont ceux de la Défense, du Travail et de l'Agriculture. Les méthodes pour rendre cet immeuble durable sont multiples. Des systèmes informatiques ouvrent et ferment les fenêtres et orientent des ailettes et des écrans de protection solaire selon la température. La masse thermique des colonnes de béton que l'on voit sert à réchauffer ou rafraîchir l'immeuble. Le GSA tente d'imposer une consommation maximum de 1908 kW/m² par an dans ses locaux. L'immeuble de San Francisco affiche une consommation inférieure à cet objectif fédéral et à celui du Titre 24 du Code de l'énergie californien. Les niveaux bénéficiant d'une ventilation naturelle peuvent se targuer d'une consommation de moins de 867 kW/m² par an. 85 % de l'intérieur du bâtiment reçoit la lumière naturelle, ce qui contribue à la réduction de la consommation d'électricité. Le GSA a également exigé que 75 % des matériaux utilisés pendant la construction soient recyclables. Actuellement, l'immeuble recycle 87 % de ses déchets. En 2007, Morphosis a remporté le premier prix international de durabilité et « d'humanité dans l'environnement bâti » du groupe Zumtobel. Thom Mayne a déclaré : « Notre objectif fondamental était de produire un immeuble axé sur la performance qui transforme fondamentalement son environnement urbain, la nature du poste de travail et l'expérience quotidienne de ceux qui y vivent, tout en pratiquant une utilisation intelligente des ressources. Pour moi, ce projet représente l'épitomé d'une architecture optimiste… »

As is often the case, the building designed by Morphosis has an unusual, one almost might say an enigmatic, mechanical appearance, a green machine in this instance.

Wie so oft bei Morphosis mutet der Entwurf ungewöhnlich, fast rätselhaft-technisierend an, wie eine – in diesem Fall grüne – Maschine.

Comme souvent le cas, le bâtiment conçu par Morphosis présente un aspect étonnant, mécanique, presque énigmatique, celui d'une « machine » écologique.

The architects excel at creating unexpected volumes and spaces, including the large urban window (left).

Die Architekten verstehen es hervorragend, überraschende Volumina und Räume zu gestalten, etwa das riesige Fenster mit Blick auf die urbane Landschaft (links).

L'architecte excelle dans la création de volumes et d'espaces surprenants, comme cette énorme fenêtre sur la ville (à gauche).

ALBERTO MOZÓ

Alberto Mozó Studio
Padre Letelier 0343
Providencia, Santiago de Chile
Chile

Tel: +56 2 494 1928
E-mail: alberto@mozo.cl
Web: www.albertomozo.com

ALBERTO MOZÓ was born in 1963 in New York and emigrated with his family to Santiago de Chile, at the age of seven. After completing college in Santiago, he graduated in 1991 from the Pontificia Universidad Católica de Chile. His first architectural projects involved the creation of interior spaces and the design of furniture for bars. He was thus in the midst of the creation of meeting places for the young generation emerging after Chile's transition to democracy. Simultaneously he worked on the restoration of old houses in Santiago. In 2002 he received an award from the Province Council of Andalucia (Spain) for the rehabilitation of old houses situated in the Ibero-American historic districts. His recent work includes the Schkolnick Photo Studio (Sur Providencia, Santiago, 1999); Yankovic House (Aculeo, Santiago, 2002); Rivadeneira House (Tunquén, Valparaiso, 2004); and the BIP Computer Office and Shop (Providencia, Santiago, 2007, published here), all in Chile.

ALBERTO MOZÓ wurde 1963 in New York geboren und zog im Alter von sieben Jahren nach Santiago de Chile. Nachdem er dort das College absolviert hatte, schloss er 1991 sein Studium an der Pontificia Universidad Católica de Chile ab. Seine ersten architektonischen Projekte waren die Gestaltung von Innenräumen und der Entwurf von Möbeln für Bars. Auf diese Weise war er unmittelbar an der Gestaltung von Treffpunkten für die junge Generation nach Chiles Demokratisierung beteiligt. Gleichzeitig arbeitete er an der Sanierung von Altbauten in Santiago. 2002 wurde er von der Provinzverwaltung in Andalusien für die Renovierung von Altbauten in ibero-amerikanischen Altstädten mit einem Preis ausgezeichnet. Zu seinen aktuelleren Projekten zählen das Fotoatelier Schkolnick (Sur Providencia, Santiago, 1999), die Casa Yankovic (Aculeo, Santiago, 2002), die Casa Rivadeneira (Tunquén, Valparaiso, 2004) sowie die Büro- und Ladenräume der Computerfirma BIP (Providencia, Santiago, 2007, hier vorgestellt), alle in Chile.

ALBERTO MOZÓ, né en 1963 à New York, s'est installé avec sa famille à Santiago du Chili quand il avait sept ans. Il est diplômé en architecture de la Pontifica Universidad Católica du Chili (1991). Ses premières commandes ont porté sur la création d'espaces intérieurs et de mobilier pour des bars. Il se trouvait ainsi au centre des lieux de rencontre de cette nouvelle génération apparue après le retour à la démocratie du Chili. Simultanément, il restaurait des maisons anciennes à Santiago. En 2002, il a reçu un prix du Conseil de la province d'Andalousie (Espagne) pour la réhabilitation de vieilles demeures dans les quartiers historiques de villes ibéro-américaines. Parmi ses réalisations récentes : le studio photo Schkolnick (Sur Providencia, Santiago, 1999) ; la maison Yankovic (Aculeo, Santiago, 2002) ; la maison Rivadeneira (Tunquén, Valparaiso, 2004) et les bureaux et boutique de BIP Computer (Providencia, Santiago, 2007, publiés ici), toutes au Chili.

BIP COMPUTER OFFICE AND SHOP

Providencia, Santiago de Chile, Chile, 2007

Floor area: 569 m². Client: Nicolas Moens de Hase. Cost: $450 000.
Team: Francisca Cifuentes, Mauricio Leal

The BIP Computer Office was built between two restored old houses and is three stories high. The architect notes that local zoning regulations encourage a building of 12 stories in this particular location, yet he determined to make his lower, essentially rectangular and laminated wood structure easily dismountable. Wood 9x34.2 centimeters in size was chosen because it is a standard dimension used in Chile for reasons of efficiency. Mozó explains: "It is important to mention that the wood utilized is an incentive for reforestation, since it is a type of wood that comes from a renewable forest. Wood is the construction material that produces the lowest carbon emissions, a significant factor with respect to global warming." The architect further states that the BIP Building is the combined result of his "vision of the next building generation," which is environmentally friendly, easy to build, transitory, and economically viable.

Das Büro für die Computerfirma BIP wurden zwischen zwei sanierten zweistöckigen Altbauten errichtet und hat drei Stockwerke. Der Architekt weist darauf hin, dass die örtlichen Bebauungspläne sogar bis zu zwölf Etagen zugelassen hätten. Dennoch entschied man sich für eine bedeutend niedrigere, im Grunde rechteckige Konstruktion aus laminiertem Holz, die sich leicht demontieren lässt. Gearbeitet wurde mit 9 x 34,2 cm starken Holzbalken, ein Standardformat in Chile und deshalb besonders effizient. Mozó erklärt: „Es ist wichtig, darauf hinzuweisen, dass das gewählte Bauholz zugleich ein Anreiz zur Wiederaufforstung ist, da es aus einem nachhaltig bewirtschafteten Waldgebiet stammt. Holz ist das Baumaterial mit den geringsten CO_2-Emissionen, ein signifikanter Faktor im Hinblick auf die Erderwärmung." Darüber hinaus ist das BIP-Gebäude nach Aussage des Architekten Ergebnis seiner „Vision für Gebäude der nächsten Generation" – umweltfreundlich in der Konstruktion, temporär und wirtschaftlich erschwinglich.

L'immeuble de deux étages de BIP Computers a été construit entre deux maisons anciennes restaurées. Les architectes font remarquer que la réglementation de zonage locale encourageait la construction de 12 niveaux et qu'ils ont décidé de faire en sorte que cette structure rectangulaire en bois lamellé soit facilement démontable. Des poutres de bois de 9 x 34,2 cm de section ont été choisies car il s'agit d'une dimension standard utilisée par l'industrie du bois chilienne pour des raisons d'efficacité. Alberto Mozó explique qu'« il est important de mentionner que le bois utilisé encourage la reforestation puisqu'il provient d'une forêt gérée écologiquement. Le bois est le matériau de construction au plus faible taux d'émissions de carbone, facteur important pour lutter contre le réchauffement global ». Cet immeuble, ajoute-t-il, est le résultat « de sa vision d'une nouvelle génération de constructions » qui sera respectueuse de l'environnement, facile à construire, transitoire et économiquement viable.

Contrary to many buildings, this office and shop is designed to be easily dismounted, a fact that contributes in a fundamental manner to its green credentials.

Anders als viele Bauten wurde dieses Bürohaus mit Ladengeschäft so entworfen, dass es leicht demontiert werden kann, ein Aspekt, der fundamental zu seinem grünen Profil beiträgt.

Contrairement à de nombreuses réalisations, cet ensemble bureaux/magasin a été conçu pour être facilement démontable, ce qui contribue de manière fondamentale à la qualité de son impact environnemental.

Stacked wood stairs and a volume
that makes the building fit into its
environment, where it might have
been as many as 12 stories high,
are part of its respectful design.

Bestandteil des umsichtigen Designs
sind unter anderem eine Treppe
aus gestapelten Holzbohlen und der
Baukörper selbst. Er wurde seinem
Umfeld angepasst, obwohl er theore-
tisch bis zu 12 Geschosse hoch
sein dürfte.

L'escalier fait de lourdes marches
de bois empilées et le volume adapté
à l'échelle du quartier (alors qu'il
aurait pu compter jusqu'à 11 étages),
font partie intégrante d'une approche
respectueuse de l'environnement.

Wooden beams and columns are repetitive but animated, in the case of the columns, by their diagonal placement. The interior space is high and bright.

Träger und Stützen aus Holz sind regelmäßig angeordnet und wirken dennoch aufgelockert – im Fall der Stützen dank ihrer diagonalen Positionierung. Der Innenraum ist hoch und hell.

La disposition répétitive des poutres et des piliers de bois est animée, dans le cas des colonnes, par leur pose croisée. Le lumineux volume intérieur bénéficie d'une grande hauteur sous plafond.

MANFREDI NICOLETTI

Studio Nicoletti Associati
Via di San Simone 75
00186 Rome
Italy

Tel: +39 06 68 805 903
E-mail: studio.nicoletti@inwind.it
Web: www.manfredinicoletti.com

MANFREDI NICOLETTI, born in Rieti, Italy, in 1930, graduated from Rome's "La Sapienza" University, and earned his M.Arch at MIT (1955), before obtaining his Ph. D. in Urban Design at Rome University. He worked in the offices of Walter Gropius, Minorou Yamasaki, and P. L. Nervi, before opening his own office in Rome, in 1960. He is a Professor at Rome's "La Sapienza" University and Vice President of the International Academy of Architecture. In 2004 Giulia Falconi and Luca Nicoletti joined Studio Nicoletti Associati as partners. Recent work includes the Palermo Sport Palace (Palermo, Italy, 1995–2001); Scientific Greenhouse for Tropical Butterflies, Catania University (Catania, Italy, 1999–2002); G8 Conference Center, Chamber of Deputies' Annex, Palazzo Marini (Rome, Italy, 2000–02); Millennium Park (Abuja, Nigeria, 2003–04); and Astana Kazakhstan State Auditorium (Astana, Kazakhstan, 2003–07). Current work includes the Nigeria National Complex, City Hall, Cultural Center, and Millennium Tower (Abuja, Nigeria, 2006–09); and the Putrajaya Precinct 4 Waterfront Development (Kuala Lumpur, Malaysia, 2008–10, published here).

MANFREDI NICOLETTI, geboren 1930 Rieti, Italien, absolvierte ein Studium an der Universität La Sapienza in Rom und erwarb einen M.Arch. am MIT (1955), bevor er an der Universität Rom in Stadtplanung promovierte. Er arbeitete für Walter Gropius, Minorou Yamasaki und P. L. Nervi und gründete schließlich 1960 sein eigenes Büro in Rom. Nicoletti ist Professor an der Universität La Sapienza in Rom und Vizepräsident der Internationalen Akademie für Architektur. 2004 schlossen sich Giulia Falconi und Luca Nicoletti dem Studio Nicoletti Associati als Partner an. Jüngere Arbeiten sind u. a. der Sportpalast in Palermo (Italien, 1995–2001), das wissenschaftliche Gewächshaus für tropische Schmetterlinge, Universität Catania (Italien, 1999–2002), das G8-Konferenzzentrum, ein Anbau an die Abgeordnetenkammer, Palazzo Marini (Rom, 2000–02), der Millenniumpark (Abuja, Nigeria, 2003–04) sowie das Staatsauditorium Astana (Astana, Kasachstan, 2003–07). Zu seinen aktuellen Projekten zählen der nigerianische Staatskomplex mit Rathaus, Kulturzentrum und Millenniumturm (Abuja, Nigeria, 2006–09) sowie die Ufererschließung des 4. Bezirks von Putrajaya (Kuala Lumpur, Malaysia, 2008–10, hier vorgestellt).

MANFREDI NICOLETTI, né à Rieti, Italie, en 1930, est diplômé de l'université de Rome « La Sapienza », M. Arch du MIT (1955), et docteur en urbanisme de l'université de Rome. Il a travaillé dans les agences de Walter Gropius, Minorou Yamasaki et P. L. Nervi, avant d'ouvrir sa propre agence à Rome en 1960. Il est professeur à « La Sapienza » et vice-président de l'Académie internationale d'architecture. En 2004, Giulia Falconi et Luca Nicoletti se sont associés dans le cadre du Studio Nicoletti Associati. Parmi leurs réalisations récentes : le Palais des sports de Palerme (Palerme, 1995–2001) ; une serre pour l'étude des papillons tropicaux à l'université de Catane (1999–2002) ; le Centre de conférences du G8, annexe de la Chambre des députés, Palazzo Marini (Rome, 2000–02) ; le Millennium Park (Abuja, Nigeria, 2003–04) et l'Auditorium national du Kazakhstan (Astana, Kazakhstan, 2003–07). Ils travaillent actuellement sur le projet du Nigeria National Complex : hôtel de ville, centre culturel et Millennium Tower (Abuja, Nigeria, 2006–09), et le développement résidentiel de la zone en bordure du lac de Putrajaya (Zone 4, Kuala Lumpur, Malaisie, 2008–10, publié ici).

PUTRAJAYA PRECINCT 4 WATERFRONT DEVELOPMENT

Kuala Lumpur, Malaysia, 2008–10

*Floor area: 200 000 m². Client: Putrajaya Holdings, Ltd. Cost: €184.166 million.
Associated Architects: Hijjas Kasturi Associates SDN*

Nicoletti takes this opportunity in Putrajaya, the administrative capital of Malaysia, as an occasion to introduce a degree of architectural and environmental inventiveness that has not yet been seen much in this new city.

Nicoletti nimmt sein Projekt in Putrajaya, der Verwaltungshauptstadt von Malaysia, zum Anlass, um architektonische und ökologische Innovationen einzubringen, die man dort so bislang nicht gesehen hat.

Nicoletti a fait de sa présence à Putrajaya, capitale administrative de la Malaisie, l'occasion d'introduire un niveau d'inventivité architecturale et environnementale assez rare dans cette ville nouvelle.

Putrajaya is the new administrative capital of Malaysia, located just south of Kuala Lumpur and founded in 1995. Manfredi Nicoletti's project was the winner of an international design competition for a waterfront area with an emphasis on allowing the permeability of building blocks of varied heights along a boulevard. The radial pattern adopted allows views to the artificial lake and boulevard and also ensures the interpenetration of architecture and landscape. "Designing an iconic residential development for Putrajaya requires a rethink to what makes Putrajaya unique in the context to the world," says Nicoletti. "The building should have a uniqueness that tells of its place of origin, which is culturally modern, Islamic, and tropical in nature…. This group of buildings is on an artificial lake, so we conceived a complex of elements like a fleet, inspired by the metaphor of eight majestic 'sails,' both light and transparent." The sustainability of the designs is a major element for the architect and the client. A double skin allows efficient sunshading and natural ventilation—the outer skin is not sealed. Balconies, vertical structural elements, and horizontal brise soleils reduce the need for cooling, and a good number of windows will be operable. Gas or biomass-fired heating and power are envisaged, as are a surface-water heat pump system, micro wind turbines, and photovoltaic cells. An emphasis is placed on natural lighting and controlled artificial lights to reduce electricity consumption.

Putrajaya ist die neue Verwaltungshauptstadt von Malaysia, die 1995 gegründet wurde und unmittelbar südlich von Kuala Lumpur liegt. Manfredi Nicolettis Projekt war Gewinner eines internationalen Entwurfswettbewerbs für ein am Ufer gelegenes Stadtviertel. Besonderer Wert wurde darauf gelegt, die entlang eines Boulevards errichteten Gebäude von unterschiedlicher Höhe durchlässig wirken zu lassen. Die radiale Anlage der Stadt erschließt Sichtachsen auf einen künstlichen See ebenso wie zum Boulevard und sorgt für eine gegenseitige Durchdringung von Architektur und Landschaft. „Um eine unverwechselbare Wohnbebauung für Putrajaya entwickeln zu können, ist es unerlässlich, noch einmal darüber nachzudenken, was Putrajaya im globalen Kontext so einzigartig macht", erklärt Nicoletti. „Die Bauten sollten Einmaligkeit ausstrahlen, die auf ihren Herkunftsort verweisen, in diesem Fall also kulturell modern, islamisch und tropisch… Die Siedlung befindet sich am Ufer eines künstlichen Sees, und so entwarfen wir einen Komplex aus Elementen, die an eine Schiffsflotte denken lassen, ließen uns von der Metapher acht majestätischer ‚Segel' inspirieren, hell und transparent." Die Nachhaltigkeit des Entwurfs war von entscheidender Bedeutung für Architekten und Auftraggeber. Eine doppelte Gebäudehaut sorgt für effizienten Sonnenschutz und natürliche Belüftung – die äußere Haut ist offen. Balkone, vertikale Strukturelemente und horizontale Sonnenblenden minimieren den Kühlbedarf, viele Fenstern lassen sich öffnen. Geplant sind außerdem eine Gas- bzw. Biomasseheizung und -stromversorgung sowie ein Wärmepumpensystem, Mikrowindkrafträder und Fotovoltaikzellen. Besonderer Wert wurde auf natürliche sowie auf computergesteuerte künstliche Belichtung gelegt, um den Stromverbrauch zu drosseln.

Putrajaya, nouvelle capitale administrative de la Malaisie, a été fondée en 1995, juste au sud de Kuala Lumpur. Le projet de Nicoletti a remporté le concours international organisé pour une zone en bordure de lac partant de l'idée de perméabilité des blocs d'immeubles de hauteurs variées le long d'un boulevard. Le plan radial adopté permet des vues sur le lac artificiel et le boulevard ainsi que l'interpénétration de l'architecture et du paysage. « Concevoir ici un ensemble résidentiel iconique a demandé de repenser ce qui pouvait rendre cette ville unique dans le contexte mondial », explique l'architecte. « L'immeuble doit avoir une originalité qui raconte son lieu d'origine, qui est moderne, islamique et de nature tropicale… Cet ensemble donne sur un lac artificiel, aussi avons-nous conçu ce complexe d'éléments comme une flotte de navires, inspirée de la métaphore de huit majestueuses "voiles", à la fois légères et transparentes. » Le caractère durable est un élément majeur de ce projet, pour l'architecte et son client. Une double peau permet une protection solaire et une ventilation naturelle – la peau extérieure n'est pas étanche. Des balcons, des éléments structurels verticaux et des brise-soleil horizontaux réduisent les besoins en climatisation et bon nombre de fenêtres sont commandées manuellement. Le chauffage et la fourniture d'énergie par gaz ou biomasse sont envisagés ainsi qu'un système de récupération de la chaleur de surface, une installation de micro-éoliennes et des cellules photovoltaïques. L'accent est mis sur l'éclairage naturel et le contrôle des sources lumineuses artificielles afin de réduire la consommation d'électricité.

The design assumes an almost biomorphic form in plan and section. Drawings above show the careful attention paid to heat and air flow throughout the structures.

In Grund- und Aufriss wirken die Formen des Entwurfs fast biomorph. Die Zeichnungen oben veranschaulichen, wie präzise Wärme- und Luftströme in den Bauten berücksichtigt wurden.

Les formes du projet sont quasi biomorphiques en plan comme en coupe. Les dessins ci-dessus montrent le soin porté à la ventilation naturelle qui parcourt les immeubles.

OFFICE DA

Office dA
1920 Washington Street, #2
Boston, MA 02118
USA

Tel: +1 617 541 5540
Fax: +1 617 541 5535
E-mail: da@officeda.com
Web: www.officeda.com

Nader Tehrani was born in England in 1963 and is of Iranian descent. He received a B. A. in Fine Arts (1985) and a B.Arch (1986) from the Rhode Island School of Design, and and M.Arch in Urban Design from the Harvard GSD in 1991. He teaches at MIT as an Associate Professor of Architecture, and has taught at the Harvard GSD, Rhode Island School of Design, and Georgia Institute of Technology, where he served as the Thomas W. Ventulett III Distinguished Chair in Architectural Design. Monica Ponce de Leon was born in 1965 in Venezuela. She received a B. A. from the University of Miami in 1989, followed by an M.Arch in Urban Design from the Harvard GSD in 1991. Ponce de Leon is a Professor at the Harvard GSD and became the Dean of the A. Alfred Taubman College of Architecture and Urban Planning at the University of Michigan in the fall of 2008. They formed their partnership in 1991 in Boston. In 2006 **OFFICE DA** designed the main library for the Rhode Island School of Design in Providence. In addition Office dA won the first-place award in the Villa Moda Competition for a mixed-use building in Kuwait, which includes housing, retail, multiplex, convention area, and sport facilities. Office dA recently completed the first LEED-certified, multi-housing building in Boston, the Macallen Building, with over 140 environmentally sensitive condominium units (2005–07, published here). Helios House, the first LEED-rated gas station, was completed in Los Angeles in 2007 (also published here).

Nader Tehrani wurde 1963 in England geboren, seine Familie stammt aus dem Iran. Er erwarb einen B. A. in bildender Kunst (1985) sowie einen B.Arch. (1986) an der Rhode Island School of Design und schließlich 1991 einen M.Arch. in Stadtplanung an der Harvard Graduate School of Design (GSD). Er lehrt als außerordentlicher Professor für Architektur am MIT und unterrichtete auch an der Harvard GSD, der Rhode Island School of Design sowie dem Georgia Institute of Technology, wo er den Thomas-W.-Ventulett-III-Lehrstuhl für architektonisches Entwerfen tätig war. Monica Ponce de Leon wurde 1965 in Venezuela geboren. Sie erwarb 1989 einen B. A. an der Universität von Miami und 1991 einen M.Arch. in Stadtplanung an der Harvard GSD. Ponce de Leon ist Professorin an der Harvard GSD und wurde im Herbst 2008 Dekanin des A. Alfred Taubman College für Architektur und Stadtplanung an der Universität Michigan. 1991 begannen die beiden in Boston ihre Partnerschaft. 2006 entwarf **OFFICE DA** die Hauptbibliothek der Rhode Island School of Design in Providence, Rhode Island. Zudem gewann das Büro den ersten Preis im Villa-Moda-Wettbewerb für einen Baukomplex mit gemischter Nutzung in Kuwait, zu dem Wohnungen, Geschäfte, ein Kino, ein Messeareal und Sporteinrichtungen gehören. Vor Kurzem konnte Office dA den ersten LEED-zertifizierten Wohnkomplex in Boston fertigstellen, das Macallen Building mit über 140 umweltgerechten Eigentumswohnungen (2005–07, hier vorgestellt). Das Helios House, die erste LEED-zertifizierte Tankstelle, wurde 2007 in Los Angeles realisiert (ebenfalls hier vorgestellt).

Nader Tehrani est né en Grande-Bretagne, en 1963, de parents iraniens. Il est B. A. en Beaux-Arts (1985), B. Arch (1986) de la Rhode Island School of Design et M. Arch d'urbanisme de l'Harvard GSD (1991). Il enseigne au MIT comme professeur associé d'architecture et a professé à l'Harvard GSD, la Rhode Island School of Design et au Georgia Institute of Technology, où il a occupé la Thomas W. Ventulett III Distinguished Chair de conception architecturale. Monica Ponce de Leon, née au Venezuela en 1965, est B. A. de l'université de Miami (1989) et M. Arch d'urbanisme de l'Harvard GSD (1991). Elle est professeure à l'Harvard GS et doyenne de l'A. Alfred Taubman College of Architecture and Urban Planning de l'université du Michigan depuis l'automne 2008. Ils se sont associés à Boston en 1991. En 2006, **OFFICE DA** a conçu la bibliothèque principale de la Rhode Island School of Design à Providence. L'agence a remporté le concours de la Villa Moda pour un immeuble mixte à Koweït, qui comprend des logements, des commerces, une salle multiplexe, un centre de congrès et des équipements sportifs. Elle a récemment achevé le premier immeuble mixte certifié LEED à Boston, le Macallen Building, qui compte plus de 140 appartements en copropriété (2005–07, publié ici). Helios House, première station-service certifiée LEED, a été achevée en 2007 (Los Angeles, également publiée ici).

HELIOS HOUSE

Los Angeles, California, USA, 2006–07

*Floor area: 975 m². Client: BP Corporation of North America.
Cost: not disclosed. Architect of Record: Johnston Marklee.
Creative and Design Firm: BIG at Ogilvy & Mather*

The idea of an ecological design for a gas station might seem contradictory, but the client and the architects have taken it up with energy and originality.

Das Konzept einer ökologisch gestalteten Tankstelle mag zunächst widersprüchlich erscheinen, doch Auftraggeber und Architekten stellten sich der Herausforderung engagiert und mit Originalität.

L'idée de conception écologique d'une station-service peut sembler contradictoire en soi, mais le client et les architectes l'ont traitée avec originalité et énergie.

Though its essential function is that of a gas station, Helios House was intended to be a "learning lab," to stimulate dialog, promote education, and foster discussion on the topic of environmental stewardship. Built to maximize sustainability and energy efficiency, the structure is located at the intersection of Robertson and Olympic Boulevards in the location of a former conventional gas station. Existing billboards and bus stops were maintained "to attract attention to the station's experimental and educational mission." The architects make reference to the rich history of gas-station architecture in America, while calling attention to "green" issues. A triangulated prefabricated steel-panel structure makes use of what the architects call "mass-customization" of the building elements. All potentially contaminated runoff water from the site is collected and placed in an underground cistern, filtered, and used to water plants. Ninety solar panels on the canopy roof "provide approximately 15 000 kWh of energy to the station—enough electricity to power two to three typical American homes for a year." Energy-efficient lights are used and the canopy was designed to reflect light, reducing electricity consumption by 16% as compared to conventional stations. Sensors further optimize the use of artificial light through a 24-hour cycle. Recycled materials were used wherever possible, and the project is LEED certified. Energy-related videos are visible for customers.

Trotz der Hauptfunktion als Tankstelle war Helios House als „Lernlabor" gedacht, um Gespräche anzuregen, Wissen zu vermitteln und Diskussionen zum Umgang mit der Umwelt anzustoßen. Die Konstruktion, bei deren Bau auf Maximierung von Nachhaltigkeit und Energieeffizienz geachtet wurde, liegt an der Kreuzung von Robertson und Olympic Boulevard, wo vorher eine konventionelle Tankstelle stand. Bereits vorhandene Werbetafeln und Bushaltestellen wurden übernommen, um „Aufmerksamkeit auf die experimentelle und informative Mission der Tankstelle zu lenken". Die Architekten nehmen Bezug auf die facettenreiche Geschichte der Tankstellenarchitektur in Amerika, jedoch mit der Besonderheit, Aufmerksamkeit auf „grüne" Aspekte zu lenken. Eine in Dreiecke segmentierte Plattenkonstruktion aus vorgefertigten Metallelementen überspannt die gesamte Anlage. Für die Produktion der einzelnen Bausegmente griffen die Architekten auf maßgeschneiderte, aber in Massenfertigung hergestellte Teile zurück. Das gesamte potenziell verunreinigte Ablaufwasser auf dem Grundstück wird in einer unterirdischen Zisterne gesammelt, gefiltert und zur Bewässerung der Bepflanzung genutzt. 90 Solarmodule auf dem Dach „erzeugen rund 15 000 kWh Strom für die Tankstelle – ausreichend Elektrizität, um zwei bis drei durchschnittliche amerikanische Eigenheime pro Jahr zu versorgen". Energiesparleuchten wurden eingesetzt, zudem wurde das Dach lichtreflektierend gestaltet, was den Stromverbrauch im Vergleich zu herkömmlichen Tankstellen um 16 % reduziert. Darüber hinaus optimieren Sensoren den Einsatz künstlicher Beleuchtung rund um die Uhr. Wo möglich, wurden für das LEED-zertifizierte Projekt recycelte Materialien verwendet. Videos zum Thema Energie werden für alle Kunden sichtbar gezeigt.

Bien que sa fonction essentielle soit d'être une station-service, Helios House avait aussi pour vocation d'être « un laboratoire d'apprentissage » pour stimuler, dialoguer, promouvoir la formation, et susciter le débat sur l'économie des sujets environnementaux. Construite avec la volonté d'optimiser sa durabilité et son efficacité énergétique, cette structure se trouve à l'angle des boulevards Robertson et Olympic à la place d'une ancienne station-service. Les arrêts de bus et les panneaux d'affichage existants ont été conservés « pour attirer l'attention sur la mission expérimentale et éducative de la station ». Les architectes se sont référés à la riche histoire des stations-service aux États-Unis, mais avec une importante nuance : attirer l'attention sur les enjeux écologiques. Une structure triangulée en panneaux d'acier préfabriqués recouvre toute la construction et les fonctions dans un effort de ce que les architectes appellent « une personnalisation massive » des éléments constructifs. Toute l'eau, potentiellement contaminée, collectée par cette structure est collectée et envoyée vers une citerne souterraine, avant d'être filtrée et de servir à arroser les plantes. Les 90 panneaux solaires placés sur le toit « fournissent environ 15 000 kWh d'électricité, suffisamment pour alimenter trois maisons américaines typiques pendant un an ». Des ampoules économiques ont été mises en place, et l'auvent a été dessiné de façon à refléter la lumière et réduire la consommation d'électricité de 16 % par rapport aux stations-service classiques. Des capteurs optimisent en permanence la consommation de l'éclairage artificiel. À chaque fois que c'était possible, des matériaux recyclés ont été utilisés et le projet a reçu une certification LEED. Des vidéos sur le thème de l'énergie informent les clients.

The articulated triangular panel canopy over the pumps morphs into the roof of the gas station itself.

Das dynamisch artikulierte Baldachindach aus dreieckigen Paneelen über den Zapfsäulen geht nahtlos in das Dach der Tankstelle über.

L'auvent des pompes, composé d'un assemblage articulé de triangles, se fond dans la couverture de la station-service.

In the image below, it is clear that the roof is also an arching protective wall, with its triangular forms becoming larger as it reaches the ground.

Im Bild unten ist deutlich zu sehen, wie sich das Dach zu einer geschwungenen Wand entwickelt, deren Dreieckselemente größer werden, je näher sie dem Boden kommen.

Dans l'image ci-dessous, le toit semble se transformer en mur de protection, les triangles s'agrandissant en se rapprochant du sol.

The folded shape of the station is seen in the drawings below, as well as in the images, which demonstrate the flexibility of the concept, bending to each planned use in the program.

Der Falt-Effekt der Tankstelle zeigt sich besonders gut an den Zeichnungen unten und den Aufnahmen, die die Flexibilität des Konzepts verdeutlichen, das sich jeder vorgesehenen Nutzung des Programms anpasst.

Les effets de pliage de la station-service sont détaillés dans les dessins ci-dessous. Les photos montrent la souplesse de ce concept qui s'adapte à chaque spécification du programme.

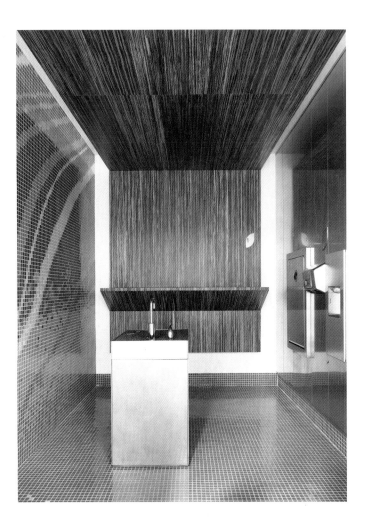

Die Architekten erläutern: „Für die Toiletten wurde mit Plantagenholz und individuell gestalteten Fliesenmosaiken aus 100% recyceltem Glas gearbeitet."

Descriptif de l'architecte : « Les toilettes sont en bois naturel et mosaïque de céramique spécialement créée en verre 100 % recyclé. »

MACALLEN BUILDING

Boston, Massachusetts, USA, 2005–07

Floor area: 18.023 m². Client: Pappas Enterprises, Inc.
Cost: not disclosed. Architect of Record: Burt Hill. Landscaping: Landworks Studio

This condominium building in South Boston was built with a "financially competitive budget." The building responds in its design to a nearby highway with a curtain wall on the western side, while brick is used on the eastern side, because of a more residential context. Bronzed aluminum panels are used on the north and south to "reflect the industrial component" of the neighborhood. A landscaped roof and terraces are part of the scheme. The architects say: "Additionally, the Macallen building was designed from the ground up to take advantage of 'green' building techniques and materials. It is the first LEED Gold certified building of its type in Boston." The large scale of this building and its complex urban site make its role as setting an example for environmentally responsible construction all the more evident. The work of Office dA in this instance also demonstrates that sustainability can go hand in hand with architectural quality.

Das Gebäude mit Eigentumswohnungen in South Boston wurde innerhalb „eines wettbewerbsfähigen Budgetrahmens" realisiert. Der Entwurf reagiert auf den nahe gelegenen Highway mit einer vorgehängten Fassade auf der Westseite des Baus, während die Ostseite mit Backstein verblendet wurde, um ihn in den Kontext des angrenzenden Wohngebiets integrieren. Im Norden und Süden wurden bronzierte Aluminiumtafeln verwendet, um „die industrielle Komponente" der Umgebung aufzugreifen. Ein begrüntes Dach und begrünte Terrassen sind Teil des Konzepts. Die Architekten erläutern: „Hinzu kam, dass das Macallen Building von Grund auf daraufhin angelegt wurde, optimal von ‚grünen' Bautechniken und -materialien zu profitieren. Es ist das erste LEED-goldprämierte Gebäude dieser Art in Boston." Die Größe des Gebäudes und seine komplexe urbane Lage lassen umso deutlicher werden, welche Vorbildfunktion die Anlage für umweltbewusstes Bauen hat. Hier beweist die Arbeit von Office dA zudem, dass Nachhaltigkeit und architektonische Qualität durchaus Hand in Hand gehen können.

Cet immeuble d'appartements en copropriété, situé dans le sud de Boston, a été réalisé « dans le cadre d'un budget très compétitif ». Sa conception a pris en compte la présence à l'ouest d'une grande voie de circulation par l'adoption d'un mur-rideau, tandis que la façade est, donnant sur une zone plus résidentielle, est en brique. Les panneaux d'aluminium de couleur bronze sur les façades nord et sud « reflètent l'aspect industriel » du quartier. Un toit paysager et des terrasses font partie du plan. « L'immeuble Macallen a été conçu, dès le départ, pour bénéficier des techniques de construction et des matériaux "verts". C'est le premier immeuble certifié LEED Or de ce type à Boston », précise l'architecte. Les grandes dimensions du bâtiment, la complexité de son contexte en font un exemple particulièrement remarquable de construction respectueuse de l'environnement. Le travail d'Office dA a été ici de démontrer que la durabilité peut aller de pair avec la qualité architecturale.

The varying scales of the building respond to its environment in the South Boston area.

Die unterschiedliche Bauhöhe des Komplexes berücksichtigt die bauliche Umgebung in Süd-Boston.

Les différences d'échelle de l'immeuble répondent à l'environnement du quartier de South Boston.

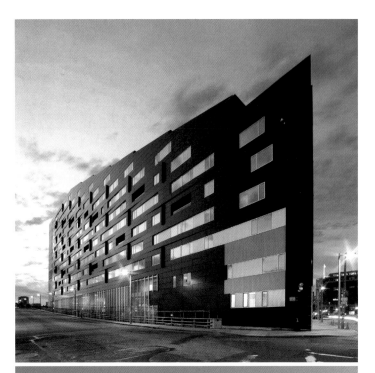

An der Ostseite stellt eine Klinkerver-
blendung Bezüge zum umliegenden
Wohngebiet her, während „das Konzept von Ladenschaufenstern und
deren auf Fußgänger zugeschnittene
Maßstäblichkeit in der Gebäudefront
aufgegriffen wird."

Côté est, l'habillage en brique reflète
celui des immeubles environnants,
« étendant la logique de ses composants à l'échelle piétonnière ou à
celle des magasins de cette façade ».

On the north and south façades, bronzed aluminum panels "reflect the industrial neighborhood component and express the structural system organization."

Bronzierte Aluminiumpaneele an den Nord- und Südfassaden „greifen die industrielle Komponente der Gegend auf und veranschaulichen die Organisationsstruktur des Baus".

Sur les façades nord et sud, des panneaux d'aluminium de couleur bronze « reflètent les composants du voisinage industriel et expriment l'organisation structurelle de l'immeuble. »

The unusual, varying façade treatments and scale, ramping up where the urban environment encourages it to do so, make this a particularly responsive building.

Die ungewöhnlich abwechslungsreichen Fassaden und Dimensionen – mit Aufstockungen, wo immer es dem urbanen Umfeld entspricht – zeigen die hohe Einfühlsamkeit des Baus.

Le traitement inhabituel des échelles et des façades, qui s'élèvent vers le ciel lorsque l'environnement urbain les y encourage, en fait un immeuble particulièrement réactif à son cadre.

DO NOT ENTER   8'-2" CLEARANCE 8'-2"

In these images, facade cladding elements emphasize the verticality of the building as opposed to the more intimate scale of the other side.

Die Verblendelemente der Fassade auf diesen Bildern unterstreichen die Vertikalität des Gebäudes, ganz anders als bei der intimeren Bauhöhe (gegenüber).

Dans ces images, les éléments d'habillage de la façade soulignent la verticalité de l'immeuble par opposition à l'échelle plus intime de ses autres composants.

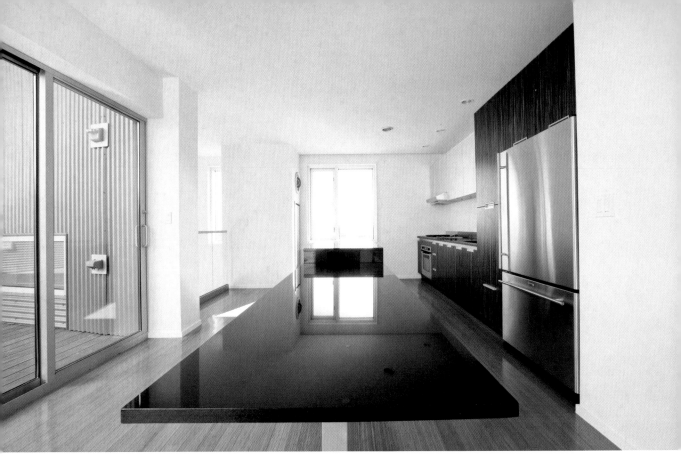

The apartment types are staggered
on top of one another, so that plumb-
ing and mechanical shafts can generate maximum structural and environmental efficiency.

Die verschiedenen Wohnungstypen
wurden übereinander gestaffelt,
sodass Installations- und Versor-
gungsschächte strukturell und
umwelttechnisch optimiert angelegt
werden konnten.

Les divers types d'appartement sont
empilés et décalés de telle façon que
les descentes techniques permettent
une efficacité structurelle et environnementale maximum.

The structural system of the building provides for versatility in apartment types ranging from studios, to lofts, to one-, two-, or three-bedroom units, duplexes, triplexes, and garden suites on the terrace.

Das Konstruktionssystem des Gebäudes ermöglicht die Realisierung verschiedenster Wohnungstypen, von 1-Zimmer-Wohnungen bis hin zu Lofts, 3- oder 4-Zimmer-Wohnungen, Maisonette-Wohnungen, Wohnungen über drei Ebenen und Gartenapartments mit Terrasse.

Le système structurel de l'immeuble permet de multiplier les types d'appartements, du studio aux lofts en passant par les 2, 3, 4 pièces, duplex, triplex et studios avec jardins sur les terrasses.

SERGIO PALLERONI

Sergio Palleroni
3134 SE Main Street
Portland, OR 97214
USA

Tel: +1 503 725 8403
E-mail: sergio@pdx.edu
Web: www.basicinitiative.org

SERGIO PALLERONI, born in Berkeley, California, in 1955, received his B.Arch degree at the University of Oregon and an M.S. in Architectural Studies (History, Theory, and Criticism) at MIT. He was Associate Professor of architecture at the University of Washington, Seattle (1993–2004), Research Fellow and Associate Professor at the Center for Sustainable Development, University of Texas, Austin (2004–08) and is currently Professor and Fellow at the Center for Sustainable Processes and Practices, Portland State University. He was Director and co-founder of the Building Sustainable Communities (BaSiC) Initiative, University of Washington, University of Texas, Penn State University, University of Wisconsin; a member of the United Nations Think Tank on Climate Change (SBCI TTWG); and of the Luce Foundation Workshop on Sustainable Development (University of Texas). Through the BaSiC Initiative, Sergio Palleroni has worked with his students to build housing, clinics, and schools in poor communities in the rural United States, Mexico, Africa, and India. He is presently Co-Principal Investigator with Jen-Hui Tsai for an Urban Development Grant, National Taipei University of Technology (NTUT, Taiwan, 2008–09).

SERGIO PALLERONI, geboren 1955 in Berkeley, Kalifornien, erwarb seinen Grad des B.Arch. an der Universität von Oregon und einen M.S. in Architektur (Geschichte, Theorie und Kritik) am Massachusetts Institute of Technology (MIT). Er war außerordentlicher Professor für Architektur an der Universität von Washington, Seattle (1993–2004), Forschungsmitarbeiter und außerordentlicher Professor am Center for Sustainable Development, Universität von Texas in Austin (2004–08), und ist derzeit Professor und Mitglied am Center for Sustainable Processes and Practices an der Portland State University. Er war Direktor und Mitbegründer der Initiative „Building Sustainable Communities" (BaSiC) der Universitäten Washington und Texas, der Penn State University sowie der Universität von Wisconsin. Palleroni war Mitglied des Think Tank der Vereinten Nationen zum Klimawandel (SBCI TTWG) und des Arbeitskreises Nachhaltige Entwicklung der Luce Foundation (Universität von Texas). Im Rahmen der BaSiC-Initiative arbeitete Palleroni gemeinsam mit seinen Studenten an Wohnungs-, Klinik- und Schulbauprogrammen in finanziell benachteiligten Gemeinden in den ländlichen Gegenden der USA, Mexikos, Afrikas und Indiens. Gegenwärtig ist er gemeinsam mit Jen-Hui Tsai Forschungsleiter für das Stipendium für Stadtentwicklung an der Technischen Nationaluniversität Taipei (Taiwan, 2008–09).

SERGIO PALLERONI, né à Berkeley, Californie, en 1955, est B. Arch de l'université de l'Oregon et M. S. en études sur l'architecture (histoire, théorie, et critique) au MIT. Professeur associé en architecture à l'université de Washington, Seattle (1993–2004), chercheur et professeur associé au Center for Sustainable Development de l'université du Texas, à Austin (2004–08), il est actuellement membre et professeur titulaire du Center for Sustainable Processes and Practices de l'université d'État de Portland. Il a été fondateur et directeur de la Building Sustainable Communities (BaSiC), initiative présente dans diverses universités : université de Washington, université du Texas, université Penn State, université du Wisconsin ; membre du Comité de réflexion des Nations unies sur le changement climatique (SBCI TTWG) et de l'atelier de la Fondation Luce sur le développement durable (Université du Texas). Dans le cadre de la BaSiC Initiative, Sergio Palleroni a travaillé avec ses étudiants sur la construction de logements, de cliniques et d'écoles pour des communautés pauvres rurales aux États-Unis, au Mexique, en Afrique et en Inde. Il est actuellement chercheur principal, avec Jen-Hui Tsai, pour le Fonds de développement urbain de l'Université nationale de technologie de Taipei (NTUT, Taïwan, 2008–09).

ZHONG-XIAO BOULEVARD
URBAN ECOLOGICAL CORRIDOR

Taipei, Taiwan, 2005–07

Site area: 50 000 m² (urban landscape and rooftops); 140 m² (building). Client: National Taipei University of Technology, Taipei City Government. Cost: not disclosed. Team: Sergio Palleroni, Jen-Hui Tsai, James Adamson

This project includes a campus garden designed and built by a group of architecture, planning, and engineering students; a "green" pavilion designed by students, built with assistance from the local construction industry, and other initiatives. An entrance to the campus along Zhong-Xiao Boulevard formerly occupied by a long wall is the location for a garden and bioswale.[1] Solar panels used as window shades on campus buildings power the pumps used for the project. Planting was carried out with the assistance of the local community. The so-called Lotus Pavilion is a large room that makes use of passive cooling and low-energy lighting. Rising almost ten meters above the ground, the structure captures passing breezes for cooling and also makes use of solar panels. The partially planted roof serves as insulation. An exterior bamboo rain screen tops the insulation, leaving a gap for air to flow through, thus further reducing solar gain. Students participating in this project went on to install various green devices, including solar panels and mesh screens for vines to grow on around the bioswale. This initiative is exemplary both in terms of student, community, and professional participation, and also in the mixture of different techniques employed, ranging from the expected passive strategies to landscape solutions.   [1] A bioswale is a landscape element designed to remove silt and pollution from surface runoff water. It consists of a drainage course with gently sloped sides filled with vegetation or compost.

Zum Projekt gehören ein Campusgarten, der von einer Gruppe von Architektur-, Stadtplanungs- und Ingenieurstudenten entworfen und gebaut wurde, sowie ein „grüner" Pavillon, der von Studenten geplant und mithilfe ortsansässiger Bauunternehmen und weiterer Initiativen gebaut wurde. Am Eingang des Campusgeländes am Zhong-Xiao-Boulevard stand früher eine lange Mauer. Heute befinden sich hier ein Garten und eine ökologisch angelegte Bodensenke, deren obere Schicht das Sickerwasser filtert.[1] Solarmodule auf den Campusbauten, die auch als Fensterläden dienen, liefern Strom für die Pumpanlagen des Projekts. Die Bepflanzung wurde mit der Hilfe von Anwohnern realisiert. Der sogenannte Lotuspavillon ist ein großer Raum, der passiv gekühlt wird und mit Energiesparlampen ausgestattet ist. Der fast 10 m über dem Boden aufgeständerte Bau fängt den kühlenden Luftzug ein und nutzt zudem Solarmodule. Das teilweise begrünte Dach wirkt dämmend. Ein außen zum Schutz vor Regen angebrachter Wandschirm aus Bambus verstärkt die Isolierung, durch eine Lücke kann Luft ziehen, was den solaren Wärmegewinn minimiert. Die am Projekt beteiligten Studenten installierten außerdem Rankhilfen im Bereich der Bodensenke, etwa Solarmodule und Drahtgitter, an denen Wein emporwachsen kann. Vorbildfunktion hat die Initiative sowohl im Hinblick auf die Einbindung von Studenten, Anwohnerschaft und Fachleuten als auch durch die Kombination verschiedener Ansätze – von den zu erwartenden Passivstrategien bis hin zur Landschaftsgestaltung.   [1] Eine ökologisch konzipierte Bodensenke ist ein Landschaftselement, um Schlick und Schadstoffe aus Stauwasser zu filtern. Sie besteht aus einem abgesenkten, mit Pflanzen oder Kompost versehenen Dränagelauf.

Ce projet comprend un jardin de campus conçu et réalisé par un groupe d'étudiants en architecture, urbanisme et ingénierie, et un pavillon « vert » dessiné par les étudiants et construit avec l'assistance d'entreprises et autres partenaires locaux. La zone d'entrée du campus donnant sur le Boulevard Zhong-Xiao anciennement masquée par un grand mur est l'emplacement choisi pour le jardin et une zone de biorétention[1]. Des panneaux solaires qui font également fonction d'écrans de protection solaire sur les bâtiments du campus fournissent l'énergie aux pompes utilisées sur place. Les plantations ont été effectuées par les gens du quartier. Le Pavillon du lotus est une vaste pièce qui bénéficie d'un refroidissement passif de l'atmosphère et d'un éclairage à faible consommation. De près de 10 m de haut, il capte les vents utilisés pour la ventilation naturelle et utilise également des panneaux solaires. Le toit en partie planté apporte une isolation thermique. Il est entouré d'un écran en bambou dont les ouvertures laissent circuler l'air et participent à la protection solaire. Les étudiants ont mis en place divers dispositifs dont des panneaux solaires et des écrans en treillis métallique sur lesquels poussent des plantes grimpantes. Cette initiative est exemplaire tant en termes de participation des étudiants, de la communauté et des professionnels locaux que d'association de techniques variées, allant de stratégies passives à des solutions qui relèvent de l'aménagement du paysage.   [1] Une zone de biorétention est un élément de paysage qui réduit le limon et la pollution des eaux d'écoulement de surface. Il consiste en plans de drainage dont les côtés, légèrement inclinés, sont recouverts de plantes ou de compost.

This intervention has turned space that was otherwise unused and uncared for into useful, ecologically productive gardens.

Diese Intervention ist zugleich die Umnutzung eines Raums, der zuvor brach lag und nicht gepflegt wurde, als ökologisch produktiver Garten.

Cette intervention a permis de transformer des lieux inutilisés et mal entretenus en jardins écologiques productifs.

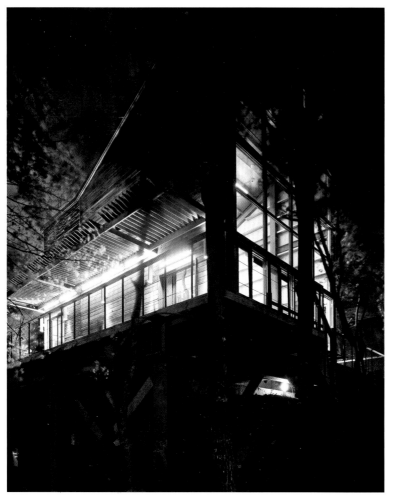

This pavilion is basically one large room, with an open loft over the southern portion. Set on steel stilts, the lightweight metal-stud structure rises to a height of 9.7 meters above the ground to catch available breezes.

Dieser Pavillon ist im Prinzip ein einziger großer Raum mit einem offenen Loftbereich über dem südlichen Abschnitt. Die Leichtbau-Metall-skelettkonstruktion erhebt sich 9,7 m hoch über dem Boden, um den verfügbaren Luftzug zu nutzen.

Ce pavillon est en fait une vaste pièce avec atelier ouvert au sud. Posée sur des pilotis d'acier, cette structure métallique légère s'élève jusqu'à une hauteur de 9,7 m au-dessus du sol pour capter la brise.

Student initiatives include a green roof on top of an existing building, and channeled water runoff to irrigate the plants.

Studenteninitiativen legten ein begrüntes Dach auf einem bestehenden Gebäude und ein Kanalisierungssystem für das Ablaufwasser zur Bewässerung der Pflanzen an.

Parmi les initiatives des étudiants figurent un jardin sur le toit d'un bâtiment existant et l'utilisation de l'eau de pluie pour irriguer les plantes.

Palleroni's initiatives in an educational environment show that ecologically
driven projects can be woven into an
existing urban environment.

Palleronis Studenteninitiativen be-
weisen, dass sich ökologisch moti-
vierte Projekte in ein bestehendes
urbanes Umfeld integrieren lassen.

Les initiatives éducatives de Palleroni
montrent que des projets de nature
écologique peuvent s'intégrer à un
environnement urbain existant.

RENZO PIANO

Renzo Piano Building Workshop
34 rue des Archives / 75004 Paris / France
Tel: +33 1 42 78 00 82 / Fax: +33 1 42 78 01 98

Via Rubens 29 / 16158 Genoa / Italy
Tel: +39 010 61 711 / Fax: +39 010 61 71 350
E-mail: info@rpbw.com / Web: www.rpbw.com

RENZO PIANO was born in 1937 in Genoa, Italy. He studied at the University of Florence and at the Polytechnic Institute (Milan, 1964). He formed his own practice (Studio Piano) in 1965, then associated with Richard Rogers (Piano & Rogers, 1971–78). Piano completed the Centre Pompidou in Paris in 1977. From 1978 to 1980 he worked with Peter Rice (Piano & Rice Associates). He created the Renzo Piano Building Workshop in 1981 in Genoa and Paris. Piano received the RIBA Gold Medal in 1989. His built work includes: Menil Collection Museum (Houston, Texas, 1981–86); San Nicola Stadium (Bari, Italy, 1987–90); the 1988–90 Extension of the IRCAM (Paris, France); Kansai International Airport Terminal (Osaka, Japan, 1988–94); Cité Internationale de Lyon (Lyon, France, 1985–96); Beyeler Foundation (Riehen, Basel, Switzerland, 1991–97); Jean-Marie Tjibaou Cultural Center (New Caledonia, 1991–98); Mercedes Benz Design Center (Stuttgart, Germany, 1993–98); Reconstruction of a section of Potsdamer Platz (Berlin, Germany, 1992–2000); Parma Auditorium (Italy, 1997–2001); Maison Hermès (Tokyo, Japan, 1998–2001); Rome Auditorium (Italy, 1994–2002); Conversion of the Lingotto Factory Complex (Turin, Italy, 1983–2003); Padre Pio Pilgrimage Church (San Giovanni Rotondo, Foggia, Italy, 1991–2004); Renovation and Expansion of the Morgan Library (New York, New York, 2000–06); New York Times Building (New York, New York, 2005–07); High Museum of Art Expansion (Atlanta, Georgia, 2005–08); and Renovation and Expansion of the California Academy of Sciences (San Francisco, California, 2005–08, published here). Current work includes the London Bridge Tower (London, UK); and Art Institute of Chicago Expansion (Chicago, Illinois).

RENZO PIANO wurde 1937 in Genua geboren. Er studierte an der Universität Florenz und der Polytechnischen Hochschule Mailand (1964). Sein Büro Studio Piano gründete er 1965, gefolgt von einer Partnerschaft mit Richard Rogers (Piano & Rogers, 1971–78). Die Arbeiten am Centre Pompidou in Paris konnte Piano 1977 abschließen. Von 1978 bis 1980 arbeitete er mit Peter Rice (Piano & Rice Associates). 1981 gründete er sein Büro Renzo Piano Building Workshop mit Sitz in Genua und Paris. 1989 wurde Piano mit der RIBA-Goldmedaille ausgezeichnet. Zu seinen realisierten Bauten zählen u. a. das Menil Collection Museum (Houston, Texas, 1981–86), das Stadion San Nicola (Bari, 1987–90), der Erweiterungsbau des IRCAM (Paris, 1988–90), der Flughafenterminal Kansai International (Osaka, Japan, 1988–94), die Cité Internationale de Lyon (Lyon, Frankreich, 1985–96), die Fondation Beyeler (Riehen, Schweiz, 1991–97), das Kulturzentrum Jean-Marie Tjibaou (Neukaledonien, 1991–98), das Mercedes Benz Design Center (Stuttgart, 1993–98), die Neugestaltung eines Abschnitts des Potsdamer Platzes (Berlin, 1992–2000), das Auditorium in Parma (Italien, 1997–2001), die Maison Hermès (Tokio, 1998–2001), das Auditorium in Rom (1994–2002), die Umgestaltung des Lingotto-Werkskomplexes (Turin, 1983–2003), die Pilgerkirche Padre Pio (San Giovanni Rotondo, Foggia, Italien, 1991–2004), die Renovierung und Erweiterung der Morgan Library (New York, 2000–06), das New York Times Building (New York, 2005–07), die Erweiterung des High Museum of Art (Atlanta, Georgia, 2005–08) sowie die Renovierung und Erweiterung der California Academy of Sciences (San Francisco, 2005–08, hier vorgestellt). Aktuelle Projekte sind u. a. der London Bridge Tower und die Erweiterung des Art Institute of Chicago.

RENZO PIANO, né en 1937 à Gênes, en Italie, étudie à l'université de Florence et à l'Institut polytechnique de Milan (1964). Il crée son agence, Studio Piano, en 1965, puis s'associe à Richard Rogers (Piano & Rogers, 1971–78). Ils achèvent le Centre Pompidou à Paris en 1977. De 1978 à 1980, il collabore avec Peter Rice (Piano & Rice Associates). Il fonde le Renzo Piano Building Workshop, en 1981, à Gênes et Paris. Il a reçu la médaille d'or du RIBA en 1989. Parmi ses réalisations : le Menil Collection Museum (Houston, Texas, 1981–86) ; le stade San Nicola (Bari, Italie, 1987–90) ; l'extension de l'IRCAM (Paris, 1988–90) ; le terminal de l'aéroport international du Kansai (Osaka, Japon, 1988–94) ; la Cité internationale (Lyon, 1985–96) ; la Fondation Beyeler (Riehen, Bâle, Suisse, 1991–97) ; le centre culturel Jean-Marie Tjibaou (Nouvelle-Calédonie, 1991–98) ; le Mercedes Benz Design Center (Stuttgart, Allemagne, 1993–98) ; la reconstruction d'une partie de la Potsdamer Platz (Berlin, 1992–2000) ; l'auditorium de Parme (1997–2001) ; la maison Hermès (Tokyo, 1998–2001) ; l'auditorium de Rome (1994–2002) ; la conversion de l'usine du Lingotto (Turin, Italie, 1983–2003) ; l'église de pèlerinage du Padre Pio (San Giovanni Rotondo, Foggia, Italie, 1991–2004) ; la rénovation et l'agrandissement de la Bibliothèque Morgan (New York, 2000–06) ; le New York Times Building (New York, 2005–07) ; l'extension du High Museum of Art (Atlanta, Georgie, 2005–08) ainsi que la rénovation et l'angrandissment de la California Academy of Sciences (San Francisco, 2005–08, publiée ici). Parmi ses projets actuels : la London Bridge Tower (Londres) et l'extension du Chicago Art Institute (Chicago, Illinois).

RENOVATION AND EXPANSION
OF THE CALIFORNIA ACADEMY OF SCIENCES

San Francisco, California, USA, 2005–08

Site area: 74 322 m². Floor area: 34 374 m². Client: California Academy of Sciences.
Cost: $370 million (including exhibition program and costs associated with the Academy's temporary housing).
Collaboration: Gordon H. Chong and Partners Architects, San Francisco

The green roof of the new building of the California Academy of Sciences is its most prominent ecological element, with a skylight visible here.

Das auffälligste ökologische Element des Neubaus der California Academy of Sciences ist das begrünte Dach. Hier ein Oberlicht.

Le toit végétalisé du nouveau bâtiment de l'Académie des sciences de Californie est son plus important atout écologique. Ci-dessous, une des verrières.

One of the ten largest natural history museums in the world, the California Academy of Sciences was founded in 1853. The institution declared: "The new CAS will be at the forefront of green building design, showcasing world-class architecture that fully integrates green building features to reflect its mission to protect the natural world." The completed structure has a LEED Platinum rating, reflecting its strategies to conserve energy and to use environmentally friendly building materials. The undulating roof of the structure, with a surface of over one hectare, is covered with 1.8 million native California plants. Careful study of the plants themselves, but also of the seismic implications of a planted roof, was part of the preparation of this aspect of the design that is open to visitors. It is calculated that the design of the roof reduces temperatures inside the museum by about 6°C. A rainwater collection system is designed to store and reuse about 13 500 cubic meters of water each year, reused for irrigation and gray water. The roof's shape and, indeed, the entire design of the museum were conceived to form a continuum with the surrounding park environment. Intended for schoolchildren and the general public, the Academy focuses on education and research on conserving natural environments and habitats.

Die 1853 gegründete California Academy of Sciences zählt zu den zehn größten Museen für Naturgeschichte weltweit. Die Institution ließ verlautbaren: „Die neue CAS wird sich als Pionier grüner Bauplanung erweisen und Weltklasse-Architektur zeigen, die grüne Gebäudetechniken umfassend integriert, um ihrer Mission, die Natur zu schützen, Rechnung zu tragen." Der fertiggestellte Bau wurde mit einer LEED-Platinmedaille ausgezeichnet, eine Würdigung der Energiesparstrategien sowie der Verwendung umweltfreundlicher Baumaterialien. Das geschwungene Dach mit einer Fläche von über einem Hektar wurde mit 1,8 Millionen einheimischen kalifornischen Pflanzen begrünt. Im Zuge der Vorbereitungen für diesen öffentlichen Gebäudeabschnitt setzte man sich intensiv mit den Pflanzen auseinander ebenso wie mit den seismischen Aspekten des begrünten Dachs. Berechnungen zufolge reduziert das so geplante Dach die Innentemperatur des Museums um rund 6 °C. Eine Regenwassersammelanlage speichert und nutzt rund 13 500 m^3 Wasser pro Jahr, die zur Bewässerung und als Grauwasser zum Einsatz kommen. Die Form des Dachs und im Grunde die gesamte Gestaltung des Museums wurden darauf angelegt, ein Kontinuum mit dem umgebenden Park zu bilden. Die Akademie, die sich an Schulkinder sowie an ein allgemeines Publikum wendet, bietet in erster Linie Bildungsprogramme an und widmet sich der Forschung zum Schutz der Umwelt und Lebensräume.

La California Academy of Sciences, un des dix plus grands musées d'histoire naturelle du monde, a été fondée en 1853. À son lancement, l'institution avait fait savoir que « la nouvelle Académie serait à l'avant-garde des constructions "vertes", grâce à une architecture de niveau international qui intégrerait pleinement les spécificités de la construction écologique, reflétant ainsi sa mission de protection du monde naturel. » Le bâtiment achevé a reçu la certification LEED Platine pour ses stratégies d'économie d'énergie et d'utilisation de matériaux écologiques. La toiture de forme ondulée qui recouvre plus d'1 ha est plantée de 1,8 million de plants de végétaux californiens. L'étude approfondie des plantes, mais aussi les implications du poids d'un toit végétal en cas de séisme, ont déterminé la conception de cette couverture fréquentée par les visiteurs. On a calculé que ce principe de végétalisation permettait de réduire la température à l'intérieur du musée de 6 % environ. Un système de collecte des eaux de pluie récupère, stocke et réutilise environ 13 500 m^3 d'eau chaque année pour l'irrigation et autres usages courants. La forme du toit et la conception du musée tout entier forment un continuum avec le parc environnant. Ouverte au grand public et aux enfants des écoles, l'Académie se consacre à l'éducation et à des recherches portant sur la conservation des environnements et des habitats naturels.

Piano's light columns and canopy are almost a signature feature here, giving the building an airiness that might seem to contrast with the earth and vegetation-covered roof.

Pianos schlanke Stützen und leichte Baldachindächer wirken hier fast wie ein Markenzeichen und verleihen dem Bau eine Luftigkeit, die geradezu als Gegenpol zur Erdmasse und Begrünung des Dach fungieren.

Les colonnes légères et l'auvent créés par Piano relèvent presque de sa signature. Ils confèrent au bâtiment une légèreté qui semble trancher avec le toit recouvert de terre et de végétation.

Piano has used dome-shaped elements in his architecture – in Turin at the Lingotto Factory and in the context of the Columbus International Exhibition in Genoa. Left, an interior view of the dome with its walkways and trees.

Bereits an anderer Stelle hat Piano Kuppeln in seiner Architektur eingesetzt – am Lingotto-Werk in Turin und der Internationalen Kolumbus-Ausstellung in Genua. Links eine Innenansicht mit Blick auf die Kuppel, ihre Laufstege und Bäume.

Piano a souvent utilisé des formes en coupole, comme à Turin (Usine du Lingotto) ou dans le contexte de l'Exposition internationale Christophe Colomb à Gênes. À gauche, vue intérieure de la coupole, avec ses coursives et ses arbres.

POLK STANLEY ROWLAND
CURZON PORTER

Polk Stanley Rowland Curzon Porter Architects
700 South Schiller
Little Rock, AR 72201
USA

Tel: +1 501 378 0878
Fax: +1 501 372 7629
E-mail: general.info@polkstanley.com
Web: www.polkstanley.com

REESE ROWLAND was born in Pomona, California. He attended the University of Arkansas School of Architecture (1986–90). He worked with Wittenberg Delony and Davidson Architects (1990–96) before joining **POLK STANLEY** in 1996. He is a Principal of the firm, responsible for project conceptual design and development. He was the project designer for the World Headquarters of Heifer International (Little Rock, Arkansas, 2004–06, published here). Born in Little Rock, **JOE STANLEY** also attended the University of Arkansas School of Architecture (1964–69). He is a founding partner and Senior Principal of the firm. He was the project Managing Principal for the Heifer Building. Amongst the significant projects of the firm, Historic Arkansas Museum (Little Rock, 2002); First Tee of Arkansas (Little Rock, 2002); Acxiom River Market Tower (Little Rock, 2004); University of Arkansas Clinton School of Public Service (Little Rock, 2004); University of Arkansas Harmon Avenue Transit Facility (Fayetteville, 2006); Acxiom Corporate Data Center (Little Rock, 2007); and the Arkansas Studies Institute (Little Rock, 2008), all in Arkansas, USA.

REESE ROWLAND wurde in Pomona, Kalifornien, geboren. Er studierte Architektur an der Universität Arkansas (1986–90). Zunächst arbeitete er für Wittenberg Delony and Davidson Architects (1990–96), 1996 schloss er sich **POLK STANLEY** an. Als einer der Partner des Büros ist er für Konzeptentwurf und Entwicklung der Projekte zuständig. Er zeichnete für den Projektentwurf der Firmenzentrale von Heifer International verantwortlich (Little Rock, Arkansas, 2004–06, hier vorgestellt). **JOE STANLEY** wurde in Little Rock geboren und studierte ebenfalls Architektur an der Universität Arkansas (1964–69). Er ist Gründungsmitglied und Seniorpartner des Büros und übernahm die Projektleitung für das Heifer Building. Zu den wichtigsten Projekten des Büros zählen u. a. das Historic Arkansas Museum (Little Rock, 2002), das First Tee of Arkansas (Little Rock, 2002), der Acxiom River Market Tower (Little Rock, 2004), die Clinton School of Public Service an der Universität Arkansas (Little Rock, 2004), der ÖPNV-Knotenpunkt der Universität Arkansas an der Harmon Avenue (Fayetteville, 2006), das Acxiom Corporate Data Center (Little Rock, 2007) sowie das Arkansas Studies Institute (Little Rock, 2008), alle in Arkansas, USA.

REESE ROWLAND, né à Pomona, Californie, a étudié à l'École d'architecture de l'université de l'Arkansas (1986–90). Il a travaillé pour Wittenberg Delony and Davidson Architects (1990–96), avant de rejoindre **POLK STANLEY** en 1996. Il est un des dirigeants de l'agence, responsable des projets de conception et du développement. Il a conçu le projet du siège mondial d'Heifer International (Little Rock, Arkansas, 2004–06, publié ici). Né à Little Rock, **JOE STANLEY** a effectué les mêmes études (1964–69). Il est associé fondateur et principal dirigeant de l'agence, et a dirigé la réalisation de l'immeuble Heifer. Parmi les réalisations les plus importantes de l'agence : l'Historic Arkansas Museum (Little Rock, 2002) ; le First Tee of Arkansas (Little Rock, 2002) ; la River Market Tower Axciom (Little Rock, 2004) ; la Clinton School of Public Service (Université de l'Arkansas, Little Rock, 2004) ; le centre de transit d'Harmon avenue (Université de l'Arkansas, Fayetteville, 2006) ; le centre informatique d'Acxiom (Little Rock, 2007) ; et l'Arkansas Studies Institute (Little Rock, 2008), toutes en Arkansas, États-Unis.

HEIFER INTERNATIONAL WORLD HEADQUARTERS

Little Rock, Arkansas, USA, 2004–06

Floor area: 9105 m². Client: Heifer International. Cost: $17.9 million.
Team: Reese Rowland, David Porter, Joe Stanley

The basic form of the Heifer International Headquarters building is a simple arc. Its lightness and transparency is apparent in these images.

Die Grundform der Heifer International Headquarters ist ein schlichter Bogen. Diese Bilder veranschaulichen ihre Leichtigkeit und Transparenz.

La forme de base du siège de Heifer International est celle d'un simple arc. Sa légèreté et sa transparence sont sensibles dans ces photographies.

Named one of the top ten green projects in the United States for 2007 (AIA/COTE), and holder of a USGBC LEED Platinum rating for its sustainability and environmental performance, the Heifer Building is located in a former rail-yard site. Built for the world hunger organization Heifer International, the landfill for the site and paving came from the former masonry and bricks of the rail facilities. Located next to the Clinton Library, the two projects form a 25-hectare green zone. Designed to "maximize sunlight and rainwater and avoid pollutants, the headquarters will see a 55% energy saving over conventional buildings. The narrow design allows for views to the green areas around the building for the 472 employees. Wetland areas and bioswales[1] are used to help with water recycling and natural cooling. The architects explain: "Structural 'tree' columns visually extend wetland trees, representing a symbiotic relationship between man-made and nature." For all of its environmental credentials the building also stands out for its obvious architectural quality—a proof that sustainability need not go hand in hand with unattractive design. The building won an AIA Honor Award (2008).   [1] A bioswale is a landscape element designed to remove silt and pollution from surface runoff water. It consists of a drainage course with gently sloped sides filled with vegetation or compost.

Das auf einem ehemaligen Verschiebebahnhof gelegene Heifer Building kam 2007 in die Top Ten der grünsten Projekte der Vereinigten Staaten (AIA/COTE) und wurde vom USGBC mit einer LEED-Platinmedaille für Nachhaltigkeit und Umweltfreundlichkeit gewürdigt. Mauerwerk und Ziegel der ehemaligen Bahnanlagen wurden genutzt, um das Grundstück, auf dem der Neubau für die weltweit im Kampf gegen Hunger engagierte Organisation Heifer International errichtet wurde, aufzufüllen und Wege zu pflastern. Die beiden neben der Clinton-Bibliothek gelegenen Projekte bilden eine 25 ha große grüne Zone. Die Firmenzentrale, die „so angelegt [wurde], dass Sonnenlicht und Regenwasser optimal genutzt werden, wird im Vergleich zu herkömmlichen Bauten eine 55 %ige Energieersparnis verzeichnen können. Der schmale Grundriss des Baus ermöglicht den 472 Angestellten im gesamten Gebäude Ausblicke auf die grüne Umgebung. Feuchtgebiete und Bodensenken[1] wurden eingesetzt, um die Wasseraufbereitung und natürliche Klimatisierung zu unterstützen. Die Architekten erklären: „Tragende baumähnliche Stützen knüpfen formal an die Bäume in den Feuchtgebieten an und stehen für ein symbiotisches Verhältnis von Natur und Menschenwerk." Abgesehen von seinen Umweltqualitäten zeichnet sich der Bau durch seine offensichtliche architektonische Qualität aus – ein Beweis dafür, dass Nachhaltigkeit keineswegs mit unattraktiver Gestaltung gleichzusetzen ist. Das Gebäude wurde 2008 mit einem Ehrenpreis des AIA ausgezeichnet.   [1] Eine ökologisch konzipierte Bodensenke ist ein Landschaftselement, um Schlick und Schadstoffe aus Stauwasser zu filtern. Sie besteht aus einem abgesenkten, mit Pflanzen oder Kompost versehenen Dränagelauf.

Désigné comme l'une des dix premières réalisations « vertes » aux États-Unis en 2007 (AIA/COTE) et détenteur d'une certification LEED Platine de l'USGBC pour sa durabilité et ses performances environnementales, cet immeuble, édifié pour l'organisation internationale contre la faim Heifer International, se trouve sur le terrain d'anciens dépôts ferroviaires. Les terrassements et les pavements proviennent d'anciennes constructions en brique existant sur place. Situé à proximité de la bibliothèque Clinton, ils bénéficient tous deux d'un espace vert de 25 ha. Conçu de façon à « optimiser l'utilisation de la lumière solaire, de l'eau de pluie, et de manière à éviter les polluants, le siège économisera 55 % de l'énergie consommée par un immeuble classique. La minceur du bâtiment permet d'offrir une vue sur la verdure environnante aux 472 employés ». Des zones humides et des zones de biorétention[1] servent à recycler l'eau et à la climatisation naturelle. Les architectes expliquent que « des colonnes structurelles en "arbre" démultiplient visuellement la présence des arbres des zones humides, tout en créant une relation symbiotique entre ce qui est dû à la main de l'homme et ce qui est naturel ». En dehors de ses performances environnementales, l'immeuble se remarque également pour sa qualité architecturale évidente, et prouve que la durabilité n'et pas toujours synonyme de « peu séduisant ». Il a remporté un Prix d'honneur de l'AIA (2008).   [1] Une zone de biorétention est un élément de paysage qui réduit le limon et la pollution des eaux d'écoulement de surface. Il consiste en plans de drainage dont les côtés, légèrement inclinés, sont recouverts de plantes ou de compost.

The building's outer curve is somewhat more closed than the inner one, as can be seen in the image above and that opposite.

Die Außenseite des geschwungenen Baus wirkt geschlossener als seine Innenseite, wie die Bilder oben und auf der rechten Seite zeigen.

La façade extérieure de l'arc est un peu plus fermée que sa façade intérieure, comme on peut le voir sur l'image ci-dessus et à droite.

Set amongst vegetation in the image above, the building seems the perfect incarnation of the green office. Below, interior views show the generous, bright spaces.

Eingebettet in die Vegetation, wie oben zu sehen, präsentiert sich der Bau als ideale Inkarnation des grünen Büros. Innenansichten (unten) zeigen die großzügigen, hellen Räumlichkeiten.

Photographié au milieu de la végétation (ci-dessus) l'immeuble semble une parfaite incarnation de l'architecture écologique de bureaux. Ci-dessous, vues intérieures montrant la lumineuse générosité des volumes.

PHILIPPE RAHM

Philippe Rahm architectes
12 rue Chabanais
75002 Paris
France

Tel: +33 1 49 26 91 55
E-mail: info@philipperahm.com
Web: www.philipperahm.com

PHILIPPE RAHM was born in 1967 and studied architecture at the EPFL in Lausanne and the ETH in Zurich. He created the firm Décosterd & Rahm associés with Gilles Décosterd in 1995 in Lausanne. Décosterd & Rahm represented Switzerland in the 2002 Venice Architecture Biennale, and received the Swiss Federal Art Prize in 2003. They worked on an atelier-residence for the artist Fabrice Hyber in the Vendée region of France, and on a project for a park in San Sebastián, Spain, with the landscape architects Gilles Clément and Joseph Andueza. Rahm and Décosterd ceased direct collaboration in 2005 and Philippe Rahm created his own firm, Philippe Rahm architectes, in Paris. Since then, he has worked on an urban design for a street (Gdansk, Poland, 2006–09); a pavilion for the École des Beaux-Arts (Nantes, France, 2006–07); an office building and shopping mall (Marghera-Venice, Italy, 2008–); and Floating Pavilions for the Voies Naviguables de France (Paris and Lyon, France, 2008); as well as the project published here, Digestible Gulf Stream (Venice Architecture Biennale, 2008), which serves as the theoretical basis of a series of new projects, including a house for the noted French artist Dominique Gonzalez-Foerster.

PHILIPPE RAHM wurde 1967 geboren und studierte Architektur an der EPFL in Lausanne und der ETH Zürich. 1995 gründete er mit Gilles Décosterd das Büro Décosterd & Rahm associés in Lausanne. 2002 vertraten Décosterd & Rahm die Schweiz auf der Architekturbiennale in Venedig und wurden 2003 mit dem Schweizer Bundeskunstpreis ausgezeichnet. Sie arbeiteten an einem Atelier und Wohnhaus für den Künstler Fabrice Hyber in der Vendée, Frankreich, und, gemeinsam mit den Landschaftsarchitekten Gilles Clément und Joseph Andueza an einem Parkprojekt für San Sebastián in Spanien. Rahm und Décosterd beendeten ihre direkte Zusammenarbeit 2005. Rahm gründete daraufhin sein eigenes Büro, Philippe Rahm architectes, in Paris. Seither arbeitet er einer Straßenplanung (Danzig, Polen, 2006–09), einem Pavillon für die École des Beaux-Arts (Nantes, 2006–07), einem Bürokomplex und Einkaufszentrum (Marghera, Venedig, 2008–), den schwimmenden Pavillons für die Voies Naviguables de France (Paris und Lyon, 2008) sowie an dem hier vorgestellten Projekt, dem Digestible Gulf Stream (Architekturbiennale Venedig, 2008), der theoretischen Grundlage für eine neue Projektreihe, in deren Rahmen auch ein Haus für die renommierte französische Künstlerin Dominique Gonzalez-Foerster geplant ist.

PHILIPPE RAHM, né en 1967 en Suisse, a étudié l'architecture à l'EPFL à Lausanne et à l'ETH à Zurich. Il a fondé, en 1995 à Lausanne, avec Gilles Décosterd, l'agence Décosterd & Rahm associés. Décosterd & Rahm ont représenté la Suisse à la Biennale d'architecture de Venise et reçu le Prix fédéral d'art en 2003. Ils ont travaillé sur une résidence atelier pour l'artiste Fabrice Hyber en Vendée (France), et un projet de parc à San Sebastián, Espagne, avec les paysagistes Gilles Clément et Joseph Andueza. Rahm et Décosterd ont cessé leur collaboration directe en 2005, et Philippe Rahm a créé sa propre agence, Philippe Rahm architectes, à Paris. Depuis, il a travaillé sur l'aménagement d'une rue (Gdansk, Pologne, 2006–09); un pavillon pour l'École des beaux-arts (Nantes, France, 2006–07); un immeuble de bureaux et une galerie marchande (Venise Marghera, Italie, 2008–); des pavillons flottants pour la société Voies navigables de France (Paris et Lyon, France, 2008); ainsi que le projet publié ici, Digestible Gulf Stream (Biennale d'architecture de Venise, 2008), qui sert de base théorique à une série de nouveaux projets, dont une maison pour la célèbre artiste Dominique Gonzalez-Foerster.

DIGESTIBLE GULF STREAM

11th Venice Architecture Biennale, Italy, 2008

Floor area: 200 m². Cost: not disclosed.
Collaboration: Piero Macola (Comic Strip); Syd Matters (Music)

In this project, presented at the 2008 Architecture Biennale in Venice, the architect further explores his conviction that the architecture of the future is not only green, but intimately and completely related to climate and physiology. The installation serves as the theoretical foundation for developing architecture based on a thermodynamic process for generating space. As Rahm wrote in the Biennale catalogue: "Architecture should no longer build spaces, but rather create temperatures and atmospheres. Here, two horizontal metal planes are extended at different heights. The lower plane is heated to 28°C, the upper one is cooled to 12°C. Like a miniature Gulf Stream, their position creates a movement of air using the natural phenomenon of convection, in which rising hot air cools on contact with the upper cool sheet and, falling, is then reheated on contact with the hot sheet, thus creating a constant thermal flow, akin to an invisible landscape." The temperatures selected are deemed to be the two extremes of "comfort"—below 12°C it is too cold and above 28°C it starts to become unpleasantly hot. The inhabitant may move around in this invisible landscape and freely choose a climate according to his or her activity or clothing. Rahm points out that there are various methods to cool an architectural space, or rather a physiological one, including the use of mint (menthol), leading him to relate architecture to gastronomy in this inventive proposal.

Mit dem 2008 auf der Architekturbiennale in Venedig vorgestellten Projekt veranschaulicht der Architekt seine Überzeugung, dass die Architektur der Zukunft nicht nur grün, sondern eng und umfassend mit Klima und Physiologie verbunden ist. Die Installation bildet die theoretische Grundlage für eine Architektur, die Raum mithilfe thermodynamischer Prozesse schafft. Im Katalog zur Biennale schrieb Rahm: „Architektur sollte nicht länger Räume bauen, sondern Temperaturzonen und Atmosphären schaffen. Hier wurden zwei horizontale Metallebenen in unterschiedlicher Höhe installiert. Die untere Ebene wurde auf 28 °C erwärmt, die obere auf 12 °C heruntergekühlt. Durch ihre Position entsteht wie bei einem Golfstrom im Kleinformat ein Luftstrom nach dem natürlichen Prinzip der Umwälzung, demzufolge die aufsteigende warme Luft durch Kontakt mit der oberen, kühlen Metallebene abkühlt und sich beim Sinken durch den Kontakt zur wärmeren Ebene wieder aufheizt. Hierdurch entsteht, wie eine unsichtbare Landschaft, ein permanenter thermischer Fluss." Die gewählten Temperaturen galten als äußerste Pole des als „angenehm" empfundenen Temperaturspektrums – unter 12 °C wird in der Regel als zu kalt, über 28 °C als unangenehm heiß empfunden. In dieser unsichtbaren Landschaft können die Bewohner sich frei bewegen und je nach Aktivität oder Bekleidung die von ihnen gewünschte Klimazone wählen. Rahm weist darauf hin, dass es verschiedene Methoden gibt, einen architektonischen oder vielmehr physiologischen Raum zu kühlen, etwa durch den Einsatz von Minze (Menthol), was ihn dazu veranlasste, Architektur und Gastronomie in seinem ungewöhnlichen Entwurf zu verknüpfen.

Dans ce projet présenté à la Biennale d'architecture de Venise 2008, l'architecte développe encore davantage sa conviction que l'architecture du futur ne sera pas seulement « verte », mais intimement et complètement liée au climat et à la physiologie. L'installation sert de point de départ théorique pour développer une architecture fondée sur un processus thermodynamique qui génère l'espace. Comme Rahm l'écrit dans le catalogue de la Biennale : « L'architecture ne devrait plus construire des espaces, mais plutôt créer des textures et des atmosphères. Ici, deux plans horizontaux en métal sont tendus à différentes hauteurs. Le plan inférieur est chauffé à 28 °C, le supérieur est refroidi à 12 °C. Comme un Gulf Stream miniature, leur position crée un mouvement de l'air par convexion naturelle. L'air chaud qui monte se refroidit au contact de la tôle d'acier plus froide, redescend, puis se réchauffe au contact de la tôle réchauffée, créant ainsi un flux thermique continu, semblable à un paysage invisible. » Les températures choisies sont censées représenter les extrêmes du confort ressenti : en dessous de 12 °C il fait froid, au-dessus de 28 °C, la chaleur commence à devenir désagréable. L'occupant se déplace dans ce paysage invisible et choisit librement le climat adapté à son activité ou à ses vêtements du moment. Rahm fait remarquer qu'il existe diverses méthodes pour refroidir un volume architectural, dont certaines sont physiologiques, comme l'utilisation de menthe (menthol), ce qui le conduit à faire un lien entre architecture et gastronomie dans cette proposition inventive.

Philippe Rahm renders the warm and cold areas of the house in schematic form (above).

Philippe Rahms schematische Darstellung der warmen und kalten Zonen des Hauses (oben).

Ci-dessus, Philippe Rahm a exprimé sous forme schématique les zones chaudes et froides de la maison.

Working with and for an artist in this instance, Rahm alternates between rather romantic views of the project (above) and more technical diagrams (right).

Rahm, der in diesem Fall mit und für eine Künstlerin arbeitete, präsentiert sein Projekt sowohl auf eher romantische Weise (oben) als auch in technischen Diagrammen (rechts).

Travaillant ici avec un dessinateur, Rahm alterne les visions assez romantiques du projet (ci-dessus) et des diagrammes plus techniques (à droite).

RAU

*RAU
Office KNSM-Laan 65
1019 LB Amsterdam
The Netherlands*

*Tel: +31 20 419 02 02
E-mail: info@rau.eu
Web: www.rau.eu*

THOMAS RAU, who is German, was born in 1960. He studied architecture and engineering at the Technical University of Aachen (1983–89). He created his present firm in 1992 in Amsterdam, after having worked in a number of offices in the same city between 1989 and 1992. The most significant projects of the firm include the City Hall Middelburg (1999–2004); Sprengeloo Technical and Vocational School (Apeldoorn, 2003–06); World Wide Fund For Nature Headquarters (Zeist, 2003–06, published here); Triodos Bank International headquarters (Zeist, 2000–07); Faculty for the University of Groningen (2003–07); De Woonplaats Office (Enschede, 2004–07); Piter Jelles Nijlân Vocational School (Leeuwarden, 2002–08); Community College (Leiden, 2003–09); Carré de Soie Offices and Housing (Lyon, France, 2007–10), all in the Netherlands unless otherwise indicated.

Der Deutsche **THOMAS RAU** wurde 1960 geboren. Er studierte Architektur und Bauingenieurwesen an der RWTH Aachen (1983–89). Sein derzeitiges Büro gründete er 1992 in Amsterdam, nachdem er dort von 1989 bis 1992 für verschiedene Büros tätig gewesen war. Zu den wichtigsten Projekten des Büros zählen das Rathaus Middelburg (1999–2004), die Technische und Berufsschule Sprengeloo (Apeldoorn, 2003–06), der World Wide Fund For Nature (Zeist, 2003–06, hier vorgestellt), die internationale Zentrale der Triodos Bank (Zeist, 2000–07), das Fakultätsgebäude der Universität Groningen (2003–07), das Büro De Woonplaats (Enschede, 2004–07), die Piter-Jelles-Nijlân-Berufsschule (Leeuwarden, 2002–08), ein Gemeindekolleg (Leiden, 2003–09) sowie der Büro- und Wohnkomplex Carré de Soie (Lyon, 2007–10), alle in den Niederlanden, sofern nicht anders angegeben.

THOMAS RAU, qui est Allemand, est né en 1960. Il a étudié l'architecture et l'ingénierie à l'Université polytechnique d'Aix-la-Chapelle (1983–89). Il a fondé son agence à Amsterdam en 1992, après avoir travaillé dans un certain nombre d'agences de cette ville entre 1989 et 1992. Parmi les principales réalisations de l'agence : le bureau municipal de Middelburg (1999–2004) ; le centre de formation technique et professionnelle Sprengeloo (Apeldoorn, 2003–06) ; le siège du WWF (Zeist, 2003–06, publié ici) ; le siège international de la banque Triodos (Zeist, 2000–07) ; le bâtiment Pôle de recherche et d'enseignement de l'université de Groningue (2003–07) ; les bureaux De Woonplaats (Enschede, 2004–07) ; le lycée professionnel Piter Jelles Nijlân (Leeuwarden, 2002–08) ; un bâtiment scolaire (Leiden, 2003–09) ; un immeuble de bureaux et de logements pour le quartier Carré de Soie (Lyon, France, 2007–10), toutes aux Pays-Bas, sauf exception.

WORLD WIDE FUND FOR NATURE

Zeist, The Netherlands, 2003–06

Floor area: 3800 m². Client: WWF Netherlands. Cost: not disclosed

WWF-Netherlands launched a project to develop a new office on the site of a former agricultural research laboratory in the Schoonoord Nature Reserve in 2003. Its initial aim was to create a carbon-neutral building. Since then, the project has evolved to apply the full set of One Planet Living principles, and is aiming to achieve a sustainable footprint. Ecological "footprinting" is a tool developed by the Global Footprint Network that measures how much land and water is needed to produce resources consumed, and waste absorption. As the architects explain: "In the moisture-balancing mud ceilings, continuous circulation through glass tubes spreads human and mechanical warmth, and—even more importantly—cooling. Through horizontal wooden blinds, a maximum amount of useful light enters. All materials were screened for environmental friendliness as well as child labor. And of course space was made for wildlife: 'bird-friendly roofing tiles' and 'bat basements.'" The former center of the 1954 building was demolished to make way for an "amorphous" central pavilion. A solar energy power station on the roof provides energy, and all installations run on vegetable oil. The building is energy self-sufficient and emits no CO_2.

2003 initiierte der niederländische WWF ein Projekt zur Entwicklung einer neuen Niederlassung auf dem Gelände eines ehemaligen landwirtschaftlichen Forschungslabors im Naturschutzgebiet Schoonoord. Anfängliches Ziel war es, ein CO_2-emmissionsfreies Gebäude zu bauen. Seither hat sich das Projekt weiterentwickelt, nun sollen die Kritierien des One-Planet-Living-Programms konsequent umgesetzt und damit ein nachhaltiger ökologischer Fußabdruck hinterlassen werden. Der „ökologische Fußabdruck" ist ein vom Global Footprint Network entwickelter Maßstab, mit dem sich ermitteln lässt, wie viel Land und Wasser benötigt werden, um die Ressourcen zu produzieren, die verbraucht werden, und um Abfälle zu beseitigen. Die Architekten erklären: „In den feuchtigkeitsregulierenden Lehmdecken sorgen Rohre für die Verteilung der Wärme, die Mensch und Maschine abstrahlen, vor allem aber auch für die Verteilung kühler Luft. Horizontale Holzlamellen regulieren das einströmende Licht. Alle Materialien wurden auf ihre Umweltverträglichkeit und ihren kinderarbeitsfreien Ursprung überprüft. Und natürlich wurde der Raum auch für Tiere gestaltet: ‚vogelfreundliche Dachziegel' und ‚Fledermauskeller'." Das ehemalige Herzstück des Altbaus von 1954 wurde abgerissen, um Platz für einen „amorphen", zentral gelegenen Pavillon zu machen. Eine Solarkraftanlage auf dem Dach liefert Strom, sämtliche Heizungsanlagen werden mit Pflanzenöl betrieben. Das Gebäude ist energietechnisch autark und CO_2-emissionsfrei.

WWF-Pays-Bas a lancé la construction d'un nouveau siège sur le site d'un ancien laboratoire situé dans la réserve naturelle de Schoonoord en 2003. Son but initial était de créer un immeuble à empreinte carbone neutre. Depuis, le projet a évolué pour mettre en œuvre les principes de One Planet Living et s'efforce d'atteindre un niveau d'empreinte pleinement écologique. Ce principe « d'empreinte écologique » est un outil mis au point par le Global Footprint Network qui mesure la quantité de terre et d'eau nécessaire pour produire les ressources consommées et l'absorption des déchets. Comme l'explique l'architecte : « Dans les plafonds de torchis à humidité stabilisée, la circulation continue d'air dans des tubes de verre diffuse la chaleur humaine ou produite mécaniquement et – plus important encore – le refroidissement. Des volets horizontaux en bois permettent la pénétration d'un maximum de lumière naturelle dans le bâtiment. Tous les matériaux ont été sélectionnés en fonction de leur impact sur l'environnement et des conditions de leur fabrication (travail des enfants). La vie sauvage a bien sûr été prise en compte : "Des tuiles de toiture favorables aux oiseaux", et des "caves pour chauves-souris". » L'ancien centre du bâtiment, construit en 1954, a été démoli pour laisser place à un pavillon central « amorphe ». Le poste de production d'énergie solaire placé sur le toit et toutes les installations fonctionnent à l'huile végétale. Le bâtiment est autonome sur le plan énergétique et n'émet pas de CO_2.

Das WWF-Gebäude, ein umweltbewusster Bau, fällt in seiner landschaftlichen Umgebung durch ein organisches Gebilde auf, das sein Herz bildet und von rechtwinkligen Büroflügeln flankiert wird.

Immeuble de bureaux répondant aux principes du développement durable, le siège du WWF s'intègre dans son cadre naturel par une forme organique centrale se projetant entre deux ailes orthogonales.

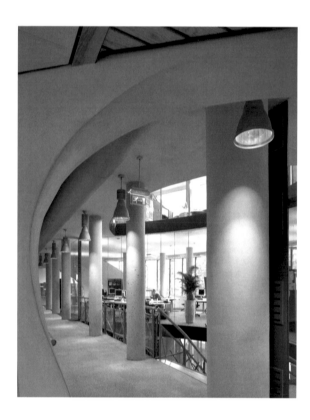

*Transparent, curving surfaces mark
the entrance and stairway seen at the
right and below. Curv-
ing walls emphasize the more organic
aspects of the design.*

Des parois de verre incurvées encer-
clent l'entrée et la cage d'escalier
que l'on aperçoit à droite et en bas.
Ces courbes renforcent les aspects
organiques du projet.

Transparente, geschwungene Linien
prägen den Eingangsbereich und das
Treppenhaus, wie rechts und unten
zu sehen. Geschwungene Wände unterstreichen die organischen Aspekte
des Entwurfs.

MICHAEL REYNOLDS

Michael Reynolds
Earthship Biotecture
P.O. Box 1041
Taos, NM 87571
USA

Tel: +1 575 751 1005
E-mail: biotecture@earthship.org
Web: www.earthship.org

MICHAEL REYNOLDS graduated with a B.Arch degree from the University of Cincinnati in 1969. He describes his own work experience as "35 years of research and development of self-sufficient housing." His concept of self-sufficiency includes the payment of little or no utilities or mortgage. He has designed and built over 300 solar structures in the United States and Canada. *The New York Times* selected him as one of its "Eco-Heroes" (April 23, 2006). He is currently working on applying his ideas to facilities for the homeless in Taos, New Mexico, and Los Angeles. A feature film about his activities, *Garbage Warrior* (www.garbagewarrior.com), has been shown in such locations as the Lincoln Center in New York (March 25, 2008) and the Museum of Modern Art (February 14, 2008). Although Reynolds is a licensed architect, his structures, long outside of the mainstream, can increasingly be considered as offering an intriguing alternative to mass-produced housing and high-energy consumption. See his Hybrid Earthship (Taos, New Mexico, 2003), published here.

MICHAEL REYNOLDS schloss sein Studium an der Universität Cincinnati 1969 mit einem B.Arch. ab. Seine Berufserfahrung beschreibt er als „35 Jahre Forschung und Entwicklung autonomer Wohnformen". Seinem Autonomiekonzept zufolge sind nur geringe oder gar keine Zahlungen für Nebenkosten und Hypotheken notwendig. In den USA und Kanada realisierte er bisher über 300 Solarbauten. Die *New York Times* ernannte ihn zu einem ihrer „Eco-Heroes" (23. April 2006). Zurzeit arbeitet er daran, seine Ideen auf Einrichtungen für Obdachlose in Taos, New Mexico, und Los Angeles zu übertragen. Ein Film über seine Aktivitäten, „Garbage Warrior" (www.garbagewarrior.com) war z.B. im Lincoln Center in New York (25. März 2008) und dem Museum of Modern Art (14. Februar 2008) zu sehen. Obwohl Reynolds Architekt ist, können seine Konstruktionen, die schon lange jenseits des Mainstreams liegen, als faszinierende Alternative zu massengefertigten Wohnbauprojekten mit hohem Energieverbrauch gelten. Das illustriert auch das hier vorgestellte Hybrid Earthship (Taos, New Mexico, 2003).

MICHAEL REYNOLDS est B. Arch de l'université de Cincinnati (1969). Il présente sa carrière professionnelle comme « 35 années de recherches et de développement sur le logement autosuffisant ». Ce concept comprend un aspect financier : le paiement de peu ou pas de charges financières d'emprunt. Il a conçu et construit plus de trois cents constructions solaires aux États-Unis et au Canada. Le *New York Times* en a fait l'un de ses « Éco-héros » (23 avril 2006). Il travaille actuellement aux applications de ses idées à des équipements pour sans-abris à Taos, Nouveau-Mexique et Los Angeles. Un documentaire sur ses activités, intitulé *Garbage Warrior* (« le guerrier des poubelles », www.garbagewarrior.com) a été présenté, dans des lieux tels que le Lincoln Center à New York, le 25 mars 2008, et le MoMA, le 14 février 2008. Bien qu'il soit architecte licencié, ses constructions, très éloignées du gros du marché, peuvent de plus en plus être considérées comme une alternative aux constructions de série à forte consommation d'énergie. A voir, pour exemple, son Hybrid Earthship (Taos, Nouveau-Mexique, 2003), publié ici.

HYBRID EARTHSHIP

Taos, New Mexico, USA, 2003

Floor area: 158 m². Client: Earthship Biotecture. Cost: $250 000

The architect lists the materials of this house as being "tires, mud, and glass." The Earthships designed (and sold) by Reynolds are intended to obey a series of "Design Principles: 1) Thermal/Solar Heating & Cooling 2) Solar & Wind Electricity 3) Contained Sewage Treatment 4) Building with Natural & Recycled Materials 5) Water Harvesting 6) Food Production." One of his favored building materials is recycled automobile tires filled with compacted earth to form a rammed-earth brick encased in steel belted rubber. As he says: "This brick, and the resulting bearing walls it forms, is virtually indestructible." Aluminum cans and glass or plastic bottles are used for interior non-structural walls. Electricity is produced with a pre-packaged photovoltaic/wind-power system. Botanical cells and an improved version of a septic tank are used to treat water that is recycled for all purposes within the house except drinking. The Hybrid Earthship and others like it have been used by Reynolds to publicize the system he has developed to build and maintain sustainable houses. Different aesthetic options are available, but the architect clearly favors rather joyously eccentric forms that make it clear that these houses are not like other residences, even those that today place an emphasis on "green" design. The concept is carried here to a level of sustainability that cannot be attained with industrially produced architecture.

Als Baumaterialien für dieses Haus nennt der Architekt „Autoreifen, Lehm und Glas." Die von Reynolds entwickelten (und vertriebenen) Earthships entsprechen einer Reihe von „Gestaltungsprinzipien": „1) Erdwärme-/Solarheizung und -kühlung; 2) Strom aus Solar- und Windkraft; 3) Unabhängige Abwasseraufbereitung; 4) Bauen mit natürlichen und recycelten Materialien; 5) Regensammelanlagen; 6) Lebensmittelproduktion". Zu seinen Lieblingsbaumaterialien zählen recycelte Autoreifen, die mit verdichteter Erde gefüllt werden, wodurch ein Stampferdeziegel mit metallverstärktem Gummimantel entsteht. Reynolds erklärt: „Dieser Ziegel und die daraus gebauten tragenden Wände sind so gut wie unzerstörbar." Für nichttragende Innenwände werden Aluminiumdosen und Plastikflaschen genutzt. Strom wird mithilfe eines Solar- und Windkraft-Fertigbausystems erzeugt. Begrünte „Zellen" und verbesserte Klärbehälter bereiten Wasser für sämtliche Nutzungszwecke auf, ausgenommen Trinkwasser. Sein Hybrid Earthship und ähnliche Modelle nutzt Reynolds, um sein System zum Bau und zur Unterhaltung nachhaltiger Häuser bekanntzumachen. Es gibt verschiedene ästhetische Varianten, dennoch scheint der Architekt ganz offensichtlich fröhlich-exzentrische Formen zu bevorzugen, die deutlich machen, dass sich diese Häuser von anderen Wohnbauten unterscheiden, selbst von solchen, die heute besonderen Wert auf „grünes" Design legen. Sein Konzept setzt Nachhaltigkeit zu einem Grad um, der mit industriell gefertigter Architektur nicht zu erreichen ist.

Selon ses propres termes, l'architecte a utilisé pour cette maison « de la terre, des pneus et du verre ». Ces Earthships (vaisseaux terrestres) conçus (et commercialisés) par Reynolds obéissent « à plusieurs principes précis : 1) chauffage et refroidissement géothermique/solaire, 2) électricité produite par le soleil et le vent, 3) traitement intégré des rejets, 4) construction avec des matériaux naturels et recyclés, 5) récupération des eaux, 6) production d'aliments ». L'un de ses matériaux de construction favoris est le pneu d'automobile recyclé rempli de terre compactée, pour former une brique prise dans un anneau de caoutchouc à armature métallique. « Cette brique, et les murs porteurs qu'elle permet de monter, est quasiment indestructible », assure-t-il. Des boîtes d'aluminium ou des bouteilles de verre ou de plastique sont utilisées dans les cloisons internes non porteuses. L'électricité est produite par un système prémonté de cellules photovoltaïques et d'éoliennes. Des cellules végétales et une version améliorée de fosse septique traitent l'eau qui est recyclée pour tous les usages domestiques, sauf la boisson. Cette maison et d'autres du même type ont permis à Reynolds de faire connaître le système qu'il a mis au point pour construire et faire exister ces résidences durables. Différentes options esthétiques sont proposées, mais l'architecte préfère à l'évidence des formes joyeusement excentriques qui expriment clairement l'originalité de ces maisons, même par rapport à celles qui mettent aujourd'hui l'accent sur leur conception verte. Le concept de durabilité est ici porté à un niveau qui ne pourrait être atteint par une construction de type industriel.

Partially buried in its desert site, the Hybrid Earthship indeed seems to be well named, evoking an almost alien presence.

Das Hybrid Earthship ist teilweise im Wüstenboden versenkt und scheint recht passend benannt zu sein, schließlich wirkt es fast außerirdisch.

En partie enterré dans le sol du désert, ce « Vaisseau terrestre hybride » justifie son nom et évoque une présence extra-terrestre.

Westend Grün (Westend Green)

ROSWAG & JANKOWSKI

Roswag & Jankowski Architekten
Lehrter Str. 57 / Haus 4
10557 Berlin
Germany

Tel: +49 30 89 73 37 73
Fax: +49 30 89 73 37 72
E-mail: kontakt@werk-a.de
Web: www.werk-a.de

Eike Roswag was born in 1969 in Gießen, Germany. He obtained his Dipl.-Ing. Architecture degree from the Technical University in Berlin (1992–2000). He worked as a partner of ZRS Architekten Ingenieure in Berlin, beginning in 2003 on projects using earth as a building material. In 2003–04 he worked on the design and construction of a rammed-earth house near Berlin (Ihlow House). Since 2006, he has been a partner with Guntram Jankowski in the firm **ROSWAG & JANKOWSKI ARCHITEKTEN** in Berlin and has taught at the Technical University there. He designed the Handmade School (with Anna Heringer) in Rudrapur (Dinajpur, Bangladesh, 2005, published on page 179), a recipient of the 2007 Aga Khan Award for Architecture. Guntram Jankowski was born in 1972 in Gräfelfing, Germany. He obtained his Dipl.-Ing. Architecture degree from the Technical University in Berlin (1993–2000). Jankowski's recent work includes the Rogge House (Berlin, 2006); and the Spindle & Klatt Big Size Club Restaurant (Berlin, 2006). Roswag and Jankowski's recent work includes the Westend Grün (Berlin, 2006–07, published here). Since 2007 they have been working on the rehabilitation of historic mud buildings and the new Oasis Restaurant made of mud blocks in the United Arab Emirates, using low-energy building technology. Since 2008 they have been working on the Built Environment Development Initiative (development of 20 learning centers) with the Aga Khan Foundation in Mozambique.

Eike Roswag wurde 1969 in Gießen geboren. Er schloss sein Architekturstudium an der Technischen Universität Berlin (1992–2000) als Diplom-Ingenieur ab. Er arbeitete als Partner bei ZRS Architekten Ingenieure in Berlin und begann 2003, Erde als Baumaterial bei seinen Projekten zu nutzen. 2003 bis 2004 arbeitete er am Entwurf und Bau eines Stampflehmhauses in der Nähe von Berlin (Haus Ihlow). Seit 2006 ist er neben Guntram Jankowski Partner im gemeinsamen Büro **ROSWAG & JANKOWSKI ARCHITEKTEN** in Berlin und unterrichtet an der dortigen Technischen Universität. Mit Anna Heringer realisierte er die Handmade School in Rudrapur (Dinajpur, Bangladesch, 2005, vorgestellt auf Seite 179), die 2007 mit dem Aga-Khan-Preis für Architektur ausgezeichnet wurde. Guntram Jankowski wurde 1972 in Gräfelfing geboren. Sein Studium an der Technischen Universität Berlin (1993–2000) schloss er als Dipl.-Ing. Architekt ab. Zu Jankowskis aktuellen Projekten zählen das Haus Rogge (Berlin, 2006) sowie das Spindler & Klatt Big Size Club Restaurant (Berlin, 2006). Unter den jüngeren Projekten von Roswag & Jankowski ist auch Westend Grün (Berlin, 2006–07, hier vorgestellt). Seit 2007 arbeitet das Büro in den Vereinigten Arabischen Emiraten an der Rekonstruktion historischer Lehmbauten und dem neuen Lehmziegel-Restaurant Oasis in Niedrigenergiebauweise. Seit 2008 sind sie an der Built Environment Development Initiative (der Entwicklung von 20 Schulungszentren) der Aga-Khan-Stiftung in Mosambik beteiligt.

Eike Roswag, né 1969 à Gießen, Allemagne, est Dipl.-Ing. Architect de l'Université Polytechnique de Berlin (1992–2000). Il a travaillé comme associé pour ZRS Architekten Ingenieure à Berlin, à partir de 2003, sur des projets utilisant la terre comme matériau de construction. En 2003–04, il a travaillé à la conception et la construction d'une maison en béton de terre près de Berlin (maison Ihlow). Depuis 2006, il est associé à Guntram Jankowski dans l'agence **ROSWAG & JANKOWSKI ARCHITEKTEN** à Berlin et enseigne à l'Université Polytechnique berlinoise. Avec Anna Heringer, il a réalisé l'école de Rudrapur (Dinajpur, Bangladesch, 2005, publiée page 179), qui a reçu le prix Aga Khan d'architecture en 2007. Guntram Jankowski, né en 1972, à Gräfelfing, Allemagne, est lui aussi Dipl.-Ing. Architect de l'Université Polytechnique de Berlin (1993–2000). Ses réalisations récentes comprennent la maison Rogge (Berlin, 2006) et le Spindler & Klatt Big Size Club Restaurant (Berlin, 2006). Le Westend Grün (Berlin, 2006–07, publié ici) est une réalisation commune de Roswag & Jankowski Architekten. Depuis 2007, tous deux interviennent sur la réhabilitation de constructions historiques en terre ainsi que du nouvel Oasis Restaurant, en briques de terre, aux Émirats arabes unis, en utilisant des technologies de construction à faible consommation d'énergie. Depuis 2008, ils travaillent au programme « Built Environment Development Initiative » (création de 20 centres d'apprentissage) avec la Fondation Aga Khan au Mozambique.

WESTEND GRÜN (WESTEND GREEN)

Berlin, Germany, 2006–07

Floor area: 187 m². Clients: Julia and Alexander von Seltmann. Cost: not disclosed

The rehabilitation of a 1930s building severely damaged during World War II started with the removal of a roof added after the war and continued with the reorganization of the entire structure, with new openings and connections added throughout. The new inner walls of the first floor are made of "mud bricks and brown mud plaster covered with white mud." Eike Roswag says: "We call the project the White Mud House. It has all the positive functions of mud buildings insofar as humidity control and fresh air are concerned. It is a very 'healthy' type of construction carried out with natural materials and no chemical-based paints or glues." The exterior is covered with 10-centimeter-thick reed thermal insulation covered with white lime plaster. This is the first building in Berlin to use such methods, which may well be inspired by Roswag's work in the developing world. A heat pump is used to reduce energy requirements, allowing the building to use only 60% of the power mandated by German standards for new buildings.

Die Sanierung des im Zweiten Weltkrieg schwer beschädigten Hauses aus den 1930er-Jahren begann mit der Demontage des nach dem Krieg aufgestockten Dachs und setzte sich in der Neuorganisation des gesamten Gebäudes fort. Hierbei wurden neue Fenster- und Türöffnungen und Raumverbindungen eingefügt. Die Innenwände im ersten Stock wurden aus „Lehmziegeln und braunem Lehmputz mit weißem Lehmoberputz" gearbeitet. Eike Roswag erklärt: „Wir nennen das Haus ‚Weißes Lehmhaus'. Es hat sämtliche positiven Eigenschaften von Lehmbauten, was Feuchtigkeitskontrolle und Frischluftzufuhr betrifft. Es ist eine sehr ‚gesunde' Bauweise mit natürlichen Baumaterialien und Farben und Klebern auf chemiefreier Basis." Den Außenbau umhüllt eine 10 cm starke Dämmschicht aus Schilfrohr mit weißem Kalkputz. Es ist das erste Haus dieser Art in Berlin, dessen Methoden durchaus von Roswags Engagement in Entwicklungsländern inspiriert sein mögen. Eine Wärmepumpe senkt den Energiebedarf, sodass das Haus nur 60 % der nach deutschen Richtlinien für Neubauten bemessenen Energiemenge verbraucht.

La réhabilitation de cette construction des années 1930, sévèrement endommagée pendant la Seconde Guerre Mondiale, a commencé par la suppression de la toiture ajoutée après la guerre et s'est poursuivie par la réorganisation de la structure tout entière, ce qui a permis de créer de nouvelles ouvertures et connexions. Les murs intérieurs du premier niveau sont « en briques de terre et torchis de terre brune recouvert de pisé blanc… Nous avons appelé ce projet "la maison en torchis blanc". Elle présente toutes les fonctions positives des constructions en terre en termes de contrôle de l'humidité et d'aération naturelle. C'est un type de construction très "sain" réalisé avec des matériaux naturels sans peintures ni colles chimiques », explique l'architecte. L'extérieur est recouvert d'une isolation thermique de 10 cm d'épaisseur en roseaux recouverts d'enduit au mortier de chaux blanc. C'est la première construction berlinoise à faire appel à ces méthodes, peut-être inspirées de l'expérience de Roswag dans les pays en voie de développement. Une pompe à chaleur réduit la consommation d'énergie, et permet à la maison de n'utiliser que 60 % de l'énergie préconisée dans les nouvelles constructions en Allemagne.

As seen from the outside, the building looks like an almost ordinary older house, but its thermally insulated surface, and indeed the heat transfer methods used by the architects as seen in the diagram to the left, make it decidedly green.

Von außen mag das Haus wie ein gewöhnlicher Altbau wirken, doch seine wärmeisolierte Außenhaut und insbesondere die Prinzipien der Wärmeübertragung (siehe Diagramm, links), die die Architekten hier anwenden, machen es zu einem höchst grünen Bau.

Vue de l'extérieur, la maison semble presque ordinaire, mais ses façades à isolation thermique et sa gestion des différences de températures (voir plan ci-contre), en font une véritable création environnementale.

Christine's House

RURAL STUDIO

Rural Studio
College of Architecture, Design and Construction / Auburn University School of Architecture
P.O. Box 278 / Newbern, AL 36765 / USA
Tel: +1 334 624 4483 / Fax: +1 334 624 6015
E-mail: rstudio@auburn.edu / Web: www.ruralstudio.org

Samuel Mockbee, born in 1945, founded Mockbee/Coker Architects, based in Canton, Mississippi, and in Memphis, Tennessee, with Coleman Coker in 1978. The firm completed a number of structures, including the Barton House and the Cook House, both located in Mississippi. They enjoy considerable reknown in the region, established through their contemporary interpretations of local architecture. Samuel Mockbee taught at Yale, at the University of Oklahoma, and was a Professor of Architecture at Auburn University beginning in 1991. He created the **RURAL STUDIO** with Dennis K. Ruth in 1993 to improve living conditions in rural Alabama and to include hands-on experience in architectural pedagogy, while "extending the study of architecture into a socially responsible context." Three programs, lasting from a semester to a year, are organized for students at Auburn. Mockbee died in 2001, but it was immediately decided that the work of the Rural Studio would continue. The studio is today under the direction of Professor Andrew Freear, who was born in Yorkshire, England. He graduated from the Polytechnic of Central London and the Architectural Association in London. He taught at the University of Illinois before joining Auburn University. Completed community projects include the Akron Senior Center in Hale County (2001–02); the Lee County AIDS Alabama House (2002–03); and the Perry Lakes Pedestrian Bridge (2003–04). Other completed houses include: Lucy House in Mason's Bend and Shiles House, both completed in Hale County in 2001–02; and the Music Man House (Hale County, 2002–03). More recent work includes Christine's House (Mason's Bend, 2005–06, published here); and the St. Luke's Church Renovation in Old Cahawba (2006–08), all in Alabama, USA.

Samuel Mockbee, geboren 1945, gründete 1978 gemeinsam mit Coleman Coker sein Büro Mockbee/Coker Architects mit Sitz in Canton, Mississippi, und Memphis, Tennessee. Das Büro realisierte zahlreiche Bauten, darunter das Haus Barton sowie das Haus Cook, beide in Mississippi. Durch ihre zeitgenössische Interpretation ortstypischer Architektur erwarb sich das Büro einen beachtlichen Ruf in der Region. Samuel Mockbee lehrte in Yale sowie an der Universität Oklahoma und war seit 1991 Professor für Architektur an der Universität Auburn in Alabama. 1993 gründete er mit Dennis K. Ruth das Büro **RURAL STUDIO**, um die Lebensbedingungen in ländlichen Gegenden Alabamas zu verbessern. Zugleich ging es ihm darum, praktische Erfahrungen in Architekturpädagogik zu vermitteln und „das Architekturstudium in den sozial verantwortlichen Bereich zu erweitern". Studenten an der Universität Auburn werden drei Programme mit einer Dauer von einem Semester bis zu einem Jahr angeboten. Mockbee starb 2001, doch man beschloss sofort, die Arbeit von Rural Studio fortzusetzen. Heute wird das Studio von Professor Andrew Freear geleitet, der in Yorkshire geboren wurde. Er studierte an der Polytechnic of Central London und der Architectural Association in London. Bevor er nach Auburn kam, lehrte er an der Universität von Illinois. Zu den realisierten Gemeinschaftsprojekten zählen u. a. das Akron Senior Center in Hale County (2001–02), das Lee County AIDS Alabama House (2002–03) sowie die Perry-Lakes-Fußgängerbrücke (2003–04). Andere Hausbauten sind das Lucy House in Mason's Bend und das Shiles House (beide 2001–02 in Hale County fertiggestellt) sowie das Music Man House (Hale County, 2002–03). Zu den aktuelleren Projekten zählen Christine's House (Mason's Bend, 2005–06, hier vorgestellt) sowie die Sanierung der Kirche St. Luke's in Old Cahawba (2006–08), alle in Alabama.

Samuel Mockbee, né en 1945, a fondé Mockbee/Coker Architects avec Coleman Coker en 1978. L'agence basée à Canton, Mississippi, et Memphis, Tennessee, a réalisé un certain nombre de projets dont la maison Barton et la maison Cook, toutes deux dans le Mississippi. Elle bénéficie d'une importante réputation dans la région grâce à ses interprétations contemporaines de l'architecture locale. Samuel Mockbee a enseigné à Yale, à l'université de l'Oklahoma et a été professeur d'architecture à l'université Auburn à partir de 1991. Il a créé **RURAL STUDIO** avec Dennis K. Ruth, en 1993, pour améliorer les conditions de vie dans l'Alabama rural et mettre en pratique une expérience directe du chantier dans sa pédagogie, tout en « étendant l'étude de l'architecture dans un contexte social responsable ». Trois programmes, d'une durée d'un semestre à un an, sont organisés à Auburn pour les étudiants. Mockbee est mort en 2001, mais il a été immédiatement décidé que Rural Studio devait continuer. Il est aujourd'hui placé sous la direction du professeur Andrew Freear, né dans le Yorkshire en Grande-Bretagne. Il est diplômé de la London Polytechnic et de l'Architectural Association de Londres. Il a enseigné à l'université de l'Illinois, avant de rejoindre celle d'Auburn. Parmi les projets communautaires achevés figurent le Centre Akron Senior dans le comté de Hale County (2001–02) ; l'AIDS Alabama House dans le comté de Lee (2002–03) et la passerelle piétonnière du lac Perry (2003–04). Parmi leurs maisons réalisées : la maison Lucy à Mason's Bend et la maison Shiles (comté de Hale, 2001–02) ; la maison Music Man (comté de Hale, 2002–03) ; la maison de Christine (Mason's Bend, 2005–06, publiée ici, et la rénovation de l'église St. Luc à Old Cahawba (2006–08), le tout en Alabama.

CHRISTINE'S HOUSE

Mason's Bend, Alabama, USA, 2005–06

Floor area: 83 m². Client: Christine Green. Cost: not disclosed.
Project Architects: Amy Green Bullington, Stephen Long. Project Instructor and Rural Studio Director: Andrew Freear.
Structural Engineer: Joe Farruggia. Environmental Engineer: Paul Stroller

Like other Rural Studio work, Christine's House was an Auburn University architectural thesis. Both the young architects involved in this house, Amy Green Bullington and Stephen Long, received their B.Arch degrees from Auburn in 2005. They took advantage of the area's abundant red clay—mixing 70% earth, 25% pulped newspaper and 5% Portland cement, poured into cardboard boxes of various sizes—to make bricks for two main walls of the house. As Amy Bullington explains: "This hybrid adobe mix, a simple modification to traditional brick making, requires few special skills and little equipment, and its high insulation value (R33 for a 30.5 cm wall) is attractive in terms of long-term client cost." A wind tower inspired by Middle Eastern designs was placed over the kitchen of the house to encourage airflow. The students carefully studied the social patterns of Mason's Bend, where a number of other Rural Studio projects have been built, so that this new addition would fit into its surroundings. Aside from the economical construction design, a clear interest in sustainability has informed this project.

Wie andere Projekte von Rural Studio war auch Christine's House eine Abschlussarbeit in Architektur an der Universität Auburn. Die zwei an der Planung des Hauses beteiligten jungen Architekten, Amy Green Bullington und Stephen Long, erlangten ihre B.-Arch.-Abschlüsse 2005. Sie nutzten die in der Gegend verbreitete rote Tonerde, um aus einer Mischung aus 70 % Erde, 25 % Pappmaschee aus Zeitungen und 5 % Portlandzement, die sie in Pappkartons unterschiedlicher Größe gossen, Ziegel für die beiden Hauptwände des Hauses herzustellen. Amy Bullington erklärt: „Dieser hybride Lehmziegelmix ist eine einfache Modifikation der traditionellen Ziegelfertigung und erfordert kaum besondere Fertigkeiten oder technische Ausrüstung, sein hoher Dämmfaktor (R33 bei einer 30,5 cm starken Wand) macht ihn für den Auftraggeber attraktiv im Hinblick auf Langzeitkosten." Ein von der nahöstlichen Tradition inspirierter Windturm wurde über der Küche installiert und fördert die Belüftung. Die Studenten hatten sich intensiv mit dem Sozialgefüge in Mason's Bend auseinandergesetzt, wo Rural Studio bereits zahlreiche andere Projekte realisiert hat, sodass sich der neueste Bau sinnvoll einfügt. Abgesehen von der sparsamen Bauweise ist das Projekt auch von einem Interesse an Nachhaltigkeit geprägt.

Comme d'autres travaux de Rural Studio, la « maison de Christine » est en réalité l'aboutissement d'une thèse d'architecture préparée à l'université Auburn. Les deux jeunes architectes impliqués dans ce projet, Amy Green Bullington et Stephen Long, ont reçu leur diplôme de B. Arch d'Auburn en 2005. Ils ont profité de la présence abondante d'argile rouge dans la région pour fabriquer des briques de diverses dimensions en mélangeant 70 % d'argile, 25 % de pulpe de papier et 5 % de ciment Portland. Elles constituent les deux murs principaux. Comme l'explique Amy Bullington : « Ce mélange hybride d'adobes, simple modification du processus traditionnel de fabrication des briques, demande peu de compétence ou d'équipement, et son pouvoir élevé d'isolation (taux d'isolation très élevé de R33 pour un mur de 30,5 cm d'épaisseur) est séduisant sur le plan du coût à long terme pour le client. » Une tour à vent, inspirée d'une typologie moyen-orientale, a été installée au-dessus de la cuisine pour faciliter la ventilation naturelle. Les étudiants ont soigneusement étudié les rapports sociaux de Mason's Bend, où un certain nombre de projets de Rural Studio ont été réalisés, pour que cette nouvelle construction s'intègre de façon appropriée. En dehors des aspects économiques de sa construction, ce projet est clairement placé sous le signe de la durabilité.

The emphasis on natural, locally obtained materials and simple methods of aeration make the house, a very basic structure, ecologically sound.

Die Konzentration auf natürliche, lokal verfügbare Materialien und einfache Belüftungsmethoden machen das Haus, eine sehr einfache Konstruktion, zu einem ökologisch verträglichen Bau.

L'accent mis sur les matériaux naturels locaux et des méthodes d'aération simples fait de cette construction très basique un exemple de solution écologique.

HIROSHI SAMBUICHI

Hiroshi Sambuichi Architects
8–3–302 Nakajima naka-ku
730–0811 Hiroshima
Japan

Tel: +81 82 544 1417
Fax: +81 82 544 1418
E-mail: samb@d2.dion.ne.jp

HIROSHI SAMBUICHI was born in 1968. He graduated from the Department of Architecture in the Faculty of Science and Technology at Tokyo University of Science. After working for Shinichi Ogawa & Associates, he established Sambuichi Architects and began design work in Hiroshima. His work includes the Running Green Project (Yamaguchi, 2001); Air House (Yamaguchi, 2001); Miwa-gama (Yamaguchi, 2002); Sloping North House (Yamaguchi, 2003); Stone House (Shimane, 2005–); and the Inujima Art Project Seirensho (Okayama, 2006–08, published here), all in Japan.

HIROSHI SAMBUICHI wurde 1968 geboren. Sein Architekturstudium schloss er an der Fakultät für Naturwissenschaften und Technik an der Tokyo University of Science ab. Nachdem er zunächst für Shinichi Ogawa & Associates gearbeitet hatte, gründete er sein Büro Sambuichi Architects und begann in Hiroshima zu praktizieren. Zu seinen Projekten zählen u. a.: Running Green Project (Yamaguchi, 2001), Air House (Yamaguchi, 2001), Miwa-gama (Yamaguchi, 2002), Sloping North House (Yamaguchi, 2003), Stone House (Shimane, 2005–) sowie das Inujima Art Project Seirensho (Inujima, Okayama, 2006–08, hier vorgestellt), alle in Japan.

Né en 1968, **HIROSHI SAMBUICHI** est diplômé du département d'architecture de la Faculté des sciences et technologies de l'Université des sciences de Tokyo. Après avoir travaillé pour Shinichi Ogawa & Associates, il a fondé l'agence Sambuichi Architects et commencé à travailler à Hiroshima. Ses réalisations comprennent le Running Green Project (Yamaguchi, 2001); l'Air House (Yamaguchi, 2001); Miwa-Gama (Yamaguchi, 2002); la Sloping North House (Yamaguchi, 2003); la Stone House (Shimane, 2005–) et le projet artistique de la raffinerie (*seirensho*) à Inujima (Okayama, 2006–08, publié ici), le tout au Japon.

INUJIMA ART PROJECT SEIRENSHO

Inujima, Okayama, Japan, 2006–08

Area: 790 m². Client: Soichiro Fukutake. Cost: not disclosed

This one-story wood-and-steel structure is located on a 5212-square-meter site on the small Inland Sea island of Inujima. The client, Soichiro Fukutake, is the head of the Benesse Corporation, which is also at the origin of Tadao Ando's projects on the nearby island of Naoshima. Like Naoshima, the island was marked by an industrial presence, in this case a copper refinery that operated between 1909 and 1919, leaving only ruins behind. The architect says: "I thought that all the existing materials are regenerable resources, such as the old architecture of the ruins, the geography, open spaces, the infrastructure of the factories, wastes, and so on. There are six different levels of height on the site, and I considered these as landscapes for making use of the necessary potential energy. I decided to use levels one to four in this project, and planned architectural figures to utilize and activate chimneys and accumulate energy for years and years." He used waste slag in the floor and walls. Timber is used above ground, as it was in the original plant, and the slag used in the floors contains iron oxide from the plant. The museum contains four main spaces, a cooling corridor that uses the heat of the earth, a sun gallery that collects the energy of the sun, an energy hall, and the chimney, and a landscape "controlling the circulation of vegetation and water." Rather than "large hidden machinery," the architect has used the energy of the earth and sun to "power" this museum.

Der einstöckige Bau aus Holz und Stahl liegt auf einem 5212 m² großen Grundstück auf der kleinen Insel Inujima in der Seto-Inlandsee. Soichiro Fukutake, Bauherr des Projekts und Direktor der Firma Benesse, war schon Auftraggeber der Tadao-Ando-Bauten auf der nahe gelegenen Insel Naoshima. Wie Naoshima so ist auch Inujima von seiner industriellen Vorgeschichte geprägt, in diesem Fall von einer Kupferraffinerie, die zwischen 1909 und 1919 in Betrieb war und von der noch Ruinen erhalten sind. Der Architekt erklärt: „Meine Überlegung war, alle vorhandenen Materialien als erneuerbare Ressourcen zu verstehen – die Architektur der Ruinen, die Geografie, die offenen Räume, die Infrastruktur der Fabriken, den Schutt und so weiter. Das Gelände hat sechs Höhenniveaus, die ich als Landschaften und potenzielle Energieerzeuger interpretiert habe. Ich beschloss, die Niveaus eins bis vier in das Projekt zu integrieren und entwarf eine Architekturkonstellation, in der sich die Schornsteine aktivieren und nutzen lassen, um so Energie auf Jahre hinaus speichern zu können." Für Böden und Wände griff der Architekt auf alte Schlacken zurück. Über Grund wurde, wie in der alten Fabrik, mit Holz gearbeitet. Die Schlacken der Bodenbeläge enthalten Eisenoxid aus dem alten Werk. Zum Museum gehören vier Bereiche, ein Kühlkorridor, der mit Erdwärme arbeitet, eine Sonnengalerie, die Solarenergie erzeugt, eine Energiehalle mit Schornstein und eine Landschaft, die „den Kreislauf von Vegetation und Wasser steuert". Statt „aufwändiger Technik hinter den Kulissen" nutzt der Architekt Erde und Sonne, um sein Museum mit Energie zu versorgen.

Cette construction en bois et acier d'un seul niveau est implantée sur un terrain de 5212 m² sur la petite île d'Inujima, dans la Mer intérieure du Japon. Le client, Soichiro Fukutake – qui dirige la Benesse Corporation – est par ailleurs à l'initiative des projets de Tadao Ando sur l'île voisine de Naoshima. Comme à Naoshima, les lieux étaient marqués par la présence d'une raffinerie de cuivre qui avait opéré de 1909 à 1919 et laissé une friche de ruines industrielles. Selon l'architecte : « J'ai pensé que tous ces matériaux abandonnés étaient des ressources réutilisables, de même que l'architecture ancienne de ces ruines, la géographie, les espaces ouverts, l'infrastructure des usines, les déchets, etc. Il existe six niveaux de hauteur sur le site que j'ai considérés comme un paysage dont il fallait extraire le potentiel énergétique nécessaire. J'ai décidé d'investir les niveaux 1 à 4, et j'ai conçu des formes architecturales pour utiliser et activer les cheminées et l'énergie accumulée depuis des années et des années. » Hiroshi Sambuichi s'est servi de scories pour les sols (mâchefer chargé d'oxyde de fer) et les murs. Le bois est utilisé pour les structures au-dessus du sol, comme dans l'usine originale. Le musée contient quatre volumes principaux, un corridor de refroidissement qui utilise la chaleur de la terre, une galerie solaire qui collecte l'énergie du soleil, un hall de l'énergie et la cheminée, et un paysage aménagé « contrôlant la circulation de la végétation et de l'eau ». Plutôt qu'une « grosse machinerie dissimulée », l'architecte s'est servi de l'énergie de la terre et du soleil pour « ancrer » cette réalisation.

The museum occupies the site of a former copper refinery on a small, remote island, giving the ruins a certain poetic presence.

Das Museum liegt auf einer kleinen entlegenen Insel, auf dem Gelände einer ehemaligen Kupferraffinerie. Die Ruinen wirken geradezu poetisch.

Le musée occupe le site d'une ancienne raffinerie de cuivre située sur une petite île isolée. Les ruines dégagent une certaine poésie.

The tall smokestack of the former refinery marks the location of the museum. The architect has deftly combined new elements with the existing architecture.

Der große Schornstein der ehema-ligen Raffinerie markiert den Standort des Museums. Gekonnt kombiniert der Architekt neue Elemente mit bestehender Architektur.

La haute cheminée de l'ancienne raffinerie signale le site du musée. L'architecte a habilement associé des éléments architecturaux anciens à des composants nouveaux.

Hiroshi Sambuichi has used natural light and energy to the exclusion of artificial sources that would have been hard to come by on this abandoned site. He mixes existing spaces and elements with new ones in a way that makes it difficult to distinguish one from the other.

Hiroshi Sambuichi nutzt natürliches Licht und Energie und verzichtet auf künstliche Energiequellen, die an diesem entlegenen Standort auch schwerlich verfügbar sind. Er kombiniert bestehende Räumlichkeiten und Elemente so geschickt mit neuen, dass kaum Unterschiede erkennbar sind.

Hiroshi Sambuichi s'est servi de la lumière et de l'énergie naturelles à l'exclusion de toute source artificielle, difficile à mettre en œuvre sur un site aussi isolé. Il a mixé les volumes existants à de nouveaux éléments d'une telle façon qu'il est difficile de les distinguer.

Located near the island of Naoshima, where Tadao Ando has built numerous art-related projects for the same client, the museum is intended to bring this abandoned industrial site back to life.

Das Museum – unweit der Insel Naoshima, auf der Tadao Ando verschiedene Kunstprojekte für denselben Auftraggeber realisierte – will das verlassene Industriegelände wieder zum Leben erwecken.

Situé non loin de l'île de Naoshima sur laquelle Tadao Ando a réalisé de nombreux projets d'ordre artistique pour le même client, ce musée devrait redonner vie à ce site industriel abandonné.

SITE

SITE
25 Maiden Lane
New York, NY 10038
USA

Tel: +1 212 285 0120
Fax: +1 212 285 0125
E-mail: info@SITEnewyork.com
Web: www.SITEnewyork.com

James Wines, founding Principal of **SITE** (Sculpture in the Environment), was born in Chicago, Illinois, in 1932 and studied Art and Art History at Syracuse University (B. A. 1956). Between 1965 and 1967 he was a sculptor. He created SITE with Alison Sky and Michelle Stone in 1970. Notable buildings include: Indeterminate Façade Showroom (Houston, Texas, 1975); Ghost Parking Lot (Hamden, Connecticut, 1978); Highway 86, Expo '86 (Vancouver, British Columbia, Canada, 1986); Four Continents Bridge (Hiroshima, Japan, 1989); Avenida 5, Expo '92 (Seville, Spain, 1992); Ross's Landing Plaza and Park (Chattanooga, Tennessee, 1992); landscape design and promenades for MCA Garden, Universal Studios (Orlando, Florida, 1996); Brinker International Chili's Restaurant, prototype restaurant design (Denver, Colorado, 1998); the Shake Shack in Madison Square Park (Manhattan, New York, 2004); interior design for Xerion Capital Partners (New York, New York, 2003); and a residential tower in Mumbai (India, 2005). More recent work includes the GwaCheon Club (Seoul, South Korea, 2007–); the Streetscape in a New World (Beijing, China, 2008); and the Fondazione Pietro Rossini Pavilion (Briosco, Italy, 2000–08), both published here.

James Wines, Gründungspartner von **SITE** (Sculpture in the Environment), wurde 1932 in Chicago, Illinois, geboren und studierte Kunst und Kunstgeschichte an der Universität Syracuse (B. A. 1956). Von 1965 bis 1967 war er als Bildhauer aktiv. 1970 gründete er SITE gemeinsam mit Alison Sky und Michelle Stone. Zu ihren wichtigsten Bauten zählen: Indeterminate Façade Showroom (Houston, Texas, 1975), Parkplatz Ghost (Hamden, Connecticut, 1978), Highway 86, Expo '86 (Vancouver, British Columbia, Kanada, 1986), Four Continents Bridge (Hiroshima, Japan, 1989), Avenida 5, Expo '92 (Sevilla, 1992), Ross's Landing Plaza und Park (Chattanooga, Tennessee, 1992), Landschaftsgestaltung und Promenaden für den MCA Garden, Universal Studios (Orlando, Florida, 1996), Brinker International Chili's Restaurant, Entwurf eines Restaurantprototyps (Denver, Colorado, 1998), der Shake Shack im Madison Square Park (New York, 2004), das Interiordesign für Xerion Capital Partners (New York, 2003) sowie ein Wohnhochhaus in Mumbai (2005). Aktuellere Projekt sind u. a. der GwaCheon Club (Seoul, Südkorea, 2007–), die „Streetscape in a New World" (Peking, 2008) und der Pavillon der Fondazione Pietro Rossini (Briosco, Italien, 2000–08), beide hier vorgestellt.

James Wines, dirigeant fondateur de **SITE** (Sculpture in the Environment), est né à Chicago, Illinois, en 1932, et a étudié l'art et l'histoire de l'art à l'université Syracuse (B. A. 1956). De 1965 à 1967, il s'est consacré à la sculpture. Il a créé SITE avec Alison Sky et Michelle Stone en 1970. Parmi ses réalisations les plus notables : le showroom à façade indéterminée (Houston, Texas, 1975) ; le parking Ghost (Hamden, Connecticut, 1978) ; le Highway 86, Expo '86 (Vancouver, Colombie britannique, Canada, 1986) ; le pont des Quatre Continents (Hiroshima, Japon, 1989) ; l'Avenida 5 à l'Expo '92 de Séville (Espagne, 1992) ; le parc et la place de Ross's Landing (Chattanooga, Tennessee, 1992) ; l'aménagement paysager et les promenades pour le jardin MCA, Universal Studios (Orlando, Floride, 1996) ; Brinker International Chili's Restaurant, restaurant prototype (Denver, Colorado, 1998) ; le Shake Shack à Madison Square Park (Manhattan, New York, 2004) ; l'architecture intérieure de Xerion Capital Partners (New York, 2003) et une tour résidentielle à Mumbai (Inde, 2005). Plus récemment ont été réalisés le GwaCheon Club (Séoul, Corée du Sud, 2007-) ; le Streetscape in a New World (Pékin, Chine, 2008) et le pavillon de la Fondation Pietro Rossini (Briosco, Italie, 2000–08), ces deux derniers projets sont publiés ici.

FONDAZIONE PIETRO ROSSINI PAVILION

Briosco, Italy, 2000–08

Floor area: 372 m². Client: Alberto Rossini. Cost: not disclosed.
Team: James Wines, Denise MC Lee, Stumo Miyazaki

As has often been the case in his work, and as can be seen in his drawings on this page, James Wines integrates an architectural design into a natural setting almost giving the impression that the new structure might be in ruins.

Wie oft in seinem Werk und wie die Zeichnungen auf dieser Seite zeigen, integriert James Wines seine Entwürfe so in ihr landschaftliches Umfeld, dass man fast meinen könnte, der Neubau wäre eine Ruine.

Comme souvent dans son œuvre, James Wines intègre un projet architectural dans un cadre naturel en donnant l'impression que la nouvelle structure pourrait être une ruine.

Intended as a memorial to the client's son, this is "an example of site-specific green architecture—a union of art, building, landscape, and exhibition space," according to the architects. The gallery space shows the family collection of modern art and the interior of the building also includes a library, lecture room, café, and meeting area. Thermal glass and cool air drawn from the ground are used in the building that is imagined as an extension of the hilly topography of the site. Recycled brick and stone gathered from the immediate area are used and a roof covered with local vegetation is also part of the design. T-shaped columns made of cast stone "visually unify the pavilion and the environment." SITE has long experimented with the interpenetration of nature and architecture and in this instance there is a conscious effort to fuse the two, making a sustainable structure in the process. The gestation period of this project has been long, but in 2008 it was "substantially completed."

Das Projekt, erbaut für den Sohn des Auftraggebers, ist den Architekten zufolge „ein Beispiel für ortsspezifische grüne Architektur – eine Verbindung von Kunst, Bauwerk, Landschaft und Ausstellungsort". Die Galerie präsentiert die Sammlung moderner Kunst der Familie, das Innere des Baus beherbergt außerdem eine Bibliothek, einen Vortragssaal, ein Café und einen Aufenthaltsbereich. Am Bau, der als Fortführung der hügeligen Landschaft des Grundstücks konzipiert wurde, kommen Wärmeschutzverglasung und dem Erdreich entzogene Kühlluft zum Einsatz. Als Teil des Entwurfs wurden außerdem recycelte Ziegel und Stein aus der unmittelbaren Umgebung verwendet, ebenfalls gibt es ein mit heimischen Pflanzen begrüntes Dach. T-förmige Stützen aus Betonwerkstein „fungieren als visuelles Bindeglied zwischen Pavillon und Umgebung". SITE experimentiert schon lange mit der gegenseitigen Durchdringung von Natur und Architektur, in diesem Fall gab es das bewusste Bemühen, beide miteinander verschmelzen und so nachhaltige Architektur entstehen zu lassen. Die Entstehungsphase des Projekts war lang, doch 2008 konnte es „weitgehend fertiggestellt" werden.

Mémorial érigé en souvenir du fils du client, il s'agit, selon les termes des architectes, « d'un exemple d'architecture verte spécifique au site, union de l'art, du bâti, du paysage et d'un espace d'exposition ». La galerie d'exposition présente la collection familiale d'art moderne et s'accompagne d'une bibliothèque, d'une salle de lecture, d'un café et d'un espace de réunions. Le bâtiment, qui se veut une extension de la topographie vallonnée du site, fait appel au verre thermique et à l'air refroidi par le sol. Les murs sont en briques et pierres recyclées, récupérées dans les environs immédiats, et le toit est planté de végétation locale. Les colonnes en pierre moulée en forme de T « unifient visuellement le pavillon et son environnement ». SITE a longtemps mené des expériences sur l'interpénétration de la nature et de l'architecture et s'est livrée ici à un effort conscient de fusion pour aboutir à une construction durable. La période de gestation du projet a été longue, mais il a été « substantiellement achevé » en 2008.

The pavilion itself might well be a sculptural work of art – precisely the intention of this project, in which different disciplines have been combined.

Fast wirkt der Pavillon selbst wie eine Skulptur – was bei diesem Projekt, das mit unterschiedlichen künstlerischen Genres bespielt wird, durchaus beabsichtigt ist.

Le pavillon pourrait s'apparenter à une sculpture, ce qui est précisément l'intention de ce projet qui associe diverses disciplines.

STREETSCAPE IN A NEW WORLD
Beijing, China, 2008

*Site area: 15 270 m². Enclosed area: 800 m². Client: New World China Land & DI Magazine. Cost: not disclosed.
Team: Li Wang, Marc Halle, Yang Yang, Ronghui Li*

This winning project was developed for the First Award concept for New World Plaza, Beijing, sponsored by New World China Land and *DI Magazine*. James Wines writes that the project "is intended as a metaphor for a growing culture and proposal for environmental improvement in a rapidly burgeoning city. The aesthetic approach is based on a similarity in the shape of the site to expanding tree branches and river tributaries." Ribbons of concrete thread through large "forest" areas, with tall trees along the perimeters of the site. Mounds and water catchments dot the area as do "forest-like compositions of LED lampposts. The main plaza includes a number of small stores and restaurants. An existing overhead bridge passes over the top of this area. The landscaped area continues as a pedestrian overpass over Lianzi Street leading to more shops." In conclusion, Wines states: "The combination of green zones, site-specific identity, and multiuse people spaces is conceived as a prototype for the mediation of scale between the city's small residential neighborhoods and its mega-sized commercial zones. Overall, the New World Plaza is interpreted as an urban forest—vertically and horizontally, physically and symbolically, experientially and ecologically."

Das Projekt gewann den First-Award-Wettbewerb für die New World Plaza in Peking, finanziert von New World China Land und *DI Magazine*. James Wines zufolge ist das Projekt „eine Metapher für eine wachsende Kultur und ein Vorschlag für die Verbesserung der Umweltqualität in einer rasch wachsenden Stadt. Der ästhetische Ansatz geht von der formalen Ähnlichkeit des Grundstücks mit sich verzweigenden Ästen oder Nebenflüssen aus." Bänder aus Beton schlängeln sich durch weitläufige „Wald"-Abschnitte, hohe Bäume säumen die Grundstücksgrenzen. Durchzogen wird das Gelände von Hügeln und Wasserbecken und „waldähnlichen Arrangements aus LED-Laternenpfählen. Am Hauptplatz liegen mehrere kleine Geschäfte und Restaurants. Eine bestehende Brücke verläuft über das Gelände. Die Grünflächen ziehen sich als Fußgängerbrücke bis zur Lianzi-Straße hinüber, wo es weitere Geschäfte gibt." Wilson fasst zusammen: „Die Mischung aus grünen Zonen, einer ortsspezifischen Identität und vielfältig genutzten Bereichen für die Bürger wurde als Prototyp entworfen, um eine Größenordnung zu finden, die zwischen den kleinteiligen Wohngebieten und den gigantischen Geschäftsgegenden der Stadt vermittelt. Insgesamt wurde die New World Plaza als urbaner Wald interpretiert – vertikal und horizontal, physisch und symbolisch, erfahrbar und ökologisch."

Ce projet a remporté le premier prix d'un concours sur le thème d'une « Place d'un monde nouveau » à Pékin, organisé par New World China Land et le *DI Magazine*. James Wines explique que « ce projet est la métaphore d'une culture en plein développement, et une proposition pour améliorer l'environnement d'une cité bourgeonnante. L'approche esthétique repose sur la similarité de formes entre les branches d'arbres et les affluents d'une rivière ». Des rubans de béton traversent de vastes zones « forestières », tandis que de grands arbres ont été plantés en bordure du périmètre du terrain. Des monticules et des captages d'eau parsèment le site, ainsi que des « compositions forestières de lampadaires à LEDs ». La place principale comprend un certain nombre de petites boutiques et de restaurants. Un pont existant surplombe la partie supérieure du site. La zone paysagée se poursuit par une passerelle piétonnière qui franchit la rue Lianzi pour conduire à d'autres installations commerciales. En conclusion, Wines assure que « cette combinaison de zones vertes, d'une identité spécifique au site, et d'espaces polyvalents est conçue comme un prototype pour la médiation d'échelle entre les petits quartiers résidentiels de la ville et ses zones commerciales géantes. Par-dessus tout, cette place s'interprète en termes d'expérience et d'écologie comme une forêt urbaine, verticalement et horizontalement, physiquement et symboliquement ».

Drawings by James Wines give a distinct impression that the project means to bring nature into the urban environment, somewhat challenging the modernist architecture of the area.

Die Zeichnungen James Wines' lassen das Ziel des Projekts deutlich werden, die Natur in das urbane Umfeld zu bringen. Eine Herausforderung angesichts der modernen Bebauung des Viertels.

Les dessins de James Wines donnent l'impression que le projet essaye d'attirer la nature dans l'environnement urbain, un défi par rapport à l'architecture moderniste de ce quartier.

ADRIAN SMITH + GORDON GILL ARCHITECTURE

Adrian Smith + Gordon Gill Architecture LLP
111 West Monroe
Suite 2300
Chicago, IL 60603
USA

Tel: +1 312 920 1888
Fax: +1 312 920 1775
E-mail: info@smithgill.com
Web: www.smithgill.com

Adrian Smith received his B.Arch degree from the University of Illinois (Chicago, 1969). He was a design Partner in the office of Skidmore, Owings & Merrill (SOM) LLP from 1980 to 2003. He was Chief Executive Officer of the SOM Partnership (1993–95) and Chairman of the SOM Foundation (1990–95), and remained a consulting design partner at the firm until 2006. He is well-known as the designer of towers such as the Burj Dubai (Dubai, UAE, 2006–09), the tallest building in the world. Gordon Gill was an Associate Partner at SOM LLP and a Director of Design for VOA Associates, before creating **ADRIAN SMITH + GORDON GILL ARCHITECTURE** with Adrian Smith in 2006. He was the designer of "the world's first net zero-energy skyscraper, the Pearl River Tower." Robert Forest received his B.Arch degree from Carleton University (Ottawa, Canada, 1994) and is the management Partner for the Masdar Headquarters. The firm's current work includes: 1 Dubai (Dubai); Burj Dubai Gatehouses and Function Island (Dubai); The Grand Boulevard at Burj Dubai (Dubai); The Mansion at Burj Dubai (Dubai); 1 Park Avenue (Dubai); Park Gate (Dubai); Masdar Headquarters (Masdar City just outside of Abu Dhabi, 2008–10, published here); Sears Tower Sustainable Systems (Chicago, Illinois, USA); Vancouver Residential Development (Vancouver, Canada); and the Verde Residences and Offices (Dubai), all in the United Arab Emirates unless stated otherwise.

Adrian Smith erwarb seinen B.Arch. an der Universität Illinois (Chicago, 1969). Von 1980 bis 2003 war er als Partner bei Skidmore, Owings & Merrill (SOM) LLP für den Entwurf zuständig. Er war Hauptgeschäftsführer der SOM-Partnerschaft (1993–95) und Vorsitzender der SOM Foundation (1990–95) und blieb dem Büro bis 2006 als beratender Partner in Entwurfsfragen verbunden. Bekannt wurde er mit seinen Hochhausbauten wie dem Burj Dubai (Dubai, 2006–09), dem höchsten Gebäude der Welt. Gordon Gill war assoziierter Partner bei SOM LLP und Chefdesigner bei VOA Associates, bevor er 2006 mit Adrian Smith das Büro **ADRIAN SMITH + GORDON GILL ARCHITECTURE** gründete. Er entwarf den „ersten Nullenergie-Wolkenkratzer, den Pearl River Tower". Robert Forest erwarb seinen B.Arch. an der Universität Carleton (Ottawa, Kanada, 1994) und ist Managementpartner für das Masdar-Headquarters-Projekt. Aktuelle Projekte des Büros sind u. a. 1 Dubai (Dubai), Pförtnerhäuser und Event-Insel für den Burj Dubai (Dubai), The Grand Boulevard für das Burj Dubai (Dubai), The Mansion für das Burj Dubai (Dubai), 1 Park Avenue (Dubai), Park Gate (Dubai), die Masdar Headquarters (Masdar City am Rande von Abu Dhabi, 2008–10, hier vorgestellt), Sears Tower Sustainable Systems (Chicago, Illinois, USA), ein Wohnbauprojekt in Vancouver (Vancouver, Kanada) sowie die Wohn- und Büroanlage Verde (Dubai), alle in den Vereinigten Arabischen Emiraten, sofern nicht anders angegeben.

Adrian Smith est B. Arch de l'université de l'Illinois (Chicago, 1969). Il a été partenaire chargé de projet chez Skidmore, Owings & Merrill (SOM) LLP de 1980 à 2003, directeur exécutif principal de SOM Partnership (1993–95) et président de la SOM Foundation (1990–95) pour qui il sera consultant en design jusqu'en 2006. Il est particulièrement connu pour être l'auteur de tours, dont le Burj Dubai (Dubaï, EAU, 2006–09), l'immeuble le plus haut du monde. Gordon Gill a été partenaire associé de SOM LLP et directeur des projets pour VOA Associates, avant de fonder l'agence **ADRIAN SMITH + GORDON GILL ARCHITECTURE** avec Adrian Smith en 2006. Il a conçu le «premier gratte-ciel zéro-énergie au monde, la Pearl River Tower». Robert Forest est B. Arch de l'université Carleton (Ottawa, Canada, 1994) et associé responsable du siège social de Masdar. Parmi les réalisations actuelles du cabinet aux Émirats arabes unis : 1 Dubai ; les Gatehouses et Function Island (tours portes de sécurité et lieu événementiel) de Burj Dubai ; le Grand Boulevard à Burj Dubai ; The Mansion à Burj Dubai ; 1 Park Avenue (Dubai) ; Park Gate (Dubai) ; le complexe résidenciel et de bureaux Verde (Dubai) ; le siège social de Masdar (Masdar City, en périphérie d'Abu Dhabi, 2008–10, publié ici). Et ailleurs : la Sears Tower Sustainable Systems (Chicago, Illinois, États-Unis) et Vancouver Residential Development (Vancouver, Canada).

MASDAR HEADQUARTERS

Abu Dhabi, United Arab Emirates, 2008–10

*Floor area: 88 000 m². Client: The Masdar Initiative, subsidiary of Abu Dhabi Future Energy Company. Cost: not disclosed.
Team: Les Ventsch (Director of Design), Ying Liu (Senior Designer). Collaboration: Environmental Systems Design (MEP Engineering),
Thornton Tomasetti (Structural Engineering)*

Masdar City is to be "the world's first zero-carbon, zero-waste city fully powered by renewable energy." The headquarters building, being designed by Adrian Smith + Gordon Gill Architecture, "will be the world's first large-scale, mixed-use 'positive energy' building, producing more energy than it consumes." Even more surprising, the building is intended to produce no waste, either liquid or solid. The structure is to include 6300 square meters of retail space, 78 000 square meters of office space, and 28 500 square meters of roof space. A large roof canopy and shaded green roofs are a first element of the sustainability strategy, as are glazed, insulating outer walls. The roof shade will have a large surface covered with photovoltaic cells, and solar thermal tubes are used to supply the building with air conditioning. Water use is strictly controlled by the most sophisticated means. Wind cones supply ventilation and direct warm air out of the building, while allowing light in. According to the architects: "The building's form is sculpted in response to an extensive environmental analysis to optimize system performance. Sustainable materials are utilized throughout and were selected based on life-cycle analysis."

Masdar wird die „erste CO_2-emissions- und abfallfreie Stadt der Welt [sein], die mit erneuerbaren Energien betrieben wird". Die eigentlichen Headquarters, entworfen von Adrian Smith + Gordon Gill Architecture, „werden das erste gemischt genutzte Gebäude mit einer ‚positiven Energiebilanz' sein, das mehr Energie produziert als verbraucht". Noch überraschender ist die Tatsache, dass das Gebäude darauf angelegt ist, weder feste noch flüssige Abfälle zu produzieren. Der Bau umfasst 6300 m² Gewerbefläche, 78 000 m² Bürofläche und 28 500 m² Dachfläche. Entscheidende Aspekte der nachhaltigen Strategie sind ein großes Baldachindach und schattige, begrünte Dachabschnitte ebenso wie eine dämmende, vorgebaute Außenhaut aus Glas. Ein erheblicher Teil der Dachfläche wird mit Solarmodulen ausgestattet, solarthermische Rohrleitungen klimatisieren das Gebäude. Der Wasserverbrauch wird mittels allerneuester Technik reguliert. Windtürme sorgen für Belüftung, dienen als Auslässe für warme Abluft und lassen zugleich Licht in den Bau. Die Architekten führen aus: „Die Form des Gebäudes ergab sich aus einer umfassenden Umweltanalyse, um die Leistung des Systems zu optimieren. Überall kamen nachhaltige Materialien zum Einsatz, die ihrer Ökobilanz entsprechend ausgewählt wurden."

Masdar City est « la première ville au monde zéro-carbone, zéro-déchets, entièrement alimentée par des énergies renouvelables ». L'immeuble du siège social du projet, conçu par Adrian Smith + Gordon Gill Architecture, « sera le premier immeuble construit au monde à la fois de grandes dimensions, mixte, à "énergie positive", c'est-à-dire produisant plus d'énergie qu'il n'en consomme ». Plus surprenant encore, il ne devrait produire aucun déchet, qu'il soit liquide ou solide. Il comptera 6300 m² de commerces de détail, 78 000 m² de bureaux et 28 500 m² de toitures aménagées. Un vaste auvent au niveau du toit et des toitures végétalisées ombragées sont les premiers éléments d'une stratégie de développement durable, de même que les murs extérieurs vitrés et isolés. Le toit sera recouvert en grande partie de cellules photovoltaïques et d'une installation d'énergie thermique solaire à tubes participant au conditionnement de l'air de l'immeuble. L'utilisation de l'eau sera strictement contrôlée par les moyens les plus sophistiqués. Des cônes à vent fourniront la ventilation naturelle et évacueront l'air chaud, tout en facilitant la pénétration de la lumière naturelle. Selon les architectes : « La forme sculptée du bâtiment est une réponse à l'analyse environnementale approfondie d'optimisation de la performance d'ensemble. Des matériaux durables seront mis en œuvre dans l'ensemble de la construction et sélectionnés en fonction de leur cycle de vie. »

The Masdar Headquarters combines an underlying Euclidian block structure with a surprising undulating roof shade used to lodge photovoltaic cells in large numbers, rendering the energy independence of the structure greater.

Die Masdar Headquarters kombinieren einen Unterbau in Form eines euklidischen Blocks mit einem überraschenden, gewölbten Baldachindach, auf dem großflächig Solarzellen installiert werden. Hierdurch wird der Bau von seinem Umfeld energetisch unabhängiger.

Le siège de Masdar associe un bloc de géométrie euclidienne à une toiture étonnamment ondulée équipée d'une multitude de cellules photovoltaïques qui accroissent l'autonomie énergétique de la structure.

Dr. Sultan Al Jaber, CEO of Masdar and client of this project, states: "In line with the Abu Dhabi 2030 Development Plan, Masdar is choosing to emphasize sustainability over height."

Dr. Sultan Al Jaber, Hauptgeschäftsführer von Masdar und Bauherr des Projekts merkt an: „Entsprechend dem Entwicklungsplan ‚Abu Dhabi 2030' wird in Masdar Nachhaltigkeit größer geschrieben als Gebäudehöhe."

Le Dr. Sultan Al Jabern, directeur général de Masdar et commanditaire du projet a déclaré : « Suivant le Plan de développement 2030 d'Abu Dhabi, Masdar a préféré le développement durable à la course à la hauteur. »

KEN SMITH
LANDSCAPE ARCHITECT

Ken Smith Landscape Architect
79 Chambers Street, Floor 2
New York, NY 10007
USA

Tel: +1 212 791 3595
Fax: +1 212 732 1793
E-mail: elizabeth@kensmithworkshop.com

KEN SMITH graduated from Iowa State University with a B. S. in Landscape Architecture (Ames, Iowa, 1975). He attended the Harvard GSD (Master of Landscape Architecture, 1986). He worked as a Landscape Architect for the State Conservation Commission in Iowa (1979–84), as a consultant for the Department of Environmental Management (Massachusetts, 1984–86), in the office of Peter Walker and Martha Schwartz (New York, San Francisco, 1986–89), and with Martha Schwartz Ken Smith David Meyer Inc. (San Francisco, 1990–92), before creating his present firm, Ken Smith Landscape Architect, in New York. His current and recent landscape work includes Lever House Landscape Restoration (New York, New York, 2000); the MoMA Decorative Rooftop (The Museum of Modern Art, New York, New York, 2004–05); 7 World Trade Center, Triangle Park (New York, New York, 2002–06); 40 Central Park South Courtyard Garden (New York, New York, 2005–06); H-12 Office Complex (Hyderabad, India, 2007); 17 State Street Plaza (New York, New York, 2008); East River Waterfront (New York, New York, 2006–); and Orange County Great Park (Irvine, California, 2007–, published here), all in the USA unless stated otherwise.

KEN SMITH schloss sein Studium an der Iowa State University mit einem B. S. in Landschaftsarchitektur ab (Ames, Iowa, 1975) und besuchte die Harvard Graduate School of Design (GSD; Master of Landscape Architecture, 1986). Er arbeitete als Landschaftsarchitekt für die staatliche Naturschutzkommission in Iowa (1979–84), als Berater für die Behörde für Umweltmanagement (Massachusetts, 1984–86), im Büro von Peter Walker und Martha Schwartz (New York, San Francisco, 1986–89) sowie für Martha Schwartz Ken Smith David Meyer Inc. (San Francisco, 1990–92), bevor er sein Büro Ken Smith Landscape Architect in New York gründete. Zu den aktuellen und jüngeren Landschaftsprojekten zählen u. a. die Grünflächensanierung am Lever House (New York, 2000), die künstlerische Gestaltung des Dachgartens des Museum of Modern Art (New York, 2004–05), der Triangle Park am World Trade Center 7 (New York, 2002–06) sowie der Garten im Hof des Hauses Central Park South 40 (New York, 2005–06), der Bürokomplex H-12 (Hyderabad, Indien, 2007), State Street Plaza 17 (New York, 2008), die East River Waterfront (New York, 2006–) und der Orange County Great Park (Irvine, Kalifornien, 2007–, hier vorgestellt).

KEN SMITH est B. S. en paysagisme de l'université d'État de l'Iowa (Ames, Iowa, 1975). Il a également étudié à l'Harvard GSD (Master of Landscape Architecture, 1986). Il a été architecte paysagiste pour la State Conservation Commission de l'Iowa (1979–84), consultant pour le Département de gestion environnementale (Massachusetts, 1984–86), et a travaillé pour l'agence de Peter Walker et Martha Schwartz (New York, San Francisco, 1986–89) et pour Martha Schwartz Ken Smith David Meyer Inc. (San Francisco, 1990–92), avant de créer son agence, Ken Smith Landscape Architect, à New York. Parmi ses interventions récentes : la restauration des jardins de la maison Lever (New York, 2000) ; le toit paysager du MoMA (New York, 2004–05) ; le Triangle Park au 7 World Trade Center (New York, 2002–06) ; le jardin de la cour du 40 Central Park (New York, 2005–06) ; le complexe de bureaux H-12 (Hyderabad, Inde, 2007) ; 17 State Street Plaza (New York, 2008) ; l'aménagement des berges de l'East River (New York, 2006–) et le Great Park du comté d'Orange (Irvine, Californie, 2007–, publié ici).

ORANGE COUNTY GREAT PARK

Irvine, California, USA, 2007–

Site area: 545 ha. Client: Orange County Great Park Corporation/City of Irvine. Cost: not disclosed.
Collaboration: Great Park Design Studio

Ken Smith is the "master designer" for this ambitious park project, which includes a "great canyon" 3.2 kilometers long and nine meters deep uncovering streams that had been carried by tunnels beneath this former air-base site. The work on the site will undoubtedly take a number of years, and began with the demolition of the structures of the former El Toro Marine Corps Air Station, which was closed in 1999. The Department of the Navy sold the entire site to a developer (Lennar Corporation) in 2005 with the requirement that the purchaser deed the 545-hectare park site to the City of Irvine. As the official description of the project has it: "The Orange County Great Park Plan will provide a wide array of active and passive uses, including a 2.5 mile [3.2 kilometer] canyon and lake, miles of walking and biking trails, a cultural terrace, Orange County's largest sports park, a botanical garden, and a tethered helium observation balloon that will be an icon for the Great Park." Opened in 2007, the Great Park Balloon and Temporary Visitor Center were the first elements of the project to be completed. The balloon, intended to allow visitors to view progress of work on the park, is anchored within a 106-meter earth berm planted with native ornamental grasses. Built areas are clad with recycled concrete from the former base runways. Planting based on local varieties, reuse of materials, and sustainability are priorities of the entire ongoing project.

Ken Smith ist „Chefgestalter" des ehrgeizigen Parkprojekts, zu dem ein 3,2 km langer und 9 m tiefer „großer Canyon" gehört, der Flüsse an die Oberfläche holt, die man zuvor in unterirdischen Tunneln unter dem ehemaligen Luftwaffenstandort hindurchgeführt hatte. Die Arbeiten auf dem Gelände, die 1999 mit dem Abriss der Bauten der ehemaligen El Toro Marine Corps Air Station begannen, werden zweifellos mehrere Jahre in Anspruch nehmen. Die Marine verkaufte das gesamte Gelände 2005 an einen Bauträger (Lennar Corporation) – unter der Bedingung, dass der Käufer das 545 ha große Parkgrundstück der Stadt Irvine überschreiben würde. Die offizielle Projektbeschreibung lautet: „Der Orange County Great Park wird eine große Bandbreite an aktiven und passiven Nutzungsmöglichkeiten bieten, darunter einen 3,2 km langen Canyon und See, kilometerlange Wander- und Radwege, eine ‚Kulturterrasse', den größten Sportpark in Orange County, einen botanischen Garten und einen Aussichtsfesselballon, eine Landmarke des Great Park." Die 2007 eröffnete Ballonanlage des Great Park und das temporäre Besucherzentrum sind die ersten bereits fertiggestellten Elemente des Projekts. Die Verankerung des Ballons, der den Besuchern erlauben soll, den Fortschritt der Arbeiten zu beobachten, wird von einer 106 m langen Böschung umschlossen, die mit einheimischen dekorativen Gräsern bepflanzt ist. Die bebauten Bereiche wurden mit recyceltem Beton der ehemaligen Landebahnen verblendet. Zu den Prioritäten des andauernden Projekts zählen die Begrünung mit heimischen Pflanzen, die Wiederverwertung von Baumaterialien sowie Nachhaltigkeit.

Ken Smith est le « concepteur principal » de cet ambitieux projet de parc, qui comprend un « grand canyon » de 3,2 km de long et des torrents de 9 mètres de profondeur dans lequel coulent des rivières amenées vers cette ancienne base aérienne via des tunnels. Les travaux dureront un certain nombre d'années et commenceront par la démolition des constructions de l'ancienne base aérienne du corps des marines d'El Toro, fermée en 1999. Le département de la Marine a vendu la totalité du terrain au promoteur Lennar Corporation en 2005, en demandant que 545 ha soient consacrés à un parc pour la ville d'Irvine. Pour reprendre les termes du descriptif officiel : « Le plan du Great Park du comté d'Orange offrira un éventail d'usages passifs et actifs, dont un canyon de 3,2 km, un lac, des kilomètres de pistes pour les piétons et les cyclistes, une terrasse culturelle, le plus vaste parc sportif du comté d'Orange, un jardin botanique et un ballon d'observation captif gonflé à l'hélium qui sera l'icône de ce grand projet. » Inaugurés en 2007, le Great Park Balloon et le Centre d'accueil temporaire ont été les premiers éléments achevés. Le ballon, qui permet aux visiteurs d'observer la progression du chantier, est ancré sur un terre-plein de 106 m de long, planté de végétaux ornementaux locaux. Les parties construites sont habillées de béton recyclé tiré du revêtement des anciennes pistes d'atterrissage. Les plantations de variétés locales, la réutilisation de matériaux et la durabilité figurent parmi les priorités de ce vaste projet en cours.

Converting a former military air base into an idyllic park setting with features that are related to its original topography, such as covered streams, is certainly an ambitious project. The Great Park Balloon (right) allows visitors to survey the entire site.

Einen ehemaligen Luftwaffenstütz-punkt in einen idyllischen Park zu verwandeln und dabei Bezüge zur ursprünglichen Topografie des Gelän-des herzustellen (etwa durch die Freilegung von überbauten Flüssen), ist zweifellos ein ehrgeiziges Projekt. Der Ballon im Great Park (rechts) ermöglicht Besuchern Überblick über das gesamte Gelände.

Convertir une ancienne base de l'armée de l'air en parc idyllique en utilisant les caractéristiques de la topographie originale comme les rivières souterraines était un projet ambitieux. Le ballon captif (à droite) permet aux visiteurs d'observer la totalité du site.

WERNER SOBEK

Werner Sobek Stuttgart GmbH & Co. KG
Albstr. 14
70597 Stuttgart
Germany

Tel: +49 711 767 500
Fax: +49 711 767 5044
E-mail: stuttgart@wernersobek.com
Web: www.wernersobek.com

WERNER SOBEK was born in 1953 in Aalen, Germany. He studied Architecture and Civil Engineering at the University of Stuttgart (1974–80) and did postgraduate research in "Wide-Span Lightweight Structures" at the University of Stuttgart (1980–86). He received his Ph.D. in Civil Engineering at the same University in 1987. He worked as a structural engineer in the office of Schlaich, Bergermann & Partner (Stuttgart, 1987–91), before creating his own office in 1991. Since 1995 he has been a Professor at the University of Stuttgart, where he succeeded Frei Otto as Director of the Institute for Lightweight Structures. His projects include: École Nationale d'Art Décoratif with Finn Geipel and Nicolas Michelin (Limoges, France, 1991–94); Façade Interbank, with Hans Hollein (Lima, Peru, 1996–99); Private Residence R128 (Stuttgart, Germany, 1998–2000); New Bangkok International Airport, with Murphy/Jahn (Thailand, 1995–2004); Mercedes Benz Museum, with UNStudio (Stuttgart, Germany, 2003–06); H16 (Tieringen, Germany, 2005–06, published here); Papal Altar (Munich, Germany, 2006); and fair pavilions for Audi and BMW. In 2007 WSGreenTechnologies was co-founded by Klaus Sedlbauer and Werner Sobek in Stuttgart. WSGreenTechnologies "offers integrated planning of buildings taking into consideration all phases of construction, use, and deconstruction. This comprises also thermal, acoustic, and visual comfort, as well as questions of biocompatibility, insofar as possible emissions of the building materials used."

WERNER SOBEK wurde 1953 in Aalen, Deutschland, geboren. Er studierte Architektur und Bauingenieurwesen an der Universität Stuttgart (1974–80) und arbeitete nach seinem Abschluss an einer Forschungsarbeit zum Thema „Flächentragwerke und Leichtbaukonstruktionen" an der Universität Stuttgart (1980–86). 1987 promovierte er an derselben Hochschule. Er arbeitete zunächst als Statiker bei Schlaich, Bergermann & Partner (Stuttgart, 1987–91) und gründete 1991 sein eigenes Büro. Seit 1995 ist er Professor an der Universität Stuttgart, wo er die Nachfolge von Frei Otto als Leiter des Instituts für Leichtbau antrat. Zu seinen Projekten zählen die École Nationale d'Art Décoratif mit Finn Geipel und Nicolas Michelin (Limoges, Frankreich, 1991–94), die Fassade der Interbank mit Hans Hollein (Lima, Peru, 1996–99), das Privatwohnhaus R128 (Stuttgart, 1998–2000), der neue internationale Flughafen Bangkok mit Murphy/Jahn (Thailand, 1995–2004), das Mercedes Benz Museum mit UNStudio (Stuttgart, 2003–06), das H16 (Tieringen, 2005–06, hier vorgestellt), die Altarüberdachung für Papst Benedikt XVI. (München, 2006) sowie Messepavillons für Audi und BMW. 2007 gründeten Klaus Sedlbauer und Werner Sobek gemeinschaftlich die Firma WSGreenTechnologies in Stuttgart. WSGreenTechnologies „bietet einen integrierten Planungsprozess für alle Arten von Gebäuden. Dieser Planungsprozess berücksichtigt alle Phasen eines Lebenszyklus des Gebäudes. Die hierbei behandelten Fragen umfassen das thermische, akustische und visuelle Wohlbefinden sowie den Bereich der Biokompatibilität z. B. in Bezug auf mögliche Emissionen durch die in Betracht gezogenen Baustoffe."

WERNER SOBEK, né en 1953 à Aalen, Allemagne, a étudié l'architecture et l'ingénierie civile à l'université de Stuttgart (1974–80), et a effectué des recherches approfondies sur les « structures légères de grande portée » dans le même cadre (1980–86). Il a reçu son diplôme de Ph.D. en ingénierie civile de la même université en 1987. Il a été ingénieur structurel à l'agence Schlaich, Bergermann & Partner (Stuttgart, 1987–91), avant de créer sa propre structure en 1991. Depuis 1995, il est professeur à l'université de Stuttgart où il a succédé à Frei Otto au poste de directeur de l'Institut des structures légères. Parmi ses réalisations : l'École nationale d'art décoratif avec Finn Geipel et Nicolas Michelin (Limoges, France, 1991–94) ; la façade de l'Interbank avec Hans Hollein (Lima, Pérou, 1996–99) ; la maison R128 (Stuttgart, Allemagne, 1998–2000) ; le nouvel aéroport international de Bangkok avec Murphy/Jahn (Thaïlande, 1995–2004) ; le musée Mercedes Benz avec UNStudio (Stuttgart, Allemagne, 2003–06) ; H16 (Tieringen, Allemagne, 2005–06, publié ici) ; l'autel pour Benoît XVI (Munich, Allemagne, 2006) et des pavillons de foire commerciale pour Audi et BMW. En 2007, Klaus Sedlbauer et Werner Sobek ont fondé WSGreenTechnologies à Stuttgart. WSGreenTechnologies « offre la programmation intégrée de bâtiments prenant en compte toutes les phases de la construction, de l'utilisation et de la déconstruction. Ceci comprend également le confort thermique, acoustique et visuel ainsi que les questions de biocompatibilité, dans la mesure de possibles émissions des matériaux utilisés dans la construction ».

H16

Tieringen, Germany, 2005–06

Floor area: 454 m². Client: Helmut and Georgia Link. Cost: not disclosed

Seen from a distance the house adapts a decidedly discreet profile, integrating glass and stone elements in an unexpected way.

Aus der Ferne gesehen beweist das Haus ein ausgesprochen diskretes Profil und kombiniert Elemente aus Glas und Stein auf überraschende Weise.

Vue à distance, la maison présente un profil volontairement discret, intégrant divers éléments en verre ou en pierre de façon inattendue.

This house is described as a logical progression and improvement on the widely published R128 house. Located south of Stuttgart, the structure seeks "maximum transparency and a minimum of structure, full recyclability … and zero emissions." Careful attention was also paid to the integration of the house into its site. An all-glass cube, shielded from the street by a hedge, contains an open living space, while a second, black cube, located below, houses private spaces. A third, light-colored cube, connected to the black cube by a steel terrace, contains the garage and utilities room. The supporting steel structure of the entire house can be dismantled "within a couple of days." The black volume is built with prefabricated architectural concrete sections. Geothermal heating with a heat pump, as well as photovoltaic panels, reduces energy consumption. The sophisticated climate control system also contributes to a minimum use of electricity. The architects write, not without a certain amount of pride: "H16 is a tribute to outstanding icons of modern architecture, such as the ones designed by Mies van der Rohe. The building combines sustainability (by zero emissions and full recyclability), state-of-the-art design, and first-class building technologies, thus making it an achievement from an architectural, technical, and aesthetic point of view."

Dieses Wohnhaus wurde als logische Fortführung und Verfeinerung des weithin publizierten R128 bezeichnet. Der im Süden von Stuttgart gelegene Bau strebt nach „maximaler Transparenz und einem Minimum an Struktur, vollständiger Reclycingfähigkeit … und Emissionsfreiheit". Besondere Aufmerksamkeit galt der Einbindung des Hauses in sein Umfeld. In einem voll verglasten Kubus, der zur Straße hin durch eine Hecke abgeschirmt ist, befindet sich ein offener Wohnbereich; in einem zweiten schwarzen, darunterliegenden Kubus liegen private Räume. In einem dritten, hellgrauen Kubus, der über eine Stahlterrasse mit dem schwarzen Kubus verbunden ist, sind Garage und Haustechnik untergebracht. Das tragende Stahlgerüst des gesamten Hauses lässt sich „innerhalb weniger Tage" demontieren. Das schwarze Volumen wurde aus Betonfertigbauteilen erbaut. Eine Erdwärmeheizung mit Wärmepumpe sowie Solarmodule reduzieren den Energieverbrauch. Auch das ausgefeilte Klimasteuerungssystem trägt zur Minimierung des Stromverbrauchs bei. Die Architekten schreiben nicht ohne Stolz: „H16 ist eine Hommage an herausragende Ikonen der Architektur, wie etwa die Bauten Mies van der Rohes. Der Bau vereint Nachhaltigkeit (durch Emissionsfreiheit und vollständige Recycelbarkeit) mit anspruchsvollem Design und erstklassigen Bauverfahren, was es zu einer Leistung in architektonischer, technischer und ästhetischer Hinsicht macht."

Cette maison est présentée comme la progression logique et le perfectionnement du projet de la maison R128 largement publié. Située au sud de Stuttgart, elle recherche « un maximum de transparence et un minimum de structure, une recyclabilité totale… et zéro émissions ». Une grande attention a été portée à son intégration dans le site. Un cube entièrement vitré, protégé de la rue par une haie, contient un séjour ouvert, tandis qu'un second cube, noir cette fois, situé en dessous, abrite les chambres. Un troisième cube, de couleur claire, connecté au précédent par une terrasse en acier contient un garage et des pièces de service. La structure en acier qui soutient l'ensemble de la maison peut être démontée « en deux jours ». Le volume noir est en béton architectural préfabriqué. Un chauffage géothermique à pompe à chaleur ainsi que des panneaux photovoltaïques réduisent la consommation d'électricité. Le système sophistiqué de contrôle de la climatisation contribue également à ces économies. Les architectes précisent, non sans une certaine fierté : « H16 est un hommage aux icônes les plus célèbres de l'architecture moderne, comme celles conçues par Mies van der Rohe. Cette construction combine la durabilité (zéro émissions et recyclabilité totale), une conception d'avant-garde et des technologies de construction de haut niveau, qui en font un accomplissement sur les plans architecturaux, techniques et esthétiques. »

Seen from below, the glass box forming the upper level almost seems to
float on its base.

Von unten betrachtet scheint die
Glasbox der oberen Etage fast über
ihrem Sockel zu schweben.

Vu en contre-plongée, le cube vitré
du niveau supérieur semble flotter
au-dessus de sa base.

The upper volume of the house is an
extremely light box made of glass,
extending out to a wooden deck.

Le volume supérieur est une boîte
vitrée extrêmement légère, qui se
prolonge par une terrasse en bois.

Der obere Baukörper des Hauses ist
eine extrem leichte Box aus Glas, an
die sich eine Holzterrasse anschließt.

As might be expected, the interior of the house is very bright and open, an impression emphasized here by the choice of modern furniture.

Wie zu erwarten, ist das Interieur des Hauses hell und offen, ein Eindruck, der hier durch die Wahl moderner Möbel noch unterstrichen wird.

Comme on peut l'imaginer, l'intérieur de la maison est très ouvert et lumineux, impression renforcée par le choix d'un mobilier moderne.

It anything, the house proves that a very modern house with large window surfaces need not be considered ecologically wasteful – in particular with an engineer such as Werner Sobek as its author.

Das Haus stellt fraglos unter Beweis, dass sich ein explizit moderner Bau mit großen Fensterflächen keineswegs mangelndes ökologisches Energiebewusstsein vorwerfen lassen muss – insbesondere, wenn ein Ingenieur wie Werner Sobek als Autor verantwortlich zeichnet.

La maison prouve, entre autres, qu'une résidence très moderne à grandes baies vitrées peut éviter les gaspillages énergétiques, en particulier lorsqu'un ingénieur comme Werner Sobek en est l'auteur.

GERMÁN DEL SOL

Germán del Sol, Arquitecto
Camino Las Flores 11441
Las Condes, Santiago
Chile

Tel: +562 214 12 14
Fax: +562 214 11 47
E-mail: contacto@germandelsol.cl
Web: www.germandelsol.cl

GERMÁN DEL SOL was born in Santiago de Chile in 1949. He graduated in 1973 from the Escuela Técnica Superior de Arquitectura de Barcelona, Spain. He created his own firm in Barcelona (1973–79) before returning to Santiago, where he worked on his own (1980–83), before spending two years in the office of R. Elmore in Palo Alto, California (1984–86). He then returned to his own practice in Santiago, where he has been based since 1986. Between 1988 and 1998, he created and directed Explora, a company dedicated to creating new travel destinations in remote places in South America. Between 1995 and 1998, he created and directed "Viña Gracia," a new Chilean vineyard. Germán del Sol then created and directed a new Hot Springs Complex, next to the Villarrica Vulcano, in Pucón (Chile, 2001–05). His built work includes: the Hotel Explora en Atacama (San Pedro de Atacama, 1998); Horse Stables (San Pedro de Atacama, 1999); Saunas and Pools (Atacama, 2000); Puritama Hot Springs Complex (Atacama, 2000); Geometricas Hot Springs Complex (Villarrica, 2004); Hotel Remota (Puerto Natales, Patagonia, 2005–06, published here); and Remota Spot (Patagonia, 2007), all in Chile. In 2008 he completed an apartment building in Vallecas (Madrid). He won the National Association of Chilean Architects Award in 2006.

GERMÁN DEL SOL wurde 1949 in Santiago de Chile geboren. Sein Studium schloss er 1973 an der Escuela Técnica Superior de Arquitectura de Barcelona in Spanien ab. Nachdem er zunächst in Barcelona ein eigenes Büro betrieb (1973–79), kehrte er nach Santiago zurück, wo er selbstständig arbeitete (1980–83), bevor er zwei Jahre lang für R. Elmore in Palo Alto, Kalifornien, tätig war (1984–86). Schließlich kehrte er zu seinem eigenen Büro in Santiago zurück, von wo aus er seit 1986 arbeitet. Von 1988 bis 1998 leitete er die von ihm gegründete Agentur Explora, die sich auf die Erschließung neuer Reiseziele an abgelegenen Orten Südamerikas spezialisiert hatte. Von 1995 bis 1998 führte er das von ihm gegründete chilenische Weingut Viña Gracia. Schließlich baute und leitete Germán del Sol auch eine Hotelanlage an den Thermalquellen am Vulkan Villarrica in Pucón (Chile, 2001–05). Zu seinen realisierten Projekten zählen das Hotel Explora en Atacama (San Pedro de Atacama, 1998), Pferdeställe (San Pedro de Atacama, 1999), Saunen und Pools (Wüste Atacama, 2000), die Thermalquellen Puritama (Wüste Atacama, 2000), der Thermalquellenkomplex Geometricas (Villarrica, 2004), das Hotel Remota (Puerto Natales, Patagonien, 2005–06, hier vorgestellt) sowie Remota Spot (Patagonien, 2007), alle in Chile. 2008 konnte ein Apartmentgebäude in Vallecas (Madrid) fertiggestellt werden. 2006 wurde er mit dem Preis des Nationalen Architektenverbands in Chile ausgezeichnet.

GERMÁN DEL SOL, né à Santiago du Chili en 1949, est diplômé de la Escuela Técnica Superior de Arquitectura de Barcelona, Espagne (1973). Il fonde son agence à Barcelone (1973–79), avant de revenir à Santiago où il travaille à son compte (1980–83). Il collabore deux années avec l'agence de R. Elmore à Palo Alto, en Californie (1984–86), puis retourne à Santiago. De 1988 à 1998, il crée et dirige Explora, société qui propose de nouvelles destinations de voyages dans des lieux isolés d'Amérique du Sud. Entre 1995 et 1998, il fonde et dirige « Viña Gracia », un nouveau domaine viticole. Il a ensuite créé et dirigé un nouveau complexe touristique autour de sources d'eau chaude près du volcan de Villarrica, à Pucón (Chili, 2001–05). Parmi ses réalisations, toutes au Chili : l'hôtel Explora à Atacama (San Pedro de Atacama, 1998) ; des écuries (San Pedro de Atacama, 1999) ; des saunas et piscines (Atacama, 2000) ; le complexe thermal de Puritama (Atacama, 2000) ; le complexe thermal Geometricas (Villarrica, 2004) ; l'hôtel Remota (Puerto Natales, Patagonie, 2005–06, publié ici) et Remota Spot (Patagonie, 2007). En 2008, il a achevé un immeuble d'appartements à Vallecas (Madrid). Il a remporté le prix de l'Association nationale des architectes chiliens en 2006.

HOTEL REMOTA

Puerto Natales, Patagonia, Chile, 2005–06

Floor area: 5215 m². Client: Immobiliaria mares del sur. Cost: $9.5 million.
Team: José Luis Ibañez, Francisca Schüler, Carlos Venegas

Inspired by the sheep farming buildings of Patagonia, the Hotel Remota has a central courtyard occupied only by several boulders at its center. The architect states: "Latin America has an ancient tradition of architecture that stands in the midst of nature, where shepherds or merchants used to pass or stay the night, or where people gather once in a while to celebrate their ancient rites." Germán del Sol describes Remota as resembling a "big black barn" from a distance with an unexpectedly refined interior. Pillars, slabs, and interior walls are made of concrete. Waterproof industrial plywood panels coated with a synthetic asphalt membrane and a 25-centimeter-thick layer of expanded polyurethane cover the building and act as insulation. Double-glazed thermal window panes "form a continuous sequence of vertical openings in the exterior walls." The natural grasses found on the site are allowed to grow wild around the building, and on its landscaped roof. The three buildings that form the hotel are connected by wooden corridors. Within, the architect has placed "Spartan" geometric dark wood furniture made by carpenters on site from dead wood culled in the Patagonian lowlands near the sea. Low-energy light bulbs, low-water consumption bathroom fittings, and an orientation intended to make use of passive solar energy are part of the overall sustainability strategy employed.

Das Hotel Remota, inspiriert von den Schaffarmen Patagoniens, hat einen zentralen Innenhof, in dem nur einige Findlinge liegen. Der Architekt erklärt: „Latein-amerika hat eine uralte architektonische Tradition von Bauten, die inmitten der Landschaft liegen, dort, wo einst Schäfer oder Händler vorüberzogen und die Nacht verbrachten oder sich Menschen versammelten, um uralte Riten zu feiern." Germán del Sol zufolge wirkt Remota aus der Ferne wie eine „große schwarze Scheune" mit unerwartet raffiniertem Interieur. Stützen, Platten und Innenwände sind aus Beton. Verkleidet und gedämmt wurde der Bau mit wasserfesten industriellen Sperrholzpa-neelen, die mit einer synthetischen Asphaltmembran und einer 25 cm starken Schicht aus Polyurethan-Hartschaum ummantelt sind. Doppelwärmeschutzfenster „bilden eine uniforme Sequenz vertikaler Öffnungen in den Außenwänden". Die auf dem Gelände beheimateten natürlichen Gräser wachsen wild um das Gebäude ebenso wie auf dem begrünten Dach. Die drei Hotelgebäude sind durch Holzkorridore miteinander verbunden. Die Innenräume stattete der Architekt mit „spartanischen" geometrischen dunklen Holzmöbeln aus, die von Schreinern vor Ort aus totem Holz aus der patagonischen Tiefebene an der Küste gefertigt wurden. Energiesparlampen, wassersparende Installationen in den Bädern und die Ausrichtung des Baus für die passive Nutzung von Solarenergie sind Bestandteil der hier angewandten Nachhaltigkeitsstrategie.

Inspiré des formes des bergers de Patagonie, l'hôtel Remota se caractérise par une cour centrale uniquement occupée en son centre par quelques rochers. L'architecte explique ainsi son projet : « L'Amérique latine possède une tradition ancienne d'architecture en pleine nature, où bergers et colporteurs séjournaient ou pas-saient la nuit, où des gens se réunissaient de temps en temps pour célébrer des rites anciens. » Il considère Remota comme « une grosse grange noire » vue de loin, mais possédant un intérieur au raffinement inattendu. Les piliers, les dalles des sols et les murs intérieurs sont en béton. Le bâtiment est habillé et isolé par des pan-neaux industriels en contreplaqué à membrane d'asphalte synthétique et couche de polyuréthane expansé de 25 cm d'épaisseur. Des fenêtres à double vitrage de verre thermique « forment une séquence continue d'ouvertures verticales dans les murs extérieurs ». Les herbes naturelles trouvées sur le site grandissent librement autour du bâtiment et sur son toit végétalisé. Les trois constructions qui constituent l'hôtel sont réunies par des corridors en bois. À l'intérieur, l'architecte a disposé un mobilier en bois de formes géométriques « spartiate », réalisé sur place par les menuisiers à l'aide de bois mort récupéré dans les marais patagonien au bord de la mer. Des ampoules à basse consommation, des équipements de salles de bains qui économisent l'eau, et une orientation qui favorise l'utilisation passive de l'énergie solaire font partie de la stratégie de durabilité utilisée.

Lying low in the ground, with its
three buildings connected by wooden
corridors, the hotel has a somewhat
austere appearance.

Das Hotel besteht aus drei durch
Holzgänge verbundenen Bauten. Es
scheint sich dicht an den Boden zu
kauern und wirkt geradezu streng.

Se détachant à peine du sol, les trois
bâtiments de l'hôtel reliés par des
corridors en bois sont d'aspect assez
austère.

Even the landscaping of the hotel participates in its overall impression of frugality generated by the architects in this sparse natural setting.

Selbst die Landschaftsgestaltung des Hotels trägt zum beinahe spartanischen Gesamteindruck bei, den die Architekten in dieser spröden Umgebung geschaffen haben.

Même l'aménagement paysager participe à l'impression générale d'économie de moyens voulue par les architectes pour ce cadre naturel sévère.

Although simple, the interiors give a greater impression of warmth than the outside of the hotel.

Trotz seiner Schlichtheit vermittelt das Interieur mehr Wärme als die Außenansicht des Hotels.

Bien que sobres, les intérieurs sont plus chaleureux que l'aspect extérieur de l'hôtel.

STUDIO TAMASSOCIATI

studio tamassociati
2731 Dorsoduro
30123 Venice
Italy

Tel/Fax: +39 0415 226 974
E-mail: info@tamassociati.org
Web: www.tamassociati.org

Raul Pantaleo was born in Milan in 1962. He attended the IUAV (Istituto Universitario di Architettura di Venezia) in Italy, and holds an international certificate in Human Ecology obtained through postgraduate studies at the University of Padua. Massimo Lepore was born in Udine, Italy, in 1960. He graduated from the IUAV. He completed postgraduate studies in urban and environmental re-qualification at the "Taller de Arquitectura y Urbanismo" (Municipality of Lleida, Spain). Simone Sfriso was born in London in 1966. She also graduated from the IUAV and now works as adviser and teaching assistant for courses in Urban Planning at the IUAV. They created **STUDIO TAMASSOCIATI** for "socially conscious design and communication" in 2001. Based in Venice, the firm works mainly for public institutions and NGOs. It is currently developing projects for public spaces and hospital projects for NGOs in the Sudan (see the Salam Center for Cardiac Surgery, Soba, 2006–07, published here), Democratic Republic of Congo, Central African Republic, and Nicaragua. Their recent work includes: Banca Popolare Etica headquarters (Padua, Italy, 2004–07); a redesign of the Marconi Square (San Giorgio Piacentino, Italy, 2007); San Giacomo del Martignone Urban Park (Anzola Dell'Emilia, Italy, 2007); and a project for a Children's Hospital (Bangui, Central African Republic, 2007).

Raul Pantaleo wurde 1962 in Mailand geboren. Er besuchte das Istituto Universitario di Architettura di Venezia (IUAV) in Italien und erwarb mit Abschluss eines Postgraduiertenprogramms an der Universität Padua ein internationales Zertifikat in Ökologie. Massimo Lepore wurde 1960 in Udine geboren. Seinen Abschluss machte er ebenfalls am IUAV. Er absolvierte ein Postgraduiertenprogramm in urbaner und ökologischer Wiederaufbereitung an der Taller de Arquitectura y Urbanismo (Lleida, Spanien). Simone Sfriso wurde 1966 in London geboren. Auch sie machte ihren Abschluss am IUAV und ist dort inzwischen als Beraterin und Lehrassistentin für Stadtplanung tätig. Gemeinsam gründeten sie 2001 das **STUDIO TAMASSOCIATI** für „sozial verantwortliche Planung und Kommunikation". Die in Venedig ansässige Firma arbeitet hauptsächlich für öffentliche Träger und Nichtregierungsorganisationen (NGOs). Derzeit wird an Projekten für öffentliche Einrichtungen und Krankenhäuser von NGOs im Sudan (Zentrum für Herzchirurgie „Salam", Soba, 2006–07, hier vorgestellt), in der Demokratischen Republik Kongo, der Zentralafrikanischen Republik und Nicaragua gearbeitet. Aktuelle Projekte sind u. a. der Hauptsitz der Banca Popolare Etica (Padua, Italien, 2004–07), die Umgestaltung der Piazza Marconi (San Giorgio Piacentino, Italien, 2007), der Stadtpark in San Giacomo del Martignone (Anzola Dell'Emilia, Italien, 2007) sowie ein Kinderkrankenhausprojekt (Bangui, Zentralafrikanische Republik, 2007).

Raul Pantaleo, né à Milan en 1962, a étudié à Venise à l'IUAV (Istituto Universitario di Architettura di Venezia), et, après des études supérieures à l'université de Padoue, a passé un diplôme en écologie humaine. Massimo Lepore, né à Udine, Italie, en 1960, est également diplômé de l'IUAV de Venise. Il a effectué des études supérieures en requalification urbaine et environnementale au « Taller de Arquitectura y Urbanismo » (Lleida, Espagne). Simone Sfriso, née à Londres en 1966, est elle aussi diplômée de l'IUAV et travaille maintenant comme conseillère et assistante d'enseignement pour les cours d'urbanisme de l'IUAV. Ils ont créé ensemble le **STUDIO TAMASSOCIATI**, « conception et communication socialement responsables », en 2001. Basée à Venise, cette agence travaille principalement pour des institutions publiques et des ONG. Actuellement, elle met au point des projets d'espaces publics et d'hôpitaux pour des ONG au Soudan (Centre Salam de chirurgie cardiaque, Soba, 2006–07, publié ici), en République démocratique du Congo, République centrafricaine et au Nicaragua. Parmi leurs récentes interventions : le siège social de la Banca Popolare Etica (Padoue, Italie, 2004–07) ; la rénovation de la place Marconi (San Giorgio Piacentino, Italie, 2007) ; le parc urbain San Giacomo del Martignone (Anzola Dell'Emilia, Italie, 2007) et un projet d'hôpital pour enfants (Bangui, République centrafricaine, 2007).

SALAM CENTER FOR CARDIAC SURGERY

Soba, Republic of Sudan, 2006–07

Floor area: 11 000 m². Client: Emergency NGO. Cost: €6 million.
Team: Raul Pantaleo, Simone Sfriso, Massimo Lepore,
Sebastiano Crescini with Pietro Parrino and Gino Strada

Emergency is an Italian NGO that provides free medical and surgical treatment to the civilian victims of war, landmines, and poverty. Emergency began work in North Darfur in 2004, and established their Center for Cardiac Surgery in Soba, 20 kilometers from Khartoum, in 2007. With a capacity of 63 beds and a 15-bed intensive-care unit, the Center is organized around a "hollow" space formed by two existing mango trees. This traditional home design device, together with the low profile of the buildings, is intended to give people a sense that they are not lost when entering the facility. Studio tamassociati insists on the homelike atmosphere of the Center, a decided contrast to many medical facilities and a useful initiative in this war-torn country. A 58-centimeter-thick wall made of two layers of bricks separated by an insulating air cavity, with small windows and high-performance glass panels, provides a first protection from local heat. Traditional thatched roofs are used for paths and rest areas. Some 1000 square meters of solar panels serve to greatly reduce energy consumption, while a system of tunnels and water vapor spray reduces ambient dust coming into the innovative chilling system. All of these measures are carefully thought-out reactions to the local situation, and to the architectural "honesty" of the project.

Emergency ist eine italienische NGO, die zivilen Opfern von Krieg, Landminen und Armut kostenfreie ärztliche und chirurgische Hilfe bietet. Emergency ist seit 2004 in Nord-Darfur aktiv und gründete 2007 ein Zentrum für Herzchirurgie in Soba, 20 km nördlich von Khartum. Das Zentrum hat eine Kapazität von 63 Betten sowie eine Intensivstation mit 15 Betten und organisiert sich um einen offenen Hof, der um zwei vorhandene Mangobäume herum entstand. Die traditionelle Wohnbauform und niedrige Bauweise sollen verhindern, dass sich die Menschen verloren fühlen, wenn sie die Einrichtung betreten. Studio tamassociati legt besonderen Wert auf die häusliche Atmosphäre des Zentrums, ein bewusst gewählter Gegensatz zu den zahlreichen medizinischen Einrichtungen in diesem kriegsgebeutelten Land. 58 cm dicke Mauern aus zwei Backsteinschichten mit einer dazwischenliegenden, isolierenden Luftschicht und kleinen Fenstern ebenso wie hochdämmende Glasscheiben sorgen für ausgezeichneten Schutz vor der Hitze. Pfade und Ruheplätze werden von traditionellen Grasdächern beschirmt. 1000 m² Solarmodule tragen dazu bei, den Energieverbrauch drastisch zu senken. Ein Tunnel- und Wasserdampfsprühsystem mindert das Eindringen von Staub in das innovative Kühlsystem. Sämtliche Maßnahmen wurden sorgsam im Hinblick auf die Gegebenheiten vor Ort und die architektonische Authentizität des Projekts ausgearbeitet.

Emergency est une ONG italienne qui fournit des services médicaux et chirurgicaux gratuits aux victimes civiles de guerres, de mines et de la pauvreté. Elle a commencé à travailler au nord du Darfour en 2004 et a fondé un centre de chirurgie cardiaque à Soba, à 20 km de Khartoum en 2007. Avec une capacité de 63 lits et une unité de soins intensifs de 15 lits, ce centre s'organise autour d'un espace « en creux » formé par deux manguiers existants. Ce plan de maison traditionnelle ainsi que la faible hauteur des bâtiments veut donner aux patients le sentiment qu'ils ne sont pas perdus dans un univers étranger lorsqu'ils arrivent au Centre. Studio tamassociati insiste sur son atmosphère de maison, contraste marqué avec beaucoup d'installations médicales et initiative louable dans ce pays déchiré par la guerre. Un mur de 58 cm d'épaisseur composé de deux pans de briques séparés par une cavité d'air, de petites fenêtres et des panneaux de verre à haute performance offrent une protection de base contre la chaleur de la région. Les toitures traditionnelles en chaume sont utilisées pour ombrager les cheminements et les zones de repos. 1000 m² de panneaux solaires permettent de fortement réduire la consommation d'électricité achetée, tandis qu'un système de tunnels et de vaporisation d'eau diminue la pénétration de la poussière dans une installation innovante de refroidissement. Toutes ces mesures correspondent aux conditions locales et traduisent l'honnêteté architecturale de ce projet.

Auf den ersten Blick wirkt das Salam Center überraschend modern, insbesondere angesichts seiner Aufgabe und Lage unweit von Khartum.

À première vue, le centre Salam semble étonnamment moderne, en particulier si on considère sa fonction et son implantation à proximité de Khartoum.

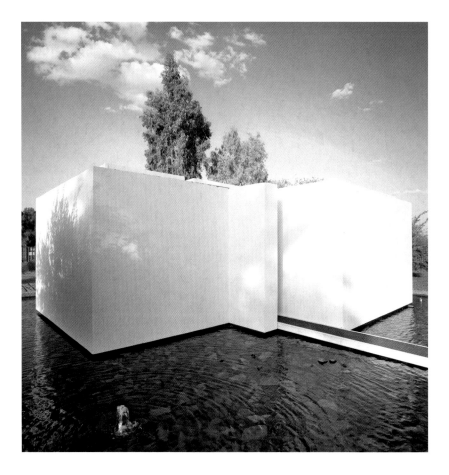

Verschiedene Aspekte des Entwurfs, wie die hier abgebildeten Sonnenblenden und die leichte, luftige Bauart, lassen die Angemessenheit dieser baulichen Intervention deutlicher werden.

Certaines caractéristiques du projet comme les pare-soleil visibles ici et le type de construction légère et aérée mis en œuvre expriment la nature bien adaptée de cette intervention.

CHRIS TATE

Chris Tate Architecture
PO Box 52051
Kingsland, Auckland
New Zealand

Tel: +64 9 630 2514
Fax: +64 9 630 2515
E-mail: chris@christate.co.nz
Web: www.christate.co.nz

CHRIS TATE was born in 1971 in Auckland, New Zealand. He received a Bachelor of Social Science in Human Service from the Auckland College of Education (1994–97) and a Diploma in Architectural Technology from UNITEC Auckland (2004–05). He did social work for various agencies from 1990 to 2001, but during that period he also bought land on an island off the coast of Auckland and designed and built a house there. He left his social work in 2001 to manage the construction of a large house on the same island designed by Richard Priest. In 2006 he created Chris Tate Architecture and completed his first project, Forest House (Titirangi, Auckland, 2006, published here).

CHRIS TATE wurde 1971 in Auckland, Neuseeland, geboren. Er erwarb einen Bachelor in Sozialwissenschaften am Auckland College of Education (1994–97) und ein Diplom in Architektur an der UNITEC Auckland (2004–05). Von 1990 bis 2001 war er für verschiedene Organisationen im sozialen Bereich tätig, kaufte währenddessen aber auch Land auf einer Insel vor der Küste von Auckland und entwarf und baute dort ein Haus. 2001 gab er seine Tätigkeit als Sozialarbeiter auf, um auf derselben Insel die Aufsicht über den Bau eines großen Hauses zu übernehmen, das er für Richard Priest entworfen hatte. 2006 gründete er Chris Tate Architecture und realisierte sein erstes Projekt, das Forest House (Titirangi, Auckland, 2006, hier vorgestellt).

CHRIS TATE, né en 1971 à Auckland, en Nouvelle-Zélande, est Bachelor en sciences humaines et sociales du Auckland College of Education (1994–97), et diplômé en technologie architecturale de UNITEC Auckland (2004–05). Il a participé à différentes interventions sociales pour diverses agences de 1990 à 2001, et pendant cette période s'est acheté un terrain sur une île de la côte d'Auckland où il s'est construit une maison. Il a quitté son travail dans les services sociaux pour diriger la construction d'une vaste maison conçue par Richard Priest sur la même île. En 2006, il a fondé l'agence Chris Tate Architecture et a achevé son premier projet, Forest House (Titirangi, Auckland, 2006, publié ici).

FOREST HOUSE

Titirangi, Auckland, New Zealand, 2006

Floor area: 100 m². Client: Chris Tate. Cost: €150 000

This house was built on a densely forested and steep 800-square-meter lot. Entering the house, visitors are required to descend 45 steps to reach the entrance. According to Chris Tate: "The site is slip sensitive, flood prone, and is protected by the local building authority as a 'Protected Environment.'" Including one bedroom, a study and a bathroom, with an open-plan living, dining, and kitchen area, the house is intended as "an interpretation of Philip Johnson's 1949 Glass House" (New Canaan, Connecticut, USA). A building platform was created on 16 poles across a gully and this glass box was set on it, cantilevered in all directions "to create a floating feeling." The precise site was selected to minimize tree removal, and New Zealand native trees were planted after construction. The house was designed to stop at a large Pururi (arched tree), saving it from being cut. A black-and-white color scheme was chosen in order to contrast with the green forest environment. Tate was allowed to build on the site because of the "low environmental impact" of the design. The floor inside the house is made of rough eucalyptus wood painted in high-gloss white.

Das Haus wurde auf ein dicht bewachsenes, steiles 800 m² großes Waldgrundstück gebaut. Besucher müssen zuerst 45 Stufen hinabsteigen, um zum Hauseingang zu gelangen. Chris Tate erklärt: „Das Grundstück ist erdrutsch- und überschwemmungsgefährdet und wurde von der örtlichen Baubehörde als Naturschutzgebiet ausgezeichnet." Das Haus mit einem Schlafzimmer, Arbeitszimmer, Bad und einem offenen Wohn-, Ess- und Küchenbereich wurde als „Interpretation von Philip Johnsons Glass House von 1949" (New Canaan, Connecticut, USA) gestaltet. Über einem Regenwasserablauf wurde eine Gebäudeplattform auf 16 Stützen aufgeständert. Hierauf wurde der Glaskubus platziert. Dieser kragt nach allen Seiten aus, um „einen schwebenden Eindruck" zu vermitteln. Die genaue Lage des Baugrunds wurde gewählt, um nicht zu viele Bäume fällen zu müssen. Nach Bauabschluss wurden heimische Bäume angepflanzt. Der Entwurf nahm Rücksicht auf einen großen herabhängenden Pururi-Baum, sodass dieser nicht gefällt werden musste. Als Kontrast zur grünen Waldumgebung entschied man sich gestalterisch für eine Schwarzweißpalette. Tate erhielt seine Baugenehmigung auch wegen des „geringen Eingriffs in die Umwelt". Der Boden im Innern des Hauses wurde aus rohem Eukalyptusholz gefertigt und glänzend weiß lackiert.

Cette maison a été édifiée sur un terrain de 800 m², incliné et abondamment planté d'arbres. Pour entrer, le visiteur doit d'abord descendre 45 marches. Selon Chris Tate : «Le site, qui pourrait être sujet à des glissements de terrain et des inondations, est classé par la réglementation locale en "environnement protégé"». Comprenant une chambre, un bureau et une salle de bains, un séjour de plan ouvert, une zone pour la préparation et la prise des repas, la maison se veut «une interprétation de la Maison de verre de Philip Johnson» (1949, New Canaan, Connecticut, États-Unis). Une plate-forme située au-dessus d'un ravin a d'abord été mise en place. Elle repose sur 16 pieux et soutient la boîte de verre, elle-même en porte-à-faux dans toutes les directions «pour créer une sensation de flottement». L'implantation précise a été déterminée de façon à limiter le nombre d'arbres à supprimer. Des arbres d'essences locales ont été replantés après le chantier. La maison s'est volontairement arrêtée devant un grand pururi (arbre arqué) pour ne pas avoir à le couper. Le noir et le blanc ont été choisis pour contraster avec l'environnement forestier vert. Tate a eu le droit de construire sur ce terrain parce que le projet n'exerçait qu'un «faible impact environnemental». Le sol intérieur est en planches brutes d'eucalyptus peintes en blanc laqué brillant.

The Forest House is indeed carefully inserted into its site, abutting the earth on one side, bridging a gully, and entirely surrounded by existing trees.

Das Forest Haus wurde außerordentlich umsichtig in sein Umfeld integriert – auf der einen Seite am Boden „andockend", überbrückt es einen Regenwasserablauf und ist rundum von Bäumen umgeben.

La «maison de la forêt» est soigneusement insérée dans son site, butant contre le relief d'un côté, franchissant un ruisseau et entièrement entourée d'arbres.

The interior of the house retains a modern if not modernist spirit, rendered more surprising by the almost invasive presence of nature all around its windows.

Das Interieur ist modern, wenn nicht modernistisch gehalten, was angesichts der geradezu invasiven Präsenz der Natur vor den Fenstern umso überraschender wirkt.

L'intérieur de la maison conserve un esprit moderne, voire moderniste, rendu plus étonnant encore par la présence presque envahissante de la nature devant les fenêtres.

MATTEO THUN

Matteo Thun & Partners
Via Appiani 9
20121 Milan
Italy

Tel: + 39 02 655 6911
Fax: + 39 02 657 0646
E-mail: info@matteothun.com
Web: www.matteothun.com

MATTEO THUN was born in 1952 in Bolzano, Italy. He studied at the Salzburg Academy with the painter Oskar Kokoschka and received his doctorate in Architecture in Florence in 1975. He began working with Ettore Sottsass in Milan in 1978 and was a co-founding member of the Memphis group with Sottsass in 1981. He was the Chair for Product Design and Ceramics at the Vienna Academy for Applied Arts (1982–96), and created his own office, Matteo Thun & Partners, in Milan in 1984. He served as creative director for Swatch from 1990 to 1993. According to his description, in his studio, Matteo Thun attempts "to offer a complete service to his international clients, developing projects covering different fields, such as architecture, design, and communication." Matteo Thun & Partners comprises a team of 40 professionals, graphic designers, product designers, and architects, who work on an interdisciplinary basis. The work of the studio ranges from hotels to low-energy prefabrication systems, to watches for Bulgari or Swatch, furniture for Kartell, or lighting systems for AEG and Zumtobel.

MATTEO THUN wurde 1952 in Bozen geboren. Er studierte an der Sommerakademie Salzburg bei Oskar Kokoschka und promovierte 1975 in Florenz in Architektur. 1978 begann er in Mailand seine Zusammenarbeit mit Ettore Sottsass, mit dem er 1981 zum Mitbegründer der Gruppe Memphis wurde. Er war Professor für Design an der Hochschule für Angewandte Kunst in Wien (1982–96) und gründete 1984 sein eigenes Büro Matteo Thun & Partners in Mailand. Von 1990 bis 1993 war er Kreativdirektor bei Swatch. Mit seinem Studio will Matteo Thun „einen Rundumservice für internationale Auftraggeber bieten und entwickelt Projekte in verschiedenen Disziplinen wie Architektur, Design und Kommunikation". Matteo Thun & Partners hat 40 Mitarbeiter, darunter Grafikdesigner, Produktdesigner und Architekten, die interdisziplinär zusammenarbeiten. Die Projekte des Studios reichen von Hotels bis hin zu Niedrigenergie-Fertigbausystemen, von Armbanduhren für Bulgari oder Swatch über Möbel für Kartell bis hin zu Lichtsystemen für AEG und Zumtobel.

MATTEO THUN est né en 1952 à Bolzano, Italie. Après avoir étudié à l'Académie de Salzbourg auprès du peintre Oskar Kokoschka, il reçoit son diplôme d'architecte à Florence en 1975. Il commence à travailler avec Ettore Sottsass à Milan en 1978, puis à participer avec lui à la fondation du groupe Memphis en 1981. Il dirige le département de design produit et de céramique à l'Académie des arts appliqués de Vienne (1982–96) et crée sa propre agence, Matteo Thun & Partners, à Milan, en 1984. Il a été directeur de la création de Swatch de 1990 à 1993. Matteo Thun & Partners propose « d'offrir à des clients internationaux un service complet de développement de projets, couvrant différents domaines comme l'architecture, le design et la communication ». L'agence emploie 40 collaborateurs, graphistes, designers et architectes travaillant sur une base interdisciplinaire. Les interventions du studio vont d'hôtels à des systèmes de construction préfabriquée à faible consommation d'énergie, en passant par des montres pour Bulgari ou Swatch, des meubles pour Kartell ou des systèmes d'éclairage pour AEG et Zumtobel.

VIGILIUS MOUNTAIN RESORT

Lana (Merano), Italy, 2001–03

Area: 11 500 m². Cost: not disclosed. Client: not disclosed

Located at an altitude of 1500 meters, this resort was designed as an extension to the existing Vigiljoch Hotel. Accessible only by funicular or on foot, the complex includes 35 bedrooms and 6 suites, together with a wellness center, swimming pool, conference room, library, and restaurants. Matteo Thun explains that the design of the new structures is based on local wood construction used in an innovative manner. Stone, wood, clay, and glass are significant building materials. Integrated into its surroundings to the greatest possible extent, the resort has a green roof covered with vegetation. Other energy-saving gestures include a façade with adjustable louvers. Large, planted terraces and an insistence on opening the architecture out onto the surrounding natural setting emphasize the close rapport between the buildings and the site. As the architect says: "The willingness to integrate completely with nature is evident in the 'Paradise Garden,'" a hill planted with larch trees in the inner part of the complex. The Vigilius Mountain Resort is a good example of the present and future potential for ecotourism, based on responsible architecture in spectacular natural settings.

Das Ferienhotel, gelegen auf 1500 Metern Höhe, ist ein Erweiterungsbau des Hotel Vigiljoch. Erreichbar nur per Seilbahn oder zu Fuß, umfasst der Komplex 35 Zimmer und 6 Suiten, ein Wellnesscenter, ein Schwimmbad, einen Konferenzsaal, eine Bibliothek und Restaurants. Matteo Thun weist darauf hin, dass das Design der Neubauten lokale Holzbautraditionen aufgreift und innovativ umsetzt. Stein, Holz, Lehm und Glas sind die bestimmenden Baumaterialien. Der Resort wurde so weit wie möglich in sein Umfeld integriert und hat ein begrüntes Dach. Zu den weiteren energiesparenden Maßnahmen zählt auch die Fassade mit justierbaren Sonnenschutzblenden. Großzügige begrünte Terrassen und die konsequente Öffnung der Architektur zur Landschaft unterstreichen die enge Beziehung von Gebäuden und Standort. Der Architekt merkt an: „Die Bereitschaft, sich ganz in die Natur zu integrieren wird auch am ‚Paradiesgarten' deutlich," einem mit Lärchen bepflanzten Hügel im Herzen des Komplexes. Das Vigilius Mountain Resort ist ein gutes Beispiel für das gegenwärtige und zukünftige Potenzial des ökologischen Tourismus, der auf verantwortliche Architektur und spektakuläre Landschaften baut.

Situé à 1500 m d'altitude, ce complexe est une extension de l'hôtel Vigiljoch. Accessible uniquement à pied ou par funiculaire, il compte 35 chambres, 6 suites, un centre de remise en forme, une piscine, une salle de conférences, une bibliothèque et des restaurants. Matteo Thun explique que la conception des bâtiments a fait appel à des principes de construction en bois locaux, mais utilisés de façon innovante. La pierre, le bois et le verre sont ainsi les principaux matériaux mis en jeu. Intégré au maximum dans son environnement, le complexe hôtelier possède un toit recouvert de végétation. Parmi les autres dispositifs d'économies d'énergie figure une façade à persiennes réglables. De vastes terrasses plantées et l'accent mis sur l'ouverture de l'architecture sur son cadre naturel soulignent les liens étroits entre les bâtiments et le site. Pour Thun : « La volonté de s'intégrer complètement à la nature est évidente dans le "jardin du Paradis", » une colline plantée de mélèzes à l'intérieur du complexe. Le Vigilius Mountain Resort est un bon exemple du potentiel actuel et futur d'un écotourisme fondé sur une architecture responsable au cœur de sites naturels spectaculaires.

Lying relatively low in its car-free isolated site, the Resort makes a strong case for "ecotourism," or the discovery of the natural environment, as opposed to ecologically unsound exploitation of a site.

Das relativ niedrige Ferienhotel liegt an einem autofreien, entlegenen Ort und ist ein eindrückliches Plädoyer für „ökologischen Tourismus" und die Entdeckung der natürlichen Umgebung, statt einer ökologisch unverantwortlichen Ausbeutung des Standorts.

Relativement discret dans ce site sans voitures, cet hôtel est un argument pour l'écotourisme ou la découverte de l'environnement naturel et s'oppose à l'exploitation anti-écologiques de certaines régions.

TNA

Makoto Takei + Chie Nabeshima/TNA
3–16–3–3F Taishidou
Setagaya-ku
Tokyo 154–0004
Japan

Tel: +81 3 3795 1901
Fax: +81 3 3795 1902
E-mail: mail@tna-arch.com
Web: www.tna-arch.com

Makoto Takei was born in Tokyo in 1974. He graduated from the Department of Architecture at Tokai University in 1997. Between 1997 and 1999 he was at the Tsukamoto Laboratory, Graduate School of Science and Engineering, Tokyo Institute of Technology, and worked with Atelier Bow-Wow. Between 1999 and 2000 he worked in the office of Tezuka Architects, before establishing **TNA** (Takei-Nabeshima-Architects) with Chie Nabeshima. Chie Nabeshima was born in Kanagawa in 1975 and graduated from the course in Habitation and Space Design, Department of Architecture and Architectural Engineering, College of Industrial Technology, Nihon University (1998), before working at Tezuka Architects (1998–2005) and co-founding TNA. Their projects include the Wood Wear House (Hayama, Kanagawa, 2005); Color Concrete House (Yokohama, Kanagawa, 2005); Ring House (Karuizawa, Nagano, 2006); Wood Ship Café (Hayama, Kanagawa, 2007) and the Mosaic House (Meguro-ku, Tokyo, 2006–07, published here), all in Japan.

Makoto Takei wurde 1974 in Tokio geboren. Sein Studium an der Fakultät für Architektur der Tokai-Universität schloss er 1997 ab. Von 1997 bis 1999 war er am Tsukamoto-Labor der Graduiertenschule für Natur- und Ingenieurwissenschaften am Tokyo Institute of Technology tätig und arbeitete für das Atelier Bow-Wow. Von 1999 bis 2000 arbeitete er für Tezuka Architects, bevor er mit Chie Nabeshima das Büro **TNA** (Takei-Nabeshima-Architects) gründete. Chie Nabeshima wurde 1975 in Kanagawa geboren und machte ihren Abschluss in Wohn- und Raumgestaltung an der Fakultät für Architektur und Bauingenieurwesen am College für Industrietechnik der Universität Nihon (1998), bevor sie für Tezuka Architects (1998–2005) arbeitete und TNA mitbegründete. Zu ihren Projekten zählen das Wood Wear House (Hayama, Kanagawa, 2005), das Color Concrete House (Yokohama, Kanagawa, 2005), das Ring House (Karuizawa, Nagano, 2006), das Wood Ship Café (Hayama, Kanagawa, 2007) sowie das Mosaic House (Meguro-ku, Tokyo, 2006–07, hier vorgestellt).

Makoto Takei, né à Tokyo en 1974, est diplômé du Département d'architecture de l'université Tokai (1997). De 1997 à 1999, il a étudié au Laboratoire Tsukamoto de l'École supérieure de sciences et d'ingénierie de l'Institut de technologie de Tokyo, et a travaillé pour l'Atelier Bow-Wow. De 1999 à 2000, il a été employé par Tezuka Architects avant de fonder l'agence **TNA** (Takei-Nabeshima-Architects) avec Chie Nabeshima. Chie Nabeshima, née à Kanagawa en 1975, est diplômée de conception de logements et d'espaces du Département d'architecture et d'ingénierie architecturale du Collège de technologie industrielle de l'université Nihon (1998), avant de travailler pour Tezuka Architects (1998–2005) et de fonder TNA. Parmi leurs projets : la Wood Wear House (Hayama, Kanagawa, 2005) ; la Color Concrete House (Yokohama, Kanagawa, 2005) ; la Ring House (Karuizawa, Nagano, 2006) ; le Wood Ship Café (Hayama, Kanagawa, 2007) et la Mosaic House (Meguro-ku, Tokyo, 2006–07, publiée ici).

MOSAIC HOUSE

Meguro-ku, Tokyo, Japan, 2006–07

Floor area: 84.5 m². Client: not disclosed. Cost: not disclosed

Built in a former parking lot for a couple with one child, this house is typical in its size of the numerous very small residences being designed in Japan, especially in densely built cities like Tokyo. Clad in white mosaic tile, the house appears to lean toward the "south sky like a sunflower." This orientation and the size of the skylight mean that the interior of the residence is flooded with light, despite its rather closed façades. The idea that nature can be present in the city and in architecture through such elements as light or wind is a particularly Japanese one, but one that is perfectly justified, especially in the urban matrix of Tokyo, where little space is left for nature in its more traditional representations (as in the gardens of the Imperial Palace). With this residence, or other realizations, such as their Ring House, the architects of TNA have shown a particular interest in nature and the environment, depending on location and their own sensitivity.

Die Größe des auf einem ehemaligen Parkplatz erbauten Hauses für ein Paar mit Kind ist typisch für die zahlreichen kleinen Wohnbauten, die in Japan entworfen werden, insbesondere in dicht besiedelten Städten wie Tokio. Das mit weißen Mosaikfliesen verblendete Haus neigt sich zum „südlichen Himmel wie eine Sonnenblume". Durch die Ausrichtung des Baus und die Größe des Oberlichtfensters sind die Innenräume trotz der eher geschlossenen Fassaden lichtdurchflutet. Der Gedanke, dass die Natur durch Elemente wie Licht oder Wind in Stadt und Architektur präsent sein kann, mag typisch japanisch sein, gerade in der urbanen Matrix Tokios ist er aber absolut gerechtfertigt, wo für die Natur und ihre traditionelleren Erscheinungsformen (etwa die Gärten des Kaiserpalasts) nur wenig Platz bleibt. Mit diesem Wohnhaus und anderen Projekten wie dem Ring House haben die Architekten von TNA je nach Lage der Grundstücke und mit dem ihnen eigenen Einfühlungsvermögen besonderes Interesse an Natur und Umwelt bewiesen.

Construite sur un ancien parking pour un couple et son enfant, cette maison est typiquement japonaise dans la petitesse de ses dimensions, fréquente dans les villes très densément construites comme Tokyo. Parée de mosaïque blanche, elle semble s'orienter vers le « Sud et le ciel comme un tournesol ». Cette orientation et la taille de la verrière signifient que l'intérieur est baigné de lumière malgré des façades assez fermées. L'idée que la nature puisse rester présente dans la ville et son architecture à travers des éléments tels que la lumière ou le vent est une vision très japonaise, mais parfaitement justifiée, en particulier dans la matrice urbaine tokyoïte où peu de place est laissée à la nature, même dans ses schémas traditionnels (comme les jardins du Palais impérial). Dans cette résidence et d'autres réalisations dont leur Ring House, les architectes de TNA montrent leur sensibilité particulière pour la nature et l'environnement en fonction du contexte.

The house quite literally takes a bow to the sky, channeling natural light inside while shielding it from excessive heat gain.

Das Haus verneigt sich buchstäblich vor dem Himmel, lässt Tageslicht in den Bau und schützt ihn zugleich vor allzu starker Wärmeentwicklung.

La maison s'incline littéralement devant le ciel, pour lui permettre de canaliser l'éclairage naturel vers l'intérieur tout en la protégeant d'un gain solaire excessif.

Contrary to external appearances that
show only a few small windows, the
house is flooded with light from
above.

Anders als die Außenaufnahmen vermuten lassen, die nur wenige kleine
Fenster zeigen, ist das Haus von
oben her lichtdurchflutet.

Contrairement aux apparences –
seules quelques petites fenêtres sont
visibles – la maison est illuminée de
lumière zénithale.

Furnished in sparse fashion, which is
typical of Japan, the house has high
spaces and is suffused constantly
with natural light.

Das Haus ist sparsam möbliert, was
für Japan typisch ist, hat hohe
Räume und ist den ganzen Tag über
mit natürlichem Licht durchflutet.

La maison est meublée avec sobriété,
à la japonaise, et ses hauts volumes
bénéficient toute la journée de
l'éclairage naturel.

UNSTUDIO

UNStudio
Stadhouderskade 113 / 1073 AX Amsterdam / The Netherlands
Tel: +31 20 570 20 40 / Fax: +31 20 570 20 41
E-mail: info@unstudio.com / Web: www.unstudio.com

Ben van Berkel was born in Utrecht in 1957 and studied at the Rietveld Academy in Amsterdam and at the Architectural Association (AA) in London, receiving the AA Diploma with honors in 1987. After working briefly in the office of Santiago Calatrava in 1988, he set up his practice in Amsterdam with Caroline Bos. He has been a Visiting Professor at Columbia and a visiting critic at Harvard (1994). He was a Diploma Unit Master at the AA (1994–95). As well as the Erasmus Bridge in Rotterdam (inaugurated in 1996), **UNSTUDIO** built the Karbouw and ACOM office buildings (1989–93), the REMU Electricity Station (1989–93), all in Amersfoort; and housing projects and the Aedes East Gallery for Kristin Feireiss in Berlin. More recent projects include an extension of the Rijksmuseum Twente (Enschede, 1992–96); the Möbius House (Naarden, 1993–98); and Het Valkhof Museum (Nijmegen, 1998); NMR Laboratory (Utrecht, 1997–2000), all in the Netherlands; a Switching Station (Innsbruck, Austria, 1998–2001); an Electricity Station (Innsbruck, Austria, 2002); the Mercedes Benz Museum (Stuttgart, Germany, 2003–06); VilLA NM (Upstate New York, 2000–07); a Music Facility (Graz, Austria, 1998–2008); the Arnhem Station (Arnhem, The Netherlands, 1986–2011); the IBG and Tax Offices (Groningen, The Netherlands, 2007–11); and Post Rotterdam (Rotterdam, The Netherlands, 2008–12), both published here. UNStudio was also a participant in the competition for the new World Trade Center in New York, in collaboration with Foreign Office Architects, Greg Lynn FORM, Imaginary Forces, Kevin Kennon, and Reiser + Umemoto, RUR, under the name of United Architects.

Ben van Berkel wurde 1957 in Utrecht geboren und studierte an der Rietveld-Akademie in Amsterdam und an der Architectural Association (AA) in London, wo er 1987 sein Diplom mit Auszeichnung erhielt. Nach kurzer Tätigkeit für Santiago Calatrava gründete er 1988 mit Caroline Bos sein Büro in Amsterdam. Er war Gastprofessor an der Columbia University in New York und Gastkritiker in Harvard (1994). 1994 bis 1995 war er Diploma Unit Master an der AA. Neben der 1996 eingeweihten Erasmusbrücke in Rotterdam baute **UNSTUDIO** in Amersfoort die Bürobauten für Karbouw und ACOM (1989–93) sowie das Kraftwerk REMU (1989–93), in Berlin entstanden Wohnbauprojekte und die Galerie Aedes East für Kristin Feireiss. Zu ihren Projekten zählen außerdem ein Erweiterungsbau für das Rijksmuseum in Twente (Enschede, 1992–96), das Haus Möbius (Naarden, 1993–98), das Museum Het Valkhof (Nimwegen, 1998) und das Labor NMR (Utrecht, 1997–2000), alle in den Niederlanden, ein Umspannwerk (Innsbruck, 1998–2001), ein Elektrizitätswerk (Innsbruck, 2002), das Mercedes Benz Museum (Stuttgart, 2003–06), die VilLA NM (im Bundesstaat New York, 2000–07), ein Musiktheater (Graz, 1998–2008), der Bahnhof Arnheim (1986–2011) sowie Büros für die IBG und das Finanzamt (Groningen, 2007–11) und Post Rotterdam (Rotterdam, 2008–12); die beiden Letzteren werden hier vorgestellt. Darüber hinaus beteiligte sich UNStudio am Wettbewerb für das neue World Trade Center in New York unter dem Namen United Architects gemeinsam mit Foreign Office Architects, Greg Lynn FORM, Imaginary Forces, Kevin Kennon und Reiser + Umemoto, RUR.

Ben van Berkel, né à Utrecht en 1957, étudie à la Rietveld Academie d'Amsterdam ainsi qu'à l'Architectural Association (AA) de Londres qu'il quitte diplômé avec mention en 1987. Après avoir brièvement travaillé pour Santiago Calatrava en 1988, il ouvre son agence à Amsterdam, avec Caroline Bos. Il a été professeur invité à l'université Columbia, New York, critique invité à Harvard en 1994, et responsable d'unité pour le diplôme de l'AA en 1994–95. En dehors du pont Érasme à Rotterdam (inauguré en 1996), **UNSTUDIO** a construit, à Amersfoort, les immeubles de bureaux Karbouw et ACOM (1989–93), la sous-station électrique REMU (1989–93) ; ainsi que des logements et la galerie Aedes East de Kristin Feireiss à Berlin. Parmi leurs projets plus récents : l'extension du Rijksmuseum Twente (Enschede, 1992–96) ; la maison Möbius (Naarden, 1993–98) ; le musée Het Valkhof (Nimègue, 1998) et le laboratoire NMR (Utrecht, 1997–2000), tous aux Pays-Bas ; un poste d'aiguillage (Innsbruck, Autriche, 1998–2001) ; une station électrique (Innsbruck, Autriche, 2002) ; le musée Mercedes Benz (Stuttgart, Allemagne, 2003–06) ; la VilLA NM (État de New York, 2000–07) ; une salle de musique (Graz, Autriche, 1998–2008) ; la gare d'Arnhem (Pays-Bas, 1986–2011) ; l'immeuble de l'IBG et de l'administration fiscale (Groningue, Pays-Bas, 2007–11) et Post Rotterdam (2008–12), tous deux publiés ici. UNStudio a participé au concours pour le World Trade Center à New York, en collaboration avec Foreign Office Architects, Greg Lynn FORM, Imaginary Forces, Kevin Kennon et Reiser + Umemoto, RUR, sous le nom de United Architects.

IBG AND TAX OFFICES

Groningen, The Netherlands, 2007–11

Floor area: 45 000 m². Client: DUO2 Consortium. Cost: not disclosed.
Team: Ben van Berkel, Caroline Bos, Gerard Loozekoot, Lars Nixdorff

The architects demonstrate with this design that even very large offices for governmental organizations can be ecologically sound, and indeed set an example for the private sector.

Mit diesem Entwurf stellen die Architekten unter Beweis, dass selbst Bürogroßbauten für Behörden ökologisch verträglich sein können und dem privaten Sektor gar als gutes Beispiel vorangehen können.

Les architectes prouvent par ce projet que même de très grands immeubles de bureaux pour des organismes gouvernementaux peuvent bénéficier de la logique écologique et donner l'exemple au secteur privé.

This design for the IBG (Informatie Beheer Groep) and Tax Offices is intended for 2500 employees and divided into spaces for the two users. Gardens, a central hall, and a pavilion for retail or commercial spaces bring those working in the building together in an informal way. In a proportion typical of the Netherlands, 1500 bicycles and 675 cars are to be accommodated in an underground garage. The architects explain: "An essential element in the design is the response to the location, adjacent to an important urban green space, known as the 'sterrenbos.' The aerodynamic form of the building has been achieved as the result of extensive sun and wind studies, which were carried out to ensure the minimum effect on this local green area." Biofuels and sunshading ensure that the building will be   neutral. UNStudio concludes: "This integrated approach to construction, material use, and management of the building fulfils government requirements stipulating that new buildings serve an exemplary function with regard to sustainable architecture."

Der Entwurf für die IBG (Informatie Beheer Groep) und das Finanzamt ist auf 2500 Mitarbeiter ausgelegt und in Räumlichkeiten für die verschiedenen Besuchergruppen unterteilt. Gärten, ein zentrales Foyer und ein Pavillon mit Ladenflächen bieten informelle Begegnungsmöglichkeiten für die Mitarbeiter. In einer Tiefgarage haben 1500 Fahrräder und 675 Pkws Platz – ein für die Niederlande typisches Verhältnis. Die Architekten erläutern: „Ein wesentliches Element des Entwurfs ist die Berücksichtigung des Standorts neben einer wichtigen städtischen Grünfläche, dem ‚Sterrenbos'. Die aerodynamische Form des Gebäudes ergab sich aus einer Reihe umfassender Untersuchungen zu Sonneneinfall und Winden, die ausgeführt wurden, um minimale Auswirkungen auf die örtliche Grünfläche sicherzustellen." Biobrennstoffe und Sonnenschutz sorgen dafür, dass das Gebäude CO_2-emissionsfrei bleibt. Abschließend merkt UNStudio an: „Diese integrierte Herangehensweise an Bau, Materialwahl und Gebäudemanagement entspricht Regierungsrichtlinien, die festschreiben, dass Neubauten im Sinne einer nachhaltigen Architektur vorbildlich sein müssen."

Ce projet pour les bureaux de l'administration fiscale et de l'IBG (Informatie Beheer Groep) est destiné à accueillir 2500 employés. Il est divisé en deux parties, une par client. Des jardins, un hall central et un pavillon pour des boutiques ou des espaces commerciaux réunissent ces deux parties de façon informelle. Dans une proportion typiquement néerlandaise, les parkings souterrains sont prévus pour 1500 vélos et 675 voitures. Pour l'architecte : «Un des éléments essentiels de ce projet est sa réponse au site, qui est adjacent à un vaste espace vert urbain, appelé le "sterrenbos". La forme aérodynamique du bâtiment est l'aboutissement d'études approfondies sur l'orientation solaire et la force des vents, afin de n'exercer qu'un impact minimum sur cet espace vert.» En terme d'émissions de CO_2, la neutralité de la construction est assurée par des protections solaires et l'utilisation de biofiouls. «Cette approche intégrée de la construction, de l'utilisation de matériaux et de la gestion du bâtiment répond aux demandes administratives stipulant que les nouvelles constructions doivent servir d'exemple dans le domaine de l'architecture durable.»

Using fluid forms generated for the overall design by studies of the wind and sun, the interior flows of the personnel are conceived to encourage casual contact and dialogue.

Die fließenden Formen gehen auf Studien zu Sonnenlichteinfall und Winden zurück. Die Bewegungsströme der Angestellten im Innenraum wurden so angelegt, dass informelle Begegnungen und Gespräche gefördert werden.

Dans un plan d'ensemble reposant sur des formes fluides issues d'études sur les vents et le soleil, les déplacements intérieurs du personnel ont été pensés pour faciliter les contacts et le dialogue.

POST ROTTERDAM

Rotterdam, The Netherlands, 2008–12

Floor area: 44 000 m². Client: Delta Projectontwikkeling, SNS Property Finance, Redevco. Cost: not disclosed.
Team: Ben van Berkel, Caroline Bos, Gerard Loozekoot, Christian Bergmann

The roof in the central hall can be adjusted in accordance with the movements of the sun and has integrated photovoltaic cells to generate extra power for the complex.

Das Dach der Haupthalle lässt sich je nach Sonnenstand regulieren und ist mit Solarmodulen ausgestattet, die zusätzliche Energie für den Komplex erzeugen.

La couverture du hall central peut se modifier en fonction de la course du soleil et intègre des cellules photovoltaïques qui produisent une partie de l'énergie utilisée par le complexe.

The architects speak in terms of "inclusive sustainability" for this "green shopping mall." "Sustainable architecture is today's foremost concern," they say. "With this project we aim to create the Netherlands' first sustainable urban retail and mixed-program complex. The integration of technical and design results in an inclusive design approach, which actively minimizes heat loads and contributes to a healthy environment." An existing structure is reused for the project, which aims for a LEED Platinum or Gold ranking. A large void above a courtyard provides natural ventilation and light. A roof on the central hall can be adjusted to direct light in specific directions and would have integrated photovoltaic cells, "which are now available in a variety of colors and degrees of translucency." The 70-meter-deep foundations below the tower allow the architects to send plastic tubes deep into the earth. Working with a vertical ground coupled chiller, the tubes allow the structure to draw either warmth or coolness out of the earth and to store the energy thus gained. The architects go a step further in their reflection, suggesting that some shops could specialize in health and nature awareness and that the public could thus be made to engage with the subject of sustainability.

Die Architekten sagen, dass die Nachhaltigkeit in dieser „grüne Shoppingmall" schon enthalten ist. „Heute gehört nachhaltige Architektur zu den wichtigsten Themen überhaupt", sagen sie. „Mit diesem Projekt wollen wir den ersten nachhaltigen, urbanen, gemischt genutzten Komplex realisieren. Technische und gestalterische Erkenntnisse werden in einem ganzheitlichen Designansatz zusammengeführt, der aktiv zur Minimierung der Wärmebelastung und zu einer gesunden Umwelt beiträgt". Das Projekt integriert einen bestehenden Altbau und strebt eine LEED-Auszeichnung in Platin oder Gold an. Die erhebliche Raumhöhe über dem Hof sorgt für natürliche Belüftung und Lichteinfall. Das Dach über der zentralen Halle lässt sich so justieren, dass Licht in verschiedene Richtungen gelenkt werden kann, und soll mit integrierten Solarzellen ausgestattet werden, „die inzwischen in verschiedenen Farben und Transparenzgraden erhältlich sind". Da es erforderlich war, das Fundament für das Hochhaus bis zu 70 m tief zu legen, konnten die Architekten Kunststoffsonden tief in das Erdreich treiben. Angeschlossen an eine Erdwärmepumpe können die Sonden Wärme und Kälte aus dem Erdreich ziehen und die so gewonnene Energie speichern. Mit ihren Überlegungen gehen die Architekten sogar einen Schritt weiter und regen an, dass sich einige Läden auf Gesundheits- und Umweltbewusstsein spezialisieren und die Öffentlichkeit so für das Thema Nachhaltigkeit begeistern könnten.

Les architectes parlent de « durabilité inclusive » pour décrire ce « centre commercial vert ». « L'architecture durable est la principale préoccupation actuelle », disent-ils. « Par ce projet, nous voulons créer le premier complexe mixte durable aux Pays-Bas. L'intégration de ces objectifs dans une approche poussée de la conception minimise les charges thermiques et contribue à un environnement plus sain. » Une construction existante a été réutilisée et le projet vise une notation LEED Platine ou Or. Un grand vide au-dessus d'une cour apporte la lumière et facilite la ventilation naturelle. Le toit au-dessus du hall central pourra s'orienter en fonction de la luminosité et sera équipé de cellules photovoltaïques intégrées « qui existent maintenant dans divers degrés de translucidité et de couleur ». La nécessité de creuser les fondations de la tour jusqu'à 70 m de profondeur a permis d'insérer dans le sol des tubes de plastique verticaux qui agissent comme refroidisseurs, et permettent d'exploiter, selon les saisons, la chaleur ou la fraîcheur du sol et d'emmagasiner l'énergie ainsi gagnée. Les architectes ont même suggéré que certains magasins pourraient se spécialiser dans la prise de conscience de la santé et de la nature, et que le public pourrait être appelé à participer aux efforts de développement durable.

The perspective below emphasises the external additions made by the architects to the existing structure. Geothermal sources are used for heating and cooling.

Die Abbildung unten lässt die Anbauten der Architekten an den Altbau erkennen. Zur Heizung und Klimatisierung des Baus wird Erdwärme genutzt.

Le dessin ci-dessous montre les extensions réalisées par les architectes. La géothermie est utilisée pour le chauffage et le refroidissement.

MICHAEL VAN VALKENBURGH

Michael Van Valkenburgh Associates, Inc.
Landscape Architects, P.C.
18 East 17th Street, 6th Floor
New York, NY 10003
USA

Tel: +1 212 243 2506
Fax: +1 212 243 2016
E-mail: mvva_ny@mvvainc.com
Web: www.mvvainc.com

MICHAEL VAN VALKENBURGH received a B. S. degree from the Cornell University College of Agriculture (Ithaca, New York, 1973) and a Master of Landscape Architecture from the College of Fine Arts at the University of Illinois (Champaign/Urbana, 1977). He oversees both the New York and Cambridge, Massachusetts, offices of the firm and is involved in some way in every project. He was Principal in Charge for the ASLA Green Roof. Other firm Principals are Matthew Urbanski, who is a lead designer for many of the firm's public projects, and Laura Solano, who is a specialist in landscape technology. Chris Counts, Project Designer and Project Manager of the project published here, received his Bachelor of Landscape Architecture from the University of Georgia, and his Master of Landscape Architecture from the Harvard GSD. He is a Senior Associate of the firm. Their work includes Harvard Yard Restoration (Cambridge, Massachusetts, 1992–2003); Tahari Courtyards (Millburn, New Jersey, 2002–03); Connecticut Water Treatment Facility (with Steven Holl, New Haven, Connecticut, 2001–05); the Teardrop Park (New York, New York, 1999–2006); and the ASLA Green Roof (Washington, D. C., 2005–06, published here), all in the USA.

MICHAEL VAN VALKENBURGH erwarb einen B. S. (Bachelor of Science) am College für Agrarwissenschaft der Cornell University (Ithaca, New York, 1973) sowie einen Master in Landschaftsarchitektur am College für bildende Künste der Universität von Illinois (Champaign/Urbana, 1977). Er betreut die Niederlassungen des Büros in New York und Cambridge, Massachusetts, und ist an jedem Projekt auf die eine oder andere Weise beteiligt. Für das ASLA Green Roof war er als Partner leitend verantwortlich. Weitere Partner sind Matthew Urbanski, Chefdesigner für zahlreiche öffentliche Projekte des Büros, und Laura Solano, Spezialistin für Landschaftsbau. Chris Counts, Projektdesigner und -manager des hier vorgestellten Projekts, erwarb seinen Bachelor in Landschaftsarchitektur an der Universität von Georgia und seinen Master in Landschaftsarchitektur an der Harvard Graduate School of Design. Er ist Seniorteilhaber des Büros. Zu den Projekten des Büros zählen u. a. die Sanierung des Harvard Yard (Cambridge, Massachusetts, 1992–2003), die Tahari-Höfe (Millburn, New Jersey, 2002–03), die Wasseraufbereitungsanlage Connecticut (mit Steven Holl, New Haven, Connecticut, 2001–05), der Teardrop Park (New York, 1999–2006) sowie das ASLA Green Roof (Washington, D. C., 2005–06, hier vorgestellt).

MICHAEL VAN VALKENBURGH est B. S. du Collège d'Agriculture de l'université Cornell (Ithaca, New York, 1973), et détient un mastère en paysagisme du Collège des Beaux-Arts de l'université de l'Illinois (Champaign/Urbana, 1977). Il dirige les bureaux de New York et de Cambridge, Massachusetts, de son agence, et s'implique dans chaque projet. Il a été responsable du projet de toit vert de l'ASLA. Les autres responsables de l'agence sont Matthew Urbanski, chargé des projets pour le secteur public, et Laura Solano, spécialiste des technologies du paysage. Chris Counts, concepteur et responsable de projets et de celui publié ici, est B. A en paysagisme de l'université de Géorgie, et M. A. de l'Harvard GSD. Il est associé senior de l'agence. Parmi leurs réalisations : la restauration du Yard de Harvard (Cambridge, Massachusetts, 1992–2003) ; les Tahari Courtyards (Millburn, New Jersey, 2002–03) ; les installations de traitement des eaux du Connecticut (avec Steven Holl, New Haven, Connecticut, 2001–05) ; le Teardrop Park (New York, 1999–2006) et le ASLA Green Roof (Washington, D. C., 2005–06, publié ici).

ASLA GREEN ROOF

Washington, D.C., USA, 2005–06

Site area: 130 m². Client: American Society of Landscape Architects. Cost: $950 000.
Team: Michael Van Valkenburgh, Chris Counts, John Gidding, Gullivar Shepard, Stephen Noone, Robert Rock, Richard Hindle

Located in central Washington, D.C., this project, though small in area, is important because of the client—the American Society of Landscape Architects (ASLA). Mounds were created with lightweight materials at the north and south ends of the roof. The existence of these largely artificial hills on the roof naturally changes the visitor's perception of the space itself, but also of the Washington skyline. One of these "waves" was planted with low varieties requiring little soil depth and the other, on the north, with "semi-intensive" (i.e. deeper rooted, higher) plants and almost two meters of soil. A special structural support suspended above the plants allows for a good number of people to be on the roof despite its high proportion of planted area. The architects write: "The project transcends its diminutive size because of the intense interest of the design community.... It is designed with an educational pedagogy in mind, as it will be the launching pad for any future ASLA effort to teach the benefits of green roof technology."

Das im Zentrum von Washington, D.C., gelegene Projekt ist zwar flächenmäßig klein, wegen des Auftraggebers – der American Society of Landscape Architects (ASLA) – aber dennoch von Bedeutung. Am nördlichen und südlichen Ende des Dachs wurden mit Leichtbaumaterialien Böschungen angelegt. Diese überwiegend künstlichen Hügel auf dem Dach lassen die Besucher nicht nur den Ort selbst, sondern auch die Washingtoner Skyline anders wahrnehmen. Eine der beiden „Wellen" wurde mit niedrig wachsenden Pflanzen begrünt, die nur geringe Bodentiefe benötigen, die nördliche hingegen mit „semi-intensiver" (also tiefer wurzelnder, höherer) Bepflanzung und einer Bodentiefe von fast 2 m. Eine spezielle bauliche Struktur schwebt über Teilen der Begrünung und macht es so möglich, dass sich trotz des hohen Grünflächenanteils vergleichsweise viele Menschen auf dem Dach aufhalten können. Die Architekten schreiben: „Dank des starken Interesses in der Architekturgemeinde wächst das Projekt über seine winzige Größe hinaus … Es wurde mit didaktischen Hintergedanken entworfen, denn schließlich wird es Grundlage für die zukünftigen Bemühungen der ASLA sein, die Vorteile von Dachbegrünung zu vermitteln."

Situé dans le centre de Washington, ce projet, bien que de faible surface, est important de par son client, The American Society of Landscape Architects (ASLA, Société américaine des architectes paysagistes). Des vallonnements ont été créés à l'aide de matériaux légers aux extrémités nord et sud de la toiture. L'existence de ces «collines», en grande partie artificielles, change naturellement la perception que le visiteur peut avoir de l'espace, mais aussi du panorama urbain de Washington. L'une de ces «vagues» a été plantée de variétés végétales de faible hauteur requérant peu de profondeur de sol, et l'autre, au nord, de plantes «semi-intensives» (à racines plus profondes) sur une épaisseur de sol de près de 2 m. Un support structurel spécial suspendu au-dessus des plantes permet au toit de recevoir un certain nombre de visiteurs malgré la forte présence des plantes. Selon les architectes: «Le projet transcende sa taille réduite par l'intense intérêt que lui porte la communauté professionnelle… Il est conçu dans un but pédagogique et éducatif, et sera la base de lancement des efforts futurs de l'ASLA pour enseigner les bénéfices de la technologie des toits végétalisés. »

The limited size of this green roof and weight constraints posed considerable challenges, but the designers succeeded in creating a convivial landscape environment where there had been only a flat surface before.

Die geringe Größe des begrünten Dachs und die gegebenen Belastungsgrenzen waren eine erhebliche Herausforderung. Dennoch gelang es den Gestaltern, ein freundliches Landschaftsumfeld zu schaffen, wo vorher nichts als eine ebene Freifläche war.

Les dimensions limitées de ce toit végétalisé et ses contraintes de poids ont posé de sérieux problèmes, mais les concepteurs ont réussi à créer un paysage convivial en remplacement d'une simple couverture plate.

WEISS/MANFREDI

Weiss/Manfredi Architecture/Landscape/Urbanism
130 West 29th Street, 12th Floor
New York, NY 10001 / USA

Tel: +1 212 760 9002 / Fax: +1 212 760 9003
Web: www.weissmanfredi.com

Marion Weiss received her B.Arch from the University of Virginia, and her M.Arch degree from Yale University. Prior to establishing her present firm, she was a designer for Cesar Pelli and Associates, Smith-Miller-Hawkinson, and Mitchell/Giurgola Architects. She is a design partner of **WEISS/MANFREDI** and a Professor of Architecture at the University of Pennsylvania's Graduate School of Fine Arts. Michael Manfredi was born in Trieste, Italy. He received his B.Arch degree from the University of Notre Dame and his M.Arch at Cornell, where he studied under Colin Rowe. Prior to his present role as a design partner of Weiss/Manfredi, he worked in the offices of Richard Meier and Michell/Giurgola Architects. He has taught at Cornell University, the Institute for Architecture and Urban Studies, the New York Institute of Technology, Princeton University, the University of Pennsylvania, and Yale University. They received the 2004 Academy Award in Architecture, an award given annually by the American Academy of Arts and Letters acknowledging the unique vision of the firm. They were also named one of North America's "Emerging Voices" by the Architectural League of New York and in 2007 their firm won the New York City AIA Gold Medal of Honor. As well as the Olympic Sculpture Park (Seattle, Washington, 2005–07) published here, current projects include the Barnard College Nexus (New York, New York, 2003–08), a multiuse arts center, and winner of an invited competition and a 2008 Progressive Architecture Award; the Brooklyn Botanic Garden Visitor Center (New York, New York, 2004–10), which will achieve LEED Gold certification; and the University of Virginia's new Arts Gateway Building, which includes a museum, an outdoor sculpture terrace, performance space, and a residence hall.

Marion Weiss erwarb ihren B.Arch. an der Universität von Virginia und ihren M.Arch. an der Universität Yale. Bevor sie ihr derzeitiges Büro gründete, gestaltete sie Entwürfe für Cesar Pelli and Associates, Smith-Miller-Hawkinson und Mitchell/Giurgola Architects. Als Partnerin bei **WEISS/MANFREDI** verantwortet sie den Bereich Entwurf und ist zugleich als Professorin für Architektur an der Graduiertenschule für bildende Künste der Universität von Pennsylvania tätig. Michael Manfredi wurde in Triest geboren. Er erwarb seinen B.Arch. an der Universität Notre Dame in Indiana und seinen M.Arch. an der Cornell University im Staat New York, wo er bei Colin Rowe studierte. Vor seiner gegenwärtigen Position als Designpartner bei Weiss/Manfredi war er bei Richard Meier und Mitchell/Giurgola Architects tätig. Er hatte Lehraufträge an der Cornell University, in New York am Institut für Architektur und Stadtplanung sowie am Institute of Technology, an der Universität Princeton, der Universität von Pennsylvania sowie in Yale. 2004 wurde das Büro für seine unverwechselbare Vision mit dem Academy Award in Architecture ausgezeichnet, einem Preis der American Academy of Arts and Letters. Darüber hinaus wurde das Team von der Architectural League in New York als eine der „aufstrebenden Firmen" Nordamerikas ausgezeichnet und 2007 mit der New Yorker AIA-Ehrengoldmedaille geehrt. Neben dem hier vorgestellten Olympic-Skulpturenpark (Seattle, Washington, 2005–07) zählen zu den aktuellen Projekten u. a. das Barnard College Nexus (New York, 2003–08), ein multifunktionales Kunstzentrum, das sich in einem eingeladenen Wettbewerb durchsetzte und 2008 den Progressive Architecture Award erhielt, das Besucherzentrum des Botanischen Gartens in Brooklyn (New York, 2004–10), das eine LEED-Auszeichung in Gold erhalten wird, und das neue Arts Gateway Building der Universität von Virginia, das ein Museum, eine Skulpturenterrasse, ein Theater und ein Wohnheim umfassen wird.

Marion Weiss est B. Arch de l'université de Virginie et M. Arch de l'université Yale. Avant de créer son agence actuelle, elle a travaillé pour Cesar Pelli and Associates, Smith-Miller-Hawkinson et Mitchell/Giurgola Architects. Elle est partenaire chargée de projets chez **WEISS/MANFREDI** et professeur d'architecture à la Graduate School of Fine Arts de l'université de Pennsylvanie. Michael Manfredi, né à Trieste en Italie, est B. Arch de l'université de Notre-Dame et M. Arch de Cornell, où il a étudié sous la direction de Colin Rowe. Avant Weiss/Manfredi, il a travaillé dans les agences de Richard Meier et Michell/Giurgola Architects. Il a enseigné à l'université Cornell, à l'Institute for Architecture and Urban Studies, au New York Institute of Technology, à l'université Princeton, université de Pennsylvanie, et université Yale. En 2004, ils ont reçu ensemble le Prix d'architecture de l'Académie de l'American Academy of Arts and Letters qui a salué la vision originale de l'agence. Ils ont été désignés parmi les « Voix émergentes » de l'Amérique du Nord par l'Architectural League of New York, et ont remporté la médaille d'or d'honneur de l'AIA de New York City en 2007. En dehors de l'Olympic Sculpture Park (Seattle, Washington, 2005–07) publié ici, leurs projets actuels portent sur le Barnard College Nexus (New York, 2003–08) ; un centre d'art polyvalent qui a remporté un concours sur invitation ; et le Progressive Architecture Award 2008 ; le centre d'information du jardin botanique de Brooklyn (New York, New York, 2004–10), qui aura une certification LEED Or, et un nouvel immeuble de l'université de Virginie sur Arts Gateway, qui comprend un musée, une terrasse pour les sculptures, un lieu de spectacles et des logements.

OLYMPIC SCULPTURE PARK

Seattle, Washington, USA, 2005–07

Park area: 3.6 ha. Floor area: 3159 m² (exhibition pavilion and garage). Client: Seattle Art Museum.
Cost: $32 million. Team: Marion Weiss, Michael Manfredi, Chris Ballentine, Todd Hoehn, Yehre Suh

The citation for this project's 2008 AIA Honor Award explains the context: "This project is located on Seattle's last undeveloped waterfront property, sliced by train tracks and an arterial road. The design connects three separate sites with an uninterrupted Z-shaped 'green' platform, descending 40 feet [12 meters] from the city to the water, capitalizing on views of the skyline and Elliott Bay and rising over existing infrastructure to reconnect the urban core to the revitalized waterfront." Formerly used by Union Oil of California as an oil transfer facility, the site required the removal of 120 000 tons of contaminated soil, capped with 51 000 cubic meters of clean fill, recuperated in part from the Seattle Art Museum's expansion site. The park includes an exhibition pavilion and its paths offer views of both the distant Olympic Mountains and of the city and beaches. The architects write: "As a 'landscape for art,' the Olympic Sculpture Park defines a new experience for modern and contemporary art outside the museum walls. The topographically varied park provides diverse settings for sculpture of multiple scales. Deliberately open-ended, the design invites new interpretations of art and environmental engagement, reconnecting the fractured relationships of art, landscape, and urban life." Aside from the American Institute of Architects, the project was recognized with an ASLA Honor Award, and was the first North American project to be awarded Harvard University's International Veronica Rudge Green Prize in Urban Design. This project was cited by *Time* as one of the top five architecture projects in their "Ten Best Architectural Marvels" of 2007.

Ein Auszug aus der Begründung für die Verleihung des AIA-Ehrenpreises 2008 erläutert den Kontext des Projekts „auf dem letzten baulich noch nicht erschlossenen Ufergelände, das von Bahntrassen und einer Hauptverkehrsstraße durchschnitten wird. Der Entwurf verknüpft drei separate Grundstücke durch eine durchgängige z-förmige ‚grüne' Plattform, die von der Stadt bis zum 12 m tiefer gelegenen Wasser hinabführt. Sie profitiert von der Aussicht auf die Skyline und die Elliott Bay, schwebt über der bestehenden Infrastruktur und bindet das Zentrum der Stadt neu an die belebte Ufergegend an." Da das Gelände von der Union Oil of California zuvor als Erdölumschlagplatz genutzt wurde, mussten 120 000 t verseuchtes Erdreich abgetragen werden. Die Fläche wurde mit 51 000 m³ unbelastetem Erdreich aufgefüllt, das z. T. vom Baugrundstück der Erweiterung des Seattle Art Museum stammte. Zum Park gehört ein Ausstellungspavillon und Wege bieten Ausblick auf die in der Ferne liegenden Olympic Mountains, die Stadt und ihre Strände. Die Architekten schreiben: „Als ‚Landschaft für Kunst' steht der Olympic-Skulpturenpark für ein neuartiges Erlebnis moderner und zeitgenössischer Kunst außerhalb von Museumsmauern. Der topografisch abwechslungsreiche Park bietet die unterschiedlichsten Standorte für Skulpturen verschiedener Größe. Der bewusst offen gelassene Entwurf regt zu neuen Formen der Kunstinterpretation und des Umweltengagements an, er bringt das von Brüchen gezeichnete Verhältnis von Kunst, Landschaft und urbanem Leben wieder zusammen." Neben dem American Institute of Architects würdigte auch die American Society of Landscape Architects (Amerikanische Vereinigung der Landschaftsarchitekten, ASLA) das Projekt mit einem Ehrenpreis. Darüber hinaus war es das nordamerikanische Projekt, das mit dem International Veronica Rudge Green Prize für Stadtplanung ausgezeichnet wurde, der von der Universität Harvard verliehen wird. Das *Time Magazine* wählte das Projekt 2007 unter die ersten fünf der „Zehn besten architektonischen Wunderwerke".

Le commentaire de l'AIA lors de la remise de son prix d'honneur en 2008 précisait le contexte de ce parc : « Ce projet est situé sur la dernière propriété non lotie en bord de mer de Seattle, parcourue de voies de chemin de fer et par une route importante. Le projet connecte trois sites séparés et une plate-forme "verte" ininterrompue en forme de Z, de 12 m de dénivelé entre la ville et l'eau, axés sur des vues du panorama urbain et d'Elliott Bay, et s'élevant au-dessus d'infrastructures existantes pour reconnecter le cœur urbain au front de mer revitalisé. » Anciennement utilisé par l'Union Oil of California pour un centre de transfert de pétrole, ce site a nécessité la décontamination de 120 000 tonnes de terre qui ont été recouvertes de 51 000 m³ de remblai propre récupéré en partie lors de l'extension du Seattle Art Museum. Le parc comprend un pavillon d'expositions et des allées qui offrent des vues sur Olympic Mountains dans le lointain, sur la ville et les plages. Pour l'architecte : « En tant que "paysage conçu pour l'art", l'Olympic Sculpture Park définit une nouvelle expérience de l'art moderne et contemporain hors des murs d'un musée. D'une topographie variée, il offre divers emplacements pour la présentation de sculptures d'échelles diverses. Laissé volontairement ouvert, ce projet invite à de nouvelles interprétations sur les interpénétrations de l'art et de l'environnement et reconnecte des relations brisées entre l'art, le paysage et la vie urbaine. » En dehors de l'Institut américain des architectes, le projet a reçu un prix d'honneur de l'ASLA, et a été le premier projet en Amérique du Nord à être récompensé par l'International Veronica Rudge Green Prize en urbanisme de Harvard. Il a également été cité par le *Time Magazine* comme l'un des cinq meilleurs projets d'architecture des « Dix plus grandes merveilles architecturales » de 2007.

The plan (opposite) and images on this page make clear that the Park is really a platform occupying a difficult site that was formerly unusable except by cars and trains.

Der Grundriss (linke Seite) und die Aufnahmen auf dieser Seite zeigen deutlich, dass der Park im Grunde eine Plattform an einem problematischen Standort ist. Abgesehen vom Zug- und Straßenverkehr war dieser bislang nicht nutzbar.

Le plan (page de gauche) et les images de cette page montrent que le nouveau parc est en fait une plate-forme occupant un site difficile jusqu'alors uniquement utilisé par des trains et des voitures.

The park includes an exhibition pavilion and garage, by no means its most visible element, carefully integrated into the overall design.

Zum Park zählen ein Ausstellungspavillon und ein Parkhaus, das keineswegs das auffälligste Element des Komplexes ist, sondern vielmehr umsichtig in den Gesamtentwurf integriert wurde.

Le parc comprend un pavillon d'exposition et un parking très peu visible, soigneusement intégré dans le plan d'ensemble.

WHY ARCHITECTURE

wHY Architecture
9520 Jefferson Boulevard
Studio C
Culver City, CA 90232
USA

Tel: +1 310 839 5106
Fax: +1 310 839 5107
E-mail: work@why-architecture.com
Web: www.why-architecture.com

WHY ARCHITECTURE was founded in 2003 by Yo-ichiro Hakomori and Kulapat Yantrasast. Hakomori received his M.Arch degree from UCLA, and his Doctorate from the University of Tokyo. Yantrasast, born in 1968 in Thailand, received his B.Arch degree in Thailand and his M.Arch degree and Ph.D. from the University of Tokyo. The two met at the University of Tokyo and they collaborated on several design competitions and research projects. After completing his studies, Hakomori worked for the late Frank Israel and for Arthur Erickson. Yantrasast became a key member of Tadao Ando's team in Osaka, working on the Modern Art Museum of Fort Worth, the Armani Teatro in Milan, the Foundation François Pinault for Contemporary Art in Paris, the Calder Museum project in Philadelphia, and the Clark Art Institute in Williamstown, Massachusetts. Their work includes the Grand Rapids Art Museum published here (Grand Rapids, Michigan, 2004–07); the Art Bridge (Los Angeles, California, 2008–09); the redesign of a number of galleries for the Art Institute of Chicago (2008–); and the Malibu Residence (Malibu, California, 2007–10), all in the USA.

WHY ARCHITECTURE wurde 2003 von Yo-ichiro Hakomori und Kulapat Yantrasast gegründet. Hakomori schloss sein Studium an der UCLA mit einem M.Arch. ab und promovierte an der Universität Tokio. Yantrasast, 1968 in Thailand geboren, erwarb seinen B.Arch. in Thailand und seinen M.Arch. an der Universität Tokio, wo er ebenfalls promovierte. Die beiden lernten sich an der Universität Tokio kennen, beteiligten sich zusammen an verschiedenen Entwurfswettbewerben und arbeiteten gemeinsam an Forschungsprojekten. Nach Abschluss seines Studiums arbeitete Hakomori für den inzwischen verstorbenen Frank Israel und für Arthur Erickson. Yantrasast wurde zu einer der Schlüsselfiguren in Tadao Andos Team in Osaka und war u. a. am Modern Art Museum in Fort Worth, Texas, dem Armani Teatro in Mailand, der Fondation François Pinault pour l'Art Contemporain in Paris, dem Calder-Museumsprojekt in Philadelphia sowie dem Clark Art Institute in Williamstown, Massachusetts, beteiligt. Zu den Projekten des Büros zählen das hier vorgestellte Grand Rapids Art Museum (Grand Rapids, Michigan, 2004–07), die Art Bridge (Los Angeles, Kalifornien, 2008–09), die Umgestaltung verschiedener Ausstellungsräume am Art Institute of Chicago (2008–) sowie die Malibu Residence (Malibu, Kalifornien, 2007–10).

L'agence **WHY ARCHITECTURE** a été fondée en 2003 par Yo-ichiro Hakomori et Kulapat Yantrasast. Hakomori est M. Arch d'UCLA et docteur de l'université de Tokyo. Yantrasast, né en 1968 en Thaïlande, a obtenu son B. Arch dans ce pays et son mastère et son doctorat à l'université de Tokyo. Ils se sont rencontrés à l'université et ont collaboré à l'occasion de plusieurs concours et projets de recherche. Après avoir achevé ses études, Hakomori à travaillé pour Frank Israël et pour Arthur Erickson. Yantrasast est devenu l'un des principaux collaborateurs de l'équipe de Tadao Ando à Osaka. Il a travaillé sur les projets du musée d'Art moderne de Fort Worth, le théâtre Armani à Milan, la Fondation François Pinault pour l'art contemporain à Paris ; le projet du musée Calder à Philadelphia ; et celui du Clark Art Institute à Williamstown, Massachusetts. Parmi leurs réalisations : le Grand Rapids Art Museum publié ici (Grand Rapids, Michigan, 2004–07) ; l'Art Bridge (Los Angeles, Californie, 2008–09) ; la rénovation d'un certain nombre de galeries pour l'Art Institute of Chicago (2008-) et la résidence Malibu (Malibu, Californie, 2007–10).

GRAND RAPIDS ART MUSEUM

Grand Rapids, Michigan, USA, 2004–07

Floor area: 11 613 m². Client: Grand Rapids Art Museum. Cost: $75 million.
Architect of Record: Design Plus

The Grand Rapids Art Museum's new building, located one block from the city center, was the first art museum in the world to receive a LEED certification. This is not surprising given the necessary temperature, lighting, or humidity controls required in art museums. In fact, obtaining LEED certification was one condition of the 2001 donation by local philanthropist Peter Wege, a known defender of environmental causes. The facility includes approximately 5000 square meters of exhibition space. A large, sheltering canopy hovers over the facility and has its lobby, restaurant, education center, and pavilions "formed like fingers extending into the green of the park." The museum also faces a sculptural work by Maya Lin called *Ecliptic*, an oval square. The main museum space is a three-level gallery tower with natural overhead lighting for the top floor. The use of natural light in the structure is planned to reduce energy consumption where possible. Ten percent of the construction materials for the project were recycled, and rainwater is recycled for toilets, plant watering, and a reflecting pool. A vapor-mist air-conditioning system emits no hydrochlorofluorocarbons. With its strong, simple lines, the Grand Rapids Art Museum makes it clear that Kulapat Yantrasast learned from a master, in particular when he worked on the Modern Art Museum of Fort Worth.

Der einen Block vom Stadtzentrum entfernte Neubau des Grand Rapids Art Museum war weltweit das erste Kunstmuseum, das eine LEED-Auszeichnung erhielt. Angesichts der in Kunstmuseen erforderlichen Steuerung von Temperatur-, Licht- und Luftfeuchtigkeitsverhältnissen erstaunt dies kaum. Tatsächlich war die Spende des ortsansässigen Philanthropen Peter Wege, der für sein Engagement in Umweltschutzfragen bekannt ist, daran gebunden, dass der Bau eine LEED-Zertifizierung erhielt. Die Einrichtung umfasst rund 5000 m² Ausstellungsfläche. Ein großes, schützendes Baldachindach schwebt über dem Bau. Lobby, Restaurant, museumspädagogische Einrichtungen und Pavillons wurden „wie Finger gestaltet, die in das Grün des Parks hineinragen". Dem Museum gegenüber befindet sich eine Skulptur von Maya Lin mit dem Titel „Ecliptic", ein ovaler Platz. Der zentrale Bereich des Museums ist ein dreistöckiger Turm mit Ausstellungsräumen, die vom obersten Stockwerk aus durch ein Oberlicht natürlich belichtet werden. Der Einsatz von natürlichem Licht soll den Energieverbrauch wo immer möglich reduzieren. 10 % der Baumaterialien sind recycelt, Regenwasser wird aufbereitet und für Toiletten, die Bewässerung der Pflanzen und ein Wasserbecken genutzt. Durch die Verdunstungsklimaanlage wird kein FCKW emittiert. Mit seinen klaren, schlichten Linien macht das Grand Rapids Art Museum deutlich, dass Kulapat Yantrasast bei einem Meister in die Lehre gegangen ist, insbesondere während seiner Mitarbeit am Modern Art Museum in Fort Worth.

Le nouveau bâtiment du Grand Rapids Art Museum, situé à un bloc du centre-ville, est le premier musée au monde à avoir reçu la certification LEED. Ce n'est pas surprenant, compte tenu de la problématique complexe de température, d'éclairage ou de contrôle de l'humidité posée par un musée d'art. En fait, l'obtention de cette certification était la condition pour recevoir une donation du philanthrope local, Peter Wege, défenseur connu de la cause environnementale. Les installations comptent 5000 m² environ d'espaces d'expositions. Un vaste auvent est suspendu au-dessus du musée dont le hall d'accueil, le restaurant, le centre éducatif et les pavillons « forment comme des doigts qui s'étendent vers l'espace vert du parc ». Le musée fait face à une œuvre sculpturale de Maya Lin intitulée Ecliptic, qui est une place de forme ovale. Le volume principal est une tour de galeries de trois niveaux à éclairage zénithal. La lumière naturelle permet de diminuer la consommation d'électricité. Dix pour cent des matériaux de construction sont d'origine recyclée, et l'eau de pluie est récupérée pour les toilettes, l'arrosage des plantes et un bassin. Un système de conditionnement de l'air à émission de brouillard artificiel n'émet aucun hydrofluorocarbone. Par ses lignes simples et puissantes, ce musée témoigne de l'influence du maître auprès duquel Kulapat Yantrasast a appris, en particulier lorsqu'il travaillait sur le projet du musée d'Art moderne de Fort Worth.

The entrance to the Grand Rapids Art Museum is clearly signaled by its great overhanging canopy roof.

Der Eingang zum Grand Rapids Art Museum wird von einem monumentalen, ausgreifenden Vordach markiert.

L'entrée du musée est fortement signalée par son grand toit en porte-à-faux.

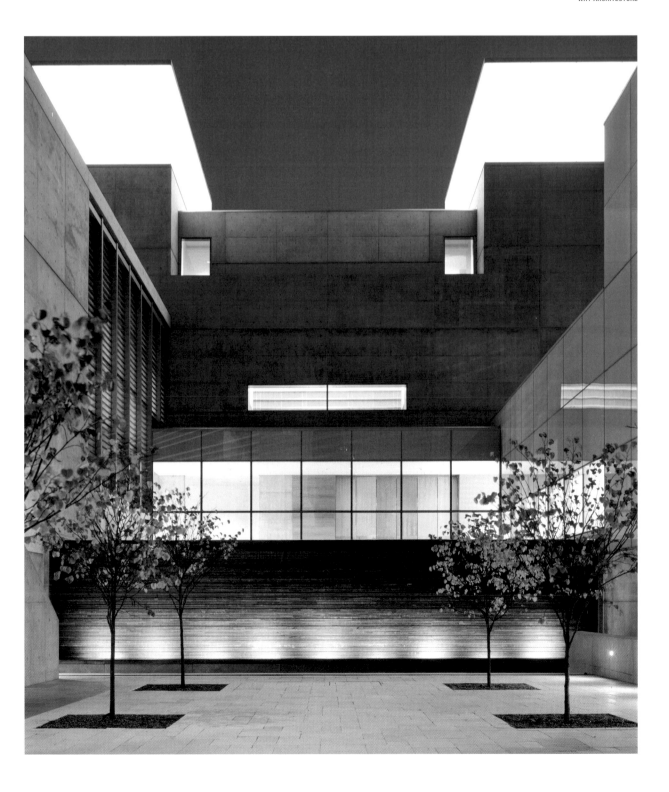

The architects have engaged in a careful assemblage of essentially Euclidean volumes, keeping in mind the ecological concerns of the client at all times.

Die Architekten schufen eine ausgewogene Komposition aus einfachen euklidischen Körpern und behielten dabei stets die ökologischen Vorgaben des Mäzens im Blick.

Les architectes ont réalisé un assemblage soigné de volumes essentiellement euclidiens en tenant compte en permanence des préoccupations écologiques de leur client.

A grand entry sequence with its ramped stairway may recall some gestures of Tadao Ando. Left, a large window opens the museum to the nearby city center.

Der beeindruckende Eingangbereich mit seiner rampenförmigen Treppe mag an gewisse Gesten Tadao Andos erinnern. Ein großes Fenster (links) öffnet das Museum zum nahe gelegenen Stadtzentrum.

L'impressionnante séquence d'entrée et le grand escalier pourraient rappeler certains gestes de Tadao Ando. À gauche, une grande baie ouvre sur le centre-ville tout proche.

KEN YEANG

T. R. Hamzah & Yeang Sdn. Bhd.
8 Jalan 1, Taman Sri Ukay
Off Jalan Ulu Kelang
68000 Ampang, Selangor
Malaysia

Tel: +60 3 4257 1948/1969
Fax: +60 3 4256 1005/9330
E-mail: trhy@tm.net.my
Web: www.trhamzahyeang.com

Born in 1948 in Penang, Malaysia, **KEN YEANG** attended the Architectural Association in London, 1966–71, and Cambridge University (Wolfson College), 1971–75. Much of his subsequent work was based on his Ph. D. dissertation in Cambridge on ecological design. His work (with Tengku Robert Hamzah as T. R. Hamzah & Yeang, created in 1976 in Kuala Lumpur) includes the Menara Mesiniaga Tower (Malaysia, 1989–92, a recipient of the 1995 Aga Khan Award for Architecture); the MBF Tower (Penang, Malaysia, 1990–93); a tower in Ho Chi Minh City (Vietnam, 1992–94); the Tokyo-Nara Tower (Tokyo, Japan, 1997); and the Menara UMNO (Penang, Malaysia, 1998). More recent work includes the Mewah Oils Headquarters (Selangor, Malaysia, 2001–03, published here), and The New National Library Board Building (Singapore, 2001–05, also published here). His published books include *The Architecture of Malaysia* (Pepin Press, Kuala Lumpur, 1992) and *The Skyscraper, Bioclimatically Considered: A Design Primer* (AD, London, 1997). Ken Yeang was President of the Malaysian Institute of Architects from 1983 to 1986. Yeang and his firm have developed a substantial reputation for designing ecologically responsible buildings on a large scale and for master planning work in numerous countries, including Dubai and China.

KEN YEANG wurde 1948 in Penang in Malaysia geboren und studierte 1966 bis 1971 an der Architectural Association in London sowie 1971 bis 1975 an der Universität Cambridge (Wolfson College). Ein Großteil seines späteren Werks baute auf seiner in Cambridge entstandenen Dissertation zum Thema ökologisches Planen auf. Zu seinen Projekten (mit Tengku Robert Hamzah als T. R. Hamzah & Yeang, Bürogründung 1976 in Kuala Lumpur) zählen der Menara Mesiniaga Tower (Malaisie, 1989–92, 1995 mit dem Aga-Khan-Preis für Architektur ausgezeichnet), der MBF Tower (Penang, Malaysia, 1990–93), ein Hochhaus in Ho-Chi-Minh-Stadt (Vietnam, 1992–94), der Tokyo-Nara Tower (Tokio, Japan, 1997) sowie das Menara UMNO (Penang, Malaysia, 1998). Jüngere Arbeiten sind u. a. die Zentrale für Mewah Oils (Selangor, Malaysia, 2001–03) sowie das New National Library Board Building (Singapur, 2001–05), die beide hier vorgestellt werden. Zu seinen Veröffentlichungen zählen *The Architecture of Malaysia* (Pepin Press, Kuala Lumpur, 1992) und *The Skyscraper, Bioclimatically Considered: A Design Primer* (AD, London, 1997). Ken Yeang war von 1983 bis 1986 Präsident des Malaysischen Architekteninstituts. Yeang und sein Büro haben sich einen besonderen Ruf für die Gestaltung umweltverträglicher Großbauten erworben sowie für die Entwicklung von Masterplänen in zahlreichen Ländern, darunter auch Dubai und China.

Né en 1948 à Penang, Malaisie, **KEN YEANG** a étudié à l'Architectural Association de Londres (1966–71), et à l'université de Cambridge (Wolfson College, 1971–75). Une grande partie de ses travaux ultérieurs est issue de sa thèse de doctorat sur la conception écologique présentée à Cambridge. Ses réalisations (avec Tengku Robert Hamzah pour l'agence T. R. Hamzah & Yeang, créée en 1976 à Kuala Lumpur) comprennent la tour Menara Mesiniaga (Malaisie, 1989–92), Prix Aga Khan d'architecture 1995; la tour MBF (Penang, Malaisie,1990–93); une tour à Ho Chi Minh-Ville (Vietnam, 1992–94); la tour Tokyo-Nara (Tokyo, Japon, 1997) et le Menara UMNO (Penang, Malaisie, 1998). Plus récemment, il a conçu le siège de Mewah Oils (Selangor, Malaisie, 2001–03, publié ici); et le nouveau bâtiment de l'administration de la Bibliothèque nationale (Singapour, 2001–05, également publié ici). Parmi ses publications: *The Architecture of Malaysia* (Pepin Press, Kuala Lumpur, 1992), et *The Skyscraper, Bioclimatically Considered: A Design Primer* (AD, Londres, 1997). Ken Yeang a été président de l'Institut des architectes malais de 1983 à 1986. Son agence et lui ont acquis une réputation grandissante dans la conception d'immeubles écologiques et de plans d'urbanisme dans de nombreux pays, incluant Dubaï et la Chine.

MEWAH OILS HEADQUARTERS

Pulau Indah Park, Port Klang, Selangor, Malaysia, 2001–03

Floor area: 16 379 m². Client: Mewah Oils Sdn Bhd. Cost: £2 million

The project is the headquarters building for a Singapore-based company that produces palm-oil products and specialty fats. The program is for a four-story office (overall height 34 meters) with a four-story packing plant, and a 32-meter-high single-volume space to house an automated warehouse. As the architects explain: "The warehouse forms a towering backdrop to the north. The office block forms a thin southern frontage in an extruded form that penetrated along its entire long section by a landscaped ramp that connects the ground floor vegetation to the roof garden and terrace. The inner public space is given full expression in the form of the building. The atrium volume is naturally ventilated by clerestories which open onto the roof gardens, at the upper western end." A linear, cascading watercourse lines the ramp-hall. Ken Yeang has always been very concerned with ecological issues and in this instance, as he says, "what could have been a regular industrial plant and office is transformed into an ecological 'green-lung' that enhances the well-being of the building's users and the biomass of the site."

Dieses Projekt ist die Firmenzentrale für einen in Singapur ansässigen Hersteller von Palmölprodukten und Spezialfetten. Das Programm umfasst einen vierstöckigen Bürobau (insgesamt 34 m hoch), eine vierstöckige Verpackungsanlage sowie eine 32 m hohe Halle, in der ein automatisiertes Lager untergebracht ist. Die Architekten erläutern: „Das Lager türmt sich als gewaltige Kulisse nach Norden hin auf. Nach Süden hin bildet der Büroblock eine schmale, sich vom übrigen Gebäude abhebende Fassadenfront, die über die gesamte Länge von einer begrünten Rampe durchschnitten wird, die die ebenerdige Bepflanzung mit Dachgarten und -terrasse verbindet. Der innen liegende, öffentliche Raum findet in der formalen Gestaltung des Baus umfassenden Ausdruck. Das Atrium wird am oberen westlichen Ende durch Obergadenfenster, die sich zum Dachgarten hin öffnen, natürlich belüftet." Ein linearer, über Stufen rinnender Wasserlauf säumt die Halle unter der Rampe. Ken Yeang hat sich schon immer intensiv mit ökologischen Fragen befasst. In diesem Fall, sagt er, „wurde das, was ein üblicher Werks- und Bürobau hätte sein können, zu einer ökologischen ‚grünen Lunge', die das Wohlbefinden der Nutzer des Gebäudes steigert und für mehr Biomasse auf dem Gelände sorgt".

Ce projet concerne le siège d'une société de Singapour spécialisée dans les produits à base d'huile de palme et les graisses. Le programme consiste en un bâtiment de bureaux de quatre niveaux de 34 m de haut, et une usine de conditionnement (de quatre niveaux également) et un volume de 32 m de haut, qui est un entrepôt automatisé. L'architecte explique que « l'entrepôt forme une masse importante au nord. Au sud, les bureaux sont protégés par une façade mince de forme extrudée, pénétrée sur toute sa longueur par une rampe paysagée qui connecte la végétation du rez-de-chaussée au jardin en toiture et à la terrasse. L'espace public intérieur trouve sa pleine expression dans la forme du bâtiment. Le volume de l'atrium est naturellement ventilé par des verrières découpées dans le jardin en toiture, à l'extrémité supérieure ouest. » Un petit ruisseau en cascade double la rampe. Ken Yeang a toujours été très concerné par les enjeux écologiques, et, à cet égard, il précise que « ce qui aurait pu n'être qu'un ensemble banal de bureaux et d'usine s'est transformé en un "poumon vert" écologique qui améliore le bien-être de ses usagers et la biomasse du site ».

Ken Yeang has long integrated green ideas into his architecture. Here, as the images below and above show, he has brought vegetation into and onto the building.

Ken Yeang integriert schon lange grüne Konzepte in seine Architektur. Wie die Abbildungen unten und oben zeigen, spielt die Begrünung hier sowohl im als auch am Bau eine Rolle.

Ken Yeang a depuis longtemps mis en pratique des concepts écologiques dans son architecture. Ici, comme le montrent les images, il a intégré la végétation dans et sur le bâtiment.

THE NEW NATIONAL LIBRARY
BOARD BUILDING

Singapore, 2001–05

*Floor area: 30 979 m². Client: National Library Board, Singapore. Cost: £80 million.
Architect of Record: D. P. Architect, Singapore*

The client provided the architect with a set of planning principles as the basis for design. These included: a place that provides the people of Singapore with an open, hospitable, and conducive learning environment; a national and civic institution with a distinctive character, reflecting Singapore's multicultural heritage and its aspirations to be a leading nation; user friendly, comprehensible to visitors and convenient for everyday staff use; an efficient building with integrated systems; a building for the tropical climate. The resulting 16-story 98-meter-high tower consists of two blocks separated by a semi-enclosed internal street. The larger block contains the library collections. The small, curved block contains exhibition, auditorium, and multimedia space. Sunshading blades, six meters deep in some locations, provide the aesthetic and functional base for the building's envelope. Over 6300 square meters are designated as green space throughout the library. Optimized day lighting and solar orientation, natural ventilation where possible, use of green or recycled materials for carpets and wall fabrics, and other strategies have been employed to make the structure ecologically responsible. Simulations were conducted on the energy consumption and building performance of the design and results showed an energy consumption rate of around 185 kWh/square meter/year, which is less than typical commercial office towers (230 kWh/square meter/year) in Singapore.

Der Auftraggeber gab dem Architekten eine ganze Reihe von Planungsvorgaben für die Gestaltung des Entwurfs an die Hand. Dazu gehörten: die Schaffung eines Orts, der den Bürgern Singapurs ein offenes, freundliches und förderliches Lernumfeld bieten sollte; eine nationale, öffentliche Institution mit unverwechselbarem Charakter, die das multikulturelle Erbe Singapurs und sein Streben, eine führende Nationen zu sein, widerspiegelt; benutzerfreundlich, nachvollziehbar für Besucher und praktisch für die tägliche Arbeit der Angestellten; ein effizientes Gebäude mit integrierten Systemen, das dem tropischen Klima angemessen ist. Das daraufhin geplante 16-stöckige, 98 m hohe Haus besteht aus zwei Blöcken, die von einer halb umbauten Straße in seinem Inneren getrennt werden. Im größeren Block befinden sich die Bibliotheksbestände. Der kleinere, geschwungene Block umfasst Ausstellungsräume, ein Auditorium und einen Multimediaraum. Sonnenschutzlamellen, an manchen Stellen 6 m tief, bilden die ästhetische und funktionale Grundlage für die Gebäudehaut. Über 6300 m² der Bibliothek wurden als Grünfläche konzipiert. Um den Komplex ökologisch so verantwortungsvoll wie möglich zu gestalten, kamen Strategien wie optimierte Tageslichtnutzung und Ausrichtung des Baus nach der Sonneneinstrahlung, weitestgehende natürliche Belüftung, grüne oder recycelte Materialien für Teppichbeläge und Wandtextilien u. a. zum Einsatz. Simulationen des Energieverbrauchs und der Energieeffizienz ergaben einen Energieverbrauch von rund 185 kWh/m² pro Jahr, was unter dem Verbrauch typischer Bürohochhäuser in Singapur liegt (230 kWh/m² pro Jahr).

Le client avait précisé dans son programme les principes de base qu'il entendait voir respecter. Ce nouveau bâtiment devait être un lieu ouvert, accueillant et adapté à l'éducation, destiné au peuple de Singapour ; une institution publique nationale à caractère particulier, reflétant le patrimoine multiculturel de la ville et ses ambitions nationales ; un lieu convivial, d'appropriation facile par les visiteurs et pratique pour le personnel ; enfin un bâtiment efficace à systèmes intégrés, prévu pour le climat tropical. La tour de seize niveaux et 98 m de haut se compose de deux blocs séparés par une rue intérieure semi-protégée. Le bloc le plus important contient les collections de livres. Le petit bloc incurvé contient des espaces d'expositions et multimédias, et un auditorium. Des brise-soleil de 6 m de profondeur à certains endroits constituent fonctionnellement et esthétiquement l'enveloppe de la bibliothèque. Plus de 6300 m² d'espaces verts ont été prévus à l'intérieur du bâtiment. L'éclairage naturel optimisé, l'orientation solaire, la ventilation naturelle partout où elle était possible, des matériaux verts ou recyclés pour les moquettes et revêtements muraux, et d'autres stratégies ont été utilisées pour rendre durable cette nouvelle structure. Des simulations sur la consommation d'énergie et les performances du bâtiment ont été menées pendant la phase de conception et les résultats ont montré une consommation de 185 kWh/m² par an, soit moins que la consommation typique des tours de Singapour qui s'élève à 230 kWh/m² par an.

Sunshading blades and the generous presence of vegetation inside the building are visible signs of Ken Yeang's green design.

Sonnenschutzlamellen und die großzügige Begrünung im Gebäude zeugen sichtbar von Ken Yeangs grüner Gestaltung.

Les lames de protections solaires et la présence généreuse de la végétation dans l'immeuble expriment l'approche écologique de Ken Yeang.

ZOKA ZOLA

Zoka Zola architecture + urban design
1737 West Ohio Street
Chicago, IL 60622
USA

Tel: +1 312 491 9431
Fax: +1 312 491 9432
E-mail: info@zokazola.com
Web: www.zokazola.com

ZOKA ZOLA was born in Rijeka, Croatia. She studied architecture at Zagreb University in Croatia and at the Architectural Association (AA) in London. She worked for David Chipperfield Architects, Sir Michael Hopkins + Partners, OMA in London; Professor Vittorio De Feo, Professor Francesco Cellini, Professor Paolo Portoghesi in Rome; and Professor Wilhelm Holzbauer in Vienna. Having qualified as an architect in the United Kingdom in 1990, Zola established her own studio in London. In 1995, she received the Young Architect of the Year Award, an annual award. She has taught Architecture as a Senior Lecturer at the Brookes University in Oxford, and was a Unit Master at the AA in London. In 1997, Zoka Zola moved to Chicago, where she first worked at De Stefano and Partners and started teaching at the School of the Art Institute of Chicago. Later, she established her own studio in Chicago and designed her own house, completed in July 2002. Her residence won the Home of the Year Award as the best home in North America. Her work includes the Pfanner House (Chicago, Illinois, 2002); Mixed-Use Development with Penthouse and Rooftop Garden (Chicago, Illinois, 2003); Zero Energy House (Chicago, Illinois, 2004); 24-Hour Mixed-Use Development with Shops, Restaurants, Housing, and Hotels along the Chicago River (Chicago, Illinois, 2008); a competition for a 200-unit housing project (Rijeka, Croatia, 2008); Rafflesia Zero Energy House (Kuala Lumpur, Malaysia, 2007–09, published here); and Solar Tower (Chicago, Illinois, 2007–, also published here), all in the USA unless stated otherwise.

ZOKA ZOLA wurde im kroatischen Rijeka geboren. Sie studierte Architektur an der Universität Zagreb in Kroatien und an der Architectural Association (AA) in London. Sie arbeitete für David Chipperfield Architects, Sir Michael Hopkins + Partners und OMA in London, für Professor Vittorio De Feo, Professor Francesco Cellini und Professor Paolo Portoghesi in Rom sowie für Professor Wilhelm Holzbauer in Wien. Nachdem sie 1990 als Architektin in Großbritannien zugelassen wurde, eröffnete Zola ihr eigenes Büro in London. 1995 wurde sie mit dem Young Architect of the Year Award, einem jährlich vergebenen Preis, ausgezeichnet. Sie unterrichtete als Privatdozentin Architektur an der Brookes University in Oxford und war Unit Master an der AA in London. 1997 zog Zoka Zola nach Chicago, wo sie zunächst bei De Stefano and Partners arbeitete und schließlich begann, Architektur an der School of the Art Institute of Chicago zu unterrichten. Später gründete sie ihr eigenes Büro in Chicago und entwarf ihr eigenes Haus, das im Juli 2002 fertiggestellt wurde. Ihr Wohnhaus gewann den Home of the Year Award als bester Wohnbau in Nordamerika. Zu ihren Arbeiten zählen das Haus Pfanner (Chicago, Illinois, 2002), ein Komplex mit gemischter Nutzung mit Penthouse und Dachgarten (Chicago, Illinois, 2003), das Nullenergiehaus (Chicago, Illinois, 2004), ein 24 Stunden geöffneter Komplex mit gemischter Nutzung mit Läden, Restaurants, Wohnungen und Hotels am Chicago River (Chicago, Illinois, 2008), ein Wettbewerbsbeitrag für ein Wohnbauprojekt mit 200 Einheiten (Rijeka, Kroatien, 2008), das Rafflesia Nullenergiehaus (Kuala Lumpur, Malaysia, 2007–09, hier vorgestellt) sowie der Solar Tower (Chicago, Illinois, 2007–, ebenfalls hier vorgestellt).

ZOKA ZOLA, née à Rijeka en Croatie, a étudié l'architecture à l'université de Zagreb et à l'Architectural Association (AA) de Londres. Elle a travaillé à Londres pour David Chipperfield Architects, Sir Michael Hopkins + Partners, OMA ; le Professeur Vittorio De Feo, le Professeur Francesco Cellini, le Professeur Paolo Portoghesi à Rome et le Professeur Wilhelm Holzbauer à Vienne. Architecte qualifiée au Royaume-Uni (1990), elle a créé son agence à Londres. En 1995, elle a reçu le prix des Jeunes architectes de l'année. Elle a enseigné l'architecture comme Senior Lecturer à l'université Brookes à Oxford, et a été responsable d'unité à l'AA à Londres. En 1997, elle est partie pour Chicago où elle a d'abord travaillé pour De Stefano and Partners et commencé à enseigner à l'École de l'Art Institute. Plus tard, elle y a créé une agence et a conçu sa propre maison, achevée en juillet 2002, qui a remporté le Home of the Year Award, prix de la meilleure maison construite en Amérique du Nord. Parmi ses réalisations : la maison Pfanner (Chicago, Illinois, 2002) ; un immeuble mixte avec penthouse et jardin sur le toit (Chicago, Illinois, 2003) ; la maison Zero Energy (Chicago, Illinois, 2004) ; un immeuble mixte avec magasins, restaurants, logements et hôtels au bord de la Chicago River (Chicago, Illinois, 2008) ; un concours pour un projet de 200 logements (Rijeka, Croatie, 2008) ; la maison Rafflesia Zero Energy (Kuala Lumpur, Malaisie, 2007–09, publiée ici) et la tour Solar (Chicago, Illinois, 2007–, également publiée ici).

RAFFLESIA ZERO ENERGY HOUSE

Kuala Lumpur, Malaysia, 2007–09

Floor area: 145 m² (interior); 30 m² (exterior). Client: YTL.
Cost: $250 000

This project was the winner of an invited competition against MAD (Beijing) and Graft (Berlin), amongst others. The architects explain: "The project is envisaged as the first showcase of Sustainable Zero Energy Housing in the world. The competition brief called for houses that work in harmony with the environment, are made from renewable materials, create their own energy, and recycle water." The house sits on 12 columns in order to allow "other species to develop around it." An analysis of wind patterns leads to the use of concave and convex walls to focus airflows. A 50-centimeter air void is set between the upper and lower roof to provide insulation from heat. Solar panels are located on 92% of the roof, generating enough electricity to run the house. Low-energy ceiling fans accelerate the existing, natural air movements. Seven independent zones allow users of the house to select their own air conditioning levels. As for the architectural design, Zoka Zola states: "Our winning design (unintentionally) looks like the Rafflesia, the largest flower in the world and a native to the rainforests of Malaysia." The house intends to integrate itself into the very specific, warm, and humid climate of Kuala Lumpur.

Das Projekt konnte sich in einem eingeladenen Wettbewerb gegen Büros wie MAD (Peking), Graft (Berlin) u. a. durchsetzen. Die Architektin führt aus: „Das Projekt wurde als weltweit erstes Vorzeigeobjekt für nachhaltige Nullenergiewohnhausbauten ausgearbeitet. Laut Ausschreibungsprofil waren Häuser gefragt, die im Einklang mit der Umwelt funktionieren, aus erneuerbaren Materialien gefertigt werden, ihren eigenen Energiebedarf decken und Wasser wieder aufbereiten." Das Haus steht auf zwölf Stützen, die es möglich machen, dass sich „andere Spezies um den Bau ausbreiten können". Eine Windanalyse gab Anlass, mit konvexen und konkaven Wänden zu arbeiten, um die Luftströme zu bündeln. Als Dämmschutz vor der Hitze wurde zwischen Ober- und Unterseite des Dachs ein 50 cm tiefer Hohlraum integriert. 92 % der Dachfläche wurden mit Solarmodulen versehen, die ausreichend Strom für das Haus produzieren. Energiesparende Deckenventilatoren verstärken die bestehenden natürlichen Luftströme. Dank sieben unabhängiger Zonen ist es Bewohnern des Hauses möglich, die Klimatisierung bedarfsgerecht zu regulieren. Zum architektonischen Entwurf merkt Zoka Zola an: „Unser Siegerbeitrag sieht (unabsichtlich) aus wie eine Rafflesie, die größte Blume der Welt, die im Regenwald von Malaysia beheimatet ist." Das Haus ist darauf angelegt, sich in das sehr spezifische, feuchtwarme Klima von Kuala Lumpur zu integrieren.

Cette maison a remporté un concours sur invitation face, entre autres, à MAD (Pékin) et Graft (Berlin). « Ce projet a été envisagé comme la première vitrine d'une maison durable Zéro Énergie dans le monde. Le programme du concours portait sur des maisons capables de créer leur propre énergie et de recycler leur eau. » La maison repose sur douze colonnes qui permettent « à d'autres espèces de se développer autour d'elle », explique l'architecte. Une analyse des vents a abouti à l'adoption de murs concaves et convexes pour concentrer leurs flux. Un vide d'air de 50 cm est aménagé entre les deux couvertures pour protéger de la chaleur. Les panneaux solaires, qui occupent 92 % de la surface de la toiture, génèrent assez d'énergie pour alimenter toute la maison. Des ventilateurs en plafond à basse consommation d'énergie accélèrent les mouvements naturels de l'air. Sept zones indépendantes permettent aux habitants de choisir leur propre niveau de climatisation. Sur la forme, Zoka Zola précise : « Notre projet ressemble (non intentionnellement) à la Rafflesia, la plus grande fleur du monde qui pousse dans les forêts humides de Malaisie. » La maison s'intègre d'elle-même dans le climat particulièrement spécifique, chaud et humide de Kuala Lumpur.

*Although air-conditioning is part of
the design, it is designed to function
only as users require, encouraging to
the free flow of air through its volumes.*

Obwohl der Entwurf auch eine Klima-
anlage vorsieht, soll diese nur nach
Bedarf von den Bewohnern genutzt
werden. Luft soll ungehindert durch
die Baukörper fließen können.

Bien que le projet utilise une climatisation mécanique, celle-ci est conçue
pour n'intervenir qu'en fonction des
besoins des utilisateurs et mobiliser
les flux de ventilation à travers les
volumes.

SOLAR TOWER

Chicago, Illinois, USA, 2007–

*Floor area: 18 116 m². Client: not disclosed.
Cost: not disclosed*

This tower is intended to capture a maximum amount of solar power. Zoka Zola states: "A majority of the towers designed these days are extravagant formal propositions. Towers are in vogue but most of them are unconcerned with the issues of today or the future. In this way, the flood of towers designed these days is outdated. Architects must seize this time of the greatest responsibility and develop sustainable strategies for towers to use all the physical and social energies of their sites; especially because towers sustain the environment maybe better than any other building type." Essentially a research project, this tower could be modified to house a variety of activities and spaces without reducing its solar capacity. Sun-tracking solar panels are mounted on horizontal poles, a system that should increase their capacity by 30% to 40%, or more, according to Zoka Zola. A subsidiary benefit of these panels is that they would shade the building's interior. The wind could also be used to generate further power. The complex surface of the building is described by the architect as a "cosmo-bio-logical looking skin."

Das Hochhaus wurde konzipiert, um maximalen Nutzen aus der Solarenergie zu ziehen. Zoka Zola erläutert: „Ein Großteil der heutzutage entworfenen Hochhäuser ist formal extravagant. Hochhäuser sind in Mode, doch die meisten stehen den Fragen der Gegenwart und Zukunft unbeteiligt gegenüber. So gesehen ist die zurzeit entworfene Flut von Hochhäusern bereits überholt. Architekten müssen diese Zeit größerer Verantwortung nutzen, um nachhaltige Strategien für Hochhäuser zu entwickeln, die die gesamte physikalische und soziale Energie ihrer Standorte nutzen, gerade weil Hochhäuser der Umwelt wahrscheinlich zuträglicher sind als jeder andere Gebäudetyp." Das Hochhaus, im Grunde ein Forschungsprojekt, ließe sich für die verschiedensten Aktivitäten und Räumlichkeiten nutzen, ohne seine solarenergetische Kapazität einzuschränken. Die Solarmodule sind auf horizontalen Stangen montiert und richten sich nach dem Sonnenstand aus, ein System, das die Leistungsfähigkeit der Module Zoka Zola zufolge noch um 30 bis 40 % oder mehr steigern könnte. Ein positiver Nebeneffekt der Module ist es, dass sie dem Innern des Baus Schatten spenden würden. Darüber hinaus könnte Windkraft genutzt werden, um zusätzliche Energie zu erzeugen. Die komplexe Oberfläche des Gebäudes wurde von der Architektin als „kosmo-bio-logisch aussehende Haut" beschrieben.

Cette tour devrait capter le maximum possible d'énergie solaire. Zoka Zola explique qu'« une majorité des tours conçues de nos jours sont des propositions formelles extravagantes. Les tours sont à la mode, mais la plupart d'entre elles ne se sentent pas concernées par les enjeux d'aujourd'hui ou du futur. La grande masse des tours conçues actuellement est démodée. Les architectes doivent prendre en main leurs lourdes responsabilités et mettre au point des stratégies de développement durable pour les tours et utiliser toutes les énergies physiques et sociales de leur site, en particulier parce que les tours peuvent profiter de l'environnement peut-être mieux que n'importe quel autre type de bâtiment. » Essentiellement projet de recherche, cette tour pourrait se modifier pour accueillir diverses activités et formes d'espace sans réduire sa capacité solaire. Des panneaux solaires à orientation réglée sont montés sur des poteaux horizontaux, système qui devrait accroître leur capacité de 30 à 40 % voire plus, selon l'architecte. Un bénéfice subsidiaire de ces panneaux est qu'ils fourniraient également de l'ombre à l'intérieur du bâtiment. Le vent pourrait également servir à produire de l'électricité. La surface complexe de l'enveloppe est décrite par Zoka Zola comme « une peau d'aspect cosmobiologique ».

The Solar Tower is an experiment in maximizing the potential of an urban building to generate electricity, above and beyond any specific consideration of its internal use.

Der Solar Tower ist ein Experiment, um das Potenzial urbaner Bauten zur Energieerzeugung zu maximieren, unabhängig vom jeweiligen Bedarf des Gebäudes und gegebenenfalls darüber hinaus.

La Tour solaire est une expérimentation d'optimisation du potentiel d'un immeuble urbain dans la production électricité, au-delà de toute considération spécifique sur son usage interne.

INDEX OF ARCHITECTS, BUILDINGS, AND PLACES

CREDITS